AFTER ELIZABETH

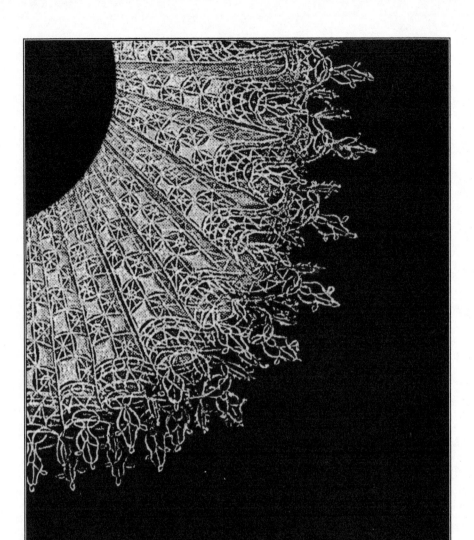

AFTER ELIZABETH

The Rise of James of Scotland and the Struggle
for the Throne of England

LEANDA DE LISLE

BALLANTINE BOOKS   NEW YORK

Published in the United States by Ballantine Books, an imprint of
The Random House Publishing Group, a division of Random House,
Inc., New York.

BALLANTINE and colophon are registered trademarks of Random
House, Inc.

Originally published in hardcover in the United Kingdom by
HarperCollinsPublishers, London, in 2005.

ISBN 0-345-45045-0

Printed in the United States of America

Book design by Simon M. Sullivan

For Peter,
Rupert, Christian and Dominic,
my cornerstones

If you can look into the seeds of time,
And say which grain will grow and which will not.
—WILLIAM SHAKESPEARE, *Macbeth*

CONTENTS

PART ONE

"THE WORLD WAXED OLD"
The Twilight of the Tudor Dynasty

"A BABE CROWNED IN HIS CRADLE"
The Shaping of the King of Scots

PART TWO

"WESTWARD . . . DESCENDED A HIDEOUS TEMPEST"
The Death of Elizabeth, February–March 1603

LIST OF ILLUSTRATIONS

SECTION 1

Sir John Harington. From *Sir John: Nugae Antiquae,* with notes by Thomas Park, 2 vols. (London, 1804).

Henry VIII, Henry VII, Elizabeth of York and Jane Seymour, by Remigius van Leemput. *Reproduced courtesy of the Royal Collection,* © *HM Queen Elizabeth II.*

Lady Katherine Seymour (neé Grey) holding her son, attributed to Levina Teerlinc. *Reproduced courtesy of Belvoir Castle, Leicestershire, UK/Bridgeman Art Library, London.*

The Infanta Isabella Clara Eugenia with a dwarf, by Frans Pourbus the Younger. *Reproduced courtesy of the Royal Collection,* © *HM Queen Elizabeth II.*

Sir Robert Cecil, by John de Critz. *Reproduced courtesy of the National Portrait Gallery, London.*

Robert Devereux, by Marcus Gheeraerts the Younger. *Reproduced courtesy of Woburn Abbey, Bedfordshire, UK/Bridgeman Art Library, London.*

Prospect of Edinburgh, by John Speed. *Reproduced courtesy of the British Library.*

James VI of Scotland, attributed to Adrian Vanson. *Reproduced courtesy of the National Galleries of Scotland.*

Map of Scotland, by John Speed. *Reproduced courtesy of the National Library of Scotland.*

SECTION 2

Anna of Denmark, by Paul Van Somer. *Reproduced courtesy of the National Portrait Gallery, London.*

Henry, Prince of Wales, by Marcus Gheeraerts the Younger. *Reproduced courtesy of the National Portrait Gallery, London.*

Princess Elizabeth, by Robert Peake the Elder. *Reproduced courtesy of the National Maritime Museum, London/Bridgeman Art Library, London.*

Lucy, Countess of Bedford, artist unknown. *Reproduced courtesy of the National Portrait Gallery, London.*

Charles Howard, first Earl of Nottingham, artist unknown. *Reproduced courtesy of the National Portrait Gallery, London.*

Coronation of James I. *Reproduced courtesy of the Art Archive.*

James I, by Paul Van Somer. *Reproduced courtesy of the Royal Collection, © HM Queen Elizabeth II.*

Mary Rogers, Lady Harington, by Marcus Gheeraerts the Younger. *Photograph © Tate, London 2004.*

Round table at Winchester. *Photograph © Ancient Art and Architecture Collection.*

Electrotype of the tomb of Queen Elizabeth I, by Elkington & Co., cast by Domenico Brucciani, after Maximilian Colte. *Reproduced courtesy of the National Portrait Gallery, London.*

Design for the new British flag, by the Earl of Nottingham. *Reproduced courtesy of the National Library of Scotland.*

AUTHOR'S NOTE

I have been asked what first drew me to the story of Elizabeth's death and the accession of James I. Initially it was the drama of events that were not then the particular subject of any book but were glimpsed in biographies and other histories. I remained fascinated, as so much that I read surprised me. The great Elizabeth emerged as fearful and isolated, her government deeply unpopular; our national hero, Sir Walter Ralegh, was despised for acts of barbarity that disgusted even the hardened stomachs of his contemporaries, and was ready to plot with Spain to overthrow the King of England; Catholic priests, far from being united in the face of oppression, were betraying each other to the authorities in a fratricidal war. And James, the slobbering fool of popular memory, was a young, astute and energetic King of Scots, while his little-known wife, Anna, was a fascinating and extraordinary queen.

The first two chapters examine the background to events in England and Scotland. The decades of the sixteenth and early seventeenth centuries then pass to the weeks and days of 1603 and a more detailed picture of the cusp of the Tudor and Stuart age emerges. There are many threads to the narrative and I am grateful to those individuals who helped weave them together. Elizabeth's godson, Sir John Harington, explains, often in his own words, the long history of the succession question and anchors it in the winter of 1602–3. He also comments on the key events that followed. The pirate William Piers plays a smaller part in the book, though an important one, as his story helps illustrate the fate of piracy, a significant feature of Elizabeth's reign, within the narrative. The journal of the Duke of Stettin serves a rather different purpose, describing England's palaces, towns and people as they were in the summer of 1602, just a few months before James saw them for the first time.

This brings me to the subject of source material. I have quoted contemporaries extensively but I have modernized the spelling so that the text reads fluently. Dates have also been modernized so that the year is dated from 1 January rather than 25 March, as it was then. Just as important as primary sources is the use of good secondary sources. I owe a great deal to the scholars whose works are listed in the bibliography, but I would particularly like to thank Dr. Kenneth Fincham for his kind and invaluable help in pointing me in the direction of useful academic articles as well as answering queries or passing questions on to Dr. Michael Questier (to whom also many thanks). Dr. Fincham read the first complete draft of the manuscript, correcting errors and making incisive suggestions about how the book could be improved. I have done my best to follow his advice. Any errors and faults that remain are obviously my own.

I would like to thank Professor John Finnis for his generosity in drawing my attention to newly discovered source material and for providing me with his personal transcriptions of documents, and Claude Blair for reading the section on the coronation, pointing out errors and drawing my attention to information of which I was unaware. If I have inserted new mistakes, I apologize. Lord Ralph Kerr read a draft of *After Elizabeth* for any errors relating to Scotland—and again any mistakes that remain are very much my own responsibility. My father-in-law, Gerard de Lisle, wrote dozens of letters to provincial libraries on my behalf, as well as giving me access to his remarkable library of rare books, while my father, Michael Dormer, helped me untangle genealogies. Without the additional patience and help of the staff of the London Library I could not have written this book.

I would also like to acknowledge most gratefully the help of the following: the staff of the British Library and the Public Record Office; Christine Reynolds, assistant keeper of the Muniments, Westminster Abbey Library; Howard Usher, the archivist at Melbourne Hall;

J. R. Webster, the archivist at Belvoir Castle; Mrs. R. J. Freedman, York City archivist; E. A. Rees, chief archivist, Tyne and Wear Archives Service; Richard Van Riel, curator of Pontefract; W. D. Butterworth, town clerk, Godmanchester Town Council; the Dunbar History Society; the archivists at St. George's Chapel, Windsor; Robert Frost, senior librarian and archivist, Yorkshire Archaeological Society; Ruth Harris, principal district archivist, West Yorkshire Archive Service; Alan Akeroyd, senior archivist, Cambridgeshire County Council; Jon Culverhouse, curator, Burghley House, Stamford; Janet Robb, librarian, North Nottinghamshire County Library; Anita Thompson, Information Services, Durham County Council; Jane Brown, search room archivist, National Archives of Scotland; Dr. Joan Thirsk; Mrs. Peter Joy; Flick Rohde; Francis Edwards, SJ; Michael Fry; Mr. and Mrs. Harold Smith; Albert Loomie, SJ; Jonathan Foyle; Mrs. H. W. G. de Capell Brooke for her translation of Henry Wotton; Giles Quarme for his advice on Theobalds; James Lowther for his information concerning his home, Holdenby House; Robin Brackenbury for information on Holmes Pierrepoint Hall; Brenda Tew; Dr. Paul Davenport and Dr. Sharon Mitchell for their medical insights into the possible causes of Elizabeth's death.

Thank you also to Peter Borland at Ballantine, who bought my book in the United States, and to Susanna Porter, who looked after me subsequently. Throughout I have enjoyed great support from my U.K. editor, Arabella Pike, who is always encouraging, helpful and enthusiastic, offering astute advice. My friend Henrietta Joy read and commented on my earliest chapters with wit and insight. My husband, Peter, was remarkably patient about sharing me with people who have been dead for centuries. Thanks to Kate Johnson for her patient editing. Finally, thank you to my agent, Georgina Capel, who saw me through hiccups of wild optimism and troughs of black despair like mother, father, nanny and friend rolled into one.

GENEALOGY

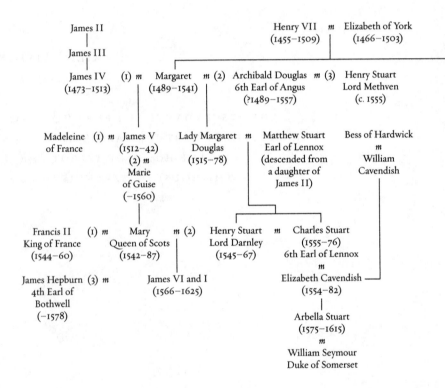

The Descendants of Henry VII

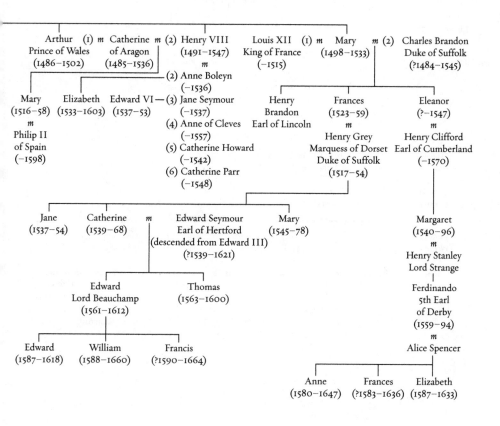

Arthur (1) *m* Catherine *m* (2) Henry VIII   Louis XII (1) *m* Mary *m* (2) Charles Brandon
Prince of Wales   of Aragon   (1491–1547)   King of France   (1498–1533)   Duke of Suffolk
(1486–1502)   (1485–1536)   *m*   (–1515)   (?1484–1545)
                        (2) Anne Boleyn
                        (–1536)

Mary   Elizabeth   Edward VI — (3) Jane Seymour   Henry   Frances   Eleanor
(1516–58)   (1533–1603)   (1537–53)   (–1537)   Brandon   (1523–59)   (?–1547)
m   (4) Anne of Cleves   Earl of Lincoln   *m*   *m*
Philip II   (–1557)   Henry Grey   Henry Clifford
of Spain   (5) Catherine Howard   Marquess of Dorset   Earl of Cumberland
(–1598)   (–1542)   Duke of Suffolk   (–1570)
                (6) Catherine Parr   (1517–54)
                (–1548)

Jane   Catherine   *m*   Edward Seymour   Mary   Margaret
(1537–54)   (1539–68)   Earl of Hertford   (1545–78)   (1540–96)
                (descended from Edward III)   *m*
                (?1539–1621)   Henry Stanley
                                    Lord Strange

        Edward   Thomas   Ferdinando
        Lord Beauchamp   (1563–1600)   5th Earl
        (1561–1612)   of Derby
                                    (1559–94)
                                    m
Edward   William   Francis   Alice Spencer
(1587–1618)   (1588–1660)   (?1590–1664)

                        Anne   Frances   Elizabeth
                        (1580–1647)   (?1583–1636)   (1587–1633)

The Royal Houses of Portugal and Spain

The Royal House of Portugal

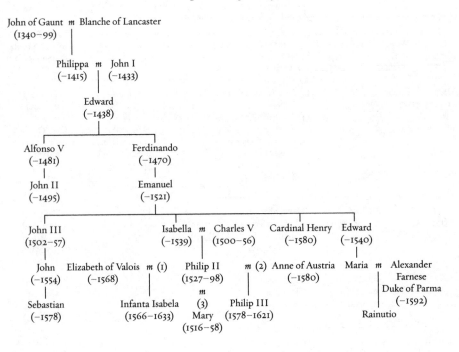

John of Gaunt *m* Blanche of Lancaster
(1340–99)

Philippa *m* John I
(–1415)   (–1433)

Edward
(–1438)

Alfonso V   Ferdinando
(–1481)   (–1470)

John II   Emanuel
(–1495)   (–1521)

John III   Isabella *m* Charles V   Cardinal Henry   Edward
(1502–57)   (–1539)   (1500–56)   (–1580)   (–1540)

John   Elizabeth of Valois *m* (1)   Philip II   *m* (2)   Anne of Austria   Maria *m* Alexander
(–1554)   (–1568)   (1527–98)   (–1580)   Farnese
                                                                                      Duke of Parma
                                            m   (–1592)
Sebastian   Infanta Isabela   (3)   Philip III   Rainutio
(–1578)   (1566–1633)   Mary   (1578–1621)
                                     (1516–58)

The Royal House of Spain

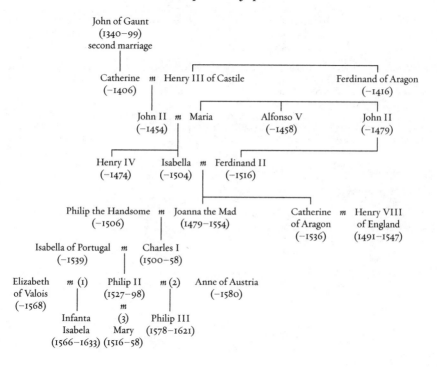

The House of Talbot

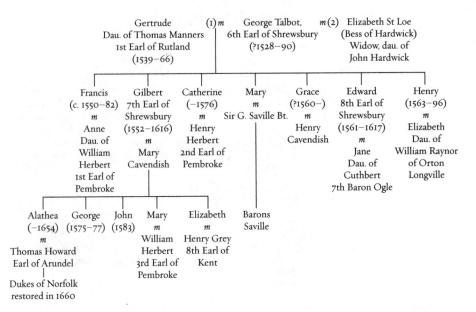

Gertrude (1) m George Talbot, m (2) Elizabeth St Loe
Dau. of Thomas Manners 6th Earl of Shrewsbury (Bess of Hardwick)
1st Earl of Rutland (?1528–90) Widow, dau. of
(1539–66) John Hardwick

Francis | Gilbert | Catherine | Mary | Grace | Edward | Henry
(c. 1550–82) | 7th Earl of | (–1576) | m | (?1560–) | 8th Earl of | (1563–96)
m | Shrewsbury | m | Sir G. Saville Bt. | m | Shrewsbury | m
Anne | (1552–1616) | Henry | | Henry | (1561–1617) | Elizabeth
Dau. of | m | Herbert | | Cavendish | m | Dau. of
William | Mary | 2nd Earl of | | | Jane | William Raynor
Herbert | Cavendish | Pembroke | | | Dau. of | of Orton
1st Earl of | | | | | Cuthbert | Longville
Pembroke | | | | | 7th Baron Ogle

Alathea | George | John | Mary | Elizabeth | Barons
(–1654) | (1575–77) | (1583) | m | m | Saville
m | | | William | Henry Grey
Thomas Howard | | | Herbert | 8th Earl of
Earl of Arundel | | | 3rd Earl of | Kent
| | | Pembroke
Dukes of Norfolk
restored in 1660

The House of Cavendish

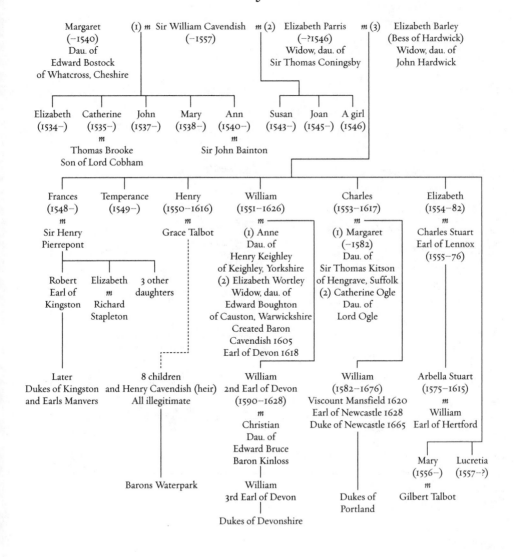

Margaret (−1540) Dau. of Edward Bostock of Whatcross, Cheshire

(1) *m* Sir William Cavendish (−1557)

m (2) Elizabeth Parris (−?1546) Widow, dau. of Sir Thomas Coningsby

m (3) Elizabeth Barley (Bess of Hardwick) Widow, dau. of John Hardwick

Elizabeth (1534−)

Catherine (1535−) *m* Thomas Brooke Son of Lord Cobham

John (1537−)

Mary (1538−)

Ann (1540−) *m* Sir John Bainton

Susan (1543−)

Joan (1545−)

A girl (1546)

Frances (1548−) *m* Sir Henry Pierrepont

Temperance (1549−)

Henry (1550−1616) *m* Grace Talbot

William (1551−1626) *m* (1) Anne Dau. of Henry Keighley of Keighley, Yorkshire (2) Elizabeth Wortley Widow, dau. of Edward Boughton of Causton, Warwickshire Created Baron Cavendish 1605 Earl of Devon 1618

Charles (1553−1617) *m* (1) Margaret (−1582) Dau. of Sir Thomas Kitson of Hengrave, Suffolk (2) Catherine Ogle Dau. of Lord Ogle

Elizabeth (1554−82) *m* Charles Stuart Earl of Lennox (1555−76)

Robert Earl of Kingston

Elizabeth *m* Richard Stapleton

3 other daughters

Later Dukes of Kingston and Earls Manvers

8 children and Henry Cavendish (heir) All illegitimate

William 2nd Earl of Devon (1590−1628) *m* Christian Dau. of Edward Bruce Baron Kinloss

William (1582−1676) Viscount Mansfield 1620 Earl of Newcastle 1628 Duke of Newcastle 1665

Arbella Stuart (1575−1615) *m* William Earl of Hertford

Mary (1556−) *m* Gilbert Talbot

Lucretia (1557−?)

Barons Waterpark

William 3rd Earl of Devon Dukes of Devonshire

Dukes of Portland

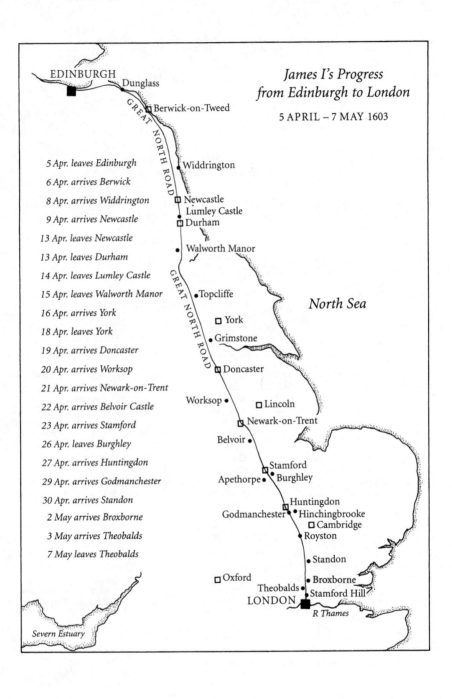

James I's Progress
from Edinburgh to London

5 APRIL – 7 MAY 1603

EDINBURGH
Dunglass

Berwick-on-Tweed

GREAT NORTH ROAD

Widdrington

Newcastle
Lumley Castle
Durham

Walworth Manor

GREAT NORTH ROAD

Topcliffe

York

Grimstone

Doncaster

North Sea

Worksop

Lincoln

Newark-on-Trent

Belvoir

Stamford
Apethorpe
Burghley

Huntingdon
Godmanchester
Hinchingbrooke
Cambridge
Royston

Standon

Oxford

Broxborne
Theobalds
Stamford Hill
LONDON
R Thames

Severn Estuary

5 Apr. leaves Edinburgh

6 Apr. arrives Berwick

8 Apr. arrives Widdrington

9 Apr. arrives Newcastle

13 Apr. leaves Newcastle

13 Apr. leaves Durham

14 Apr. leaves Lumley Castle

15 Apr. leaves Walworth Manor

16 Apr. arrives York

18 Apr. leaves York

19 Apr. arrives Doncaster

20 Apr. arrives Worksop

21 Apr. arrives Newark-on-Trent

22 Apr. arrives Belvoir Castle

23 Apr. arrives Stamford

26 Apr. leaves Burghley

27 Apr. arrives Huntingdon

29 Apr. arrives Godmanchester

30 Apr. arrives Standon

2 May arrives Broxborne

3 May arrives Theobalds

7 May leaves Theobalds

PART ONE

There are more that look, as it is said,
to the rising than to the setting sun.

—ELIZABETH I

CHAPTER ONE

"THE WORLD WAXED OLD"

The Twilight of the Tudor Dynasty

Sir John Harington arrived at Whitehall in December 1602 in time for the twelve-day Christmas celebrations at court. The coming winter season was expected to be a dull one, though the new Comptroller of the Household, Sir Edward Wotton, was trying his best to inject fresh life into it. Dressed from head to toe in white, he had laid on dances, bear baiting, plays and gambling. The Secretary of State, Sir Robert Cecil, lost up to £800 a night—an astonishing sum, even for one who, according to popular verse, ruled "court and crown." Behind the scenes, however, courtiers gambled for still higher stakes. Harington observed that Elizabeth I, the last of the Tudors, was sixty-nine and although she appeared in sound health, "age itself is a sickness."[1] She could not live forever, and after her reign of forty-four years the country was on the eve of change.

To Elizabeth, Harington was "that witty fellow my godson." Courtiers knew him for his invention of the water closet, his translations of classical works, his scurrilous writings on court figures and his mastery of the epigram, which was then the fashionable medium for comment on court life. In the competition for Elizabeth's favor, however, courtiers were expected to reflect her greatness not only in learning and wit but also in their visual magnificence. They did so by dressing in clothes "more sumptuous than the proudest Persian." A miniature depicts Harington as a smiling man in a cut silk doublet and ruff, his long hair brushed back to show off a jeweled earring that hangs to his shoulder. Even a courtier's plainest suits were worn with beaver hats and the finest linen shirts, gilded daggers and swords, silk garters and show roses, silk stockings and cloaks.[2]

This brilliant world was a small one, though riven by scheming and distrust. "Those who live in courts, must mark what they say," one of Harington's epigrams warned. "Who lives for ease had better live away."[3] Harington, typically, knew everyone at Whitehall that Christmas, either directly or through friends and relations.[4] Elizabeth herself was particularly close to the grandchildren of her aunt Mary Boleyn, a group known enviously as "the tribe of Dan." The eldest, Lord Hunsdon, was the Lord Chamberlain, responsible for the conduct of the court. His sisters, the Countess of Nottingham and Lady Scrope, were Elizabeth's most favored Ladies of the Privy Chamber. But Harington also had royal connections, albeit at one remove. His estate at Kelston in Somerset had been granted to his father's first wife, Ethelreda, an illegitimate daughter of Henry VIII. When Ethelreda died childless the land had passed to John Harington senior. He remained loyal to Elizabeth when she was imprisoned following a Protestant-backed revolt against her Catholic sister Mary I, named after one of its leaders as Wyatt's revolt, and when Elizabeth became Queen she rewarded him with office and fortune, making his second wife, Harington's mother, Isabella Markham, a Lady of the Privy Chamber. It was the hope of acquiring such wealth and honor that was the chief attraction of the court.

Harington once described the court as "ambition's puffball"—a toadstool that fed on vanity and greed—but it was one that had been carefully cultivated by the Tudor monarchy. With no standing army or paid bureaucracy to enforce their will, the monarchy had to rely on persuasion. They used Arthurian mythology and courtly displays to capture hearts, while patronage appealed to the more down-to-earth instincts of personal ambition. Elizabeth could grant her powerful subjects the prestige that came with titles and orders, and the influence conferred by office in the Church, the military, the administration of government and the law; there were also posts at court or in the royal household. She could bestow wealth with leases on royal lands and palaces, offer special trading licenses and monopolies or bequeath the ownership of estates confiscated from traitors.[5] Those who gained most from Elizabeth's patronage were themselves patrons, acting as conduits for the Queen's munificence.

Harington and his friends worked hard to ingratiate themselves with the great men at court, often spending years, as he complained, in "grinning scoff, watching nights and fawning days."[6] When a great patron fell from grace a decade of personal and financial investment could be lost. The precise standing of all senior courtiers was therefore tracked and discussed by gossips and intelligencers. Every tiny fluctuation in their fortunes stoked what one observer described as "the court fever of hope and fear that continuously torments those that depend upon great men and their promises."[7] The "fever" reached a pitch when the health of the monarch was a cause for concern since her death could mean a complete revolution in government.

Harington arrived at court having completed, on 18 December, his *Tract on the Succession to the Crown*—a subject on which the pulse of the nation was now said to "beat extremely" but which was strictly forbidden. As Harington had recorded in his tract, Elizabeth had "utterly suppressed the talk of an heir apparent" in the year of his birth, 1561, "saying she would not have her winding sheet set up before her face." Her concern, he explained, was "that if she should allow and permit men to examine, discuss and publish whose was the best title after her, some would be ready to affirm that title to be good afore hers."[8]

Forty years earlier there had been those who had claimed that Elizabeth's Catholic cousin, Mary, Queen of Scots, had a superior claim to the English throne; others asserted that it belonged to her Protestant cousin Catherine Grey. Both claimants had since died: Catherine in a country house prison in 1568, Mary on the executioner's block in 1587. But their sons, James VI of Scotland and Lord Beauchamp, had succeeded them as rivals to her throne, together with more recent candidates such as James's cousin Arbella Stuart and the Infanta Isabella of Spain. The dangers to Elizabeth were such that the publication of any discussion of the succession had been declared an act of treason by Parliament only the previous winter. Her advancing age meant, however, that an heir would soon have to be chosen, if not by her, then by others.

Harington had dedicated his tract to his preferred choice, James VI, the Protestant son of Mary, Queen of Scots. As the senior descendant of Henry VIII's elder sister, Margaret, and her first husband, James IV, he was Elizabeth's heir by the usual dynastic rules of primogeniture, but James was far from being the straightforward choice that this suggests.

The Stuart line of the Kings of Scots was barred from the succession under the will of Henry VIII, which was backed by Act of Parliament. James was also personally excluded under a law dating back to the reign of Edward III precluding those born outside "the allegiance of the realm of England." His hopes rested on the fact that the claims of his rivals were equally problematic. Elizabeth had declared Catherine Grey's son, Lord Beauchamp, illegitimate, and, as men had delved ever deeper into the complex question of the right to the throne, the numbers of potential heirs had proliferated. By 1600 the sometime writer, lawyer and spy Thomas Wilson had counted "twelve competitors that gape for the death of that good old princess, the now queen."[9] Spain, France and the Pope all had their preferred candidates, while the English were divided in their choice by religious belief and contesting ambitions.

Courtiers feared that the price of Elizabeth's security during her life would be civil war and foreign invasion on her death—but the future was also replete with possibilities. A new monarch drawn from a weak field would need to acquire widespread support to secure his or her position against rivals. That meant opening up the royal purse:

there would be gifts of land, office and title. Harington's tract was a private gift to James made in the hope of future favor. The gamble was to invest in the winning candidate—for as Thomas Wilson observed, "this crown is not likely to fall for want of heads that claim to wear it, but upon whose head it will fall is by many doubted."[10]

❋   ❋   ❋

The Palace of Whitehall, built by Cardinal Wolsey and extended by Henry VIII, sprawled on either side of King Street, the road linking Westminster and Charing Cross. On the western side were the buildings designed for recreation: four covered tennis courts, two bowling alleys, a cockpit, and a gallery for viewing tournaments in the great tiltyard. Up to 12,000 spectators would come to watch Elizabeth's knights take part in the annual November jousts held to celebrate her accession. When the jousts were over the contestants' shields were hung in a gallery, where that summer the visiting German Duke of Stettin-Pomerania had been directed to admire the insignia of Elizabeth's last great favorite, Robert Devereux, the second Earl of Essex. He had broken fifty-seven lances in the course of fighting fifteen challengers during the Accession Tilts of 1594. There was, however, much more to Essex than his prowess at the tilt. He had represented the aspirations of Harington's generation, born after Elizabeth became Queen and kept from office by her stifling conservatism.

Elizabeth is still remembered as the Queen who defied the Armada in 1588, and as the figure of Gloriana encapsulated in Edmund Spenser's *The Faerie Queene* the following year. But as one court servant warned, this was to see her "like a painted face without a shadow to give it life."[11] Elizabeth had reached the apogee of her reign in the 1580s. Thereafter came a decline that lasted longer than the reigns of her siblings, Mary I and Edward VI, put together. Her victory over the Armada was tarnished by the costs of the continuing war with Spain and the woman behind the divine image had grown old. To Essex's vast following of young courtiers Elizabeth was a dithering old woman, dominated by her Treasurer, Lord Burghley, and his corrupt son, Sir Robert Cecil. Her motto, *"Semper eadem"* (I never change), once perceived as a promise of stability, came to be taken as a challenge.

When Burghley died in August 1598, Essex hoped to become the new force in Elizabeth's government but within weeks a long-simmering rebellion in Ireland turned into a war of liberation. Essex, as Elizabeth's most experienced commander, was made Lord Deputy of Ireland and sent to confront the rebel leader, Hugh O'Neill, Earl of Tyrone. Instead, in September 1599, in defiance of royal orders, Essex arranged a truce and returned to court. Elizabeth was furious, and as Essex fell into disgrace he turned his hopes to finding favor with the candidate he hoped would succeed her. In February 1601 he led 300 soldiers and courtiers in a palace revolt to force her to name James VI of Scotland her heir and overthrow Robert Cecil together with his principal allies, Henry Brooke, Lord Cobham and Sir Walter Ralegh. The revolt quickly failed and the Earl was executed, but Essex remained a popular figure in national memory. Stettin's journal records that ballads dedicated to Essex were being "sung and played on musical instruments all over the country, even in our presence at the royal court though his memory is condemned as that of a man having committed high treason."[12] They mourned England's "jewel ... The valiant knight of chivalry," destroyed, it was said, by the malevolence of the Cecil faction.

> *Brave honour graced him still,*
> *Gallantly, gallantly,*
> *He ne'er did deed of ill,*
> *Well it is known*
> *But Envy, that foul fiend,*
> *Whose malice ne'er did end*
> *Hath brought true virtue's friend*
> *Unto his thrall.*[13]

Beneath the smiles of the courtiers as they played cards that Christmas lay the deep bitterness of old enemies: those who had admired Essex and those who had rejoiced in his downfall.

The gallery above the tiltyard where Essex had jousted was linked to the second group of buildings through a gatehouse over King Street.

Here, in the Privy Gardens, thirty-four mythical beasts sat on thirty-four brightly colored poles overlooking the low-railed pathways. The buildings had a similar fairy-tale quality. They were decorated in elaborate paintwork, the Great Hall in checkerwork and the Privy Gallery in black and white grotesques. The theme of these distorted animal, plant and human forms extended into the interior, where they were highlighted with gold on the wood pillars and paneling. The visiting Duke of Stettin thought the ceilings rather low and the rooms gloomy. Elizabeth's bedroom, which overlooked the Thames, "was very dark" with "but little air." Nearby in Elizabeth's cabinet, where she wrote her letters, Stettin observed a marvelous silver inkstand and "also a Latin prayer book that the queen had written nicely with her own hand, and, in a beautiful preface, had dedicated to her father."[14]

Harington had been granted an audience with the Queen soon after his arrival at Whitehall. As usual, he was escorted from the Presence Chamber, where courtiers waited bareheaded to present their petitions, along a dark passage and into the Privy Chamber, where his godmother awaited him.[15] A mural by Hans Holbein the Younger dominated the room. The massive figure of Henry VIII stood, hands on hips, gazing unflinchingly at the viewer. His third wife, Jane Seymour, the mother of his son, Edward VI, was depicted on his left; above him was his mother, Elizabeth of York, with his father, Henry VII. The mural boasted the continuity of the Tudor dynasty, a silent reproach to the childless spinster Harington now saw before him. Contemporaries remarked often on Elizabeth's similarity to her grandfather. When she was young they saw it in her narrow face and the beautiful long hands of which she was so proud. As she grew older she developed her grandfather's wattle, a "great goggle throat" that hung from her chin.[16] But she did not now look merely old. She appeared seriously ill.

Harington was shocked by what he saw and frightened for the future. Elizabeth had been increasingly melancholic since the Essex revolt, but he was now convinced that she was dying. He confided his thoughts in a letter to the one person he trusted: his wife, Mary Rogers, who was at home in Somerset caring for their nine children.

Sweet Mall,

I herewith send thee what I would God none did know, some ill bodings of the realm and its welfare. Our dear Queen, my royal godmother, and this state's natural mother, doth now bear signs of human infirmity, too fast for that evil which we will get by her death, and too slow for that good which she shall get by her releasement from pains and misery. Dear Mall, How shall I speak what I have seen, or what I have felt?—Thy good silence in these matters emboldens my pen . . . Now I will trust thee with great assurance, and whilst thou dost brood over thy young ones in the chamber, thou shalt read the doings of thy grieving mate in the court.[17]

Elizabeth received Harington seated on a raised platform. Her "little black husband," John Whitgift, the Archbishop of Canterbury, whose plain clerical garb contrasted so starkly with her bejeweled gowns and spangled wigs, was beside her.* It was believed that Elizabeth used her glittering costumes to dazzle people so they "would not so easily discern the marks of age," but if so, she no longer considered them enough. Increasingly afraid that any intimation of mortality would attract dangerous speculation on her successor, she had taken to filling out her sunken cheeks with fine cloths and was also "continually painted, not only all over the face, but her very neck and breast also, and that the same was in some places near half an inch thick."[18] There were some things, however, that makeup could not hide. When Elizabeth spoke it was apparent that her teeth were blackened and several were missing. Foreign ambassadors complained it made her difficult to understand if she spoke quickly. But during Harington's audience this was not a problem; her throat was so sore and her state of mind so troubled that she could barely speak at all.

The rebellion in Ireland that had cost Elizabeth so much in men,

---

*Elizabeth, who was conservative in religious matters, wanted a single man as her senior cleric. After Whitgift's appointment Harington recalled how Whitgift had always cut a dashing figure. When he was Bishop of Worcester, he would arrive at Parliament attended by large numbers of retainers in tawny livery. When another bishop asked how he could afford so many menservants Whitgift quipped, It was by reason he kept so few women—a reference to the fact he had remained unmarried (Harington, *State of the Church*, pp. 7–8).

money and peace of mind was near its end. The archrebel Tyrone was offering his submission, but it brought Elizabeth no joy; memories of Essex's betrayals were crowding in. She whispered to Whitgift to ask Harington if he had seen Tyrone. Harington had witnessed Essex making the truce with Tyrone in 1599 and later met him in person. He still trembled at the memory of Elizabeth's fury with him about it when he had returned to England, and he now answered her carefully, saying only, "I had seen him with the Lord Deputy." At this, Elizabeth looked up with an expression of anger and grief and replied, "Oh, now it mindeth me that you was one who saw this man elsewhere," and she began to weep and strike her breast. "She held in her hand a golden cup, which she often put to her lips; but in sooth her heart seemed too full to lack more filling," Harington told his wife.

As the audience drew to a close Elizabeth rallied and she asked her godson to come back to her chamber at seven o'clock and bring some of the lighthearted verses and witty prose for which he was famous. Harington dutifully returned that evening and read Elizabeth some verses. She smiled once but told him, "When thou dost find creeping time at thy gate, these fooleries will please thee less; I am past my relish for such matters. Thou seeest my bodily meat doth not suit me well; I have eaten but one ill-tasted cake since yesternight."[19] The following day Harington saw Elizabeth again. A number of men had arrived at her request only to be dismissed in anger for appearing without an appointment: "But who shall say that 'Your Majesty hath forgotten'?" Harington asked Mall.

No one dared to voice openly the seriousness of Elizabeth's condition but Harington did find "some less mindful of what they are soon to lose, than of what they may perchance hereafter get."[20] He told his wife that he had attended a dinner with the Archbishop and that many of Elizabeth's own clerics appeared to be "well anointed with the oil of gladness." But the spectacle of Elizabeth's misery amid the feasting pricked Harington's conscience. In his *Tract on the Succession* he had wasted no opportunities to dwell on the unpopularity of her government and to contrast her failings as an aged Queen with James VI's youth, vigor and masculinity. Now he could not suppress memories of all the kindness she had shown him; "her watchings over my

youth, her liking to my free speech and admiration of my little learning . . . have rooted such love, such dutiful remembrance of her
princely virtues, that to turn askant from her condition with tearless
eyes, would stain and foul the spring and fount of gratitude."[21]

Harington's eyes, however, tear-filled or not, remained as fixed on
the future as those of everyone else, and he was comforted by the re-
alization that his examination of the succession issue had been completed with exquisite timing.

❈   ❈   ❈

The question of the succession had dominated the history of the
Tudor dynasty and would shape events to come. The first Tudor king,
Henry VII, had been a rival claimant to a reigning monarch until his
army killed Richard III at the battle of Bosworth Field in 1485. The
victory came at the end of a long period of civil strife in which Harington's great-grandfather, James Harington, was allied with the losing side—an error that cost the family much of their land in the north
of England. Henry was fearful that such families would rise against
him if a rival candidate for his crown emerged and so he worked hard
to achieve a secure succession. He had two sons to ensure the future
of his line and he bolstered his claim by creating a mythology that an-
chored the Tudors in a legendary past.

Henry VII claimed that his ancestor Owen Tudor was a direct descendant of Cadwallader, supposedly the last of the British kings.
This made the Tudors the heirs of King Arthur and through them, it
was said, Arthur would return.[22] Henry even named his eldest son
Arthur, but the boy died at age fifteen, not long after his marriage to
Catherine of Aragon. It was thus his second son, Henry VIII, who inherited the crown, as well as his brother's bride. Henry and Catherine
had a daughter, the future Mary I, but no sons. Henry saw this lack of
a male heir as an apocalyptic failure, fearing that the inheritance of
the throne by a mere queen regnant could plunge England back into
civil war. He became convinced that God had punished him for having married his brother's wife and sought an annulment from the
Pope. When the Pope, under pressure from Catherine's Hapsburg
nephew, Charles V, denied it to him, he made himself the head of the

Church in England. Justifications for Henry's new title were found in the various "histories" of Arthur, but his actions had coincided with the revolution in religious opinion in Europe begun by the German monk Martin Luther. One of Henry's chief researchers was a keen follower of Luther's teachings, and although Henry had once written against Luther he chose to reward Thomas Cranmer's service in "discovering" the royal supremacy by making him Archbishop of Canterbury. Centuries of Catholic culture and belief were to be overturned in favor of new Protestant ideas as Henry divorced Catherine, declared Mary illegitimate and married "one common stewed whore, Anne Boleyn," as the Abbot of Whitby called her.

The Reformation changed England forever. The simple fact that the country was no longer part of the supranational Roman Church encouraged a stronger sense of separateness from the Continent and enabled Henry to develop a full-blooded nationalism to which his dynasty was central. Elizabeth, the child of this revolution, was not, however, her father's heir for long. Anne Boleyn was executed before her daughter was three years old and Elizabeth, already a bastard in the eyes of the Catholic Church, was declared illegitimate by her father in order that any children of the marriage to his new love, Jane Seymour, should take precedence over her, as Elizabeth had once done over her sister, Mary. When Jane Seymour had her son, Edward, in 1537, it seemed to Henry that the question of the succession was answered. As Henry had no further children by the three wives who succeeded Jane Seymour, he eventually restored Elizabeth and Mary in line to the succession after Edward, in default of Edward's issue or any further children by his last wife, Catherine Parr. His decision was confirmed in the Act of Succession in 1544—the year before Elizabeth made her father the gift of the prayer book that the German Duke later saw on her desk.

The Act of Succession allowed the King to alter the succession by testament, that is, in his will. This was significant, for Henry's will wrote into law who Elizabeth's heirs should be if all his children died without issue. Henry had sought Elizabeth's heirs among the descendants of his sisters, Margaret of Scotland and Mary Brandon, Duchess of Suffolk. Margaret, the eldest, had married James IV of Scotland, who was killed fighting the English at Flodden in 1513. Their son,

James V, died after losing a later battle against the English and left his infant daughter, Mary Stuart, as Queen of Scots. She should have been Elizabeth's heir under the laws of primogeniture, but Henry's will disinherited the Stuart line in favor of that of the Suffolks in vengeance for the Stuart enmity to England and the Scots' refusal to marry their Queen to his son.

Harington's tract explained that the Scots had feared that if Mary Stuart married Prince Edward their country would have become a mere province of England. In the winter of 1602–3 the English had similar concerns that if James VI of Scotland inherited the throne their country might be subsumed into a new kingdom called "Britain." Machiavelli had argued that changing a country's name was a badge of conquest and Harington warned James that "some in England fear the like now." The name "Britain" had an unpleasantly Celtic ring and people believed that the creation of a new united kingdom could nullify English Common Law.

Many believed that James was also precluded from the succession by the medieval law excluding heirs born outside "the allegiance of the realm."[23] Edward VI had brought attention to this law in drawing up his will in 1553, which also excluded the Stuart line. Harington's tract attempted to counter it by arguing that Scotland was not really a foreign country at all, since all Englishmen considered it "subject to England in the way of homage." But it was a view with which James himself was unlikely to concur.*

❊   ❊   ❊

Elizabeth had inherited the throne in 1558, following the death of her Catholic half-sister, Mary I. As a woman, the twenty-five-year-old Queen fitted awkwardly into the chivalric legend of the Tudors being the heirs to Arthur, but Elizabeth proved adept at reshaping it. From the day of her coronation, where she greeted the crowds with "cries, tender words, and all other signs which argue a wonderful earnest

---

*Thomas Wilson had also observed that the law against foreigners inheriting the English throne need not apply to James if it "be alleged that the King of Scots is no alien, neither that Scotland is any foreign realm, but a part of England, all be it the Scots deny it" (Wilson, *State of England in 1600*, p. 8).

love of most obedient servants," Elizabeth worked to build an image that was at once feminine and supremely majestic. She became the mother of her people; the wife married to her kingdom; the unobtainable love object of the knights and nobles; a Virgin to rival the Queen of Heaven, to whom medieval England had once been dedicated; the summation of the dynasty's mythology.

Even in 1558, however, courtiers were considering the vital question of who would succeed her. The last three reigns had seen violent swings in religious policy, from Henry VIII's Reformation to the radical Protestantism of Edward VI and then the Catholicism of Mary. No one had believed Elizabeth would be able to bring stability to a kingdom still bitterly divided by religion unless she produced an heir to guarantee the future of her Protestant supporters: men such as Elizabeth's closest adviser, William Cecil, the future Lord Burghley, who had sat on Edward VI's Privy Council but lost his post when Mary I succeeded him. A petition urging Elizabeth to marry was drawn up by the House of Commons on the first day of her first Parliament. Her reply was that she preferred to remain unmarried. Whether she intended this to be her last word on the subject is questionable, but, in the event, the dangers of making a bad or divisive choice would always outweigh any advantages of love and companionship. Fear and jealousy arose in one quarter or another whenever a potential bridegroom looked to be a likely candidate for her hand. Harington, however, could not see that Elizabeth's decision might be a consequence of their own prejudice that a woman was invariably ruled by her husband. Instead he shared the widespread view that her disinclination to marry was the result of some personal failing.

Harington claimed that Elizabeth had a psychological horror of the state of marriage and "in body some indisposition to the act of marriage," but he admitted that she had made the world think that she might marry until she was fifty years old and "she has ever made show of affection, and still does to some men which in court we term favourites."[24] These flirtations or dissimulations took some of the pressure off her to produce an actual spouse, but in the absence of one she was continually pushed to name a successor. It was only with hindsight that Harington realized Elizabeth had given her definitive answer, that she would never name an heir, in August of 1561, the year when she was confronted by the claims of her Suffolk heir, the Protestant Lady Catherine Grey, and her Catholic Stuart rival, Mary, Queen of Scots.

On 10 August Elizabeth had learned that the twenty-year-old Catherine was heavily pregnant and that the father was Edward Seymour, Earl of Hertford. He was young, dark and handsome, and, more significantly, he was also a descendant of Edward III and the heir of Edward VI's uncle, the Protector Somerset, who had ruled England during Edward's early minority. A marriage between such a couple would be a very suitable royal match—too suitable from Elizabeth's perspective, since any son of such a union would have become her de facto heir and a possible rival. It was to Elizabeth's horror, then, that Catherine confessed they had wed in a secret ceremony in December 1560. Angry and fearful, Elizabeth had her sent to the Tower and Hertford joined her soon after.

While Elizabeth was considering what to do next, an envoy arrived at court from the likely beneficiary of this fiasco, her cousin Mary, Queen of Scots. In 1561 James's mother was a charming, willowy eighteen-year-old who at five foot eleven towered over most of her contemporaries. She had been raised the adored daughter of the French court, destined to be Queen of France, and at sixteen that destiny was fulfilled when she married Francis II. Francis, however, had died the previous December and that August she had returned to the violent country of her birth. Scotland had undergone its own Reformation the previous year, making Mary the Catholic Queen of a Protestant country. It was a possible template for her future as Queen of England, and Mary's emissary, William Maitland of Lethington, hoped that Elizabeth's anger with Catherine Grey would encourage her to name Mary her heir. Instead Elizabeth announced that she would never name her successor.

"I was married to this kingdom, whereof always I carry this ring for a pledge," she informed Maitland, pointing to her coronation ring, "and howsoever things go I shall be queen of England so long as I live, when I am dead let them succeed who have the best right."[25] Maitland stayed at court hoping to change Elizabeth's mind, but in the days that followed she only expanded on her motives for refusing to name an heir. "I know the inconstancy of the people," she told Maitland, "how they loathe always the present government; and have their eyes continually set upon the next successor; and naturally there are more that look, as it is said, to the rising than to the setting sun." She recalled how malcontents had looked to her when Mary I was on the throne and concluded such men might now feel differently toward her. A prince, she warned, could not even trust "the children who are to succeed them."[26] She would certainly not trust those of Catherine Grey or Mary, Queen of Scots.

On 21 September 1561, Catherine gave birth in the Tower to a son, Edward, Lord Beauchamp, heir to the throne under the will of Henry VIII and under English law. Elizabeth was, however, already working toward the destruction of his claim. Catherine and Hertford were closely questioned about their marriage. It emerged that the only witness to the ceremony and the only person who knew the name of the priest had subsequently died. There was, therefore, only the couple's word that they had been married and that was hardly likely to be enough. Their son was declared illegitimate by a church commission later that autumn.*

Over the next four decades Elizabeth's own former illegitimacy kept alive the hope that Beauchamp's might also be reversed, and William Cecil would remain an advocate of Beauchamp's claim until his death. But Elizabeth's actions had undoubtedly damaged the Suffolk cause and its immediate effect was to strengthen that of Mary, Queen of Scots. Elizabeth's brush with smallpox in 1562 reminded the Protestant elite that their wealth and power were entirely dependent on her life, and the Commons once again drew up a petition begging Elizabeth to marry. It drew attention to the dangers of civil war and foreign invasion if England were to be disputed among rival claimants of different religions after her death; France—where Huguenots and Catholics were fighting a savage civil war—illustrated just how grim

---

*It was, perhaps, because Elizabeth was seriously ill with smallpox in 1562 that she did not think to ensure that Edward and Catherine were kept apart in the Tower. In consequence another "illegitimate" child, Thomas, was born on 10 February 1563. Edward was fined £15,000 and Elizabeth made sure that he never saw Catherine again.

that fate would be. Elizabeth assured them that there was time for her to marry, but in 1565 it was the Queen of Scots who made a dynastic marriage with the English crown in mind.

Mary Stuart's husband, the twenty-year-old Henry Darnley, was descended from Margaret Tudor through her second marriage to Archibald Douglas, Earl of Angus. He was, therefore, second only to Mary herself in the line of succession. His English birth was a significant bonus, as it went some way to answering objections about Mary's foreign birth. Harington used it to counter fears that James VI would give official posts and royal land to Scots, arguing: "It is without all question that he which is . . . by both his parents descended of English blood will in England become English and a favourer chiefly of Englishmen"—a popular argument amongst James's supporters. Whatever the dynastic advantages of the marriage, however, it would prove fatal for Mary. Darnley was a handsome youth: six foot one, fair-haired, "beardless and lady faced," but he was also insufferably arrogant and the strain of playing second fiddle to his wife soon proved too much for him. He began to drink heavily and conducted several affairs. Mary, anxious not to give him any real power, refused to grant him the crown matrimonial and instead invested her trust in her personal secretary, the Italian musician David Riccio.

In March 1566, when Mary was six months pregnant, the jealous Darnley and a group of nobles came for her secretary. They walked into the tiny room off the Queen's bedchamber where she was having supper with the Countess of Argyll and Riccio, demanding he leave the room. The terrified man grabbed Mary's skirts, but with a pistol pointing at Mary's pregnant belly, he was dragged away screaming to be stabbed to death. James survived the trauma to his mother and was born at Edinburgh Castle on 19 June 1566, between nine and ten in the morning. A caul was stretched over James's face in what has traditionally been seen as a sign of good fortune. The first sign of it came later that morning when his father recognized his legitimacy with the seal of a kiss, but a rapid series of events followed that endangered his life and then that of his mother.

When James was nine months old, Darnley's house was destroyed by gunpowder and his body was found strangled in grounds nearby.

Three months later Mary married his suspected murderer, the Earl of Bothwell. The scandal triggered a revolt led by her Protestant lords, including Bothwell's former ally in the murder of Darnley, James Douglas, Earl of Morton. It ended with her thirteen-month-old son put on her throne in her place, to be raised a Protestant. Mary fled to England in May 1568. Elizabeth had warned that a prince could not even trust the children who were to succeed him, but she could hardly rejoice at being proved right. Catherine Grey had died only four months earlier. Her younger sister, known as "Crookback Mary," was in custody after secretly marrying Thomas Keyes, the Master of the Revels.* But Elizabeth was now confronted with a far greater threat than that posed by the Grey sisters, for here was a queen regnant and no mere subject.

William Cecil dissuaded Elizabeth from helping Mary regain her throne and since Elizabeth could not risk allowing Mary to leave for Europe, where she might have raised support for an invasion force, she was left with no choice but to keep her cousin imprisoned in a succession of great houses in the English Midlands. There Mary became a focus for Catholic discontent fueled by envy of Cecil's power and influence. Mary was barely south of the border before the great Catholic families of the north, the Earls of Northumberland and Westmorland, backed the Duke of Norfolk's secret bid to marry her and return with her to Scotland. Elizabeth discovered the plan and the earls, fearing execution, led the north in rebellion in November 1569. It was crushed with great savagery and in its wake a still greater disaster fell on English Catholics. Pope Pius V issued a bull excommunicating Elizabeth and releasing her subjects from their obedience to her.[†]

A divide that had existed since the Reformation began widening

---

*Mary Grey married in 1565. Within months it was discovered, and she was placed in custody until her husband died, after which she lived an impoverished and childless life until her own death in 1578.

†The subsequent ruin of many Catholics was remembered in the 1930s as the Vatican considered how best to confront Adolf Hitler. Voices recalled the terrible effects of the bull and the Pope backed off from issuing a condemnation of Nazism (Diarmaid MacCulloch, *Reformation: Europe's House Divided*, p. 334).

once more. The Pope's bull allowed William Cecil—Lord Burghley from 1571—to paint Catholics as traitors by virtue of their faith. New laws were immediately introduced to prevent Catholics entering Parliament and they began to be ousted from local power in towns and counties. This appeared to be justified when, late in 1571, Mary and Norfolk were discovered to be involved in a plot to depose Elizabeth with the possible backing of a Spanish invasion. Norfolk was executed for his role and Elizabeth was put under pressure from her Councilors to behead Mary as well. She refused to set a precedent of regicide but the Protestant elite was soon fearful that the Catholic threat was growing ever greater.

In 1574 a new breed of secular priest (the equivalent of today's diocesan priests) arrived in England as missionaries from the continent. Protestant hopes that Catholicism would die out were dashed and the reaction was ferocious, with the first of many priests to be executed dying in 1577. In June 1580 the Jesuits arrived in England spearheaded by Robert Persons and Edmund Campion. The pair would convert such important figures as the Queen's champion Robert Dymoke and set up a printing press to disseminate Catholic literature and propaganda. Professional priest hunters were quickly put on their trail and in 1581 Persons was forced to flee back to the Continent. Campion, however, was caught. "In condemning us," he told his judges, "you condemn all your ancestors, all the ancient priests, bishops and kings, and all that was once the glory of England." He was hung, cut down while still alive, drawn of his bowels, castrated and quartered.

Campion's terrible death marked the beginning of the harshest yet period of repression. Those Catholics who refused to attend Protestant services—known as recusants (from the Latin recusare, "to refuse")—faced ever more ruinous fines, while priests and those who harbored them were executed every year for the rest of Elizabeth's reign. This did not stamp out Catholicism. Even three generations after the Reformation, Wales and the north of England remained predominantly Catholic. The west of England had a substantial Catholic minority and as much as 20 percent of the entire nobility and gentry were Catholic. But it did radicalize Catholics and it also gained the sympathies of many young Protestant courtiers. The explosion of opinion and argument that followed the Reformation led not only to wars of religion but also to the skeptical humanism of the late Renaissance. By 1602 it was illustrated in the works of Shakespeare and Montaigne and found political expression in Henri IV's secular state in France and a desire in English court circles for toleration of religion.

Harington, who although a Protestant had many Catholic friends and relations, would refer to Campion's death in his *Tract* with the comment that "men's minds remain rather the less satisfied of the uprightness of the cause; where racks serve for reasons."[27] It was, however, the older generation who remained in power in the 1580s and they remained convinced that the persecution was a matter of personal survival.

In 1584 Burghley and Elizabeth's then Secretary of State, Sir Francis Walsingham, took steps to block Mary's accession, drafting a so-called Bond of Association whose members agreed to murder Mary if Elizabeth's life was threatened. The wording indicated that if James VI claimed the throne his life would also be forfeit. Burghley had hoped to follow this with a neo-republican law that would bring a Great Council into effect on Elizabeth's death with the power to choose her successor. Elizabeth put paid to that scheme but in 1585 she did agree to sign a statute decreeing that anyone who plotted against her—or whose supporters plotted against her—would lose his or her right to the throne.[28] It was often used against James's claim, for in 1586 Mary was at last found in correspondence with a rich young Catholic traitor called Anthony Babington. In essence Babington and his co-conspirators were accused of planning a Catholic uprising backed by an invading army financed by Spain and the Pope. Elizabeth was to be deposed and assassinated. Here at last was the means for Burghley to dispose of Mary and, with the help of Walsingham, he seized it with both hands.

Mary was tried and convicted for her involvement in the Babington plot and in February 1587, at three strokes of the axe, the Protestant James VI became the leading Stuart candidate for the throne. The majority of Catholics conceded that all hope for the restoration of Catholicism had died with Mary, Queen of Scots. But some others—idealists, zealots and leading Jesuits—remained determined to have a Catholic monarch, if necessary by force of arms. And already the number of Elizabeth's possible heirs was increasing.

❈   ❈   ❈

Mary, Queen of Scots made Philip II of Spain a written promise that she would bequeath him her right to the English succession the year before her execution. In the event she never did so, but her death left him the leading Catholic candidate for the succession. As a descendant of John of Gaunt and Edward III, he had English royal blood; as king of the greatest power in Europe, he had the might to back his right; and in 1587 he was already building the Armada with which he intended to invade England.

Elizabeth needed allies in Europe, but at fifty-four she was too old to gain them by offering her hand in a marriage alliance. She therefore introduced a new candidate for the succession: James's English-born first cousin, the eleven-year-old Arbella Stuart, who remained a serious rival to his claim. Her father, Charles Stuart, was the younger brother of Mary, Queen of Scots's husband, Henry Darnley. She was therefore a great-great-granddaughter of Margaret Tudor. Her mother was the daughter of a courtier called William Cavendish, whose formidable wife, known to posterity as Bess of Hardwick, remained Arbella's guardian.

Bess had been a friend of Catherine Grey and she had used the example of Catherine's marriage to plan that of her daughter Elizabeth with Charles Stuart. They too were married in secret, but Bess made sure that this union had plenty of witnesses. It never paid out the prize of a male heir, but Arbella was legitimate, royal and English-born. When Arbella was orphaned at the age of six in 1581, Bess—who was then married to the sixth Earl of Shrewsbury—took her in and gave her a Protestant education suitable for a future ruler. Elizabeth, in addition to seeing her as a pawn in European politics, saw her as a rather useful counterpoint to James's ambitions and she was the focus of considerable curiosity when Elizabeth invited her to court early in the summer of 1586. Elizabeth was then based at Burghley's palace,

Theobalds, in Hertfordshire, where the Earl of Essex had begun to supplant Sir Walter Ralegh as the Queen's favorite.

Arbella arrived at court accompanied by her Cavendish aunts and uncles, a slim, full-faced girl with dark blond hair and slightly bulging blue eyes. Elizabeth allowed her the honor of dining in the Presence Chamber and courtiers showered the eleven-year-old with attention. Essex talked to Arbella loudly of his devotion to the Queen and Burghley invited her to supper. Arbella went accompanied by her youngest uncle, Charles Cavendish, who reported all that passed in a letter to his mother.[29] Ralegh, whose fate would later become strangely bound up with Arbella's, was sitting next to Burghley, the elder states-man with his long gray beard; Ralegh was dark and sleek, "long faced and sour-eye lidded."[30] Cavendish was struck by how polite, even in-gratiating, Ralegh was with Burghley: the fading favorite needed a powerful ally to match the support that Essex had in his stepfather, Elizabeth's first and greatest love, the aging Earl of Leicester.

Burghley "spoke greatly in Arbella's commendation, as that she had the French and the Italian; danced and writ very fair" and wished "she were fifteen years old." Cavendish then saw him whisper in Ralegh's ear. Ralegh replied in his distinctive low voice and Devonshire accent that "it would be a happy thing."[31] The two men appeared to be dis-cussing a possible marriage. The name soon circulating as the most likely groom was that of Rainutio Farnese, son of the Duke of Parma, Philip II's lieutenant in the Spanish Netherlands, and, like him, a de-scendant of John of Gaunt. Elizabeth hoped that personal ambition might dull Parma's effectiveness in the coming invasion. She also hoped that the promise of marrying Arbella to a Catholic might salve feeling about the death of Mary, Queen of Scots, and with this in mind she advertised to the French ambassador's wife that Arbella "would one day be as I am." The ambassador duly reported the conversation home, observing that Arbella "would be the lawful inheritress of the crown if James of Scotland were excluded as a foreigner."[32]

Childish and spoiled, Arbella was delighted "that it pleased her Majesty to ... pronounce me an eaglet of her own kind," but she would soon discover that her position depended on the prevailing po-litical climate. When the Armada was defeated in August 1588, Arbella ceased to be seen as useful, though she failed to sense the change in her circumstances and continued to play the role of Elizabeth's heir. On one notorious occasion she insisted on taking precedence over all the other ladies at court. Elizabeth seized on it as an excuse to order her to return home to Derbyshire.

In December 1591 Burghley began pursuing fresh attempts for a settlement with Spain. Burghley had always been the most enthusiastic advocate for peace and his chief rivals from the war party, Leicester and Walsingham, were now dead (Leicester had died in September 1588 and Walsingham in November 1591). New plans were made for Arbella's marriage to Farnese, and in order to underscore her importance in the line of succession she was invited back to Whitehall for the Christmas celebrations.

Harington recalled that Arbella had matured into an attractive young woman. He often admired her elegance of dress, "her virtuous disposition, her choice education, her rare skill in languages, her good judgement and sight in music."[33] Elizabeth, however, began to fear that a party was building behind her and, according to Harington, Essex or his followers had made some "glancing speeches" that suggested she had cause for concern. When the Duke of Parma died the following December, Elizabeth let the marriage plans drop. The friendship with Farnese was now of no use to her and she decided to put the eighteen-year-old Arbella back in her Derbyshire box. She would not be invited back to court during Elizabeth's lifetime. While Arbella's name continued to be mentioned in connection with the latest political gossip—a Catholic plot to kidnap her, a new husband who had been found for her—it was only as a bit part in a much bigger story.

In 1593, the first year of Arbella's exile, the twenty-five-year-old Earl of Essex was appointed to the Privy Council. The average age of his fellow councilors was almost sixty, with the sclerotic Burghley holding a position of unrivaled authority. The only other young member was Burghley's son, Robert Cecil, who had been appointed to the Privy Council in 1591, when he was twenty-eight. Just as Leicester had marked Essex out as his heir, so Burghley was grooming Cecil for his. A contemporary described Cecil as having a "full mind in an imperfect body."[34] He was short—no more than five foot two—and hunch-backed. His face was almost feminine, with large, vivid eyes that suggested his quick wit. Elizabeth would sometimes refer to Cecil as her "pygmy" and sometimes as her "elf." Others preferred the sobriquet "Robert the Devil."

Unfailingly polite, watchful and measured, Cecil had been raised as a courtier from infancy. He was therefore completely familiar with the complex network of human relations that bound people at court by blood, marriage, love, friendship, honor and dependency and he was precisely attuned to its mores. Here the normal rules of morality did not apply. Harington complained that you ended up a fool at court if you didn't start out a knave—but this did not trouble Cecil. As one discourse argued: "The courtier knows the secrets of the court, judges them not, but uses them for his particular advantage."[35] Essex did his best to push his young clients forward for high office, but as Elizabeth's old Councilors died she preferred to leave their posts vacant rather than replace them, arguing that younger men were too inexperienced—and Burghley was no keener on finding new talent than the Queen. He surrounded himself with fifth-rate men who could pose no threat to him. In this stagnant pool corruption flourished.[36]

Burghley's servant John Clapham admitted that "purveyors and other officers of [the Queen's] household, under pretence of her service, would oft-times for their own gain vex with many impositions the poorer sort of the inhabitants near the usual places of her residence." And it wasn't only the poor who suffered. "Certain it is," he recalled, "that some persons attending near about [the Queen] would now and then abuse her favour and make sale of it, by taking bribes for such suits as she bestowed freely."[37] There had always been bribery: since official salaries were very low it was expected, but the scale shocked court and country alike. Burghley claimed to be dismayed by it, but his son was well known for his predilection for taking large bribes and Burghley himself covered up or ignored financial scandals involving his appointees at the Treasury and the Court of Wards. Some cost the crown tens of thousands of pounds.[38] This mismanagement, combined with the problems of an outdated system of taxation, encouraged Elizabeth's carefulness with money to become obsessive.

As the Jacobean bishop Godfrey Goodman later wrote, the aging queen "was ever hard of access, and grew to be very covetous in her old days ... the court was very much neglected, and in effect the people were weary of an old woman's government."[39]

Harington's tract complained that a few servants got everything and he had observed even then that "envy doth haunt many and breed jealousy."[40] The old Catholic chivalric families, who had lost most to the "goose-quilled gents" in the Cecilian elite, remained particularly resentful and they joined their Protestant peers in turning to Essex as the new leader of the nobility. Essex's stepfather, Christopher Blount, was a Catholic, but his own religious allegiance was advertised by his having a Puritan chaplain. The term "Puritan" had been coined as an insult, implying extremist views, and the Puritans referred to themselves simply as the "hotter sort" of Protestant or as "the Godly."* Some had all the bullying fanaticism we associate with the term. There was a joke recorded in the winter of 1602–3 that a Puritan was "a man who loved God with all his soul and hated his neighbour with all his heart."[41] But what attracted Essex was their integrity.

Even the Jesuit Robert Persons admitted: "The Puritan part at home in England is thought to be most vigorous of any other ... that is to say most ardent, quick, bold, resolute, and to have a great part of the best captains and soldiers on their side."[42] Many Puritans hoped for political reforms that would sweep away corruption in public life, as well as for religious changes on Calvinist lines. Elizabeth had expected and even hoped that Essex and Cecil would hold differing views and attitudes. She had often used the arguments between Leicester and Burghley to give her the freedom to choose her own path. But Essex and Cecil became more than mere rivals in the Council. They dominated opposing factions, with Cecil shoring up his father's preeminence and his agenda of peace with Spain while Essex promoted the aggressive foreign policy previously advocated by Leicester.

Essex often tried to bully and badger Elizabeth into accepting his

---

*Puritans wanted to see the restitution and continuation of Edward VI's reforms, dispensing with "papist" rituals such as the cross in baptism, and instituting sermons in order to achieve a more godly church and society.

policies, but his view that she "could be brought to nothing except by a kind of necessity" was not the best way to gain her trust. It became increasingly clear to Essex that Elizabeth was becoming more, rather than less, reliant on Burghley and the only hope for change would lie with her successor. The first determined attempt to browbeat the Queen into naming her heir had come in February 1593 when the Puritan MP Peter Wentworth petitioned Elizabeth to name her successor. Her reply was to put him in the Tower.

Harington recalled how from his cell Wentworth wrote "to tell [the Queen] that if she named not her heir in her life her body should lie unburied after her death."[43] He remained in the Tower for four years, until his death, all the while stubbornly refusing to keep silent on the issue of the succession—a promise that would have given him his liberty.

Meanwhile, beneath the surface of public life, opposing groups continued to make frantic efforts to secure the succession. The question, after all, was not merely one of who would inherit the throne but also who would be the leading men in their government. In the autumn of 1593 Catholic exiles approached Ferdinando Stanley, Earl of Derby (a junior descendant of Henry VIII's younger sister, Mary Brandon). Derby was known to have Catholic sympathies and the group appeared to hope that he would accept the role of a candidate for the succession. Derby, however, took their letter to the Queen. The incident had all the hallmarks of an attempt by Robert Cecil to "waken" a plot with agents provocateurs, a much-used method of gaining kudos with Elizabeth and destroying enemies, particularly Catholics. Derby's action may have saved him from the scaffold, but within a few months he was dead anyway, having endured a violent sickness in which he produced vomit colored "like soot or rusty iron."[44] The description indicates bleeding in the stomach and the rumor was that he had been poisoned.* Some said the Jesuits had murdered Derby in revenge for his betrayal of them, others that the Cecils had arranged it in order to clear the path for Beauchamp. Eliz-

*Though the bleeding from the stomach might equally have been caused by stomach cancer or an ulcer, or a result of porphyria inherited through his mother, Eleanor Brandon.

abeth had become dangerously ill with a fever and the issue of the succession had taken on a new urgency.

Renewed efforts were being made to have the decision on Lord Beauchamp's legitimacy reversed and the following year Sir Michael Blount, the Lieutenant of the Tower, was caught stockpiling weapons for Beauchamp's father, the Earl of Hertford, in the event of Elizabeth's death. The Earl was put in the Tower with his son. The Cecils and Hertford's brother-in-law, the Lord Admiral, Charles Howard of Effingham (later the Earl of Nottingham), worked hard for their release, which came remarkably quickly in January.

Essex was by now firmly allied to James, with whom he had been in correspondence since 1594.* The King's candidature appealed to Essex on several levels. The first was that he was a man. Essex once voiced the view that "they laboured under two things at this court delay and inconstancy which proceeded chiefly from the sex of the Queen."[45] Second, James, unlike Beauchamp, was indisputably royal. Third, James disliked the Cecils, blaming Burghley for his mother's death and resenting his championship of Beauchamp's cause; and last, but significantly, it was believed he could attract support from across the religious spectrum. James had already shown himself to be sympathetic to the Puritan cause. In 1590, for example, he had ordered that prayers be said in Scotland for those in England suffering for the "purity" of religion. Catholics, meanwhile, saw James in terms of his being the son of Mary, Queen of Scots, whom they regarded as virtually a martyr. Some hoped that he might convert when he left Scotland and there was widespread belief among Catholics and Protestants that, at the very least, he would offer Catholics toleration. Harington observed that James had never been subject to a papal excommunication and "had no particular cause to persecute any side for private displeasure." James's accession, therefore, offered a golden opportunity to "establish an unity, and cease the strife among us if it be possible."[46]

Perhaps the most effective enemy of this vision of religious freedom came, however, from among the Catholics themselves: the for-

*The Earl's followers had approached the King as early as 1589, but James had not shown any interest in Essex's offers of loyalty until he had his place on the Privy Council.

mer missionary Robert Persons. Since Campion's death, Persons had risen to be Prefect of the English Jesuits and was usually resident in Rome, where he was described as a courtly figure of "forbidding appearance." To Persons any Catholic hopes of toleration were a threat to the higher goal of a total restitution of Catholicism, and he was now to use his talents as a brilliant propagandist to change the whole basis of arguments on the succession. In November 1595 a book entitled *A Conference About the Next Succession to the Crown of England* appeared in England published under the pseudonym "R. Doleman."* It took advantage of the fact that the Tudors had failed to assert the strict hereditary principle, and claimed that "ancestry of blood alone" was not enough to gain a crown. A monarch should have all the attributes of honor necessary to majesty and, the book argued, there was no such candidate within the Tudor family. The Doleman book took advantage of every consideration ever raised against the Tudor candidates, crystallized popular prejudices and added new disqualifications. Readers were invited to reflect that in the Suffolk line, Beauchamp and Lord Derby had damaged their royal status by marrying the daughters of mere knights (the daughters of Sir Richard Rogers and Sir John Spencer respectively).[47] Beauchamp and Derby were therefore simply not royal enough to command respect. Of the senior Stuarts, Arbella was said to be of illegitimate descent because Margaret Tudor's second husband, the Earl of Angus, had another wife living at the time of their marriage, while James was disqualified under the Bond of Association. The book further argued that James's Scots nationality made him a particularly undesirable choice—and here Persons had hit on a raw nerve.

Historically, Scotland was "the old, beggarly enemy," and although the Scottish Reformation of 1560 had ended three centuries of armed conflict the English still despised their impoverished northern neighbor.[48] For many, the idea of a Scot becoming King of England suggested a ridiculous reversal of fortune. Doleman played up to these feelings, claiming that there was no possible advantage to England in joining with an impoverished country whose people were known for

---

*The name probably represented a team of writers.

their "aversion and natural alienation . . . from the English" and for their close ties with England's Irish and French enemies: James would fill English posts with Scottish nobles and might even oppress the English with foreign armies.

Furthermore, Doleman warned, while some claimed that England and Scotland shared the same religion, the truth was that Scottish Calvinism was "opposite to that form which in England is maintained," with its rituals and bishops. If James became king the nobility would find the Church hierarchy torn down and themselves subject to the harangues of mere Church ministers.[49] His words echoed something the Earl of Hertford had once said of the Puritans: "As they shoot at bishops now, so they will do at the nobility also, if they be suffered."[50] The fact that episcopacy had been abolished in Scotland in 1593 added credence to the claims.

Having thus dismissed all the Tudor candidates as unworthy, the Doleman book announced that in seeking a successor to Elizabeth "the first respect of all others ought to be God and religion."[51] If this seems a strange argument now it is worth remembering that the rights of the present royal family have been based on this premise since the reign of William and Mary. It held still greater force at a time when kings were believed to rule by divine right.

The Doleman book accepted that each faith would prefer to choose a monarch of its own religion, but it expressed no doubt that a Catholic choice would win since Catholics were strengthened by the persecution "as a little brook or river, though it be but shallow . . . yet if many bars and stops be made therein, it swells and rises to a great force."[52] It was a belief shared within the Protestant establishment. Even Walsingham had once observed that the execution of Catholics "moves men to compassion and draws some to affect their religion." The book's comments were not, however, designed to spread dismay among Protestants so much as to attract the attention of Catholics. Doleman informed Catholics that they were not only bound to choose a Catholic candidate as a religious duty but also blessed with an excellent choice: Philip II's favorite daughter, the Infanta Isabella Clara Eugenia. Her claim through her father (and thus Edward III) was strengthened by that of her mother, Elizabeth of Valois, a descendant of the Dukes of Brittany, to whom William the Conqueror had pledged feudal obedience.

The book claimed Isabella also had the personal attributes necessary in a great monarch. She was "a princess of rare parts both for beauty, wisdom and piety" and, as she came from a rich kingdom, she was less likely to "pill and poll" her English subjects than a poverty-stricken Scot.[53] The arguments made the Infanta a powerful and believable candidate overnight. As a final touch, Persons mischievously dedicated the book to Spain's leading enemy at court, the Earl of Essex—he who had attracted such a large Catholic following. "No man is in more high and eminent place or dignity," Doleman wrote; "no man likes to have a greater part or sway in deciding this great affair."

❈   ❈   ❈

In his *Tract* Harington recalled that as the pivotal year of 1598 opened, the English universities of Oxford and Cambridge "did both light on one question that bewailed a kind of weariness of the time, *mundus senescit,* that the world waxed old."[54] The Privy Council was half the size it had been at the beginning of Elizabeth's reign and Burghley was so old and ill he had to be carried into meetings in a chair. He still pursued the cause of peace with Spain without success and the costs fell on a country burdened by a growing population and a series of harvest failures. As food prices rose, wages fell, men impressed for the war returned to vagrancy and theft, and sedition increased. There were reports of the poor claiming that Philip II of Spain was the rightful King of England and that life had been better under his wife Mary I. The greatest danger for Elizabeth, however, was the discontent at court.

Years of simmering resentment between the Cecil and Essex factions reached boiling point in June when Philip II was dying and there were new hopes of peace. Burghley was keen to press ahead with negotiations with Spain. There was another terrible famine and he warned of "the nature of the common people of England [who are] inclinable to sedition if they be oppressed with extraordinary payments." Essex, however, realized the power of Spain was waning and wanted to push home the advantage. The Queen supported the Cecils, and Essex's irritation with her came out into the open in dramatic fashion at a Council meeting attended by Sir Robert Cecil, the Lord Admiral, and Sir Francis Windebank, Clerk of the Signet. The pretext for the argument was the choice of a new deputy for Ireland. Elizabeth's choice was Essex's uncle and principal supporter in Council, Sir William Knollys. Essex tried to dissuade her. When he knew he had failed he lost his temper and as the others looked on with horror Essex suddenly revealed his pent-up contempt for the Queen, turning his back on her with a scornful look. Furious, Elizabeth hit him around the head and ordered him to be gone and be hanged. His hand went to his sword. Admiral Nottingham grabbed him and Essex checked himself, but he swore that he would not have put up with such an indignity from Henry VIII himself.

As Elizabeth absorbed the implications of her favorite's behavior Burghley left court for Bath hoping to recover his deteriorating health. Harington also was making use of the medicinal waters when Elizabeth sent Lady Arundel with a cordial for Burghley's stomach along with a message "that she did intreat heaven daily for his longer life—else would her people, nay herself stand in need of cordials too." Burghley's death shortly afterward, on 4 August, came as a crushing blow to the Queen, all the more so when it was followed within weeks by the massacre of her troops at Yellow Ford in Ireland. For a decade the administration in Ireland had tried to curtail the power of Ulster's greatest chieftain, the Earl of Tyrone, feudalizing land tenure and centralizing power. Tyrone had kept his freedom of action for a time by bribing corrupt officials and fighting proxy wars through followers he claimed he could not control. He had even seduced and married the young sister of Ulster's chief commissioner, Sir Henry Bagenal, in an attempt to trap him in a blood alliance. This phony war had ended on 16 August as Tyrone led an all-out fight for liberation, leaving Sir Henry Bagenal among the 2,000 loyalist dead.

The events that followed haunted Harington, as they did the Queen. Essex and his army had reached Dublin in mid-April 1599. The Irish Council advised him against attacking Tyrone in Ulster before the late summer and so he led the army south into Leinster, "the heart of the whole kingdom," before going on into Munster. It was an arduous and bloody campaign. Harington wrote home thanking God "that among so many as have been hurt and slain . . . and some shot even in the very ranks I was of, I have escaped all this while without bodily hurt." Essex furthermore was no longer the confident, handsome young soldier he had once been. At thirty-two his hair had grown thin and he had to wear it short, except for one long lock behind his left ear, which he tucked into his ruff. His once round and amiable face was pinched, "his ruddy colour failed . . . and his countenance was sad and dejected."[55] He suffered terrible headaches—possibly a symptom of syphilitic meningitis—and certainly his sense of judgment was abandoning him.

When Essex heard that his military successes were ignored at court and that he was being criticized for his failure to take on Tyrone directly, he considered bringing the army back from Ireland. He intended to use it to force Elizabeth to name James her heir and dispose of Cecil, Cobham and Ralegh once and for all, but his friend Henry Wriothesley, Earl of Southampton, and his stepfather, Sir Christopher Blount, dissuaded him. Instead Essex made the fateful decision to make a truce with Tyrone against royal orders and return to court to secure royal support for his military strategy. In the months that followed Essex's subsequent arrest, his supporters approached James, asking him to invade England in support of the Earl. While James worked to raise the necessary funds they published pamphlets justifying Essex's actions in Ireland. In the autumn of 1600 Elizabeth responded to these paper darts by stripping the Earl of his right to collect a tax on sweet wines. It left him facing financial ruin, and Harington looked on aghast as Essex shifted "from sorrow and repentance to rage and rebellion so suddenly, as well proves him devoid of good reason or right mind." He had guessed what lay ahead: "The Queen well knows how to humble the haughty spirit; the haughty spirit knows not how to yield."[56]

Increasingly unstable, Essex was ready to accept the most paranoid theories about Cecil. He knew his rival must be looking for a stronger candidate than Lord Beauchamp, whose candidature had been seriously weakened by the Doleman book. The Jesuit Robert Persons believed that Cecil was interested in Arbella's claim. Cecil's wife had died in 1598 and there were rumors in Europe that he even wanted to marry Arbella. Essex, however, became convinced that Cecil was plotting to place the Infanta Isabella on the throne together with her husband and co-ruler of the Netherlands, the Archduke Albert.* He reasoned that Cecil was the leading exponent of peace with Spain and his suspicions were raised further by the mysterious appearance of Cobham and Ralegh at a peace conference that took place in Boulogne in July 1600. They had not been sent in any official capacity and Essex was convinced they were acting with Cecil to make a secret deal with the Infanta and her husband.

Essex's paranoia was fueled by those around him, notably his sister Penelope Rich and his secretary, Henry Cuffe. The latter pointed out that Cecil was placing men he could trust in the crucial offices on which the defense of the realm rested. Ralegh had been given the governorship of Jersey in September 1600, "there to harbour [the Spaniard] upon any occasion." Meanwhile, "in the east, the Cinq Portes, the keys of the realm," were in the hands of Lord Cobham, "as likewise was the county of Kent, the next and directest way to the Imperial city of this realm." The navy and Treasury were in the hands of Cecil's allies, Admiral Nottingham and Lord Buckhurst, and Cecil had "established his own brother, the Lord Burghley," as President of the North.[57] Essex ignored the obvious point, made by the intelligence gatherer Thomas Phelipps, that Cecil was too closely associated with the persecution of Catholics to risk promoting a Catholic claim. Instead he decided to preempt Cecil's supposed plans and seize the court.

On 7 February 1601 one of Essex's inner circle of friends, the Welshman Sir Gilly Merrick, paid Shakespeare's company 40 shillings to perform *Richard II*, the story of a feeble and indecisive king who al-

---

*One of Philip II's last actions had been to create the new kingdom of the Netherlands. The Spanish had been fighting the Dutch rebels in the Netherlands for twenty-five years without making progress. Philip hoped that a sovereign state that included the Franche-Comté of Burgundy, as well as the Netherlands south of the Maas and Waal, would be better able to defeat the Dutch rebels and would remain allied to Spain. He planned to marry Isabella to her first cousin, the Archduke Albert, who was already Governor of the Netherlands. The Act of Cession creating the kingdom was made on 6 May 1598 and that autumn, shortly after Philip's death, the Infanta married Albert.

lows the country to go to rack and ruin and is deposed by a glorious subject who then becomes king himself. Cecil had introduced Essex to Shakespeare's play during a brief reconciliation in 1597 and it had since become something of an obsession with the Earl. This was doubtless what Cecil intended: it was part of his modus operandi to give his enemies the rope with which they later hanged themselves.

The next day, a Sunday, 300 armed men gathered in the courtyard at Essex's house. About a third of the rebels were soldiers who had served alongside Essex at one time or another. Many were Catholic, and they included several names later associated with the Gunpowder Plot: Robert Catesby, Thomas Wintour, Francis Tresham. Others were Puritan; some, like Sir Henry Bromley, had City connections. A few were blood relatives of Essex. Most strikingly, however, the rebels included what the courtier John Chamberlain called the "chief gallants" of the time: the young Earls of Southampton and Rutland, Lords Lumley and Monteagle among them, united above all by hatred of Cecil.

Essex led his followers through Ludgate toward Paul's Cross. A small black taffeta bag containing a letter from the King of Scots hung around his neck. The streets were too narrow for the rebels to ride their horses and so they walked, brandishing their swords and crying out: "For the Queen! For the Queen!" People came out from their tall, narrow, shop-fronted timber-and-plaster houses and crowds began to gather—but no one came forward. Essex, sweating freely, shouted that Ralegh, Cobham and Cecil were plotting to put the Infanta on the throne and murder him, but the people simply gaped and "marvelled that they could come in that sort in a civil government and on a Sunday."[58] They did not hold Elizabeth responsible for the actions of her officials, as the court did.

At noon Essex paused at the churchyard of St. Paul's. He had intended to make a speech but by the time he reached it he knew the revolt had failed. Within a fortnight Elizabeth had signed a warrant for Essex's execution. She had it recalled, but if she was waiting for her onetime favorite to beg for mercy he did not oblige. When the final warrant was signed his only request was to be executed in the privacy of the Tower, so as not to stir up the multitude.

Early on the morning of 25 February 1601, Ash Wednesday, the Lieutenant of the Tower, Sir John Peyton, "gave the Earl warning as he was in his bed to prepare himself to death." At seven or eight he conducted him to the scaffold. Ralegh, as Captain of the Guard, was obliged to be present at the execution, but the atmosphere was so charged he withdrew to watch from a window in the Armory. When Essex had finished praying he took off his doublet. His secretary in Ireland, Fynes Moryson, had noticed that he suffered from the cold, but no one saw him shiver in the winter air, nor did he move after the first of the three blows it took to sever his head from his body. The long lock of hair Essex grew in Ireland was cut off and kept as a relic.*

Elizabeth was careful to show mercy to the young noblemen who had followed Essex. His friend the Earl of Southampton was imprisoned in the Tower, where he still remained. Of the rest, only four of the principal conspirators were executed: Essex's stepfather, Sir Christopher Blount; another Catholic, called Sir Charles Davers; his secretary, Henry Cuffe; and fellow Welshman Sir Gilly Merrick. Blount made amends to Ralegh and Cobham on the scaffold for accusing them of supporting the Infanta's claim. Their names, he said, had been used only "to colour other matters." He also confessed that he and others had been prepared to take things as far as the shedding of the Queen's blood. But neither Elizabeth's mercy nor this confession did anything to dent the Earl's posthumous reputation. When the official version of what had occurred was delivered in a sermon at the Cross at St. Paul's weeks later it was "very offensively taken of the common sort" and the minister fled the pulpit in fear of his life.[59]

In subsequent months Ralegh was accused of having blown smoke in Essex's face as he mounted the scaffold and Cecil's life was threatened in places as far apart as Wales, Surrey and Mansfield. But although this anger was not directed against the Queen it was she who felt it most. A few years earlier a French ambassador recorded that Elizabeth had given him "a great discourse of the friendship that her people bore her, and how she loved them no less than they her, and

---

*His daughter, Frances Devereux, Duchess of Somerset, wore it along with his ruby earring when she sat for a portrait by Vandyke, both of which are still preserved at Ham House. Her husband was Lord Beauchamp's younger son, William Seymour.

she would die rather than see any diminution of the one part or the other."[60] Now she believed the bond between them was broken, a view encouraged by those in her government who did not wish to see blame cast upon themselves.

❀   ❀   ❀

In the months following the Essex revolt Elizabeth's health and spirits deteriorated markedly and by the time Harington saw her at court in October 1601 she had reached a state of physical and mental collapse. She was eating little and was disheveled and unkempt. A sword was kept on her table at all times and she constantly paced the Privy Chamber, stamping her feet at bad news, occasionally thrusting her rusty weapon in the tapestry in blind fury. Every message from the City upset her, as if she expected news of some fresh rebellion. Eventually she sent Lord Buckhurst to Harington with a message: "Go tell that witty fellow, my godson, to go home: it is no season now to fool it here."[61] He did as he was told and so missed the opening of Elizabeth's last parliament, in November 1601, when she almost fell under the weight of her ceremonial robes.

The Spanish had invaded Ireland in September, hoping to take advantage of Tyrone's rebellion and gain a stepping-stone to England. Subsidies were needed for the war and MPs soon granted them, but many of the subsequent parliamentary debates saw furious attacks launched against the granting of monopolies. During the 1590s Burghley had altered the system of royal patronage based on the leasing and alienation of crown lands in their favor in order to shift the cost of reward away from the crown. It had since fallen on ordinary people. The price of starch, for example, had tripled over the three years that Cecil had held the monopoly on it.[62] He railed in the Commons against those "that have desired to be popular without the house for speaking against monopolies" and Ralegh defended his monopoly in tin so vehemently that it almost brought the debate to a halt. Elizabeth, however, was sufficiently concerned by the attacks on her prerogative to promise to abolish or amend them by royal proclamation.[63] When the news was announced MPs wept and cheered.

A few days later Elizabeth received a deputation in the Council

Chamber at Whitehall. Once they had delivered their thanks, she took the opportunity to remind them of what was later seen as the central philosophy of her reign.

> *Mr Speaker, We perceive your coming is to present thanks to us. Know I accept them with no less joy than your loves can have desire to offer such a present, and do more esteem it than any treasure or riches; for these we know how to prize, but loyalty, love and thanks, I account them invaluable. And although God hath raised me high, yet this I account the glory of my crown, that I have reigned with your loves . . . Of myself I must say this: I never was any greedy, scraping grasper, nor a strict, fast-holding prince, nor yet a waster; my heart was never set upon worldly goods but only for my subjects' good. What you do bestow on me, I will not hoard up, but receive it to bestow on you again; yea, my own properties I account to be yours, to be expended for your good, and your eyes shall see the bestowing of it for your welfare.*[64]

They were described as "golden words" but Elizabeth was only too aware that things had changed, and when Parliament was dissolved in December she recalled the bitter truth of "so many and diverse stratagems and malicious practises and devises to surprise us of our life."[65] That spring, Elizabeth began complaining of an ache in one of her arms. A doctor suggested that her discomfort was rheumatism and might be helped with ointments. She reacted furiously, telling him he was mistaken and ordering him from her presence, but it was soon reported that "the ache in the Queen's arm is fallen into her side." She was "still thanks to God, frolicy and merry, only her face showing some decay," yet sometimes she felt so hot she would take off her petticoat while at other times she would shake with cold.[66] Depression dogged her and in June Elizabeth was overheard complaining desperately to Cecil about "the poverty of the state, the continuance of charge, the discontentment of all sorts of people."[67] She told the French ambassador, the Comte de Beaumont, that she was weary of life. Then, sighing as her eyes filled with tears, she spoke of Essex's death, how she had tried to prevent it and failed.[68]

By August Elizabeth's pains had gone to her hip. Defiantly she continued to hunt every two or three days, but a Catholic spy writing under the name "Anthony Rivers" reported that a countrywoman who saw her on her progress had commented that the Queen looked very old and ill. A guard terrified the woman by warning that "she should be hanged for those words." Courtiers, however, were less easily intimidated and whispers about the succession were on everyone's lips.[69] The spy described how James's agents were working hard to gather support from powerful families offering "liberty of conscience, confirmation of privileges and liberties, restitution of wrongs, honours, titles and dignities, with increase according to desert etc." Individuals were responding with shows of affection: "for the most part it is thought rather for fear than love." He named Cecil as one such, adding, "All is but policy it being certain he loves him as little as the others."[70] It is now believed that the spy "Rivers" was William Sterrell, secretary to the Earl of Worcester, which would have placed him at the heart of Elizabeth's court.[71] His letters to Persons and others make it clear that few actively wanted a Scots king, and he reported that a group of courtiers was planning to marry Arbella Stuart to Beauchamp's seventeen-year-old elder son, Edward Seymour, "and carry the succession that way." To all outward appearance, however, it was business as usual.

In October 1602 Cecil entertained Elizabeth at his new house on the Strand and presented her with ten gifts, mostly jewels. She left in excellent spirits, refusing any help to enter the royal barge. As she climbed aboard, however, she fell and bruised her shins badly. It left her in considerable pain. She began to talk of moving from Whitehall to the comforts of Richmond Palace, but in the end the lassitude of depression kept her at Whitehall, where Harington found her weeping at Christmas.

Now that Elizabeth's godson was certain she was dying he intended to follow the *Tract on the Succession* sent to James in Scotland with a gift for New Year's, the traditional time for giving presents. He designed a lantern constructed as a symbol of the dark times of Elizabeth's last years and the splendor that was to come with James's rising sun. It was engraved with the words "Lord remember me when thou comest into thy kingdom" and, a little underneath, "After the cross, light."[72]

CHAPTER TWO

"A BABE CROWNED IN HIS CRADLE"

The Shaping of the King of Scots

William Shakespeare is said to have written *Macbeth* to flatter James. It certainly did not flatter Scotland. The play, which was first performed in 1606, depicted a violent, medieval country inhabited by witches. It was supposedly set in the eleventh century but as Shakespeare knew, many at the English court believed the picture held true of the Scotland of their day—and not without some reason. For the most part Scottish society was divided between feudal lairds and their tenantry. What meager surpluses the land produced were used to feed the lairds' private armies before any remainder could be traded in the towns. These consequently remained small and trade was underdeveloped, while an inordinate amount of energy was expended on the detection and killing of witches. There were, however, signs of growing wealth and improvement.[1]

The thirty-six-year-old James VI had been King of Scotland for almost as long as Elizabeth had been Queen of England, and his reign had brought a measure of peace to what had been a notoriously volatile country. In 1598 legislation was carried through the Scots Parliament that encouraged the resolution of feuds through the royal courts. With it the tradition of the feud began to die out and by January 1603 James's efforts were culminating in the resolution of one of the last of the great feuds: that between George Gordon, the sixth Earl of Huntly, and Huntly's enemies, the Earls of Argyll and Moray. A marriage between their children was set for the following month. This lessening civil disorder had allowed trade to improve and in the towns stone houses were gradually replacing those of wood. Although witches were being strangled and burned in numbers never remotely matched in England, this too was considered an advance. Medieval Scotland had been comparatively lax with its witches, the true danger they posed having been revealed only by modern theological works to which Scotland's highly educated King had himself contributed. Meanwhile at court, thanks in part to James's patronage, Scotland had become a center of cultural importance for poetry and music. There were also developments in the sciences, with John Napier of Merchiston, the discoverer of logarithms, already working on his inventions.[2]

That January, 1603, James's court was at Holyroodhouse in Edinburgh. Scotland's capital was modest in size but dramatic in appearance, as the Earl of Essex's former secretary Fynes Moryson described:

> *The City is high seated, in a fruitful soil and wholesome air, and is adorned with many noblemen's towers lying about it, and abounds with many springs of sweet waters. At the end towards the East is the King's palace joining to the monastery of the Holy Cross, which King David the first built, over which, in a park of hares, conies and deer, a high mountain hangs, called the chair of Arthur. From the King's palace . . . the City still rises higher and higher towards the west, and consists especially of one broad and very fair street . . . and this length from the East to the West is about a mile, whereas the breadth of*

*the City from the north to South is narrow, and cannot be half a mile. At the
furthest end towards the West, is a very strong castle which the Scots hold un-
expugnable . . . And from this castle, towards the West, is a most steep rock
pointed on the highest top, out of which this castle is cut.*[3]

Holyrood itself was also striking, with its gray stone courtyards and
towers emulating the chateau of Chambord. It was reported to be in
an "altogether ruinous" state in 1600, but repairs costing £1,307 13
shillings and 10 pence had since been carried out and it had been furnished with several new items, including gold cloth curtains, a £20 silver water pot, several velvet chairs, eight silver chandeliers and a gilded
plate worth £86. James's private chambers were on the second floor of
the northwest tower, built by his grandfather James V. There was an
outer chamber to the east and an inner bedchamber to the west—the
door and window frames having been painted red during his grandfather's time. Directly above these rooms were those of James's wife,
Anna, the twenty-eight-year-old youngest daughter of Frederick II of
Denmark. A new brass chandelier hung outside her door.[4]

There were no Christmas celebrations as there were at Whitehall:
the Kirk had abolished them when James was nine. Nor were there
some of the usual court entertainments. Plays, which were an English
obsession, were frowned on. There were, however, pageants and fire-
works, visits to the royal lion house and hunting in the park. The
structure of court life was relaxed, much closer to the informality of
the French model than the English. While Harington complained
that Elizabeth lived "shut up in a chamber from all her subjects and
most of her servants," James's courtiers wandered in and out of his
rooms quite freely, and dozens had open access to his bedchamber.
Royal meals were another striking point of comparison. Elizabeth did
not eat in public. Instead a great table was set near her throne in the
Presence Chamber. A cloth was laid and a courtier entered with one
of her ladies. They brought the cover to the table and made elaborate
obeisance. After the food was tried some of it was carried through to
the Privy Chamber, where Elizabeth would eat and drink with her habitual restraint. Royal meals in Scotland, by contrast, were convivial
affairs with plenty of wine drunk and coarse language heard.

"Anyone can enter while the King is eating," the English diplomat Sir Edward Wotton reported after a visit in the winter of 1601–2; "the King speaks to those who stand around while he is at table . . . and they to him. The dinner over, his custom is to remain for a time before retiring, listening to jests and pleasantries. He is very familiar with his domestics and gentlemen of the bedchamber."[5] Most of these domestics had served James since he was a child—his valet William Murray had been with him since he was two.

The royal table was laden with roasted game and boiled mutton, wine and ale, but did not include any of the fine food that was commonplace in a great English house. Fynes Moryson complained that the Scots had "no art of cookery, or furniture of household stuff but rather rude neglect of both." Most Scots ate "red colewort and cabbage, but little fresh meat" and even at the house of an important courtier he found the table "more than half furnished with great platters of porridge, each having a little piece of sodden meat."[6] James, however, liked his food simple, just as he declared that he preferred "proper, cleanly, comely and honest" clothes over being "artificially trimmed and decked like a courtesan." His courtiers wore plain English cloth, "little or nothing adorned with silk lace, much less with lace of silver or gold," and the style was French—"all things rather commodious for use than brave for ornament."[7]

James particularly disliked the wearing of earrings and was impatient of the fuss required to dress long hair. He kept his own reddish locks cropped short and his suits were usually dark and adorned with nothing more than a few enamel buttons. Wotton described the King as having a youthful face—he "does not seem more than twenty-eight, or thereabouts"—and of being average in height, with broad shoulders and a "vigorous constitution." He would go hunting whenever he could, often spending six hours a day galloping cross-country with a loosened bridle. Although it was a common pursuit among monarchs, and one his mother had enjoyed, her former emissary, Monsieur de Fontenay, complained that James's passion for hunting amounted to an obsession and that he put this recreation before his work. James admitted in return that he did not have much stamina for business, but he claimed he could achieve more in one hour than others in a day; that he could speak, listen and watch simultaneously and some-times do five things at once. He was certainly a mass of nervous en-ergy. He paced his rooms ceaselessly, fiddling with his clothes, hating to stay still even for a moment. An Englishman later described James's twitching as resembling that of a man sitting on an anthill.[8] But if James was unable or unwilling to concentrate on routine administra-tive work, Fontenay had to agree with the King that his mind was ex-ceptionally quick:

> *Three qualities of mind he possesses in perfection: he understands clearly, judges wisely and has a retentive memory. His questions are keen and penetrat-ing and his replies are sound. In any argument, whatever it is about, he main-tains the view that appears to him most just, and I have heard him support Catholic against Protestant opinions. He is well instructed in languages, sci-ence, and affairs of state, better, I dare say than anyone else in his kingdom. In short he has a remarkable intelligence, as well as lofty and virtuous ideals and a high opinion of himself.[9]*

James's childhood friend, the Earl of Mar—whom James nick-named "Jocky o'Sclaittis"—had been telling the English court that the King's body was as agile as his mind, but, as fit as James was, this was very far from the truth. Sir Edward Wotton tactfully described the lower half of James's body as "somewhat slender." In fact his legs were so weak he could barely walk before the age of seven and he never did so normally. Fontenay observed he had an "ungainly gait" and others mention he meandered in a circular pattern and leaned on the shoul-der of one of his courtiers as he walked. The muscles in James's face and mouth also appear to have had some weakness and his manner of eating and drinking was judged crude. One infamous memoir claims that James had "a tongue too large for his mouth, which made him drink very uncomely, as if eating his drink, which came out into the cup of each side of his mouth."

Such descriptions suggest that James may have suffered from cere-bral palsy, caused by damage to the brain before, during, or shortly after his birth.[10] But there is another aspect to the kind of brain dam-age James suffered that is, perhaps, worth exploring. About 60 percent of individuals with cerebral palsy have emotional or behavioral difficulties. James's restlessness, his inability to concentrate on routine administrative work, his hyperconcentration on what did interest him and his passion for a high-stimulation activity like hunting are all characteristic of the contentious attention deficit/hyperactivity disorder, which, like cerebral palsy, is said to have a neurological basis.

James's mother endured a long and difficult labor and it is possible that this is when the brain damage occurred. Many contemporaries, however, believed that his disabilities were caused in utero at the time of Riccio's murder. The trauma to his mother might indeed have been sufficient to have damaged James—and whatever the true cause of his disabilities, he had to live with the psychological effects of being told that this was the case. The childhood that had followed James's birth was steeped in danger and he might easily have emerged from it as a brute, but despite his having physical defects to remind him of the possible effects of violence on him, Wotton saw "in his eyes and in the outward expression of his face . . . a certain natural goodness," and the English courtier Roger Wilbraham later claimed James had "the sweetest, pleasantest and best nature that ever I knew." His experiences had filled him less with anger than with the desire to resolve conflict. He chose the Old Testament's King Solomon as his role model and picked as his motto words from the Sermon on the Mount—"*Beati pacifici*" (blessed are the peacemakers).

James was convinced it was his destiny to unite the old enemies, the crowns of England and Scotland. He sometimes pointed out the lion-shaped birthmark on his arm said to fulfill the words of a Welsh prophecy, quoted by Harington in his *Tract on the Succession:* "a babe crowned in his cradle; marked with a lion in his skin; shall recover again the cross; [and] make the isle of Brutus whole and imparted . . . to grow henceforward better and better."[11]

In James's mind the phrase "recover the cross" referred to his intention to heal religious divisions. First James intended to reform the Church of England on lines that would satisfy all except the most extreme conservatives and Puritans, for example, by developing a preaching ministry, but keeping the hierarchy of bishops. His ultimate ambition, however, was to encourage the reform of the Church of

Rome and make it acceptable to moderate Protestants. It was the divisions in Christendom that lay at the heart of so much conflict across Europe and he hoped that differences could be thrashed out at a Grand Council. James often said that he revered the Catholic Church as the mother church—comments that fueled Catholic hopes that he might convert—but he also saw it as "clogged with many infirmities and corruptions."[12] Chief among them was the office of the papacy and he described the Pope as the Antichrist. "Does he not usurp Christ his office, calling himself universal bishop and head of the church?" he once asked.[13] He intended to do what other Protestants had failed to and knock the triple crown from the Pope's head, reducing him to the rank of the first bishop of the church, "but not head or superior."[14]

❋   ❋   ❋

James, as he was wont to remind people in later years, was a "cradle king," crowned at the age of thirteen months on 26 July 1567. The Protestant lords who had overthrown his mother placed their infant king in the guardianship of John Erskine, Earl of Mar, the father of his childhood friend Jocky o'Sclaittis, whom he had at his side in 1603. It was at Mar's castle, perched on a sheer rock face above the town of Stirling, that James spent his formative years. The omens for James's survival in this fortress had not been good. Harington quoted a popular saying in his *Tract:* "A king in Scotland . . . die[s] rarely in his bed." The Stuart crown he had usurped was as weak as the Tudor crown was strong. There had been a succession of child kings and despised women rulers, and the great lairds retained the military power that had been stripped from the English nobles by the Tudors. James's book of instruction on matters of kingship, the *Basilikon Doron*, dedicated to his eldest son in 1598, recalled them as robber barons who drank

> *in with their very nourish milk, that their honour stood in three points of iniquity; To thrall by oppression the meaner sort that dwells near them . . . to maintain their servants and dependers in any wrong . . . and for any displea-*

sure that they apprehend to be done unto them by their neighbour, to take up
plain field against him; and (without respect to God, King or commonweal) to
bang it out bravely, he and all his kin against him and all his.[15]

Scotland was riven by private wars as well as religious differences, and the usurping of Mary's crown had offered opportunities to settle many old scores as well as new ones. All save one of James's regents were to die violently. The first, James Stewart, Earl of Moray, the illegitimate half-brother of Mary, Queen of Scots, was assassinated in the streets of Linlithgow on 22 January 1570, when James was three. The murder apparently pleased Mary so much that thereon she paid her brother's assassin a yearly pension. However, her old enemy, James's paternal grandfather the Earl of Lennox, was named the next regent as Scotland descended into civil war. Battles raged around Stirling as by night the four-year-old James slept in a bed draped in black damask, a picture of his grandfather James V on the wall, and by day he was coached by his two Calvinist tutors. The junior of these, Peter Young, remained close to James. He had been a kindly and encouraging teacher to a bright and sensitive pupil. But James's senior tutor had proved a brutal master.

George Buchanan was the finest Latin scholar in Europe: a poet, dramatist, humanist and founding father of Presbyterianism, he arrived at Stirling a man with a mission. The ink was barely dry on his tract *Detectio Mariae Reginae,* a vitriolic attack on the reign of Mary, Queen of Scots, and he was determined to raise a very different type of monarch. In this he succeeded, but at a price. He instilled in James learning that surpassed that of any other monarch in Europe, but he used the rod to do it. He espoused high, democratic ideals of kingship but he despised courtly manners and regarded women with contempt. He allowed James to grow up as timorous as his mother was bold, as boorish as his mother was refined, as contemptuous of women as she was charming to men. James ended up resenting Buchanan and much of what he stood for, but he was every inch his pupil. Inspired by Buchanan's example, James wrote several impressive theological and political works, in which his theories on the divine right of kings countered Buchanan's quasi-republican view that kings took their authority from the people and could be lawfully deposed—views that James had come to believe were a recipe for instability.

After just a year of Buchanan's tutoring James had been ready to open the Scottish Parliament with an address in Latin. The events that followed were to be imprinted on his memory. He once said that he had learned to speak Latin before he learned Scots and even aged five he spoke it with confidence. His voice was naturally loud and in 1603, after years of speech-giving, his language was often grave and sententious, but then it doubtless still had the squeak of a small boy. After his speech James had sat among the lairds, squirming in his chair until his sharp eyes and probing fingers discovered a hole, either in a tablecloth or in the roof over his head. He then made a childish observation: "This parliament has a hole in it!" The words were flung back at him as prophetic when only days later his grandfather, the Earl of Lennox, was brought into the castle dying of wounds received in a raid by his mother's supporters.[16] James never forgot his grandfather lying with his bowels cut open, and perhaps because of talk of his having foreseen it, he developed a keen interest in the supposed gift of foresight.[17]

But Lennox's bloody death was not the only murder James witnessed at Stirling. The old Earl of Mar had held the regency for only a short time before it passed on to the Earl of Morton, one of James's father's murderers. He held it until a few months before James's twelfth birthday, when on 4 March 1578, two great Highland earls, Argyll and Atholl, appeared at Stirling Castle dressed in full armor. They informed James that in Scots tradition he was now of age and should abolish the regency. James's remarkable education and royal status had ensured he never suffered from undue modesty and he was already quite willing to take on the full mantle of a king, but Morton proved reluctant to relinquish his power without a fight. On 26 April 1578 James was woken in his room at Stirling Castle by the sound of clashing steel in the hall. Morton and James's former playmate, twenty-year-old Jocky o'Sclaittis, had returned to seize the castle and James. Possession of the person of the monarch brought with it authority and the threat of kidnap had been a constant one until very recently. As James watched the fight he witnessed Mar's uncle trampled to death. Terrified, he tore at his hair, shouting that "the Master was slain," but the fight continued until it concluded in victory for Morton and Mar.[18]

James had problems sleeping for some time afterward, and for the rest of his life he trembled at the sight of armed men. It would be a mistake, however, to label James a coward, as many Englishmen later would. As a teenager he learned to use his intellect and cunning to manipulate the fearsome warriors who wished to control him, developing a close and secretive side to his otherwise expansive character and growing perversely proud of a talent to deceive.

In 1579 Buchanan had left James as he arrived, with a treatise for the boy to ponder on. *De jure regni apud Scotos* promulgated the Presbyterian view that God had vested power in the people, who could resist and depose the monarch if he ruled tyrannically or failed to promote the "true" religion. That September, however, a new and long-lasting influence had entered James's life—one who represented everything Buchanan detested: James's Catholic cousin, Esmé Stuart, Seigneur d'Aubigny.

❊   ❊   ❊

D'Aubigny was a handsome, red-bearded father of four in his late thirties. He had returned from the court in France to deal with a dispute over the title and estates of the Lennox earldom, and the newly adolescent James was fascinated by his sophisticated relative. He would stay up late with him, drinking and joking. D'Aubigny reciprocated with displays of affection and James, who had no other close family, became passionately devoted to him. D'Aubigny's influence expanded rapidly. He reorganized James's court and household on the French model and encouraged his interest in poetry. James in turn lavished money and titles on him, ostensibly converting him to Protestantism and eventually making him Duke of Lennox.

The English agent Sir Henry Widdrington had looked on appalled at Lennox's growing power, convinced that he was using his conversion as a cover for plotting with the Catholic powers. He sent letters south warning that James was "altogether persuaded and led" by Lennox, so that "he can hardly suffer him out of his presence, and is in such love with him, as in the open sight of the people, often times he will clasp him about the neck, with his arms and kiss him." The Kirk went further and later declared that "the Duke of Lennox went about to draw the King to carnal lust."[19]

Beyond seventeenth-century descriptions of James's "lascivious" kisses with his favorites, the exact nature of the sexual activity James enjoyed with Lennox and later male favorites is unknown. But the view of one (admittedly hostile) witness—that a man who showed so little restraint in public was unlikely to do so in private—seems a reasonable one.[20] James was a tactile man and the chief arguments against his having been a practicing homosexual fail to convince. The first is that seventeenth-century Protestants regarded sodomy with ferocious disapproval and that James himself condemned it to his son as a sin so horrible "that ye are bound in conscience never to forgive [it]."[21] Homosexual sex is not, however, limited to sodomy, and James was also well known for his blasphemous oaths and his failure to live up to much advice he gave his son. The second argument is that James's marriage to Anna had demonstrated physical passion (as proven by her frequent pregnancies). But while it is notable that James had no great male favorites during the period in which he was fathering children, it is also evident that after the birth of his last child, Sophia, in 1606, his attraction for young men reasserted itself and his sexuality became a matter of significance in English political life, with the appearance of Robert Carr in 1607 and then George Villiers in 1614.[22]

It is not known whether the English court knew of James's sexual preferences in 1602–3, or if so, precisely how it was regarded. In the sixteenth and seventeenth centuries there was no real concept of "homosexuality"; sex between men was simply viewed as an act of depravity, along with all other sexual acts that took place outside marriage. It was, however, understood that some men had a particular taste for it. Burghley would have passed on everything he knew about James to his son Cecil before his death in 1598, and although there is no reported gossip on the matter in the winter of 1602–3, there are hints in comments by Sir John Harington and Sir Edward Wotton, both of whom praise James's "chastity" with regard to women. Harington could not resist pointing out that it was thought a little strange that James had no mistresses, confessing that in England to call a courtier chaste, "specially if it were afore his Mrs," was considered an insult worthy of a stabbing. If anything was suspected, however, such worldly courtiers were unlikely to be shocked. The Earl of Essex's closest friend, the Earl of Southampton, enjoyed the sexual companionship of both men and women without earning great opprobrium.

What really mattered to courtiers was how a king's sexual preferences impacted on politics. Wotton and Harington praised James's "chastity" because in not keeping mistresses he was not creating bastards to rival his legitimate children. Male lovers, however, could hold direct power in a way that a mistress could not, and the power that Lennox held foreshadowed that of James's later favorites in England. Safe in the knowledge of James's devotion, Lennox had moved against the regent Morton, a trusted ally of England. Elizabeth had made a formal approach to James demanding that he get rid of "the professed Papist," Seigneur d'Aubigny, but although James was usually wary of offending Elizabeth, on this he stood his ground.

James's stance sealed Morton's fate and the last regent was executed during the summer of 1581, ostensibly for his part in Darnley's murder. "That false Scots Urchin!" Elizabeth is said to have exclaimed when the news of Morton's death reached her. "What can be expected from the double dealing of such an urchin as this!"

The following year the sixteen-year-old James was kidnapped by allies of the Kirk led by William Ruthven, first Earl of Gowrie and son of Patrick Ruthven, whose servant had held the pistol to the belly of Mary, Queen of Scots during the Riccio murder. The captured king had been forced to look on as Lennox fled into exile in France, where he died in 1583. But in due course James used his cunning to escape his captors and effect a countercoup with Gowrie's rivals. Gowrie, having been initially pardoned, was executed in May 1584, after attempting to stage a second coup; leading Presbyterian ministers were forced to flee to England and the Scottish Parliament ordered all copies of Buchanan's *De jure regni*, with its arguments against the divine right of kings, to be handed in to the authorities so that they could be purged of offensive material.[23]

It was at this time that Monsieur de Fontenay, the emissary of Mary, Queen of Scots, had visited James's court. Fontenay thought the eighteen-year-old king "for his years the most remarkable Prince who ever lived." But he also described a very damaged individual, "an old young man," both wary and childishly self-indulgent. There were three aspects of James's personality that particularly concerned the Frenchman: James's arrogance, fanned by his superior education, blinded him to his "poverty and insignificance" on the world stage. He was "overconfident of his strength and scornful of other princes"—a characteristic that was still more true of him in 1603, when he had two decades of successful rule in Scotland behind him. Last, Fontenay made his observations about James's addiction to hunting. The sport seems to have given him a sense of release from his disabilities matched by no other physical pursuit apart from sex, but his attachment to it was as uncontrolled as his love for his favorites, and this incontinence was evident in other aspects of James's life.

He regularly spent money he did not have (a common problem in adults with ADHD). Elizabeth, not known for her generosity, bailed out her profligate neighbor in a series of payments totalling around £58,000, from 1586 to 1603.[24] He also appeased his lairds with gifts of titles without concern that he might degrade their value: by 1603 Scotland had as many nobles as England, though a population only a quarter of the size.[25]

Mary, however, was also curious to know not only about her son's character but also about his religious views. It was evident that he felt his mother's chief enemies, Presbyterians such as Buchanan, had also proved dangerous to him, and she hoped that James might invite her back to Scotland. Fontenay, however, forewarned her that although James had indeed grown to dislike his Presbyterian ministers and regarded the Kirk as the chief threat to royal rule, he despised the Pope and showed no obvious affection for her. Mary nevertheless remained desperate to believe that James would recognize her right to be sovereign of Scotland if she offered to legitimize the title of king that he had usurped from her. She made contact with her son to argue that such a deal was greatly to his advantage since the Catholic powers would then support his candidature for the English succession. But in

1585 she discovered James had made an agreement with Elizabeth that made him a pensioner of the English crown* and left her in her prison at Tutbury Castle, Staffordshire. Terrified that she was going to be left in England to be murdered under the Bond of Association, Mary threatened to disinherit him. He never contacted her again. The following year Sir Francis Walsingham began gathering the evidence to convict Mary of involvement in Babington's plot against Elizabeth. Only the threat that James would break Scotland's treaties with England and turn to France or Spain to avenge his mother's death could have saved her. But while James pleaded for Mary's life after her conviction, he never threatened to break Scotland's treaties with England. He may have rested his hopes on Elizabeth's reluctance to commit regicide, but he was certainly prepared to take the risk that his mother would be killed. While Elizabeth did not want to take responsibility for Mary's death, she had asked Mary's jailers to murder her so that she could cast the blame there. When they refused she signed Mary's death warrant and then suspended it as she redoubled her efforts to have Mary killed under the Bond of Association. Burghley, however, ignored her orders and convened a meeting of the Privy Council to ensure that the warrant was put into effect. James learned the grim details of his mother's death firsthand when her servants returned to Scotland.

After eighteen years confined to a series of houses in England, Mary's elegant frame had become thickset and her face hung with double chins. But her courage and dignity remained. On 8 February 1587 in the fire-lit hall of Fotheringay she approached the scaffold smiling, having cast herself in the role of a Catholic martyr with "an Agnus Dei about her neck, a crucifix in her hand, and a pair of beads at her girdle with a golden cross at the end of them."[26] The death of a common traitor nevertheless awaited her, and it was not to be a dignified one.

Mary's French physician, Monsieur Bourgoing, recorded in his journal that once she had been blindfolded and her prayers said she had

*The Treaty of Berwick, signed in July 1586, entitled James to an annual pension of £4,000; James seems to have interpreted it as recognition of his claim to the English throne.

lifted her head "thinking she would be decapitated with a two-handed sword (according to the privilege reserved in France for Princes and gentlemen)." Henry VIII had granted such a privilege to Anne Boleyn and, when Elizabeth's life had been under threat in the aftermath of the Wyatt revolt against Mary I, she had expressed the hope that if it came to it, she would be executed in the same manner. But Mary, who had been Queen of France, was led to the block and butchered with an axe, "like those with which they cut wood," Bourgoing noted with disgust. It took the nervous executioner three strokes to take off Mary's head and when his companion raised it up, with the shout "God save the Queen," he found himself, in a moment of grim farce, holding a chestnut wig, as her gray head rolled on the floor.

Mary's weeping servants had stayed after the official witnesses left the room and watched the executioners strip the stockings from Mary's corpses (it was usual for the executioners to sell any clothes from the corpses of their victims; even their hair could be cut from their heads). As the men pulled and ripped, Mary's little dog, a Skye terrier, dashed out from under her skirts. "The poor creature, covered with blood, rushed up and down the body, howling plaintively," Bourgoing recalled. Confused, it had lapped at the pools of blood on the floor before being taken away.[27]

After Mary's servants had finished recounting their story James was silent, and he quickly retired to his room. He had once said that Scotland could never be without faction while Mary was alive, but the manner of her death was a bitter humiliation for him and for his country: a high price to pay for Elizabeth's crown. With his noblemen demanding vengeance, James immediately cut all contact with England. South of the border, meanwhile, Elizabeth went into mourning; Burghley was banned from her presence and Sir William Davison, who had delivered the death warrant, was thrown into the Tower. Elizabeth then sent her cousin Sir Robert Carey to Scotland with a letter in which she swore that she had signed Mary's death warrant on the understanding that it would be put into effect only in the event of the arrival of an invasion force. But Carey was stopped at the Scottish border and was forced to wait for days before James agreed to see him.

The storm did pass, however, as Elizabeth and James knew it would.

James accepted Elizabeth's story, with English money sweetening the pill. Elizabeth for her part forgave Burghley but not Davison, whom she made the scapegoat for what had occurred.

James seized the opportunity offered by Mary's death to heal the divisions in Scotland. Thereafter he had rewarded and protected his mother's servants and in the *Basilikon Doron* James advised his son that he had found those who served his mother among his most loyal subjects.[28] It was a lesson he would carry with him to England.

❀   ❀   ❀

James had chosen the future Queen of Scots and England with care. In 1589 Anna was a Protestant princess, with a generous dowry comprising £150,000 and various territories including the Orkney and Shetland Isles, pawned to Scotland in the previous century. A miniature had also shown the fourteen-year-old to be very pretty, with fair hair and ivory skin. There had been an exchange of letters in French during which the lonely James fell so in love with his future companion that when the ship bringing her to Scotland was caught in storms and forced to head to Norway, he set sail to fetch her, committing "himself and his hopes Leander-like to the waves of the ocean, all for his beloved Hero's sake."

As soon as he arrived in Norway, James had made his way along the coast by ship and horse until he reached Oslo and the bishop's palace. There he dashed to see Anna "with boots and all." The minister David Lindsay, who was with James, declared her "a princess both godly and beautiful." Anna was tall for her age, with a determined set to her chin, and James was immediately "minded to give the Queen a kiss after the Scottish fashion, which the Queen refused as not being the form of her country; but after a few words privily spoken between his majesty and her, familiarity ensued."[29] The royal couple were married the following Sunday before traveling to Denmark to enjoy a second wedding and several months of honeymooning among Anna's relatives. It was here, amid the rich and sophisticated Danish court, that James was introduced to the modish European theories on witchcraft he later expounded in his *Daemonologie,* a treatise he published in support of the persecution of witches.

The Danish admiral who had escorted Anna to Norway had blamed the storms on the wife of a Copenhagen burgess with whom he had quarreled. She confessed under torture that she was a witch and was burned alive in September 1590 along with several others whom she had named. The Kirk had long been obsessed with witchcraft, but they had been unable to persuade James to take an interest in it until he returned from Denmark. Investigations, however, now led to the unmasking of a coven in Berwick that, it was claimed, had plotted to kill the King. James attended the trials and was astonished to hear the accused witches describe what he believed to be private conversations he had had with Anna in Norway. The first of the great waves of witch killing in Scotland had soon followed.

Anna had also found herself subject to the Kirk's disapproval, with her Lutheran faith proving to be an early source of friction. Even her coronation as Queen of Scotland proved a controversial affair. James's had been the first Protestant coronation in Scotland, but it was rushed and had kept many Catholic features. Anna's offered an opportunity to design a more purely Protestant ceremony and the ministers of the Kirk were anxious to get rid of the anointing, which they condemned as a "Jewish" ritual. James was equally determined to keep it since it reflected his view that kings drew their rights from God and not the people. When he threatened to ask one of his remaining bishops to carry it out they gave way, but tensions remained when the coronation took place in the abbey church of Holyrood on 17 May 1590.

The ceremony began with a grand procession of trumpeters and nobles. James followed, dressed in deep red, with five earls carrying his long train. Behind them came Anna. She joined James on a throne placed on a raised platform and hymns were sung. Later, after a short oration by the minister Robert Bruce, the moment came for the anointing.[30] A witness recorded that "the Countess of Mar went up to the queen and bared a little of the queen's right arm and shoulder. Robert Bruce immediately poured the queen's oil onto her bare arm and shoulder." Anna was then taken away and dressed in new robes of red velvet and white Spanish taffeta before being returned to her seat. "Silence was called for. Then his majesty had the crown delivered to her . . . Immediately afterwards his majesty delivered the sceptre to Robert Bruce that he might pass it to the queen." As he did so he acknowledged Anna as queen and pledged obedience, but his speech concluded, "We crave from your majesty the confession of the faith and religion which we profess." Anna had been promised the free exercise of her Lutheran faith, but from that moment it was apparent that she would be pressured into accepting the lower-church Protestantism of Scottish Calvinism.[31] Anna, however, proved to be very much her own woman.

The Duke of Sully described Anna's character as "quite the reverse of her husband's; she was naturally bold and enterprising; she loved pomp and grandeur, tumult and intrigue."[32] Even at just fifteen and unable to speak Scots,* Anna had made her presence felt. She had been raised in one of the most prestigious kingdoms in Europe and she encouraged a new formality at James's court. "Things are beginning to be strangely altered," it was reported. "Our Queen carries a marvellous gravity, which, with the reserve of her national manners, contrary to the humour of our people, has banished all our ladies clean from her."[33] Anna also made it plain that she enjoyed traditional courtly pursuits and she quickly earned herself the sobriquet the "dancing queen," as well as the anger of the Kirk, which condemned her "night waking and balling."[34]

James, however, found that Anna had a warm and generous temperament and the early years of the marriage were happy ones, with Anna joining him hunting and he indulging her love of fashion and jewelry. In January 1603 her wardrobe included gold-on-peach gowns with silver sleeves and her hair was habitually adorned with Scottish pearls strung on coronets worn on the back of the head. Every New Year, James added new jewels to the collection of "my dearest bedfellow": necklaces fringed with diamond drops, jeweled flower and butterfly brooches and a large number of diamond ciphers. Her favorite was "A" for Anna—the name she always used, although James preferred to call her "my Annie."[35] She quickly learned to write as well as

---

*The dialect of northern English spoken in the south and northeast of Scotland. This was not the uneducated brogue some English appeared to think, but rather the language of some of the most beautiful poetry of the day.

speak Scots and by the time she was eighteen she was also politically active. A member of the Mar family later complained that Anna's friends "generally happened to be of a contrary party to those whom the King thought his faithfulest friends." James, however, recognized that she was uniquely placed to intercede for those who felt cut off from royal favor and he demonstrated that he appreciated her role by listening to, if not always agreeing with, her opinions.[36]

Gradually it was noticed that Anna had become close to her French-educated courtiers: she had depended on them for conversation before she learned Scots and she appreciated their refinements, as did James. Many were Catholic and, although Anna had sworn an oath at her coronation to "work against all popish superstition," she was reported to be leaning toward Catholicism as early as 1593.[37] The Countess of Huntly, who gave her a Catholic catechism, was believed to be the main source of influence. The Countess was part of a group that backed the reunification of the Churches and Anna may have been aware that this was an area that interested her husband. In any event the Countess's conversation doubtless made an attractive contrast to the lectures Anna received at the hands of the Kirk. The turning point in Anna's religious life came in about 1600 when the chaplain she had brought with her from Denmark became a Calvinist.

Since Anna could not tolerate becoming a Calvinist herself, she sacked her chaplain and turned to her Catholic friends for advice. They smuggled the Jesuit priest Robert Abercrombie into a secret room to give Anna instruction. She duly visited him for three days and on the last she heard mass and received the sacrament as a Catholic. Anna later described to Abercrombie how James confronted her about rumors of her conversion when they were in bed together, asking if it was true that she had "some dealings with a priest." She had immediately confessed. "Well, wife," James apparently told her, "if you cannot live without this sort of thing, do your best to keep things as quiet as possible; for, if you don't, our crown is in danger."[38] James's response, if accurately reported, seems a remarkably mild one, but he must have been as aware of the potential benefits of his wife's conversion to his image abroad as he was of its dangers to his popularity at home.

Since the publication of the Jesuit-penned *Conference About the Next Succession,* James had sought to deflect interest from the candidacy of the Infanta Isabella. He hinted to English Catholics, to the Vatican and to the new King of France, Henri IV, that he would offer toleration of religion in England and that he might even convert. Anna's own conversion added considerable credence to his claims and according to the Duke of Sully she became "deeply engaged in all the civil factions, not only in Scotland in relation to the Catholics, whom she supported and had even first encouraged, but also in England."[39] Robert Abercrombie was allowed to stay in Scotland until 1602, during which time Anna received the sacrament from him a further nine times. She would come to him early in the morning while the rest of the household slept and he recalled that afterward she would stay and talk with him and that "sometimes she expressed her desire that her husband should be a Catholic, at other times her son should be educated under the direction of the Sovereign Pontiff."[40] It was, however, the Mar family and not Anna who was raising James's heir—a matter over which she felt deep resentment.

Prince Henry, the first of James and Anna's children, was born in February 1594 and soon afterward Anna discovered that James intended for Henry to be raised at Stirling Castle, as he had been. It meant that if anything happened to James during Henry's minority the Earl of Mar would become regent of Scotland instead of the queen, which was the norm in Europe. James was once overheard trying to explain to Anna that he was concerned that "if some faction got strong enough, she could not hinder his boy being used against him, as he himself had been against his unfortunate mother."[41] Anna refused to accept this and pleaded with James to change his mind, reminding him how she had "left all her dear friends in Denmark to follow him."

Anna usually got her way but on this James flatly refused to yield; he even gave written orders to Mar that he was to keep Prince Henry until he was eighteen unless he himself instructed otherwise.[42] In 1596 Anna gave birth to a daughter, Elizabeth, who was sent to be raised by Lord and Lady Livingstone, along with her younger sister, Margaret, who died at the age of two. James and Anna's second son, Charles, was born in 1600 and subsequently placed with Lord Fyvie.

In May 1602 a third son, Robert, followed but died four months later. These sad separations may have served to sour the royal marriage, but it was above all Anna's lasting hatred for the Mar family that explains her reaction to that mysterious episode in Scottish history, the Gowrie affair—an episode that concluded in the destruction of all significant opposition to James and the Mar faction.

❉   ❉   ❉

By the autumn of 1599 James had become desperately worried that he was about to lose his chance of inheriting Elizabeth's throne. His principal supporter at Elizabeth's court, Essex, was under house arrest. Essex's followers had warned him that Sir Robert Cecil would destroy his claim to the succession once Essex was out of the way, and there was evidence to support their view. In 1598 an English Catholic called Valentine Thomas had hinted in a confession that King James of Scotland had asked him to assassinate the Queen. The 1585 statute precluding those who plotted against Elizabeth from the succession was still extant and James was convinced that Cecil was behind Thomas's confession, just as Lord Burghley had been behind the statute, which had been aimed at his mother. Elizabeth assured James that she did not believe Thomas, but when she ignored his demands for a public statement of his innocence, James listened to Essex's supporters in their call for him to raise an army to back plans to overthrow the Queen.

That October James told his Parliament that he "was not certain how soon he should have to use arms but whenever it should be, he knew his right and would venture crown and all for it."[43] It had proved difficult, however, to raise the money for such an army. James's financial situation, which had begun to improve three years earlier, was once again in desperate straits.*

*The improvement followed the employment of a committee of eight Exchequer auditors known as the Octavians. They had taken control of all areas of royal finance and reduced James's handouts to courtiers. A group of disappointed courtiers had, unsurprisingly, united in determination to get rid of them and James had eventually done so—but for a price. The legislation he had sought to encourage the resolution of feuds through the royal courts was passed in June 1598 by the courtiers in exchange for his getting rid of the Octavians. After this the tradition of the feud began to die out.

James was forced to raise new taxes and debase the coinage, but there was a danger that the Kirk would move to take advantage of growing public anger. James had infuriated the Kirk with plans to reintroduce episcopacy—an answer to the Jesuit accusation that he would introduce a presbytery to England. It had also learned that his *Basilikon Doron* raged about the power it had wielded in his youth. In November 1599 the Master of Gray wrote to Cecil that between the anger of the poor and that of the Kirk "there was in men's breasts such a desire of reformation that nothing lacked save one gallant man for uniting grieved minds."[44] The ministers had already settled on the twenty-two-year-old John Ruthven, third Earl of Gowrie, and the minister Robert Bruce was sent to fetch him from France, where he was studying. By this time James appeared to have forgiven the Ruthven family for their role in the attack on his mother during Riccio's murder and for the exile of his beloved Lennox. Several of the children of the first Earl of Gowrie, who led the Ruthven raid, were now in the royal household and Anna counted three of the sisters of the third Earl among her ladies-in-waiting.* She was especially fond of the eldest, Lady Beatrice, and their brother, nineteen-year-old Alexander, was a favorite of both James's and Anna's. Gowrie had, however, willingly agreed to the Kirk's request, first traveling to England, where he arrived at Elizabeth's court on 3 April 1600.

The English ambassador to Paris had written a ringing commendation of Gowrie for Cecil. He was "exceedingly well affected both to the common cause of religion and particularly to her majesty" and "one of whom there may be exceedingly good use made." Gowrie had spent time in secret conferences with both the Queen and Cecil before arriving back in Edinburgh in May 1600. A huge crowd of supporters welcomed him, but James, watching, was overheard making the observation that there had been a still larger crowd for the execution of Gowrie's father. Within three months Gowrie was dead, slain in his own house by the King's men.

James's explanation of these deaths was almost literally unbelievable. He insisted that on 5 August 1600 Alexander Ruthven had lured

*John Gowrie's elder brother, James, the second Earl, died in 1588.

him from a day's hunting to Gowrie House in Perth, claiming his brother had captured a man carrying a large amount of foreign gold. As the rest of the hunting party ate their dinner with Gowrie, Alexander had tricked James into following him until he came to a room "where a man was, which the King thought had been the man had kept the treasure."[45] Alexander then grabbed James and drew his dagger, saying that James had killed his father and now he would kill him. James pleaded for his life, but Alexander replied that words could not save him and ordered the man in the room to kill him. The man had seemed unwilling and a struggle followed, during which James was spotted screaming for help at the window. His men dashed to his aid and killed first Alexander and then Gowrie as he fought to avenge his brother.

James ordered the Kirk's five Edinburgh ministers to repeat this story to their congregations so that they might thank God for his deliverance, but they refused. Robert Bruce, the minister who had crowned Anna and fetched Gowrie from France, made it clear that he believed James had plotted to kill the brothers, either because of his hatred for the family or because Anna was having an affair with one of them (there was talk that she had a flirtation with Alexander). James's reply to these accusations was blunt and compelling: "I see Mr Robert," he told Bruce, "that ye would make me a murderer. It is known very well that I was never blood-thirsty. If I would have taken lives, I had causes enough; I need not to hazard myself so."[46] James was certainly not the kind of man to place himself in the middle of a violent situation.

When the ministers persisted in refusing to accept James's story he had them replaced: four later capitulated and were forced to tour the country offering their humble submission in public places, while the fifth, Robert Bruce, refused and was sent into exile. The Kirk was informed that thereafter 5 August was to be celebrated as a national holiday with special services to give thanks for the King's survival.

At home and abroad, however, people remained unconvinced by James's version of events. The English ambassador, Sir William Bowes, thought that James, finding himself alone with Alexander—"a learned, sweet and artless young gentleman"—had made some mention of the boy's father, "whereat the youth showed a grieved and expostulatory countenance." James had taken fright and shouted for help, and after the boy was killed, he made up his story to conceal his embarrassment.[47] More recent theories have suggested that Alexander offered James sexual favors or the cancellation of a debt to lure him from his protectors and kidnap him. When James had realized what was happening he shouted in terror that he was being murdered. The Kirk certainly had strong motives for supporting another kidnap attempt and there was a suggestion at the time that England was involved.* Gowrie's servants were, however, severely tortured in an effort to uncover a conspiracy and all denied any knowledge of one. The man whom James had seen in the tower swore he had just been told to go there and wait upon events. An explanation for this comes from Gowrie's tutor, William Rynd, who reported that he had once heard young Gowrie say that the best way for a man to keep a plot secret was to keep its existence to himself. But it is possible that James did indeed plot against the Ruthvens. In London in the winter of 1602 a character named Francis Mowbray appeared claiming that he had evidence of the Ruthvens' innocence. He was handed over to James that January and died in February 1603, having fallen, it was reported, from the window of his cell in an escape attempt.

Whatever the truth behind the Gowrie mystery, the significance of it lies in James's determination to use the incident to demonstrate that neither Kirk nor nobleman would be able to control him as they had done in the past, and those who tried would suffer for it. His action against the remaining members of the Ruthven family began immediately. As soon as the King's party returned to Falkland Palace that night he had the three Ruthven sisters thrown out into the driving rain, despite Anna's protests. She refused to believe the Ruthvens had attempted to kill her husband and saw the event entirely in terms of a triumph for the Mar faction. She stayed in bed for two days afterward, refusing to eat or speak. When she eventually did so she shouted at her husband to beware how he treated her, for she was not the Earl of Gowrie. On another occasion she "hoped that heaven would not visit her family with the vengeance for the sufferings of the Ruthvens."

*It is notable that one of Gowrie's first actions in Scotland had been to oppose James's proposal to raise the taxes to pay for an army in the Scots parliament.

James, aware that Anna was pregnant, took her abuse without complaint, but he was not deflected from his pursuit of vengeance.

On 6 August a party of men were sent to seize the surviving Ruthven brothers, William and Patrick, who were still only schoolboys. They escaped over the border and in June 1602 were said to be hiding in Yorkshire. James complained to Elizabeth and, with some reluctance, she agreed to have them banished. William fled abroad early in 1603, leaving Patrick behind. In Scotland, meanwhile, in the autumn of 1600, the decaying corpses of John and Alexander were tried for treason. They were found guilty; the Ruthven estates and honors were forfeited and their name proscribed. On the day their bodies were being gibbeted, quartered and exposed throughout the country, Anna gave birth to the future Charles I. James hurried to Dunfermline, where she was lying with her child, and in the New Year he presented Anna with a jewel worth 1,333 Scottish pounds. There were those among the Mar faction who wanted her imprisoned for her support for the Ruthvens; James would hear none of it "but . . . does seek by all means to cover her folly," a witness reported.[48]

That January 1603 Sir Thomas Erskine, the Captain of the Guard, warned James that Anna had smuggled Beatrice Ruthven into her rooms at Holyrood and talked to her for hours just feet from where he slept. Beatrice left laden with gifts to support her in exile in England. James was shaken and angry but again he refused to punish Anna. He simply ordered workmen to seal up "all dangerous passages for coming near the King's chamber." There were other matters to think about than the Ruthvens, as the question of the succession had returned to center stage.

❖   ❖   ❖

The aftermath to the Gowrie conspiracy had found James's ally at Elizabeth's court, the Earl of Essex, still disgraced and Secretary Cecil with total domination over the Privy Council. In December 1600, however, Cecil's agents made an unexpected gesture of reconciliation. They claimed that "the Earl of Leicester or Sir Francis Walsingham were the only cutters of [Mary Stuart's] throat."[49] James had ignored them. Aware of the unpopularity of Elizabeth's government, he was convinced that she would soon be facing an uprising and in February 1601 he sent the Earl of Mar and a diplomat named Edward Bruce to aid Essex in his plans to raise a revolt.* But by the time Mar and Bruce arrived in London Essex had already been tried and beheaded.

James's fear was that Cecil would now use the Essex revolt to achieve what the confession of Valentine Thomas had failed to do, namely, link him directly to a plot against Elizabeth. Fortunately the black bag containing his last letter to Essex, which the Earl wore on the day of the revolt, had disappeared. It was probably destroyed either by Essex himself or by the Lieutenant of the Tower, Sir John Peyton, who soon offered James his loyalty. With no solid evidence against him, James sent instructions for Mar and Bruce to ask the "present guiders" in England to declare that he was untouched by any actions against the Queen. They were to offer his future favor to those courtiers who supported him and his eternal displeasure to those who did not. He was particularly keen for the message to get through to Cecil, who, he observed, "is king there in effect." With Essex dead, however, the kaleidoscope of faction was shifting once more. Cecil made clear to the envoys that he had every intention of backing the Stuart cause. The rules of primogeniture underpinned the laws of inheritance to which the entire political elite was subject and the majority had never been comfortable with overturning them, still less now when James's dynastic rivals were particularly weak. Even a foreigner such as the French ambassador, André Hurault, Sieur de Maisse, had observed that "it is certain the English would never again submit to the rule of a woman"; that ruled out James's cousin Arbella Stuart and the Earl of Derby's daughter, Lady Anne Stanley. Meanwhile the claim of Lord Beauchamp had been all but destroyed by the Doleman book and his failure to marry someone of suitable status.

Essex was right to believe that Cecil had needed to have a rival candidate to James in the late 1590s. The evidence suggests Cecil had considered marrying Arbella to Beauchamp's elder son, Edward Seymour, so uniting the lines of Henry VIII's sisters Margaret and Mary

*The latter was to be made Lord of Kinloss on 22 February 1603, a mark of his continued importance.

Tudor. His ally, Beauchamp's father, the Earl of Hertford, had certainly done so and Cecil's interest in the match may have been behind the rumors in Europe that he wanted to marry Arbella himself. But Elizabeth would never have permitted a Seymour-Stuart union and the sensible thing for Cecil to do now that Essex was dead was to present himself to James as his greatest champion and suggest that Essex had really wanted the crown for himself. This appears to be exactly what he did. Bruce and Mar were delighted to have caught such a fish and tactfully dropped James's demands for a public statement of his innocence of any plotting against the Queen. Instead they organized a code to enable Cecil to correspond in secret with the Scottish King. Names were to be represented by numbers: James, for example, was 30 and Cecil 10.

Cecil insisted that absolute secrecy be maintained over their correspondence for, as he later put it, "if Her Majesty had known all I did . . . her age and orbity, joined to the jealousy of her sex, might have moved her to think ill of that which helped to preserve her."[50] He had a narrow escape from being discovered only that summer. Elizabeth's Treasurer, Lord Buckhurst, later described how the Queen was walking in Greenwich Park when she "heard the post blow his horn." She asked that the bag of letters be brought to her, and Cecil, knowing that it would contain letters from Scotland, fell on his knees and begged her not to look at them. He told her that if she did people would think "it to be out of a jealousy and suspicion of him" which would leave him disgraced and unable to continue working for her effectively.[51] Elizabeth chose not to look in the bag, but Cecil remained so nervous of discovery that he risked insulting his future Queen by asking James not to tell Anna of their correspondence.

Cecil's first letter to the King assured him that Elizabeth was a dynastic legitimist, not at all inclined to "cut off the natural branch and graft upon some wild stock," but he warned that Elizabeth would perceive any demand for a public recognition of his right as a threat. Furthermore, if he invaded England as Essex had suggested, all Englishmen would unite against him. James was happy to agree to Cecil's requests, but in turn he required that Cecil work with two Englishmen he trusted. The first, Lord Henry Howard, was the embittered younger brother of the Duke of Norfolk, beheaded for plotting to marry James's mother—and thus a member of a family that had proven its loyalty to the Stuart cause. The second was Edward Somerset, Earl of Worcester, who like Howard was a Catholic, though Elizabeth had famously said of him that he "reconciled what she believed to be impossible, a stiff papist to a good subject." Where Howard was a brilliant academic but a tedious companion, Worcester was handsome and charismatic—the perfect courtier—and when Elizabeth had sent him to Scotland in 1590 to congratulate James on his marriage he had impressed the King so much that they had remained in contact thereafter.

James hoped that as a leader of the English Catholics Worcester was well placed to reconcile his co-religionists to the King's inheritance. Cecil had therefore helped engineer Worcester's promotion to the Privy Council in the summer of 1601, along with two other new members: Arbella Stuart's maternal uncle, Gilbert Talbot, Earl of Shrewsbury, and Cecil's protégé, Sir John Stanhope, an old enemy of Shrewsbury's.* Howard assured James that Shrewsbury had been picked only because Elizabeth felt she had to respond to complaints that the nobility were underrepresented on the Council, adding bitchily that Elizabeth never listened to his advice on anything. In fact James and Cecil recognized the need to have an ally within the Arbella camp on the Council and Cecil had chosen Stanhope as his counterweight. Thomas Wilson's State of England described how Cecil maintained a tradition of pairing rival with rival in all the great offices of state so that "each having his enemies eye to over look him, it may

---

*The origin of Shrewsbury and Stanhope's enmity was a long-running dispute over whether the Stanhopes had a right to build a weir on the River Trent. Such questions were considered matters of honor, as they reflected on a family's status within their county, and the argument had run to bloodshed on more than one occasion. The most recent incident had taken place in 1599. Stanhope and a band of twenty armed and mounted men had attacked Mary Shrewsbury's favorite brother, Charles Cavendish, his two attendants and his page. Cavendish and his men had fought off Stanhope's party, killing two or three of their assailants and wounding two others, but Cavendish had been left injured with a bullet in the thigh. Even in Elizabethan England, where duels and brawls were commonplace, such an incident was scandalous, but the hatred it created clearly had its uses to Cecil.

make him look more warily to his charge, and that if anybody should incline to any unfaithfulness . . . it might be spied before it be brought to any dangerous head." They in turn were supported only by "base pen clerks . . . that cannot conceive his master's drifts and policies."[52]

As Thomas Wilson observed, Cecil was like his father, "of whom it was written that he was like an aged tree that lets none grow which near him planted be."[53] It was already clear that it would be more difficult for Cecil to maintain his political hegemony under James, but he was determined to cut two of his old allies down to size: his former brother-in-law, Lord Cobham, and Elizabeth's Captain of the Guard, Sir Walter Ralegh. One of Elizabeth's Maids of Honor, Meg Radcliffe, had predicted years before that the anti-Essex alliance would break up after the Earl's death and so it was proving. Cobham and Ralegh were not of any further use to Cecil; if anything, they were a liability, unpopular with almost everybody. The women of the court detested Lord Cobham, an ill-tempered individual later described by a courtier as "but one degree from a fool," and the men loathed Ralegh, whom they considered an arrogant upstart.

Born the younger son of a mere tenant farmer from an old but impoverished Devonshire family, Ralegh had caught Elizabeth's attention early in the 1580s. According to one telling story, Ralegh had been called before the Privy Council to explain why he had fallen out with his commanding officer in Ireland, Lord Grey of Wilton. Ralegh was already an experienced soldier, having spent his teenage years fighting for the Protestant cause in France. Wilton, however, was a notorious one. His infamy rested on his having ordered the cold-blooded killing of 600 mainly Italian and Spanish prisoners at Smerwick Fort, just north of Dingle Bay. Even in an era of endemic violence this massacre had shocked: "Truly I never heard of such a bloody barbarous action, as the Lord Grey . . . committed in Ireland upon the Spaniards," the Jacobean bishop Godfrey Goodman later recalled, "for whereas they had submitted himself to their mercy, he put some four or five hundred of them [in effect the whole number] into a yard, weaponless; and then were soldiers sent in with clubs, bills and swords, and slew everyman of them."[54]

This massacre was not, however, the subject of Ralegh's complaints to the Council. The boy who had seen the horrors of the wars in France did not become the man to blanch in Ireland. Ralegh was one of two officers who had led the companies that carried out the killings. Ralegh was instead at the Council table to present his own ideas about winning the war in Ireland and, as the writer John Aubrey described it, he "told his tale so well, and with so good a grace and presence that the Queen took especial notice of him, and presently preferred him." Elizabeth liked to surround herself with a particular type of man—"proper men" was how Aubrey put it, and Ralegh exemplified this ideal, as one contemporary recalled: "For touching his shape and lineaments of body, they were framed in so just a proportion and so seemly an order, as there was nothing in them that a man might well wish to have been added or altered. In such gifts of the mind as the world generally esteems, he not only excelled most, but matched even the best men of his time."[55]

The Queen had showered Ralegh with gifts and honors: the estates of the young Catholic traitor who had given the Babington plot its name, a prized knighthood and the Bishop of Durham's crumbling palace in London. Ralegh renovated the palace and made it the center of an intellectual circle that discussed science and religion. From here he also planned his great expeditions, including the one that founded the first English colony in the New World at Roanoke Island. Elizabeth bestowed the name "Virginia" on it and all things from the New World became fashionable, from smoking tobacco in silver pipes to eating potatoes, which were considered an aphrodisiac. Ralegh, who was said to "love a wench well," had little need of sexual fillips, but he had disadvantages as a courtier. Being an outsider, he had no network of powerful relations to protect his interests. He had befriended Lord Cobham because he was an immensely rich peer with all the social contacts that Ralegh himself lacked. He might, however, have acquired more friends with better judgment if his sarcasm and "damnable pride" had not earned him so many enemies. It was said that "he was commonly noted for using of bitter scoffs and reproachful taunts which bred him much dislike" and "was so far from affecting popularity as he seemed to take a pride in being hated of the people."

Ralegh took great pleasure in annoying those less quick-witted than himself and even ignored religious sensibilities, teasing the pious by "perverting the words and sense of Holy Scripture." Many assumed he was an atheist, something considered almost synonymous to being evil.[56] There was considerable relief, therefore, when Essex replaced Ralegh as Elizabeth's favorite in 1587, and no little delight when he fell into disgrace in May of 1592 after he married one of Elizabeth's Maids of Honor behind the Queen's back and then lied to her about it. It was Cecil who had eventually smoothed Ralegh's path back to royal favor. In 1597 he had returned to his former post as Captain of the Guard and thereafter he had proved a ruthless ally of Cecil's in the factional struggle with Essex. He had even suggested that Cecil murder Essex in January 1600 when there appeared to be a danger that the Queen might accept him back in favor.

The beginnings of the split between the old allies came the following summer, when Ralegh and Cobham turned up uninvited at the peace conference of Boulogne—the event that had convinced Essex that Cecil was seeking to come to an accommodation with the Archdukes of the Netherlands, the Infanta Isabella and her husband, Albert. In fact, as Cecil complained to a friend, they had kept him ignorant of their activities.[57] What they appear to have been involved in were unilateral negotiations concerning a collection of treasure known as the "Burgundy jewels." It had belonged to ancestors of the Archdukes who once ruled the ancient Kingdom of Burgundy, a traditional ally of England against France. The jewels had been given to Elizabeth in pawn by the Dutch rebels in exchange for a loan of £28,000, a fraction of the value of the treasure, and Albert and Isabella were desperate to redeem them.[58] They hoped that paying generously would help pave the way for better relations with England and perhaps even lead to a revival of the old Anglo-Burgundian alliance—something that might have appealed to Ralegh, who recognized, as Essex did, that Spanish power was in decline. The debts of the Spanish crown were escalating and the population dropping, with plague and famine killing hundreds of thousands. Their new King, Isabella's half-brother Philip III, was a slow, fat, pink-skinned man, incapable of energizing his country, and the national mood was encapsulated in Cervantes's Don Quixote, the hero who tilted at windmills. France, by contrast, was emerging as a great power. Henri IV had restored royal authority after decades of civil war and the peace made with Spain in 1598 allowed French trade to flourish. "France," Ralegh had warned in 1600, "is already one of the greatest kingdoms in Europe, and our farthest friend."[59]

But Ralegh's actions were not all about politics. He was also keen to make money and Cobham, whom Elizabeth had employed to negotiate for peace with the Archduke's emissary, the Count of Aremberg, since 1597, was easy to manipulate. In the event, however, the negotiations came to nothing and Ralegh only succeeded in losing Cecil's trust.

The first indication of Secretary Cecil's anger came in 1601. After Cecil's wife died in 1598, the Raleghs had often taken care of his son, William. The boy adored Ralegh, whom he called his "captain," but he was now taken away from their home for good. Cecil, however, was careful to disguise his ill will toward his erstwhile allies: "in show we are great," he told a friend, "and all my revenge shall be to heap coal on their heads."[60] Cobham and Ralegh were therefore shocked to find that they were not among those invited to join the Privy Council in the summer, though Ralegh still hoped that he would be made a councillor when Parliament opened in November 1601.[61] Just before then an opportunity arose for the two friends to make contact with James, as Cecil had done.[62]

James's latest envoy, Ludovic Stuart, Duke of Lennox, son of his beloved Esmé, had arrived at Dover. Cobham, as Warden of the Cinque Ports, was there to attend on him. He seized the opportunity to express to Lennox his wish to forward James's claim, but unfortunately he then boasted about it to Cecil, who, after listening to his excitable brother-in-law, delivered an icy warning. He told Cobham that if James informed Elizabeth of what he had done, he would be in terrible trouble. Cobham protested that he had only spoken from excessive zeal, to which Cecil piously retorted that he hoped the Queen would outlive him and that no dealings with James would thus be necessary. Cobham and Ralegh were desperate to retain the Queen's favor, which appeared to be mysteriously evaporating, and it was a shaken Cobham who relayed Cecil's words to Ralegh. He fell straight into the Secretary's trap. Instead of pursuing Lennox, Ralegh told Cecil that Lennox had approached him, but he had told him that he was "too deeply engaged . . . to his own mistress" to seek favor elsewhere.[63] Come November, however, Ralegh still did not have a place on the Privy Council and it was an embittered figure that took his seat in Parliament that month.

As Cecil spelled out Elizabeth's requests for subsidies to support the war in Ireland to Parliament, Ralegh made sarcastic interventions. Infuriated, Cecil resolved to blacken Ralegh's and Cobham's names with James, telling Howard that these "two hedgehogs . . . would never live under one apple tree" with him.[64] Howard was happy to do the dirty work and the Scottish King was soon complaining about the "ample, Asiatic and endless volumes" that Howard sent him on the wickedness of Ralegh, Cobham and a third figure, an old friend of Ralegh's, Henry Percy, the ninth Earl of Northumberland. "You must remember," Howard wrote on 4 December 1601, "that I gave you notice of the diabolical triplicity that is Cobham, Ralegh, and Northumberland, that meet every day at Durham house." He claimed they had hatched a plan that "Northumberland . . . a sworn enemy to King James," should pretend to Cecil that he supported his candidature. This ploy had failed, Howard continued, so Northumberland had told his wife: "He had rather the King of Scots was buried than crowned."[65]

Northumberland's marriage to one of Essex's sisters was an unhappy one and it seems she was content to betray her husband's confidences—or even to invent stories against him. And she wasn't the only wife to do so. Howard found another useful instrument in Cobham's wife, the widowed Countess of Kildare. Born Frances Howard, she was the daughter of Cecil's ally the Earl of Nottingham and had married Cobham in 1600—as the tenth richest man in England he had one obvious attraction to an ambitious woman. Like several other Howard women of the day, Lady Kildare (it was usual to keep the name of one's first husband in cases where the first husband's title was superior) was beautiful but scheming and she had a reputation as a vicious gossip. Essex had once labeled her "the spider of the court," and whether she intended to harm her husband or not, she provided

Howard with plenty of ammunition against him, complaining that he and Ralegh frequently railed against James's title. Cecil's letters to James supported Howard's efforts, praising the "wisdom and sincerity" of "faithful 3 [Howard]," and assuring James that if he did not "cast a stone into the mouths of these gaping crabs [Cobham and Ralegh] they would not stick to confess daily how contrary it is to their nature to resolve to be under your sovereignty."[66]

As James absorbed these missives, Howard began to suggest to Cecil ways in which Ralegh and Cobham might be finished. Elizabeth was extremely anxious about the unpopularity of her government and Howard suggested that she be encouraged to be suspicious of Cobham and Ralegh and "taught the peril that grows unto princes by protecting, countenancing or entertaining persons odious to multitudes."[67] Ralegh and Cobham soon felt the deepening royal chill and struggled to retrieve the Queen's good opinion, on one occasion complaining to Elizabeth that the prisoners from the Essex revolt were being treated too leniently and on another drawing up a paper supporting her decision not to name an heir.[68] Such actions took them further from any hope of James's favor and Howard intended that in the longer term other matters could be used against them. Howard had discovered that Cobham and Ralegh had decided to divide their labors so that if the policy of peace with Spain prospered, Cobham would benefit; if war, then Ralegh. Howard hoped that Spain could be used to bring them both down: "The glass of time being very far run, the day of the queen's death may be the day of their doom," he wrote to Cecil in June 1602.[69] Northumberland, however, was going to prove more difficult to destroy.

❈   ❈   ❈

The thirty-eight-year-old Northumberland was an unconventional figure with an equally unconventional background. His father, Thomas Percy, the eighth Earl, had faced execution for his involvement in the 1569 revolt of the northern earls but was found dead in his cell from gunshot wounds. It was said to be a suicide, although some had suspected murder. Either way his escape from the executioner saved his vast estates from being forfeited to the crown under the rules of attainder, and young Northumberland inherited land stretching over eight counties across England and Wales. His immense wealth had allowed him to stand apart from the Cecil and Essex factions during the 1590s, which was just as well since he cared for neither of them. He saw Cecil, who was descended from Welsh farmers, as a social upstart and felt no commensurate warmth for Essex, whose enemy, Ralegh, shared his interests in navigation, astronomy and mathematics.

Science was a risky area for study at a time when it was confused with magic, and Howard had deliberately laced his letter to James with references to diabolic meetings at Durham House to stir up James's horror of the occult. To Howard's dismay, however, James was anxious to gain the support of a man who might otherwise have blocked his route south and in the winter of 1602–3 they were in close contact. Northumberland used his links with James to defend Cobham and Ralegh from accusations of disloyalty to James's cause but he did not wish to be too closely associated with them and told James that Ralegh "will never be able to do you much good nor harm": in other words, that he was expendable. Northumberland had a much bigger agenda than Ralegh's career to consider—the cause of toleration of religion. While Northumberland was content to conform in religious matters, Catholicism remained strongly rooted in the north of England where he had most of his land base and he saw himself as a natural protector of Catholics.

As Elizabeth's health deteriorated, Northumberland offered James a detailed analysis on how toleration would help achieve a bloodless and successful accession. According to Northumberland, there were two outstanding questions that concerned James's supporters: would he succeed peacefully without opposition, and would he invade England and try to seize the crown before Elizabeth was dead?

Northumberland explained to James that widespread fear of a Scots invasion sprang from the knowledge that the Scots had invaded England in the past, that they had many allies among England's traditional enemies and that England was vulnerable. Large numbers of her military men were employed in Ireland, in the Netherlands and on the high seas, while in England itself "all men are discontented in

general [and] . . . look rather for the sun rising than after the sun setting." In his *Tract* to the King Harington had suggested that things
were so bad a Scots invasion might succeed, but Northumberland
warned James that even if it did, a small country like Scotland would
never be able to maintain its domination of its richer southern neighbor. It would be best for James to wait for nature to take its course
with Elizabeth, for "it is most certain young bodies may die, but old
ones must out of necessity."[70] Once Elizabeth was dead, Northumberland was certain James's cause would prove a powerful one:

> When we look into your competitors at home we find the eyes of the world,
> neither of the great ones nor the small ones, cast towards them, for either in
> their worth they are contemptible, or not liked for their sex, wishing no more
> Queens, fearing we shall never enjoy another like to this.[71]

Northumberland acknowledged, however, that James's candidature had two obvious problems. The first was that he was Scots.
He warned—as Harington had—that "the better sort" feared James
might give public office to the Scots, while ordinary people found
"the name of Scots is harsh in the ears." He advised therefore that
James enter England as an Englishman; if he succeeded in keeping
"the better sort" happy, ordinary people would also accept him "and
the memories of the ancient wounds between England and Scotland
will be cancelled."[72]

The second potential source of serious opposition James might
face, Northumberland wrote, was from the Catholic population. Harington had told James that "a great part of the realm, what with commiseration of their oppression, and what with the known abuses in
our own church and government, do grow cold in religion and in the
service of both God and prince."[73] Northumberland confirmed "their
faction is strong, their increase is daily." Indeed, so many young men
were being drawn to the Catholic seminaries on the Continent that
there were now too many English priests to be supported at home.
The number of converts was also growing and they were found even
in the families of the most bitter enemies of Catholicism: Leicester's
son became a Catholic, as would Walsingham's daughter, while the

children of recusant-hunting bishops such as the Bishop of Durham, Tobie Matthew and John Thornborough had already done so.[74] Northumberland admitted that "the purer sort" of these Catholics—those influenced by the Jesuits—preferred the candidature of the Infanta Isabella to that of James. "I will dare say no more," Northumberland concluded, "but it were a pity to lose so good a kingdom for not tolerating a mass in a corner."[75] The unspoken advice was clear enough: the moderates needed to be encouraged—but James already knew that well enough.

❊   ❊   ❊

The English Jesuits, led by their Principal, the Somerset-born Robert Persons, were the most determined and dangerous opponents of James's succession. They had been behind the Doleman book on the succession and in February 1601 had persuaded Philip III to promote the candidature of the Infanta Isabella despite her own opposition to it.

Three main issues governed the Spanish Council's outlook in matters of foreign policy, and as the Jesuits were aware, their relations with England affected them all: the first—the Dutch rebellion in the Netherlands—was backed by England; the second—trade in the Indies—was frequently interrupted by English privateers; the third—the threat posed by France—had been countered in earlier centuries by an Anglo-Spanish alliance. It was vitally important, therefore, for Spain to have a friendly monarch on the English throne. The Infanta and Albert believed this would be best achieved by peaceful relations with whomever naturally succeeded Elizabeth; but Scotland was a traditional enemy of Spain and the Jesuits had persuaded the Spanish Council that if they did not provide a candidate themselves the English Catholics would support James in return for toleration, and that would be a disaster for Spain. Philip III followed their advice and the Infanta's objections were overruled.

Spain's invasion of Ireland in September 1601 followed. Intended as a stepping-stone to an invasion of England, it proved to be a military fiasco and in December Spanish forces were obliged to surrender to Essex's replacement in Ireland, Lord Mountjoy. By the early summer of 1602, however, the Spanish Council had devised new plans to invade England in the following March and started laying groundwork, giving the soldier and spy Thomas Wintour a large sum of money (100,000 escudos) to try to buy the loyalty of discontented Catholics. Within weeks, the Archduke Albert had admitted he was in touch with James and had offered his support in the hopes of future friendship. Clearly the Catholic campaign for the English throne required a new and more convincing candidate.

In Rome, English and Welsh Catholics were still petitioning the Pope to consider a marriage between Arbella Stuart and a member of the Farnese family, to whom she had been linked before the death of Alessandro Farnese, the Duke of Parma, in December 1592. Others suggested she marry the young Earl of Arundel, whose father had died in the Tower and who was considered a Catholic martyr.[76] Even Robert Persons accepted that a new candidate was required, one who might fulfill the Pope's desire to choose someone on whom Spain, France and the Vatican could all agree—and here he had a stroke of good fortune. Henri IV had always been a strong advocate of James's claim. The Scots King had a French grandmother, their countries were traditional allies and Henri had hoped to gain goodwill from the Pope by encouraging James to grant toleration of religion to Catholics, as he had offered it to Protestants in France. Henri's attitude, however, underwent a revolution in the summer of 1602.

After discovering that Cecil was working for James, Henri had realized that if James became king, it might mean a settlement between Spain and England, a cause that had always been close to Cecil's heart. Although France and Spain were at peace, it was an uneasy one and Henri spent half his revenue on defense. Not only did he fear better Anglo-Spanish relations, but under James the English and Scots crowns would be united and France would lose the benefits of the Auld Alliance, which he called France's "bridle on England." In October 1602 Spanish spies reported home that Henri IV of France was "no less worried about the King of Scotland than we are." Robert Persons approached the leader of the curia's French faction, Cardinal D'Ossat, and urged him to encourage the opening of discussions between Spain, France and the Papacy. The Pope meanwhile had issued a secret brief to his nuncio in Flanders ordering all English Catholics to oppose any Protestant successor to Elizabeth "whensoever that wretched woman should depart this life."

Alarmed by the prospect of Jesuit plots in England, James wrote a furious letter to Cecil in January, attacking his pursuit of peace with Spain. If any treaty were achieved, he complained,

> it would no more be thought odious for any Englishman to dispute upon [i.e. argue for] a Spanish title; . . . the king of Spain would . . . have free access in England, to corrupt the minds of all corruptible men for the advancement of his ambitions . . . and lastly, Jesuits, seminary priests, and that rabble, with which England is already too much infected, would then resort there in such swarms as the caterpillars or flies did in Egypt, no man any more abhorring them.[77]

He demanded to know why Cecil had not carried out a royal proclamation issued in November ordering the expulsion of all priests from England.

> I know it may be justly thought that I have the like beam in my own eye, but alas it is a far more barbarous and stiff-necked people that I rule over. Saint George surely rides upon a towardly riding horse, where I am daily struggling to control a wild unruly colt . . . I protest in God's presence the daily increase that I hear of popery in England, and the proud vaunting that the papists make daily there of their power, their increase and their combined faction, that none shall enter to be king there, but by their permission.[78]

Cecil tried to put James's mind at rest. He insisted he was indeed ferocious in his pursuit of Jesuits—"that generation of vipers"—and if he was reluctant to see the secular Catholic priests "die by dozens" it was because by and large they shared moderate Catholic opinion. Many were loyal to James's candidature and they were useful tools against the Jesuits. Some secular priests had published pamphlets accusing the Jesuits of treason and even were prepared to betray them to their deaths.[79] Unconvinced, James replied with what amounted to an order:

I long to see the execution of the last edict against [the priests], not that
thereby I wish to have their heads divided from their bodies but that I would be
glad to have both their heads and their bodies separated from this whole land,
and safely transported beyond the seas, where they may freely glut themselves
on their imagined Gods.

James explained that he was not interested in "the distinction in their
ranks, I mean betwixt the Jesuits and the secular priests." Both were
subject to the Pope, he pointed out, arguing that if the secular priests
appeared harmless, it actually made them more dangerous.[80]

On 20 January 1603 the Spanish Council finally submitted their
recommendations on the succession issue to Philip III. They suggested that an English candidate should be chosen because it would
satisfy the "universal desire of all men to have a King of their own nation . . . whilst the King of France will have reason to be satisfied, and
to refrain from helping the King of Scotland, as it cannot suit him for
Scotland and England to be reunited." The Marquis de Poza added
that if the English could not agree on a Catholic candidate "it would
be better to have any heretic there rather than the King of Scotland."
The Count de Olivares agreed:

the worst solution of the question for us may be regarded as the succession of
the King of Scotland. He is not only personally to be distrusted, but the union
of two kingdoms, and above all the increment of England . . . with the naval
forces she possesses, would be a standing danger to your Majesty in a vital
point, namely the navigation to both Indies. To this must be added the hatred
which has always existed between the crowns of Spain and Scotland and the old
friendship of the latter with France.

The Council noted that there was a faction within the curia that
believed James might be converted. It recommended that English
Catholics might be informed that the truth was otherwise. They
pointed out that James was notoriously dishonest and Henri IV's
ambassador was complaining that it was being made difficult for him
to hear mass in Edinburgh. Furthermore, "there is a strong belief that

he consented to the killing of his mother, and at least he manifested no sorrow or resentment at it."[81] They advised that their new candidate should support religious toleration for Protestants and observed that Catholics and Protestants shared "a common ground of agreement . . . their hatred of the Scottish domination," and concluded that "the greatest aid to success will be . . . the liberal promises made to Catholics and heretics, almost without distinction, particularly to other claimants and their principal supporters, who should be given estates, incomes, offices, grants, privileges, and exemptions, almost, indeed, sharing the crown amongst them"—as James was already doing.

The Council then emphasized to Philip that the means of approaching France had to be decided immediately, "in case the Queen dies before we are fully prepared. If this should happen we should not only be confronted with the evils already set forth, but the Catholics, who have placed their trust in your Majesty, will be handed over to the hangman and religion will receive its death blow."[82] Orders were made "that the building and fitting out of high ships should be continued with high speed, and also that the [military] efforts already recommended to be made in Flanders should proceed."

News of a buildup of Spanish forces had already reached England. On 17 January an English courtier wrote to a friend that a former prisoner in Spain had described military preparations and that the Queen's ships had captured several vessels heading to Spain laden "with arms and munitions."[83]

There was also shocking news about Arbella Stuart emerging at court. That Christmas she had at last attempted to escape from her grandmother's house, Hardwick Hall in Derbyshire. It was said that she had planned a marriage with Edward Seymour, the senior grandson of the Earl of Hertford and Catherine Grey. Hertford had betrayed her plan and Cecil had tried to assure James that, as far as he knew, Arbella was no Catholic, just a lonely spinster. Courtiers in England now anxiously prepared for whatever violence lay ahead. Northumberland added fifty-three warhorses to his stables. The Earl of Hertford reinforced the gateways to his house and erected defensive structures. Bess of Hardwick's elder son, Henry Cavendish, began stocking Chatsworth with new pikes and other arms.[84] Cecil, meanwhile, busily began shoring up his personal financial position. Even the prospect of a peaceful Stuart inheritance did not make his future secure. James might sack or demote him after he had served his purpose and if that occurred he would be brought down by the weight of his debts. The building of his new grandiose palace on the Strand had almost bankrupted him. Harington had heard a rumor in the summer that Cecil was being forced to sell Theobalds, the fabulous palace in Hertfordshire that his father had left him. Cecil denied it, but the Secretary of State was in a delicate position and the easiest way for him to make money was to take it from the crown.

Cecil had never been above making money from Elizabeth in morally dubious ways: when he offered his ship the *True Love* for an official expedition to the Azores in 1597 he had charged the Queen twice for the victuals. He now sold her his unprofitable estates for £5,200 and acquired the valuable royal Great and Little Parks of Brigstock in Northamptonshire behind the back of Elizabeth's cousin and Lord Chamberlain, Lord Hunsdon, the lessee. His action, he hoped, would offer some security of income, whatever lay ahead.

As James looked on watchfully from Scotland, the final duel between Cecil and Persons for the English crown was about to begin.

PART TWO

That strange outlandish word "change."
—THOMAS DEKKER, *A Wonderful Year*

CHAPTER THREE

"WESTWARD...DESCENDED A HIDEOUS TEMPEST"

The Death of Elizabeth, February–March 1603

On the thirty-first day of January Elizabeth finally left Whitehall for Richmond.[1] Wind and rain lashed the party on their journey, the last Elizabeth would ever make. Richmond Palace with its stone towers surmounted by fourteen "cloud capped" cupolas has now gone; only the gatehouse at the entrance from the green still stands, and above it the stone plaque bearing the arms of Henry VII, the first Tudor king.

Richmond was Henry VII's finest palace, a place of courtyard gardens overlooked by light and spacious double-storied galleries. Even in Elizabeth's time tourists would come to see his famous library and a genealogy on a vellum roll, twenty feet long, tracing the Kings of England back to Adam and Eve. Another hung between the windows in the great hall, culminating on the left with a picture of Henry VII himself.[2] There were also fantastic reminders of his son Henry VIII. Some visitors were shown a room with blood-spattered walls where Henry VIII's entrails were said to have been thrown three times, in accordance with instructions he had left to be carried out after his death. Another tall tale was spun about a magic mirror in which "he could see everything passing in the world."[3] The mirror was said to have broken at Henry's death but Elizabeth was also reputed to have wonderful mirrors that would not show her age.[4]

The supernatural pressed in on the natural world in sixteenth-century England and even the most hardheaded citizens believed in the power of magic. When Arbella Stuart was first at court her worldly grandmother Bess Shrewsbury used to demand she send her hair clippings for the casting of spells. The Earl of Northumberland, whose scientific experiments earned him the sobriquet "the Wizard Earl," once owned a crystal ball and Elizabeth herself both owned and gave away magic jewelry, such as a ring she had made for Essex to protect him from thieves.[5] We cannot be certain that Elizabeth also owned an unusual mirror but her aversion to seeing a clear reflection of herself in later years was often commented on. This may have been a consequence of public awareness of the false image she presented to the world in her costumes and makeup, as well as of her legendary vanity, but aged and ill though she was, her dramatic appearance still worked a kind of alchemy. The Duke of Stettin thought she did not look ugly when seen from a distance and although close up she was obviously very old she could still look impressive, as another foreign visitor to Richmond Palace found.

The Venetian ambassador Giovanni Carlo Scaramelli was given an audience with Elizabeth at Richmond early in February 1603. His country had previously refused diplomatic ties with Elizabeth on the grounds that she was a heretic. English piracy was, however, delivering hammer blows to Venetian trade in the Mediterranean and they needed to make every effort to persuade the English government to bring the situation under control. This was not going to be easy since most Privy Councilors profited from it.

The problem had its origin in the war with Spain. Elizabeth had no professional navy, and since the 1580s private interest and public duty had worked together with the government's issuing of "letters of reprisal" to legitimize acts of piracy against enemy shipping. It had proved very successful, with Elizabeth taking half the profits from each enterprise, Admiral Nottingham a tenth, and the sailors and investors the rest. The English fleet expanded and the publication of Richard Hakluyt's descriptions of the exploits of English sailors allowed the wider nation to share in the romance of their escapades. Eventually, however, the financial incentive to piracy had a corrupting effect. By 1598 Englishmen had begun to prey on neutral shipping and despite several royal proclamations forbidding attacks on Venetian trade, incidents involving Venetian ships increased, with Cecil, Nottingham, Cobham, Ralegh and Elizabeth's Treasurer, Lord Buckhurst, all involved in it.

Scaramelli found Elizabeth seated on a chair placed on a small square platform with two steps. She had recovered from her depression at Christmas and was dressed in silver and white taffeta trimmed with gold. Musicians had just stopped playing and the room was full of ladies and gentlemen who had until that moment been dancing. At Elizabeth's feet Scaramelli recognized the Archbishop of Canterbury, John Whitgift, Admiral Nottingham, the "omnipotent" Secretary Cecil (as he described him) and most of the rest of the Privy Council. Scaramelli had heard they lived like princes. Now their benefactress rose to greet him:

> Her hair was of a colour never made by nature and she wore great pearls like pears round the forehead. She had a coif arched round her head and an imperial crown, and displayed a vast quantity of gems and pearls upon her person; even under her stomacher she was covered with golden jewelled girdles and single gems, carbuncles, balas-rubies, diamonds; round her wrists in place of bracelets she wore double rows of pearls of more than medium size.[6]

Scaramelli cut a severe figure as he knelt down to kiss Elizabeth's robe. Venetians covered their suits with a "black cloth gown buttoned close at the neck" and kept their hair short.[7] Elizabeth raised him, extended her right hand to be kissed and welcomed him with the comment that it was "high time that the Republic sent to visit a queen who has al-

ways honoured it on every possible occasion." Scaramelli congratu-
lated Elizabeth on her health and assured her that the entire Serene
Republic wished her every prosperity and satisfaction. Then it was
down to business.[8]

Scaramelli had with him a letter concerning the Serene Republic's
latest tribulations at the hands of a pirate, William Piers of Portsmouth.
Piers was in his early twenties and captained a stocky man-of-war of
medium tonnage, with twenty or thirty guns and a crew of around
sixty men. Piers had recently attacked the Venetian ship the *Veniera*
and had captured booty worth around 100,000 ducats. There were
no Venetian galleys able to follow in pursuit of Piers because the
crews were infected with what the Provveditore at Zante, Piero Bonumier, described as "repulsive diseases." Bonumier had therefore applied to three English ships in the area for help. Their commanders
refused, claiming that their merchantmen were unsuited to the task,
so the *Veniera*'s crew hired a vessel to go after Piers themselves. They
then encountered another English pirate who stole everything that
Piers had left them.[9] The whole farce had "greatly annoyed" the Senate and Scaramelli handed Elizabeth the letter asking that Piers "or
others who commit such villainous deeds" be punished and their
booty restored to their rightful owners as soon as possible.

Elizabeth, now seated, passed the Senate's letter to Cecil. Only
weeks earlier Cecil had personally invited Ralegh and Cobham to join
a new pirate venture against Venice, one he hoped would raise ready
cash and keep Ralegh away from court as he prepared their ship, the
Fortune, for sea. Cecil opened the Senate's letter in silence before passing it back to the Queen. Elizabeth then read it and as she returned it
to her secretary, she rose again to her feet. Her expression, which had
been up to now "almost smiling," was grave. "I cannot help feeling
that the Republic of Venice, during the forty-four years of my reign,
has never made herself heard by me except to ask for something," she
pronounced. To Scaramelli's relief, however, her bitter words concluded with a promise: "As the question touches my subjects . . . I will
appoint Commissioners who shall confer with you and report to me,
and I will do all that in me lies to give satisfaction to the Serene Re-

public, for I would not be discourteous."[10] Scaramelli departed Richmond Palace into icy rain, happy with what he had achieved. But he knew that the Queen's word would hold good only for as long as she lived.

A few days after Scaramelli's audience, a small but significant event took place at Richmond Palace: the ring Elizabeth had worn since her coronation, with which she been "married to this kingdom," was filed from her finger, where it had grown into her flesh. The news of the ring's removal was received as an omen, "as if it portended that her marriage with the kingdom, contracted by the ring, would now be dissolved."[11] A state of acute anxiety took hold at court and, as at all times of threat, Catholics encountered renewed hostility.

On 17 February a priest called Anderson, betrayed by another as having been friendly with the Jesuits, was tried and executed at Tyburn. The Catholic spy Anthony Rivers reported that Anderson had "prayed for the Queen and showed great courage, yet with mildness and discretion; many pitying him and inveighing against the cruelty of the Lord Chief Justice for he had not a day's liberty to provide for his death, as even common thieves have." Rivers added in a separate letter that the Chief Justice "would have put more to death at Bury but the Queen forbad it."[12]

❈   ❈   ❈

Many were by now convinced that the mysterious business of Arbella's plot to marry Edward Seymour had been an attempt on the throne. Although Cecil had assured James that this was not the case, the truth was that he himself remained uncertain. The news and details of Arbella's escape venture first reached Cecil on 31 December 1602. His old ally, the Earl of Hertford, had sent to him in London, under guard, a long-serving servant to Arbella's grandmother, Bess Shrewsbury. It transpired that this man, John Dodderidge, had appeared at the Earl's house in Tottenham the previous day, asking to see the Earl alone. Hertford, suspecting that it might concern his grandson, insisted that he come to the public dining room. There the kneeling servant delivered a message from Arbella. It referred to the previous interest Hertford had shown in a possible Stuart-Seymour marriage and described a plan that would enable her to marry his grandson in secret.

Arbella proposed that Seymour should come to Hardwick Hall disguised as the son or nephew of "some ancient grave man" who wished to sell the Countess land or borrow money from her: "if they come like themselves they shall be shut out of the gates, I locked up, my grandmother will be the first shall advertise and complain to the Queen." Since Arbella had never met Seymour she asked that he was to bring, by way of identification, "some picture or handwriting of the Lady Jane Grey whose hand I know. She sent her sister a book at her death which were the very best they could bring."[13] The book Arbella referred to was a Greek testament inscribed with the last thoughts of "Queen Jane" on the eve of her execution half a century before. The dying Edward VI had left Jane Grey the crown in a failed attempt to prevent the accession of his Catholic sister Mary I or Elizabeth, whom he suspected would not usurp Mary's place. After Jane was overthrown she was placed in the Tower and following Wyatt's revolt Mary ordered her beheading. The doomed girl had tried to comfort her fourteen-year-old sister, Catherine—Seymour's grandmother— assuring her that she was going to immortal happiness before bidding her farewell: "Your loving sister . . ." She faced her executioner only hours later.

Jane's book was a grim reminder of the possible fate of those with ambitions for the crown, and Hertford, "mightily distasting and disliking, grew impatient" with Dodderidge. He told the servant to write down everything he knew and warned that he was "to prepare himself for punishment." The next day, still terrified, Dodderidge confessed again to Cecil.

Dodderidge was fond of Arbella, whom he had known since her childhood, and he described how she had spent three weeks working to persuade him to carry her message. First she had told him that Hertford had sounded out a relative of hers, one David Owen Tudor, on a possible marriage between Seymour and herself. She asked him to take a message in response to this suggestion to Hertford's lawyer, Mr. Kyrton. Seeing Dodderidge hesitate, she changed her mind and requested he go to Hertford's house in Tottenham. She assured him that he would be welcomed and that her Cavendish uncles supported her plans. He had left Hardwick on Christmas Day, riding a horse borrowed from Arbella's eldest uncle, Henry Cavendish, who lived near Hardwick at Chatsworth.

Cecil was aware there was a revived interest in Arbella's candidature in Europe and a close watch had been put on the young Earl of Arundel, who had been suggested to the Pope as a possible spouse for Arbella. He was also aware of reports the previous autumn that there was a group of courtiers interested in placing Arbella and Edward Seymour on the throne: the letter the spy Rivers had written describing what he had heard had been intercepted. But since the Earl of Hertford had given up any idea of a possible marriage between Arbella and his grandson, no extra security had been considered necessary for him. If there was a serious conspiracy to marry Arbella to Seymour, Cecil knew, it would have to be backed by another nobleman. The obvious name was that of Gilbert Shrewsbury, whose wife was Arbella's aunt Mary Cavendish. Lady Shrewsbury was a Catholic convert who might have persuaded Arbella to promise toleration of religion in exchange for Catholic support for her marriage. She was also a friend of Lady Ralegh, whose husband was likely to be interested in a Seymour-Stuart match.[14]

The intelligence gatherer Thomas Phelipps had noted in 1600 that Ralegh supported the choice of a Seymour candidate, "seeing Essex leans to the Scot."[15] There was no reason for him to have changed his view since he had fallen out with Cecil, who in turn now supported James. But whatever Ralegh's inclinations, Shrewsbury was a Privy Councilor, well placed to earn James's gratitude for his support, and he had a lot to lose by taking the risk of backing his niece. Sir John Harington, who knew the Shrewsburys well, had assured James in his *Tract*, "It is least likely that when it comes to trial they will hazard so great estates, so contented lives, so gentlemanly pleasures, so sweet studies, to advance their niece against law, reason, probability, yea possibility."[16] Cecil took the same view and it was apparent that Dodderidge could name only Owen Tudor, a family chaplain called James Starkey and Arbella's Cavendish uncles as having helped her. Furthermore, Dodderidge admitted he had not discussed anything with her uncles himself. The only evidence was the loan of Henry's horse and Cecil knew that Henry was quite capable of deciding to help Arbella for no better reason than to annoy his mother. The dowager Countess had engaged Henry in a deeply unhappy marriage to Shrewsbury's sister, Grace Talbot, and he had never forgiven her for it.

To find out exactly who was behind Arbella's attempt Cecil picked the Queen's Commissioner, Sir Henry Brouncker, to interview her. Brouncker had entrusted the care of his family to Cecil eight months earlier when he had thought he was dying "with the stone." He could be relied on to be discreet about anything that emerged about earlier approaches to Owen Tudor. The Queen briefed Brouncker personally before he left Whitehall and three and a half days later, on 4 January, he arrived at Hardwick. Arbella's grandmother had no idea of what had happened. Horrified by the sketchy outline she was given, she promptly agreed to Brouncker's request to interview Arbella. Brouncker warned the terrified Arbella that the time had come to confess all and ask forgiveness: "I . . . demanded whether she had had no late intelligence with the Earl of Hertford or employed any man to him." Flushing, she denied everything. Brouncker advised her again to tell the truth. When she continued to lie he pulled from his pocket a confession signed by John Dodderidge.[17]

Arbella told Brouncker angrily that the servant must have gone to see Hertford of his own volition. He was a "bold, lewd fellow" and would do anything for gain. Brouncker ignored her comments and insisted she must tell him "who was the first mover of this marriage." Arbella, realizing that she had to concede something, told Brouncker that it was "a man of the Earl of Hertford's to one Owen Tudor, servant to my grandmother." Brouncker retorted, "That was moved long since, but I desired to know how it was lately renewed." At this Arbella became so distressed that her replies were at first incomprehensible. Eventually, however, she corroborated Dodderidge's account, "saving that she faintly denied that her uncles were acquainted with the matter." She promised Brouncker that she would write everything down if he would "promise to conceal it from her grandmother."[18]

The sharp-tongued Bess Shrewsbury held more fears for Arbella than even the Queen, who could have had her life.

Brouncker was now convinced that Arbella was the tool of others. After leaving Hardwick he took his horse and explored the area around the estate. He noticed a number of gentlemen who did not live locally, including Mary Shrewsbury's servant Mr. Hacker, Henry Cavendish and a Catholic gentleman he simply referred to as Stapleton from Yorkshire—most likely Richard Stapleton, the recusant Catholic husband of Arbella's first cousin Elizabeth Pierrepont.[19] It was his presence that concerned Brouncker the most and he advised Cecil that Owen Tudor should be interviewed to find out more.

Cecil's network of contacts soon tracked Owen Tudor to Anglesey. Owen Tudor was the elder of two brothers, the younger of whom was fighting for the Spanish. He told Cecil's men that Hugh Owen, a brother-in-law of the traitor, the eighth Earl of Northumberland, had raised the subject of Arbella marrying Edward Seymour many years before. He thought that his own son, who was now working as Arbella's page, might have told her some of the details. Dodderidge had also named James Starkey as someone willing to help Arbella and he too was interviewed. What emerged was a picture of a lonely and deeply unhappy young woman. Arbella had spent the prime of her life, from eighteen to twenty-eight, in the Derbyshire countryside. From 1597, when she was twenty-three, she lived at her grandmother's new home, Hardwick Hall, which still stands "more glass than wall." Bess was by then looking for immortality in the descendants of her sons and the houses she had built, not in founding some royal dynasty. She topped Hardwick with her initials, "ES," for Elizabeth Shrewsbury, but Arbella, educated to rule a kingdom, did not even have a bedroom she could call her own. Too young, her life was one of memories: her time at court and the stories she had heard about the secret marriage of Catherine Grey to the Earl of Hertford, as well as that of her parents. They had become an obsession.

A turning point had come the previous spring. Arbella had been led to believe she was going to be invited to meet the Duke of Nevers, a French nobleman of royal blood who was coming to court at Easter.

The rumors were that he hoped to marry her, but in the event his visit had been a short one and she had spent another Easter at Hardwick. Starkey had often found her crying over her books and she asked him to help her leave Hardwick. He refused, but he did agree to carry out some of her requests.

Arbella had told Starkey she was frightened that her grandmother would take her jewels, and once tearfully gave him a key and asked him to look after a valuable pearl that belonged to her. She told him she had already sent most of her jewels to Yorkshire—the home of Elizabeth Pierrepont and Richard Stapleton.[20] But although the Stapleton connection was troubling, the Starkey interview, like the others, had only linked Arbella's action with members of her family and a few servants. Cecil judged that it was therefore safest to leave her in the care of her grandmother—safer, certainly, than placing her in the Tower, where her presence might attract a little too much interest. But Bess Shrewsbury wanted nothing more to do with Arbella and begged Cecil and the Vice Chamberlain, Sir John Stanhope, to take her granddaughter off her hands. They refused and so Bess put Arbella under close watch: she was allowed no choice in the company she kept or the things she did, her letters were intercepted, and her angry grandmother would regularly pinch her nose and abuse her.

Arbella's letters to Brouncker asked bitterly "if the running on of years be not discerned in me only," that she should be treated worse than an infant.[21] When her complaints were ignored she went on a hunger strike, refusing to eat until she was moved from Hardwick. By the second week of February 1603 she was obviously unwell and "enforced to take much phisick."[22] In this weakened state she heard some grim news. Starkey had been unable to bear the shame and terror of the interviews and early in February he had hanged himself. Arbella was so distressed by his death that Bess finally agreed to move her to the house of her uncle William Cavendish, who lived at nearby Owlcotes, on condition that she start eating again.

At court, meanwhile, the news of Starkey's suicide fueled the speculation that someone was making an attempt to put Arbella on the throne. Indeed, the rumors had reached the Venetian ambassador, Scaramelli, who had written to the Senate describing the relative strengths of James and Arbella's claims, how they were perceived and where their support lay.

James was known to be clever, extravagant and ambitious to the point, Scaramelli wrote, "that his ambition helps him to swallow the shedding of his mother's blood." It was widely said he would grant toleration of religion when he was crowned, but Scaramelli judged that James's most significant support came from Elizabeth's Privy Council. It was clear that they were not prepared to see another woman crowned and it was noted that Cecil had already made moves to secure James's route south—making his elder brother, Thomas Cecil (since his father's death Lord Burghley), President of the North as well as placing people James trusted "as governors of all the strong places in those parts." There was, however, much talk about the legal objections to James's candidature: "first that he was not born in the kingdom and is therefore ineligible for the crown; and the second, that his mother, after her execution was declared a rebel by Parliament, and incapable of succession, and this incapacitates her son." These impediments, Scaramelli explained to the Senate, made Arbella (or "Arabella," as Scaramelli called her in the Italian manner) a serious candidate.

The Venetian had learned from courtiers that Arbella was "of great beauty and remarkable qualities, being gifted with many accomplishments, among them the knowledge of Latin, French, Spanish and Italian, besides her native English." She, like James, he wrote, was raised in the belief that she would succeed to the crown, but she had been forced to live in relative poverty, far from London.[23] Many courtiers seemed to believe that Spain was behind Arbella's attempted marriage to Seymour, and Scaramelli reported that Starkey had "killed himself because of his intrigues."[24] The Queen was said to be deeply distressed by Arbella's recent actions and it was even being suggested that Arbella might lose her head.

❈   ❈   ❈

By the third week of February Elizabeth had sunk into the same state of depression and paranoia that Harington had found her in at Christmas—and once more it expressed itself in matters concerning Ireland.

The Lord Deputy, Mountjoy, was pressing for Elizabeth to grant Tyrone a pardon so that the war could be concluded. Cecil supported him, arguing that if they were to defend themselves from the Spanish, Ireland needed to be secure. Elizabeth, however, had turned down Mountjoy's request, informing him that she would not accept any submission from "the author of so much misery to our loving subjects." The Irish rebels had indeed been cruel. The wives of English settlers in Munster had been forced to watch their own children being slain, and had then been raped, had their noses slit and were whipped as they ran naked down the roads. But now the rebel army was ruined and the Irish people were starving. Essex's former secretary in Ireland, Fynes Moryson, recorded "no spectacle was more frequent in the ditches of towns, and especially in wasted countries, than to see multitudes of these poor people dead with their mouths all coloured green by eating nettles, docks, and all things they could rend up above ground."[25] Harington described the famine as "so terrible . . . as no chronicle of Jew or Gentile hath the like."[26] No purpose, not even revenge, could be served by continuing the war.

Cecil enclosed a letter of his own with Elizabeth's instructions to Mountjoy, confiding his belief that the Queen was "almost in conflict with herself" as to what to do about Tyrone. He believed her fundamental concern was her own position and "how to terrify future traitors when so horrible a traitor [as Tyrone] is received."[27] The long shadow of the Essex revolt still hung over Elizabeth; she knew that even now—perhaps especially now—she might not be allowed to die peacefully in her bed. When Cecil continued to try to persuade her to pardon Tyrone she turned on him, claiming it "most dishonourable to pardon a rebel that had made seven years war with her; whereas she could not be permitted to spare Essex's head for one day's delict."[28] Eventually Cecil succeeded in getting her agreement to the pardon, but her depression worsened. Letters were arriving from Arbella claiming that she had a secret admirer at court—a man whose credit was "great with her Majesty."

As Elizabeth pondered who this potential new traitor might be, her misery was compounded by the death of her cousin Elizabeth Carey, Countess of Nottingham. The Countess had been Elizabeth's longest-

serving Lady of the Bedchamber and the Queen's grief was insupport-
able. She disappeared to her room, the dancing at court stopped and
the gossip on her state of health grew louder. "And now Brouncker is
again sent unto [Arbella] and it is thought will bring her to Woodstock, where she shall be kept," Anthony Rivers informed his Jesuit
contacts in Europe. "What the design may be cannot yet be discovered." He had noticed the Shrewsburys were in close contact with
Cecil: "many secret meetings are made between them, where, after serious consults, they dispatch messengers and packets of letters, and
this sometimes twice in a week."[29] The old rumors of Cecil's interest
in marrying Arbella were revived and Rivers thought it possible that
Cecil was behind Arbella's action, for "so subtle is the Secretary that
hardly can it be judged which way he will take, and as yet he rules
all."[30]

❖   ❖   ❖

Arbella had begun to eat again at Owlcotes and by the beginning of
March she was well enough to return to Hardwick for a new round of
interviews with Brouncker. She was delighted that her invention of an
admirer had brought Brouncker back and she answered all his queries
about the identity of her friend with the answer "the King of Scots,"
the one man she could name without harm to anyone. Brouncker
quickly realized that they had been duped and, angry to have been
lured from court at such a crucial time, announced that he would be
returning to Richmond immediately. Distraught at the idea of being
left again at Hardwick, Arbella wrote to the Queen, apologizing for
her recent behavior, in tones of the greatest bitterness. She realized,
she told Elizabeth, that her life was to be more unfortunate than she
had ever thought possible and only death could make her "absolutely
and eternally happy."

    After Brouncker had gone, Arbella went to the long gallery where
he had first interviewed her, this time with her young cousin Mary
Talbot, the daughter of Mary and Gilbert Shrewsbury. The fire was
smoking and it stung their eyes as they walked "sullenly as if our
hearts had been too great to give one another a good word, and so to
dinner." After Arbella had eaten she went to ask her grandmother's

blessing, as part of her nightly routine. She was met with a "volley of most bitter and injurious words" from Bess and a stream of questions from her uncle William. She ran to her study. They followed her and watched as she started writing a letter, demanding to know whom the letter was to. She told them it was to Brouncker and read it aloud before running back to the long gallery to find a servant to carry it. Arbella found the household warming themselves by the fire. As she burst in they shrank back "as if they had been afraid of me." She had already caused the death of one servant and the ruin of another, but one man who "stood with his hat in his hand and my glove in his hat" offered to take her letter to Brouncker.[31]

It was a long, rambling missive and Cecil marked it with the comment, "I think she has some strange vapours to her brain." Many other letters followed as Brouncker made his way back to Richmond. Sometimes she wrote twice a day, often letters of thousands of words, pouring forth a great spate of misery and recrimination. "If you think to make me weary of my life and so conclude it according to Mr Starkey's tragical example you are deceived," she wrote in one. "I recommend my innocent cause to your consideration, and God's holy protection . . . for all men are liars. There is no trust in man whose breath is in his nostrils."[32]*

Brouncker arrived back at court just as Elizabeth emerged from her room. She was described as in such "a deep melancholy that she must die herself," but the business of government went on. The Treasurer, Lord Buckhurst, was telling her that her coffers were empty and that immediate funds were required for Ireland, while the City of London pressed hard for the repayment of her debts. She became so testy and impatient that soon only Cecil dared approach her.[33] Elizabeth appeared suspicious that some men around her were "ill affected" and she complained frequently about Arbella and whoever might be sup-

---

*Some have since blamed Arbella's mental collapse on variegate porphyria, a disease that she and Mary, Queen of Scots, are reputed to have inherited through Margaret Tudor, and which eventually caused the "madness" of George III. Symptoms include loss of appetite and abdominal pain as well as anxiety, depression, confusion and restlessness. But the diagnosis, which is necessarily speculative when a patient has been dead so long, may only serve to make us underestimate her anguish.

porting her.[34] On 9 March Cecil wrote to the English ambassador in Edinburgh, George Nicolson, warning that Elizabeth's ill health and depression had become so serious that her life could be measured in months at most. The Queen was eating little and although she did not have a cough or a fever, her mouth and tongue were dry and her chest hot. She couldn't sleep and would not stay in bed or take physic; instead, to everyone's dismay, she had spent the previous three days walking restlessly in the garden.[35]

The spy Rivers gave his contacts additional information on the Queen's state of health. Every day, he wrote, Elizabeth would complain of some new infirmity, "as imposthumation near her head, aches in her bones, and continual colds in her legs, besides a notable disease of judgement and memory insomuch as she cannot abide discourses of government and state, but delights to have old Canterbury tales to which she is very attentive." When the Venetian Scaramelli sought a second audience with the Queen he was amazed to be sent a message that she wished to discuss only "pleasant topics" and that if he wanted to return to the matter of Piers the pirate he would have to wait for the report of her Commissioners. The mood at court was gloomy: "all are in a damp," Rivers reported: "Matters of succession are now ordinary discourse, both in court and country, but no appearance of any likely to prevail but the King of Scots, upon whom the far greater part of the realm seem to have fixed their hopes. Many have utter aversion that way, and would be opposite had they any potent competitor."

Arbella was seen as James's chief rival and his supporters were doing their best to damage her reputation, encouraging rumors that she was mad. Scaramelli observed that the kings of Spain and France were, nevertheless, publicly well disposed toward her. Henri IV was particularly active and tried to deflect Elizabeth's mistrust of Arbella's supporters by informing her that several members of her nobility were in secret contact with James. This she easily believed, according to the historian William Camden, as "some of the Lords of the Court (to say nothing of the Ladies), who had the least reason of all to have done it, ungratefully . . . forsook her."[36] They included the Countess of Nottingham's sister, Lady Scrope, a lady of the Privy Chamber, and Elizabeth's pampered godson, Sir John Harington, who railed at dinners about the shortcomings of her government. Some courtiers were even overheard arguing that James should be sent for.

As the sense of impending crisis deepened, the head of the Jesuits in England, Henry Garnet, showed a group of former soldiers the secret papal brief ordering all Catholics to oppose the crowning of a heretic. They included the Essex rebel and future gunpowder plotter Robert Catesby. The Jesuit faction was desperate for the Spanish to fulfill their promises to carry out an invasion that month and a son of Lord Buckhurst, the Catholic Thomas Sackville, was on his way to Rome to try to hurry preparations. The Spanish, however, were only now composing a letter to Rome confirming their support for an English-born candidate. A Scots invasion seemed more likely and it was variously reported that James would bring 14,000 or 30,000 troops into the field to secure the succession. Rivers heard that troops had been made ready in the north to confront them: "My Lord Burghley, the President, is sent down to see this done, and all this to withstand the Scot."[37] Work was meanwhile going ahead for the defense of London: "the Council have consented to have thirty thousand quarters of wheat to be put by, laid up in our storehouses of London, and that the ditches shall be cleansed and enlarged two feet."

But the Council's immediate fear was not, in fact, of invasion by Scotland or even Spain. It was of revolution in England. The previous decade had seen much social unrest. In rural areas public anger centered on the enclosure and intensive use of common land by the larger landowners. During the famine year of 1596 there had been riots and disturbances in Derbyshire, Northamptonshire, Somerset and Oxfordshire, where, it was said, peasants hoped "to knock down the gentlemen and rich men."[38] London, however, had also seen violence. On 27 June 1595 large numbers of London apprentices, angry that the rich were evading their share of taxation, had gathered in Leadenhall and Cheapside: 1,800 people marched to the Mayor of London's house and erected a gallows in front of his door. Two days later the Attorney General saw a further thousand armed with "guns . . . pikes, pole axes, swords, daggers, staves and such like" rioting on Tower Hill. Elizabeth had declared martial law but it was several days before the situation was brought under control.[39] The elite feared that Elizabeth's death could now be the trigger to revolution, since it was widely believed that during an interregnum no legitimate government existed. It would be weeks, or months, before James could be installed and during that period England could be in a state of anarchy.

It was only a matter of time before news of Elizabeth's poor health reached the wider public. The ideal opportunity for the government to quash rumors and issue warnings was through the sermon delivered on 13 March, the first Sunday of Lent, at the Pulpit Cross in the churchyard of St. Paul's. The Cross marked the heart of the capital and the site had been used to disseminate information and propaganda for generations. Henry III had consulted with Londoners at Paul's Cross in the thirteenth century; sermons were being recorded at the beginning of the fourteenth, and under Henry VIII Paul's Cross became the platform for a state-sponsored revolution. Every note in the cacophony of opinion released at the Reformation was, at one time or another, expressed on the octagonal, framed stage where the preachers stood. The area was also a hotbed for gossip, bustling with courtiers and apprentices, actors and aldermen, spies and lawyers. Some came for the books sold hot off the presses in nearby streets, others to exchange news or views with friends and self-proclaimed experts on court affairs. The Lenten sermon could thus preempt any dangerous talk on Elizabeth's health and be used to recite punishments that might be expected by troublemakers. But instead of ensuring that they had a man on whom they could rely in the pulpit, on Sunday the thirteenth, a Puritan divine called Richard Stock took to the churchyard stage and prepared to deliver what he knew would be a controversial sermon.

Most of Stock's congregation stood in the open air, with gentlemen sitting at the front, their hats on their heads. At the very back, however, were those to whom his sermon was to be aimed: the dignitaries in their private boxes in the galleries built up against the transept and choir of the old Gothic cathedral. They included the Mayor of London, his aldermen, noblemen, Privy Councilors and their wives. For two hours Stock lectured them on their greed and venality: "I have lived here some few years, and every year I have heard an exceeding outcry of the poor that they are much oppressed of the rich of this city, in plain terms, of the Common Council. All or most charges are raised by your fifteenths, wherein the burden is more heavy upon a mechanical and handicraft poor man than upon an alderman, proportion for proportion," he reminded them. "You are magistrates for the good of them that are under you, not to oppress them for your own ease. I would speak to him who is chief of the city for this year. What is past cannot be remedied, but for the future, as far as lies in your power, prevent these things."[40]

The subject matter of Stock's sermon was all too reminiscent of the trigger for the riots of 1595. The Lord Mayor, Robert Lee, was furious. But he also knew that punishing Stock could spark the disorder the government was anxious to avoid and so Stock was let alone.* The Mayor and Privy Councilors would, however, be more careful about who gave the key sermons in the next few weeks.

The Council had by now decided that it was time something was done about Arbella's stream of letters and complaints, the latest of which had just arrived. It was her longest yet and, disturbingly, it appealed for help from the old Essex faction. The letter was dated 9 March, Ash Wednesday, the second anniversary of Essex's execution, "and the new dropping tears of some might make you remember it, if it were possible you could forget," she wrote. Arbella drew attention to the parallels between Essex's fate and her own. He had been allowed to die at the hands of his enemies; now her life was threatened by the same anti-Essex faction. "You saw what a despair the greatness of my enemies . . . drove innocent, discreet, learned and Godly Mr. Starkey into"; Cecil, Stanhope and Hertford, she implied, now hoped for her suicide, and she accused the Queen of taking their side against hers, just as she had taken their side against Essex.

Arbella asked all those who loved Essex to come forward in her defense. He had been her "noble friend" in difficult times and "I never

---

*Stock enjoyed a respected career as a parochial public speaker until his death in 1626. He even returned to the subject of the oppression of the poor in a sermon at the election of another lord mayor near the end of his life when he remarked that "a grayhead spake now what a greenhead had done formerly": *Dictionary of National Biography* (CD-ROM, 1995).

Left Elizabeth's witty godson, Sir John Harington, supported James's accession but was in prison when he was crowned.

Below Mural of Henry VIII, Henry VII, Elizabeth of York and Jane Seymour, boasting the continuity of the Tudor dynasty.

Right Lady Katherine Seymour, Countess of Hertford (née Grey), and her son Edward Seymour, Lord Beauchamp—Elizabeth's heir under the will of Henry VIII, as backed by the Act of Succession.

In 1602 the Spanish planned to invade England and place the Infanta Isabella Clara Eugenia on the throne. This portrait was sent as a gift to James after his accession in 1603.

Above Robert the Devil: Principal Secretary to Elizabeth, Sir Robert Cecil, in 1602–3.

Left The last favorite: Robert Devereux, second Earl of Essex, led a revolt to force Elizabeth to name James VI her heir. His continuing popularity after his execution left Elizabeth fearful and depressed. In 1603 James called Essex his "martyr," but the memory of Essex as a warrior against the Spanish would come to haunt him.

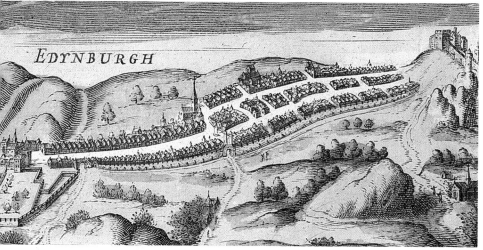

John Speed's Prospect of Edinburgh, 1610.

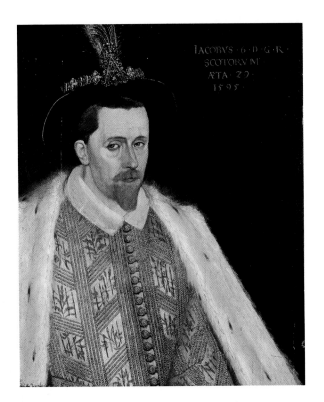

Left James VI. This portrait of 1595, attributed to Adrian Vanson, gives a much better sense of the watchful, clever young King who came south in 1603 than later portraits painted in England.

Below John Speed's map of Scotland is framed with portraits of James, Anna and their sons Henry and Charles in 1610.

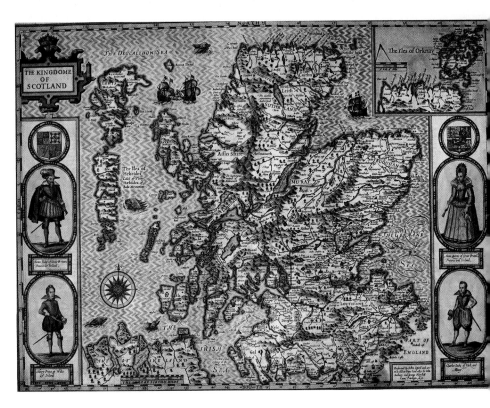

Anna, the first Queen of Scots and Queen of England. James's remarkable wife is wearing pearls that had belonged to Queen Elizabeth I. (John de Critz, c. 1605)

Left Robert Persons, SJ, the most dangerous enemy of James's accession as King of England.

Right Sir Walter Ralegh and his son Wat in 1602, when Ralegh put his estates in the boy's name, apparently to avoid them being lost should he be attainted of treason.

Above Richmond Palace, where Elizabeth spent her last traumatic weeks.

Left The dying Elizabeth in February/March 1603. The subject of this portrait by Nicholas Hilliard is a matter for debate, but the face resembles portraits of Elizabeth from this period, notably the Rainbow portrait. Above her head are the Latin words for "By the love of virtue," an attribute that in women was associated with chastity.

Above Arbella Stuart tried to flee Hardwick Hall in Derbyshire in December 1602 and March 1603, in what many believed was an attempt on the crown.

Right Arbella Stuart at age thirteen, with her books at her hand.

ARBELLA STVARTA
COMITISSA·LEVINIÆ
ÆTATIS·SVÆ·13·ET·4·
ANNO·DÑI·1589·

had nor shall have . . . the like time to this to need a friend in court." It was Hertford's own plans that had inspired her attempted marriage, she pleaded: "What fair words have I had of Courtiers and Councillors and lo they are vanished into smoke. Who is amongst you all dare be sworn in his conscience I have wrong? And dare tell the Earl of Hertford he hath done it? and the 2 Councillors [i.e., Cecil and Stanhope] they wrong their estate . . . to let innocence be thus oppressed and truth suppressed."[41]

On Monday 14 March, Cecil drafted a letter to Arbella's grandmother insisting that "as much as maybe, her sending up and down such strange letters may be forborne." It asked for William Cavendish to take Arbella back to Owlcotes, where she might be happier and quieter. But the ink was barely dry when Cecil and Stanhope received shocking news from Arbella's grandmother. The very same day Arbella had written the letter, she had sent her page, the fourteen-year-old son of Owen Tudor, to an inn in Mansfield. There Henry Cavendish and Richard Stapleton were waiting to conclude arrangements for another escape attempt. On Thursday the tenth, Cavendish and Stapleton rode to the hamlet of Hucknall, half a mile from the gates of Hardwick, with six other horsemen. A further band of forty or so armed men waited in woodland nearby. Arbella was expected to find an excuse to go out for a walk and join them sometime before noon. Midday came and went, however, without any sign of Arbella.

Arbella had tried to leave Hardwick, saying she wished to go for her walk, but her grandmother had pointed out it was "dinner time" and obliged her to stay in the house. Cavendish waited at Hucknall until nearly two o'clock before deciding to fetch Arbella himself. He had fought the Spanish in the Netherlands, but at the gates of Hardwick he proved no match for his septuagenarian mother. Bess agreed "my bad son Henry" could enter, but she refused to allow Stapleton or the other horsemen through the gate. Arbella, seeing that her opportunity of escape was slipping away, asked her grandmother if she could speak with Stapleton. Bess refused. Arbella demanded to know if she was a prisoner, "and said she would see and so went to the gate, and would have gone out, but was not suffered."

In desperation Arbella had shouted through the bars telling Stapleton to go back to Mansfield until he heard from her. Cavendish gesticulated back, trying to arrange a time for them to meet the following day, but Arbella was by then being dragged off and was unable to reply. When she heard her uncle and Stapleton ride away she became hysterical and tried to follow them, begging to be allowed to go for a walk, "which I thought not convenient she should do," Bess noted in her letter to court, "and so she stayed."[42]

Exasperated, Cecil sent Brouncker north once more, this time to interview Richard Stapleton and Henry Cavendish as well as Arbella. Elizabeth was informed, but she was growing weaker by the day and her doctors were warning "that if this continues she must needs fall into a distemper, not a frenzy, but rather a dullness and a lethargy."[43] Those who had thought she might live for months now revised their estimate to weeks and, inevitably, the news began to leak beyond the court. People studied the faces of the Councilors as they came and went from Richmond, sometimes looking anxious, as if they feared for Elizabeth's health, sometimes cheerful, as if she might be recovering. According to one court servant, everyone knew that Elizabeth was dying when Councilors, fearful of their impending loss of authority, dropped the harsh tone they habitually used to those asking them for favors, "changing into a mild and affable demeanour, saluting by name such as they met, even of the meaner sort, and giving very gracious answers and ready dispatch to all suitors."

Once tongues were set wagging some spoke openly about Elizabeth dying; others went so far as to claim she was already dead, giving the very hour that she had died and insisting it was being kept secret for the security of the state. The result was just as the government had anticipated: "the wealthier sort feared sudden uproars and tumults, and the needy and loose persons desired them."[44]

On 15 March the Privy Council was convened in perpetual session at Richmond; guards were doubled at the royal palace, pensioners were armed and the peers summoned. According to a French report, the Earl of Northumberland arrived at Richmond at the head of a hundred men declaring that he would kill anyone who opposed James's succession. The only other peers present were Lord Thomas Howard, nephew to James's correspondent Henry Howard, and Lord

Cobham, who sent word to Ralegh in Plymouth to return to court immediately.

After the meeting, Northumberland wrote to inform James that Elizabeth's death was imminent and to reassure him that the Council had come out in support of him as Elizabeth's heir. He reported that orders were being made for the suppression of rumors and disturbances in the provinces and that the rest of the nobility had been called for. Potential troublemakers were being press-ganged into the army and sent to the Low Countries, known recusants such as Robert Catesby were locked up and the City of London was ordered "to keep strong watch lest discontented persons make any head there."[45] The change there was felt immediately. A Londoner noted in his diary that guards were put at "every gate and street" and Scaramelli reported that 500 vagrants were seized from the taverns and placed under lock and key in one night alone.

The rich took advantage of the new security, carrying their plate and treasure from the suburbs to safehouses in the City, and the crown jewels were locked away in the Tower. Admiral Nottingham closed the ports and the navy was placed on alert against any foreign attempts.[46] Thus far, however, everything was peaceful, and Northumberland emphasized:

> In all this likelihood of so mighty a change, not one man hath stirred save Sir Edward Baynham, a wild and free-speaking youth, who braving it, and protesting that he would lose his life and so would forty thousand Catholics more, ere your Majesty should come in. This man is committed to prison, and I assure your Majesty condemned by all of them, or the most part, that are Catholicly inclined.[47]

The rumor mill was, however, grinding ever more furiously, fueled by the contents of Arbella's last letter. On Wednesday the sixteenth, Scaramelli wrote to the Senate claiming that the Queen had begun to have doubts about Essex's treachery in Ireland, that "her dear intimate, might have been quite innocent after all; for ... he concluded an agreement with Tyrone that was more advantageous for the kingdom, and more honourable for the Queen than the present one."[48] This was, of course, nonsense. Essex's truce had left Tyrone's armies intact while Mountjoy had utterly defeated him. But Scaramelli had been told that Elizabeth had felt so deeply about her supposed misjudgment of Essex that on the anniversary of his execution, she had "burst into tears and dolorous lamentation, as though for some deadly sin she had committed and then fell ill of a sickness which the doctors instantly judged to be mortal."[49] The symptoms he describes give us some clues as to what she was dying from:

> The Queen's illness is want of sleep, want of appetite, labour of the lungs and heart, cessation of the natural motions, irresponsiveness to remedies. There is but little fever but also little strength; nor are there any good symptoms except that a slight swelling of the glands under the jaw burst of itself, with a discharge of a small amount of matter.[50]

The burst swelling was probably a ruptured abscess. Elizabeth's teeth were in poor condition and an infection in a rotten tooth could have turned into a fatal condition called Ludwig's angina. With this illness Elizabeth would have been generally unwell for some time. Abscesses under the tongue and in the throat would then have made it difficult to swallow, speak or breathe. At this stage death would follow within days.[51] Two days later, on 18 March, the French ambassador, de Beaumont, described Elizabeth as being unable to speak for long periods. She sat on her cushions, staring at the ground, her finger in her mouth. James's agents now made frantic last-minute efforts to gain waverers to his cause. One arrived at Scaramelli's residence that same day "with great secrecy; looking carefully round about him so as not to be noticed."[52]

Once inside, the agent showered compliments on the Serene Republic, telling Scaramelli that James called it the "Splendour of the World." Eventually he asked whether Venice would support James's succession. Scaramelli gave a neutral reply and mentioned his concerns about English piracy. The agent promptly "professed a profound hatred of the English, and declared that when it came to his master's turn he would put an end to this general buccaneering." Scaramelli observed that he "spoke quite openly and with absolute confidence of his master's succession to the throne, and went to the length of saying that there was not a family of any importance wherein, by promises and hopes, he had not won over father, brother or so." The Scottish agent had also let slip James's fear that Henri IV was in some way involved in Arbella's rebellion.[53]

The agent pressed Scaramelli as to how long he would be staying in England. "I told him that if the Queen got better I hope to finish my business in two audiences; that would occupy April and a few days of May. He said, 'That is a long time; you may hear great news before that.' "[54]

Brouncker, meanwhile, had arrived in Derbyshire. He found no stocks of pikes or shot, no groups of armed men in the villages around Hardwick, no evidence of a powerful conspiracy in support of Arbella. Henry Cavendish had met Brouncker and he had agreed to travel to court to be interviewed by Cecil. Brouncker's only concern was that Richard Stapleton had fled to London. He wrote to warn Cecil that Stapleton "had long practised to convey my Lady Arbella into Norfolk, and there to keep her amongst seminaries and priests, and to defend her by a strong party if need required, as Arbella herself told me, though after she would have denied it."

Arbella had shut up like a clam when she had heard that the Queen was dying, and she warned Brouncker that he would have no right to hold her after the Queen's death. He asked Cecil anxiously what he could do without a warrant under the Great Seal: "I know not how to direct my course unless you advertise me whether anything be resolved concerning a successor."[55] But there was no time for a reply. Events were overtaking the post horse.

❈   ❈   ❈

The playwright Thomas Dekker's *Wonderful Year of 1603* recalls the harbingers of Elizabeth's decline as "a hideous tempest, that shook cedars, terrified the tallest pines, and cleft asunder even the hardest hearts of oak." Dekker's storm takes on an almost physical form: "her thighs being whirlwinds and her groans thunder" to deliver a "pale, meagre, weak child, named Sickness." When Sickness is fully grown Death makes him his herald—without even a bribe, Dekker jokes ("and that's a wonder in this age"). The herald is then ordered "to go into the Privy Chamber of the English Queen, to summon her to appear in the Star Chamber of heaven." Dekker describes him as being sent dressed as a courtier. He did not name which one, but Sir Robert Carey would have been appropriate.

Carey was the youngest grandson of Elizabeth's aunt Mary Boleyn. It was he whom Elizabeth had sent to Scotland in 1587 with the letter assuring James that she was not responsible for Mary, Queen of Scot's death. Carey arrived at Richmond on Saturday 19 March; when he left he was carrying another message to the waiting King. He later claimed that he had traveled to court from Northumberland for no better reason than to catch up with friends. But it is more likely that his sister, Lady Scrope, had sent him a warning that the Queen was dying. As soon as Elizabeth was informed that her cousin was at court she asked to see him. Carey recalled that he found her

> in one of her withdrawing chambers, sitting low upon her cushions. She called me to her. I kissed her hand, and told her it was my chiefest happiness to see her in safety and health which I wished might long continue. She took me by the hand and wrung it hard and said: "No Robin I am not well" and then discoursed with me of her indisposition, and that her heart had been sad and heavy for ten or twelve days and, in her discourse she fetched not so few as forty or fifty great sighs. I was grieved at the first to see her in this plight: for in all my lifetime before I never knew her fetch a sigh but when the queen of Scots was beheaded.[56]

Carey tried to raise the Queen's spirits but found that her "melancholy humour . . . was too deep rooted in her heart; and hardly to be removed."

It was clear that the Queen was dying, and as Carey left that evening he anxiously considered "in what a wretched estate I should be left; most of my livelihood depending on her life." As a younger son, Carey had inherited only "that which the cat left on the malt heap." Earlier in his life the Queen had hoped that Carey would improve his situation by marrying an heiress; instead he had fallen in love with and married the widowed Elizabeth de Widdrington, whose fortune was as modest as his tastes were expensive. Elizabeth had been very angry at the time but eventually she had forgiven him. Now he enjoyed the rewards of her favor, among which was his office as Warden of the Middle Marches. If he did not gain favor with her successor, he could lose everything.

Carey was aware that James had given Lady Scrope a sapphire ring with instructions for it to be returned on the Queen's death. She may have suggested to him that a possible answer to his problems was to be the man to carry it to Scotland. In any event, immediately after supper Carey wrote to tell James that Elizabeth would not last above three days and that when she did die, he "would be the first man that should bring him news of it." As Carey retired to bed that night his sister remained with the Queen, along with two other ladies-in-waiting from the so-called tribe of Dan: his niece Lady Kildare and his great-niece, the sixteen-year-old Elizabeth Southwell. For weeks the women had watched the Queen weaken. "I am not sick," she would sometimes exclaim; "I feel no pain, and yet I pine away."[57] It had seemed mysterious and rumors of foul play had begun to circulate. "They even name the person," Scaramelli noted, "and say that actions of this magnitude begin in danger and end in reward."[58]

Bizarre stories abounded, many said to have been spread by Catholics. None were recorded at the time but Elizabeth Southwell recounted several strange tales in her memoirs. She accused Cecil and "his familiar," the Vice Chamberlain, John Stanhope, of killing the Queen by witchcraft, claiming that they gave Elizabeth an enchanted coin to hang around her neck and that playing cards were found with nails struck through the head of the queen of hearts. She also recalled that Lady Gifford said that she had seen Elizabeth's ghost walking abroad while her physical body was sleeping in bed. Elizabeth's ladies would have expected to see strange things: supernatural signs were widely believed to mark great events such as the death of a ruler. In Shakespeare's Hamlet—the earliest known version of which appeared in print in 1603—the death of Julius Caesar was foretold by the dead walking in the streets and by "stars with trains of fire and dews of blood." But some have since taken the view that Southwell embroidered her recollections with the supernatural in order to smear Cecil and the heretic Queen. The young Maid of Honor converted to Catholicism after eloping with Leicester's son Robert Dudley in 1605 and only subsequently did she describe the details of Elizabeth's last days. Southwell's accusations do, however, show the sense of widespread paranoia during Elizabeth's last days—and much of what she wrote is echoed in contemporary reports and other memoirs.

The Jacobean bishop Godfrey Goodman and Burghley's servant John Clapham both related versions of another of Southwell's supernatural stories. Elizabeth was lying in bed at night when she caught sight of her wasted body in the firelight. Come the morning she demanded to see a true mirror for the first time in twenty years. Horrified by her reflection, she railed against the flatterers who had lied to her, and fell "into an extremetie." Here Elizabeth's supposed preference for false mirrors is no longer a comment on her vanity or unease at the false image she gave to the world. The Queen is recognizing that she has been listening to dishonest men and not to her true servants. As with the story Scaramelli repeated, in which Elizabeth regrets executing honest Essex at the behest of false men, her heart breaks at the moment she realizes her mistake.

Such allegories would not have been lost on contemporaries. Listening to the "wrong" people was an error courtiers were anxious for her successor to avoid, and time and again in the following weeks they would express fears that James would be seduced by flatterers and government corruption would persist.

On the morning of Sunday 20 March, Carey returned to Richmond Palace from his lodgings expecting to see the Queen in the Royal Chapel for the morning service. He waited with the rest of the congregation in the long, narrow room with its handsome cathedral seats and pews until "after eleven o'clock one of the Grooms [of the Chambers] came out, and bade make ready for the Private Closet." The Private Closet was in the passageway between the Privy and Presence Chambers, and near to her sleeping quarters. Elizabeth, however, was incapable even of going that far. She never arrived at the Private Closet. Instead "she had cushions laid for her in the Privy Chamber, hard by the Closet door; and there she heard service."[59] When it was finished Elizabeth remained on her cushions, unable to speak, refusing to go to bed, convinced "that if she lay down she should never rise."[60] The congregation, however, went home, taking their news with them.

London was ringing with the sound of bells. The Duke of Stettin, traveling around England the previous summer, had remarked how popular bell-ringing was in England. He was told that Elizabeth enjoyed hearing them even when the bells rang late into the evening, considering it "a sign of the health of the people." Stettin also learned that when someone was in extremis the parish bells were "touched gently with the clappers," which was taken as a signal for everyone in the street and in their house to fall on their knees and pray for the invalid.[61] As word spread of Elizabeth's condition, however, the bells were not tolled but stilled. The Jesuit William Weston, who was in the Tower awaiting banishment, noticed a strange silence descending on the city, "as if it were under interdict and divine worship suspended. Not a bell rang out. Not a bugle sounded—though ordinarily they were often heard."[62]

Elizabeth remained on her cushions all that Sunday night. On Monday Scaramelli reported that "Her Majesty's life is absolutely despaired of, even if she is not already dead. For the past six days she has become quite silly and indeed, idiotic." The reservations many felt about James's inheritance came to the fore, with Catholics condemning him as a schismatic and Protestants rejecting him as a foreigner and threatening death to all foreigners. People dashed hither and thither, tying up their affairs before shutting themselves in their houses, while at Richmond Palace Elizabeth remained immobile, refusing medical help and food. Eventually Admiral Nottingham persuaded her to take some broth and Cecil told the Queen that "to content the people her majesty must go to bed." Elizabeth, however, merely smiled and told him "the word must was not to be used to princes," adding pointedly: "Little man, little man, if your father had lived ye durst not have said so much but thou knowest I must die and that makes thee so presumptuous."[63] She then asked him to leave the room.

According to Elizabeth Southwell, when Cecil had gone, Elizabeth turned to Admiral Nottingham, "to whom she shook her head and with a pitiful voice said, 'My lord I am tied with a chain of iron about my neck...I am tied and the case is altered with me.' " Her comments were taken to refer not merely to the swelling and pain around her neck but also to the power ebbing into the hands of her leading Councillors.*

On Tuesday 22 March Elizabeth's death was reported in Leicester, though the suspected culprits were soon arrested. Elizabeth was still on her cushions, refusing to go to bed until that evening, when at last Admiral Nottingham helped pull her up onto her feet.[64] She stood rock still for what seemed like hours until, "What by fair means, what by force he got her to bed."[65]

The next day Elizabeth's chaplain, Dr. Parry, invited his friend John Manningham to dine in the Privy Chamber. Manningham, a young lawyer from the Middle Temple, found the clerics in garrulous form on the subject of the Queen's health. There had been "some whispering that her brain was somewhat distempered," but they told him that although Elizabeth had sat "very pensive and silent" over the past two days, her eyes fixed on one object for hours at a time, she had kept her senses and her memory. The only thing that suggested confusion to them was her stubborn refusal to accept any medical help—possibly she remembered how her half-brother Edward VI suffered at the hands of doctors during his last days. Manningham closed his diary for the day with the comment, "A royal majesty is no privilege against death."[66]

❈   ❈   ❈

The knowledge that Elizabeth had not named her successor weighed heavily on everyone; without her word her father's will, sanctioned by Parliament, remained extant and it excluded the Stuart line. Admiral Nottingham suddenly recalled a conversation he had with the Queen

---

*Bishop Goodman's memoirs quote Elizabeth as saying, "They have yoked my neck—I can do nothing—I have not one man in whom I can repose trust," and William Camden's as "They have yoked my neck; I have none whom I can trust; my condition is turned strangely upside down." Both may simply be repeating Southwell, but other ladies could also have told them the same story. Note regarding Ludwig's angina that the word "angina" comes from the Latin *angere*, which means "to strangle."

on the journey to Richmond. He claimed that in response to his questioning she had told him: "My throne has been the throne of kings, neither ought any other than he that is my next heir succeed me," but this was worthless without the corroboration of witnesses. A decision was therefore made to ask the dying queen to name her heir one last time.

That afternoon, 23 March, Elizabeth responded to the Council's request to see her and called for them. She lay on a walnut bed, carved with gilded and painted beasts. Above her were hung ostrich plumes spangled with gold. Elizabeth asked for liquid to ease her sore throat in order that she might speak, but, seeing her in pain, the Councilors suggested that she instead raise a finger when they named the successor "whom she liked."[67]

Elizabeth Southwell recalled that when they named Lord Beauchamp, Elizabeth croaked: "I will have no rascal's son in my seat but one worthy to be a king."[68] These are the last words Elizabeth is said to have spoken. There are differences of opinion about what then occurred. Southwell claims the Council named "the King of France and the King of Scotland at which she never stirred." Carey, on the other hand, tells us that Elizabeth put "her hand to her head when the King of Scots was named to succeed her." A similar story was repeated by the court servant John Clapham, who wrote that Elizabeth turned her hand "in the form of a circle," but he added the skeptical rider, "These reports, whether they were true indeed or give out of purpose by such as would have them so to be believed it is hard to say. Sure I am they did no hurt."

The Council was set on James and the course of Elizabeth's life suggests she would have supported his candidature. As Cecil wrote to one of his Scots contacts in January, although Elizabeth took "no pleasure in [James's] rising, yet she would be sorry of his perishing."[69]

At six o'clock on Wednesday night the Archbishop of Canterbury, John Whitgift, and Elizabeth's other chaplains went to pray with the dying queen. "I went with them," Carey recalled, "and sat upon my knees full of tears to see that heavy sight." Elizabeth was lying on her back with one arm hanging out of the bed. The Archbishop told her that although she had been a great queen on earth, she now had to yield her account to the King of Kings. Then he prayed. Hours later, exhausted, he blessed her and rose to leave. She gestured for Whitgift to stay, which he did for a further half hour, whereupon the scene was repeated. "By this time it grew late and everyone departed; all but the women that attended her." As Carey left he told a servant at the Palace that he wanted to be called when Elizabeth died and he gave the porter a coin saying he must let him through the gate when he returned from his lodgings. Between one and two in the morning on the eve of the feast of the Annunciation of the Blessed Virgin the servant arrived at Carey's lodgings with the message that the Queen was dead.

Parry, Elizabeth's chaplain, told his friend John Manningham she had "departed this life, mildly like a lamb, easily like a ripe apple from the tree." There was, however, little peace for the living that March morning. Carey went straight to the gate of Richmond Palace to see his sister and collect James's blue ring. The porter, despite his bribe, refused to admit him, saying that the Council had "commanded him that none should go in or out, but by warrant from them." At that moment Sir Edward Wotton, the Comptroller of the Household, who had kept the court in such good spirits over Christmas, appeared at the gate. He offered to let Carey in. Carey asked him how the Queen was. "Pretty well," Wotton lied. Carey retorted, "Good night!" and turned on his heel. Wotton quickly tried another tack, promising Carey that if he came in he would let him out of the gate whenever he wanted. Carey remained suspicious, but he followed Wotton inside.

Carey was taken to his sister in one of the household rooms, where he found "all the ladies weeping bitterly." Lady Scrope was unable to pass him the ring under Wotton's gaze but they exchanged a few quiet words before he was led on to the Privy Chamber, where most of the Council was assembled. It was apparent that they were aware of Carey's intentions and he was "caught hold of and assured I should not go to Scotland until their pleasures were further known." The Councilors then made their way to Cecil's chamber to give him the news of the Queen's death. As they walked they ordered the porters that no one should leave the palace save the servants who were to prepare their coaches and horses for London. Carey trailed behind until he was out of sight and then headed off to wake his brother, Lord

Hunsdon. The old peer was seriously ill—he would die in September—but loyally he got up, dressed quickly and dashed after the Council's servants to the gate.

The porter, recognizing Hunsdon as the Lord Chamberlain, let him out, but when Carey pressed after him the porter stopped him. Hunsdon shouted angrily at the porter, "Let him out, I will answer for him," and to Carey's great relief the porter let him go. Carey's sister Lady Scrope had by now left her weeping companions and was watching the scene from a room above the gate. She tossed down the sapphire ring that James had asked to be returned on Elizabeth's death and Carey snatched it up. With the ring in his pocket he rode at speed to the lodging of his friend the Knight Marshal at Charing Cross and waited for the Councilors to arrive at Whitehall to proclaim James king. He hoped now that he had the ring they would accept his role as messenger as a fait accompli and give official approval to his journey.

At nine o'clock the Councilors arrived at Whitehall and Carey asked the Knight Marshal to tell them he awaited their instructions. Carey's friend found them very relieved that Carey had not yet left for Scotland and he was told that yes, he should tell Carey they would immediately dispatch him to Scotland with the necessary papers. But as Sir Arthur Savage rode off to send for Carey, another of Elizabeth's cousins, Sir William Knollys, whispered a warning to the Knight Marshal that if Carey arrived, they would hold him and send their own choice of messenger. He promptly made some excuse and left. Carey was almost at Whitehall when he spotted his friend on the road. He pulled up his horse to greet him. His friend quickly relayed what had happened and advised him to leave immediately for Scotland. Carey did not hesitate. Within the hour he was mounted on a fresh horse and galloping north.[70]

At around ten o'clock the Councilors emerged from Whitehall onto the green opposite the tiltyard where Essex used to joust for the Queen. The diminutive figure of Cecil was carrying the proclamation that would name James king. He had sent a copy of the proclamation to Scotland for approval several days earlier. James read it that very morning, and declared to those near him that the music of its words sounded so sweetly in his ears that he could not alter one note "in so agreeable a harmony." It had been signed and approved by representative peers, gentry, and Councilors, a novel procedure that is followed to this day.

The signatories included the Lord Mayor, Robert Lee; the Treasurer, Lord Buckhurst; Admiral Nottingham; his brother-in-law Lord Scrope; the young Lord Grey of Wilton (the son of the soldier-butcher of Smerwick Fort); Arbella's uncle, the Earl of Shrewsbury; his enemy Sir John Stanhope; Carey's cousin Sir William Knollys; the Comptroller, Sir Edward Wotton; the Earl of Worcester, who was both a stiff papist and a good subject; Sir Robert Cecil; Lord Cobham; the Earl of Northumberland, and twenty-six other peers, gentry and Privy Councilors. Ralegh's name, however, was absent: he was still hurriedly making his way to court from the West Country.[71]

As a crowd gathered Cecil began to read from the document the news of Elizabeth's death and the accession of the King of Scots:

> *Forasmuch as it has pleased Almighty God to call to his mercy out of the transitory life our Sovereign Lady, the High and Mighty Prince, Elizabeth late Queen of England, France and Ireland, by whose death and dissolution, the Imperial Crown of these two realms aforesaid are now absolutely and solely come to the High and Mighty Prince, James VI of Scotland, who is lineally and lawfully descended from the body of Margaret, daughter to the High and Renowned Prince, Henry the seventh King of England, France and Ireland . . . We therefore the Lords Spiritual and Temporal of this realm, being here assembled, united, and assisted with those of her late Majesty's Privy Council, and with great numbers of other principal gentlemen of quality in the kingdom, with the Lord Mayor, Aldermen and citizens of London, and a multitude of other good subjects and commons of this realm do now hereby with one voice and consent of tongue and heart, publish and proclaim, that the High and Mighty Prince, James VI King of Scotland is now by the death of our late sovereign, Queen of England of famous memory, become also our only, lawful, lineal and rightful Liege James the first, King of England, France and Ireland, defender of the faith.[72]*

The justification of James's right as coming entirely through descent from Henry VII's eldest daughter, Margaret, of course ignored the problem of James's foreign birth. When Elizabeth was first Queen she had been greeted in a sermon at York as "born mere English amongst us and therefore most natural unto us." Cecil was using the argument of the Jesuit-inspired Doleman book that a king should have outstanding qualities. James was welcomed as having "the rarest gifts of mind" and, rather inaccurately, "of body." No one on the green at Whitehall was certain how the people would react and the proclamation forcefully reminded officials of their duty to prevent "any disorderly assemblies" or attempts on James's right.

When Cecil finished reading the nervous Councilors took their places in procession behind the Garter and heralds. They walked down the Strand past the great palaces on the Thames: Durham House, which Elizabeth had leased to Ralegh in the 1580s, Cecil House, newly built at such expense that it had nearly bankrupted him, and Essex House, now rented by the Earl of Northumberland. They passed on to Fleet Street, the same route that Essex had taken on the day of his revolt. The gathering crowds hummed with the news of Elizabeth's death and the proclamation of James's accession. They were struck by how the Queen, "born on the eve of the Nativity of the . . . Blessed Virgin," had died on the eve of the Annunciation. The Lord Mayor, Robert Lee, represented another pleasing coincidence: he had the same name as his predecessor at the time of Elizabeth's accession. Manningham recalled a joke about him: three things that made other men poor had made the Mayor rich, namely, "wine, women and dice; [for] he was fortunate in marrying rich wives, lucky in great gaming at dice, and prosperous in sale of his wines."[73]

At Ludgate the procession found the gates and portcullis shut. The Mayor stood on the other side alongside his aldermen and announced that the gates would not be opened unless James was declared king. Lord Buckhurst took off the image of St. George that formed part of the insignia of his Order of the Garter and pushed it through the gate together with the parchment of the proclamation. The Lord Mayor accepted it and allowed the procession through, into the City. In contrast to the formal palaces on the river, the City was a huddle of tall, narrow timber and clay houses, five or six stories high. Many had been divided into several dwellings—a practice that had been made illegal in the previous summer in an attempt to ameliorate overcrowding.[74]

At eleven o'clock the procession stopped at the west side of the High Cross at Cheapside. John Manningham found "an extraordinary and unexpected number of gallant knights and brave gentlemen of note well mounted, besides the huge number of common persons." Like many foreign visitors, the Duke of Stettin was struck by the good looks of the English, "the most beautiful people, men as well as women, of good proportion, and of a healthy natural colour." Even ordinary citizens in the crowds were dressed well "in splendid silken stuffs . . . Nothing is too expensive for them, and the ladies especially look very clean with their linen and frills all starched in blue."[75] They listened intently as Cecil reread the proclamation "distinctly and audibly." When he had finished they cried, "God save the King!" but with little enthusiasm. One witness described the mood as "flat" and the Venetian Scaramelli deduced "that there was evidently neither sorrow for the death of the queen, nor joy for the succession of the king." The playwright Thomas Dekker ascribed this to shock:

> Having brought up (even under her wing) a nation that was almost begotten and born under her; that never shouted any other Ave but for her name, never saw the face of any Prince but herself, never understood what that strange outlandish word "change" signified: how was it possible, but that her sickness should throw abroad a universal fear, and her death an astonishment?[76]

People were frightened that they were now on the cusp of the long-feared civil war. As the news of Elizabeth's death spread the price of meal rose, quadrupling by the end of the day.[77] When night fell, however, Manningham noted in his diary that there was "no tumult, no contradiction, no disorder in the city; everyman went about his business as readily as peaceably, as securely as if there had been no change, nor any news ever heard of competitors." Celebratory bonfires sprang up across the city, and London was once more filled with the sound of bells. The French ambassador expressed his dismay at the apparent absence of mourning, but as one court official observed: "Such is the condition of great princes more unhappy in this respect than their own subjects, in that, while they live, they are followed by all men, and at their death lamented of none."[78]

The sun had finally set on the faded brilliance of Gloriana and a new era was about to dawn. Manningham caught the mood of the evening: "The people is full of great expectation, and great with hope of [the King's] worthiness, of our nation's future greatness; everyone promises himself a share in some famous action to be hereafter performed, for his Prince and Country."[79]

CHAPTER FOUR

"LOTS WERE CAST UPON OUR LAND"

The Coming of Arthur, March–April 1603

O n the morning of Friday 25 March, Elizabeth's Privy Councilors and a number of other prominent individuals met at Admiral Nottingham's house in Chelsea.[1] Ralegh was among them. He had arrived at Richmond within hours of Elizabeth's death. Everyone was acutely aware that the Council was about to hand the crown to the King of Scots and that Cecil must have been allied to James's cause for some time. Diaries, memoirs and seventeenth-century histories give us only flashes of what occurred, but it seems tensions were running high between those who had hopes that they would gain personally from James's accession and those who feared they would not.

At the top of the agenda was the wording of the messages the Council was to send to James. Cecil produced a note written by the

Earl of Essex that suggested "to some private friends, that when the time came the King of Scots might be accepted with some conditions." It would have been possible, for example, to refuse James the power to give the Scots offices in England, but to say so was to risk his future disfavor. It was classic Cecil. "Here is the rope," his action said, "now who will take it?" He may have warned some of his friends to keep their mouths shut. Prompted by Cecil's action, the elderly Chancellor of the Exchequer, Sir John Fortescue, asked "very moderately and mildly...whether any conditions should be proposed to the King."[2] The young and hot-tempered Lord Grey of Wilton immediately answered "like a zealous patriot" and "desired that articles might be sent to the King for the preservation of the liberties and fundamental laws of the kingdom."[3]

Grey of Wilton was a deadly enemy of Essex's friend Southampton. The bitterness dated back to an incident in Ireland in May 1599. There was a skirmish in which Southampton had advanced "in most soldier like order, with a small troop of horse and foot," pushing back 200 rebels into the bogs and woods. Wilton, however, "being carried to the rebel by heat of valour," had recklessly charged the enemy contrary to his commander's orders.[4] Essex punished him with a night's imprisonment and Wilton never forgave the insult. The following year he had attacked Southampton in a London street. The Queen had been furious and he had left shortly afterward to fight on the Continent. When Cecil intervened on his behalf Cobham and Ralegh used the excuse of passing on the good news for their secretive trip to Ostend that summer. Grey returned to England to exact his final revenge by leading Elizabeth's troops against the Essex rebels in 1601, something that was bound to sit uneasily with the new regime.

Fortescue, who was a cousin of Elizabeth's and unlikely to be particularly favored by James, supported Wilton's motion, as did Cobham and Ralegh. They had guessed that it would be a struggle for them to gain favor under James and Ralegh had taken steps to pass his Dorset estate on to his son, thus protecting the boy's inheritance from attainder if he were ever to be accused of treason. No one else, however, was prepared to risk James's wrath by supporting Wilton's motion.

Cecil then suggested that Ralegh resign his post of Captain of the

Guard to make way for James's existing Captain, Sir Thomas Erskine of Gogar.[5] London was rife with the gossip over the next few days that this triggered a huge row between Cecil and Lord Cobham.[6] The quarrel may also have prompted the outburst John Aubrey later described, in which Ralegh "declared his opinion, 'twas the wisest way for them to keep the government in their own hands and set up a Commonwealth, and not to be subject to a needy beggardly nation." In any event Northumberland put an end to the arguments, turning on Ralegh, Cobham, Fortescue and Grey with "a protestation, that if any man should offer to make any proposition to the King, he should instantly raise an army against him."[7] He then addressed the Council, declaring that with the Queen dead they had no legal authority and that the nobility had been treated with contempt for too long and would tolerate it no longer: it was up to them to take charge.

The Lord Keeper, Sir Thomas Egerton, attempted to calm Northumberland by proposing that all those who were not peers should resign their seats at the table to the lords. Admiral Nottingham and the other non-peers declined the invitation, but a more moderate line was now taken. Ralegh was instructed to keep his post of Captain of the Guard until James's will was known, and was invited to sign the copy of the proclamation that was to be sent to Scotland.[8]

Northumberland's brother, Sir Charles Percy, and the Earl of Worcester's son, Thomas Somerset, were picked as the Council's official messengers and left with the Council's papers late that morning. Percy and Somerset were a full day's ride behind Sir Robert Carey, who had reached Doncaster on Thursday, rested for the night, collected a fresh horse and set off again. Post horses were established every ten miles between London and Berwick and they were renowned for being strong and fast. Those on unofficial business could usually rent them for around threepence a mile, Percy and Somerset half a penny less. Another threepence would pay for a guide and his horse, but Carey knew the route too well to need them.[9] As a young man he had once won a wager of £2,000 that he could walk to Berwick from London in twelve days.[10] He was now in his early forties and not quite as fit as he once was, but by Friday night Carey had reached his home at Widdrington Castle in Northumberland.

Widdrington was a rambling edifice with an ancient gothic tower finished with four round turrets, standing on land overlooking Coquet Island. A brook ran to the north and there was a village of the same name nearby. The castle had stood against raiding parties of Scots since the reign of Edward I, and as such it was an appropriate base for the Warden of the Middle Marches. The north of England was divided into three Marches, East, Middle and West, each ruled by a Warden whose job it was to contain the chronic lawlessness of the region. The Scots had proved particularly troublesome during the 1590s, when the cash-strapped James had used violence as a form of blackmail to extract his pension from Elizabeth when she proved slow to give it. Many of the raids were led by Carey's opposite number, the Warden of the Scottish Middle March, Robert Kerr of Cessford.[11] This had stopped, however, in 1600, after Essex's friends warned James that he might need to bring an army south to take his crown. James had since worked hard to ingratiate himself with border magnates such as the Earls of Northumberland and Cumberland, the northern gentry and Wardens, and Cessford had punished Scottish thieves rather than leading them.

If there was to be trouble now, Carey feared, it would come from English criminal families taking advantage of the interregnum. As Carey dismounted he called his deputies, and gave them the news of Elizabeth's death and orders for keeping the peace. On Saturday morning he drew up instructions for James to be proclaimed King of England at Morpeth, Alnwick and Berwick. His brother, Sir John Carey, read the proclamation in Berwick that afternoon, one of only three men bold enough to take the risk of proclaiming James without a warrant.[12] The second was Henry Hastings, the Mayor of Leicester, the city where the Queen had been pronounced dead two days prematurely. Hastings was of royal Plantagenet descent and had good reason to prove his loyalty, as did the third man, Sir Benjamin Tichborne, the Sheriff of Hampshire and a Catholic.

By about noon Carey had reached the pink sandstone of Norham Castle, a border outpost he held in his right as Warden. He calculated that if he maintained his pace he would be with the King by suppertime, but as he raced on toward Edinburgh he had a fall from his horse, who kicked him in the head. The injury left him bleeding heavily and he had to slow his pace. The country Carey rode through had been notorious for its feuds, but it was now only in the Gaelic-speaking areas of the west that such cycles of revenge posed problems. The linguistic divisions in Scotland reflected a deepening national divide. In the south and northeast, where Middle Scots was spoken, people considered themselves to be Anglo-Saxon and regarded the Gaelic-speakers of the west as lawless savages. James divided them into two sorts: "the one, that dwells in our main land, that are barbarous for the most part, and yet mixed with some show of civility: the other, that dwells in the Isles, that are utterly barbarous, without any sort or show of civility."[13]

James intended to see the Highland clans of the mainland assimilated and those in the Isles colonized, a policy he would eventually extend to his new kingdom of Ireland. In the meantime they had recently boasted two bloody massacres: the Glengarry Macdonalds had burned to death a congregation of Mackenzies in a church at Kilchrist on 7 February. Their piper reportedly walked around the building taunting those inside by playing a clan pibroch as they screamed and died. More significantly—since it involved the deaths of a small number of Lowlanders close to the court—a band of up to 200 Colquhouns of Luss was killed in the same month by the Macgregors at Glenfruin, the so-called Glen of Sorrow. The punishment of the Macgregors was decided at a secret meeting at Holyrood eight days later, when the Scots Privy Council proscribed the entire clan, "that the whole persons of that clan should renounce their name and take them some other name, and that they nor none of their posterity should call themselves Gregor or Macgregor thereafter, under pain of death."[14]*

---

*The law against the Macgregors would not be repealed until 1774, during which time supplementary laws were passed that no more than four Gregors could meet together at any time or carry any weapon, save a pointless knife for their meat. Their enemies were encouraged to hunt them down with bloodhounds known as "black dogs." If any of the Macgregors were caught, their heads were sold to government officials or they were sent into slavery in America. The survivors hid in the hills and became known as "the Children of the Mist."

It was nearly midnight when Carey reached the city walls of Edinburgh. They were described as built of "little and unpolished stones [that] seem ancient, but are very narrow, and in some places exceeding low, in others, ruined." The hovels in the south of the city were crowded with the poor but as Carey rode toward the Royal Mile he passed the homes of the gentry, which the "Water Poet," John Taylor, claimed had stone walls eight or ten feet thick—"exceeding strong, not built for a day, a week, or a month or a year; but from antiquity to posterity, for many ages." On the Royal Mile were other large houses "of squared stone, five six and seven storeys high," with wooden galleries offering fine views of the city's main thoroughfare.[15] James had already retired to bed when Carey reached the gates of Holyrood, but he had been expecting him since that morning, when he received the letter sent from Richmond.[16] Carey was immediately escorted to James's chambers. There he fell to his knees before his new king "and saluted him by his title of 'England, Scotland, France and Ireland.' " It was the moment James had waited for all his life, and Carey recalled he gave him his hand to kiss and "bade me welcome."

After Carey had relayed the details of Elizabeth's illness and death James asked whether he had letters from the Privy Council. He confessed he did not and described his escape from London with "a blue ring from a fair lady, that I hoped would give him assurance of the truth that I had reported." James took the ring and, having examined it, said: "It is enough: I know by this you are a true messenger." He then committed Carey to the care of Lord Home and sent for surgeons to dress his injuries. Carey kissed his hand and James assured him, "I know you have lost a near kinswoman and a mistress; but . . . I will be as good a master to you, and will requite this service with honour and reward."[17] Thanks to Carey, James was now certain Elizabeth was dead, but without papers from the Council he did not yet know whether he had been proclaimed king, if they were demanding conditions, what the public reaction had been, or whether there was any threat of invasion.

After years of fearing the Infanta Isabella, James was confident that there were not going to be any problems with the Netherlands. A week earlier the Archduke Albert's emissary, Nicholas Scorza, had promised to back James's efforts to claim the English throne with men and money, should it prove necessary.[18] It was possible, however, that his opponents would unite behind some other candidate—one that would be backed by France if not Spain. James spent an anxious night and on Sunday morning, desperate for information, he sent the Abbot of Holyrood to Berwick to find out what was happening there. He had not, however, forgotten Carey. At 10 a.m. he sent Lord Home to tell him that he could name his reward for his endeavors. Carey asked to be admitted as a Gentleman of the Bedchamber. Carey's sisters had done well from equivalent posts under Elizabeth and he knew that it would guarantee him the most immediate possible access to the King. To his delight James immediately sent word back that "with all his heart" he could have his request.

The Council's messengers, Percy and Somerset, arrived at Holyrood later that day, carrying furious complaints that Carey had left London "contrary to such commandment as we had power to lay upon him, and to all decency, good manners and respect which he owed to so many persons of our degree."[19] James, however, was more interested to read that he had been proclaimed King of England at Whitehall and Cheapside without any problems. Overwhelmed with relief and gratitude, he immediately composed a note to Cecil thanking God and his friends for what had passed, adding in his own hand: "How happy I think myself by the conquest of so faithful and so wise a counsellor I reserve to be expressed out of my own mouth to you."[20] The Council had requested settlement of government and James prepared instructions for all Councilors and senior officers to remain in their posts "during the royal pleasure."[21] One immediate break with the past was made, however. A note was sent to Sir John Peyton, the Lieutenant of the Tower of London, instructing him to release the Earl of Southampton. The Earl of Essex was now being openly referred to as James's "martyr," a phrase that sat strangely with James's evident goodwill toward Cecil. Some hoped it meant that Cecil would find himself out of the Council when the King reached London. Others, however, had concluded that Cecil had, in fact, convinced James that Essex had really wanted the crown for himself.

The Council's other messengers were arriving at destinations across the kingdoms of England, Wales and Ireland, carrying copies of the proclamation of James's accession. In Dublin, the Lord Deputy of Ireland, Lord Mountjoy, decided to keep the news quiet for a while. He had offered the Earl of Tyrone safe conduct to Mellifont Abbey to offer his submission and the Earl was due to arrive at any time. Mountjoy did not want any complications. In England, meanwhile, many town mayors heard that James was to be proclaimed but refused to take action until they received official instructions. In Kingston upon Hull, for example, Lord Clinton and a group of ten gentlemen arrived at the mayor's house at six that morning and spent several hours trying and failing to convince the mayor to proclaim James. The most the mayor would agree to do was to send a messenger to Cecil's brother, Lord Burghley, President of the North, to ask for guidance.

The messenger from Hull arrived at Lord Burghley's house in York at the same time as the Privy Council's man. Inside, Lord Burghley was having difficulties similar to those Clinton had encountered in Hull: he was insisting that he had heard the news of the Queen's death from a "secret friend" at court and the mayor of York and his aldermen were refusing to do anything about it. On the delivery of the Council's papers, however, the mayor agreed to carry out the proclamation. It was read in the market square before a nervous crowd.

York was at the heart of the Catholic north. But there was no earl of the stature of Northumberland's father willing to lead a rebellion and no call for it among ordinary Catholics: the hopes inspired by James's promises had prevailed. That night York remained quiet and a greatly relieved Lord Burghley wrote to Cecil, that "the contentment of the people is unspeakable, seeing all things proceed so quietly, whereas they expected in the interim their houses should have been spoiled and sacked." Sir George Carew, who was on his way to Scotland with personal messages from Cecil, wrote to him from Coventry with similar news to that of Lord Burghley. Everyone was thanking God that "the opinions of the wisest, who for many years past trembled to think of her Majesty's decease," had now been proved wrong.

The messenger who had been sent from Hull that morning returned to Lord Clinton with a copy of the York proclamation—one of seven Lord Burghley had ordered to be delivered to local towns. An

accompanying letter instructed the mayor that after James was proclaimed the townspeople should express their joy by lighting bonfires
and suchlike. Nothing could be left entirely to chance as anti-Scots
feeling was not far from the surface. Lord Burghley's letter to Cecil
had included a report that a Scottish woman had been heard saying
that "nothing did discontent them more than that their king should
be received peaceably," since it meant they would not be getting their
hands on the attainted land of those Englishmen who dared oppose
him.[22]

A little before noon on Monday the twenty-eighth the Mayor,
Recorder and aldermen, Lord Clinton and his gentlemen, processed
through Kingston upon Hull to the marketplace. James was proclaimed to rolling drums and blasting trumpets; free drink was dutifully given to the crowd, bonfires lit and bells rung. Similar carefully
choreographed scenes of celebration were being repeated across England, "whereupon the people both in City and Country finding the
just fear of forty years, for want of a known successor, dissolved in a
minute did so rejoice, as few wished the Queen alive again," one
courtier recorded in his journal.[23] The Abbot of Holyrood assured
James that Berwick had welcomed him with the greatest warmth and
it was soon apparent that any disorder was going to be criminal rather
than political in nature.

Just as Carey had feared, criminal families from the East and West
Marches were already looting the countryside, riding in companies of
300–400 men, with their colors displayed. Between Sunday 27
March and 7 April, a period that came to be known as the "Busy
Week," they destroyed an estimated £10,600 worth of goods.[24]
Carey, still suffering from the injuries he sustained when he fell from
his horse and anxious to stay close to James, sent two of his deputies
to organize the troops to confront them.

On Thursday the thirty-first, a week to the day after Elizabeth's
death, Carey saw James proclaimed at Edinburgh's Cross.[25] A large
crowd gathered for the ceremony, the poorer citizens and country
folk in coarse, plaid cloaks, the Scots courtiers in plain English cloth,
their servants in rough gray wools and broad, flat hats.[26] They were
proud that their rich southern neighbor was to be ruled by their king,

but an English witness recorded that they were also concerned about what they were to lose. Scotland had become richer and more stable under James's rule. He was still in the prime of life, with young sons on which to focus their hopes for the future. His leaving meant the future suddenly looked more uncertain, "and such a universal sorrow was amongst them, that some of the meaner sort spoke even distract-edly and none, but at his departing expressed such sorrow, as in that nation hath seldom been seen the like."[27] Their shouts of pride min-gled with groans as the proclamation of James's accession was read. That night, however, doubts were put on one side, the bonfires were lit and the town enjoyed a night of feasting.

As the city of Edinburgh celebrated James's triumph, Sir Robert Carey was sworn in to his new office in the Bedchamber. He was now an English cuckoo in a Scottish nest filled by men who had known James all their lives: They included his old antagonist, Robert Kerr of Cessford. "Now was I to begin a new world," he recalled. It was not going to be an easy one.

❈   ❈   ❈

The Puritan MP Peter Wentworth had warned Elizabeth that if she did not name a successor, she would remain unburied at her death. This was not an idle threat. Elizabeth's officials could keep their wands of office only until her funeral; if she did not name an heir the funeral had to be delayed until a successor was chosen and crowned, something that could take weeks or even months. Elizabeth, however, had laid a plan to force a prompt burial. She left instructions that her body was not to be disemboweled. By tradition her body had to be at-tended by her ladies, day and night, and Councilors would have to consider the unpleasantness and dangers to them in attending on a rapidly decomposing corpse. The attendants were, after all, their own wives, daughters and granddaughters.

Elizabeth's order was public knowledge but the reasons for it could only be guessed at. Ben Jonson teasingly suggested that she wished to hide that she "had a membrane on her which made her incapable of man, though for her delight she tried many." Stories that Elizabeth was physically incapable of sex had been commonplace for years. Harington had repeated the rumors in his tract, and they have since led to all sorts of exotic theories. One medical historian has claimed that Elizabeth represented a case of testicular feminization—that she was in fact a man![28] In 1603 such enjoyable speculation distracted attention from the real problems that Elizabeth's order posed. James could not be crowned until he had made the long journey to London and it was possible people would begin to question his right before he was safely installed. On the morning of Saturday the 26th the Council was presented with a genealogy drawn up by Sir Robert Cotton (and most likely commissioned by his patron, Henry Howard) "proving" James's descent from the last British king. In the absence of a strict legal right the Council wanted to reinforce James's dynastic credentials. They also made the decision that Elizabeth's funeral would not be held for a month. What then were they going to do about Elizabeth's rotting body?

Distressing rumors were leaking out that the corpse had been left unguarded at Richmond and that "mean persons" had access to it. It appeared Elizabeth's body had been forgotten—but there is an explanation for the seeming indifference of the Council. According to Elizabeth's young Maid of Honor, Elizabeth Southwell, Cecil countermanded Elizabeth's orders that she was not to be disemboweled. Contravening her instructions had to take place in secret, which explains why Elizabeth's body was left unguarded and the "mean persons" in all probability were the embalmers. But it proved to be a mistake to leave them to work on their own. They were not well paid and without anyone to watch over them they had pocketed some of the money they were given to buy cerecloth. Consequently it was reported that Elizabeth's body was wrapped "very ill."[29] This was a grim irony when, at the same time, the huge value of Elizabeth's Wardrobe was the talk of the town. People boasted the late Queen had "made no will, nor gave anything away," so her successor could inherit a "well-stored jewel house and a rich wardrobe of 2,000 gowns."[30]

Elizabeth had her every button, petticoat and fan listed in inventories in 1600: "Item: one gown of black velvet with a broad guard of black velvet embroidered with pearls of silver . . . Item: one jewel of gold like a cross bow garnished with diamonds . . . Item: Buttons of gold each set with . . . pearls and one garnet in the middest." They recorded 1,900 items of clothing, not far from what the gossips estimated; included was a jeweled heart presented to her by Sir John Harington's father in the hope of recovering some of the land lost to the family for espousing the cause of Richard III.[31]

On Saturday night, as Elizabeth's cousin Sir Robert Carey rode unsteadily into Edinburgh, her body was placed in a simple oak coffin and carried onto a barge draped in black. A small number of Privy Councilors and Ladies of Honor accompanied the coffin for its slow journey down the Thames to Whitehall. Torches lit the way, while other barges filled with pensioners and officers of the Household followed behind. They disembarked at the steps to the palace and Elizabeth's coffin was carried into the Withdrawing Chamber, where six of her ladies were to wait by it day and night. The Venetian ambassador, Giovanni Scaramelli, was told that her court would carry on until her funeral "with the same ceremony, the same expenditure, down to her very household and table service, as though she were not wrapped in many a fold of cerecloth, and hid in such a heap of lead, of coffin, of pall, but was walking as she used to at this season, about the alleys of her gardens."[32]

The following morning the young lawyer John Manningham arrived at the black-draped royal chapel for the Sunday service. He expected to see Giles Thomson, Dean of Windsor, deliver the sermon, but the evangelical preacher John King, the Vicar of St. Andrew's in Holborn, stood in the pulpit in his place. There were to be no more mistakes like that made on 13 March at Paul's Cross. John King delivered a firm warning against "intestine discord," as well as offering thanks for the peaceful transfer of power witnessed so far.[33] Many feared there could yet be a Catholic uprising, an invasion at one of the ports, or a rebellion in favor of an English candidate for the succession. In Hampshire nervous locals were discussing the recent work done to the Earl of Hertford's house, that "great iron bars and bolts were made for the doors . . . that the glass windows were boarded up, that divers pieces of ordnance were new scoured and made ready for present service and that one Thomas Smith a gunner . . . had been there . . . making bullets for shot." Others reported that Hertford had told a watchman that "there might be another King within these six days" and that one of his men had said the Earl was "able to raise 6,000 men in arms at an hour's warning." In the West Country meanwhile people spoke darkly about Ralegh having ordered up horses, as if preparing for a possible revolt.[34]

By Monday 28 March rumors were rife that Lord Beauchamp had taken Portsmouth with 10,000 men, that he had French backing and that Catholics had risen in his support all over the country. As the hours passed, however, no Frenchmen appeared and that evening John Manningham was making light of the panic: " 'He is up,' said one. 'He is risen,' said another. 'True, I think,' said I, 'he rose in the morning and means to go to bed at night.' "[35] An embarrassed Lord Beauchamp explained that the rumors had sprung from a misunder-standing. He claimed that he had loyally taken a large band of men to proclaim James king at the High Cross in Bristol and people had wrongly assumed he was gathering support for himself. Not everyone was convinced. A friend of Manningham's argued that "to muster men in these times is as good a colour of sedition, as a mask to rob a house."[36] The fact remained, however, that no one had rallied to Beauchamp's colors—or those of any other of James's rivals.

❖ ❖ ❖

As the fears of disorder subsided again people began to reflect on Elizabeth's reign, exchange anecdotes about her and speculate about the new king. Manningham recorded an entirely trivial, but delight-ful, story about Elizabeth and a dog-loving cousin:

> *Mr Francis Curl told me how one Dr Boleyn, the Queen's kinsman, had a dog which he doted on so much that the Queen, hearing about it, requested that he must grant her one desire, and he should have whatsoever he should ask. She demanded the dog; he gave it and "Now Madam" quoth he, "You promised me my hearts desire." "I will" quoth she, "Then I pray you give me my dog again."[37]*

Manningham, however, had also picked up a curious piece of gossip that would become the basis of a legend that would persist until after the Civil War. The Queen's chaplain at Richmond, Dr. Parry, told Manningham that the Countess of Kildare had assured him that when Elizabeth had her coronation ring cut from her finger she had replaced it with "a ring which the Earl of Essex gave her."[38] On the face of it Kildare had little reason to invent such a story. Not only was she the wife of Essex's enemy, Lord Cobham, she was also the daughter of another enemy—Admiral Nottingham. But whether true or not, it inspired a reworking of the myth Scaramelli described, in which Elizabeth realized that Essex had been innocent of treachery in Ireland and was the victim of his enemies after all. The legend focused on whether or not Essex had ever pleaded for his life. In the summer of 1601, Elizabeth had told the French ambassador, de Biron, that she might have spared Essex's life if he had asked her to do so.[39] Her comments were designed to deflect criticism of her actions by highlighting Essex's arrogance, but according to the legend, she discovered when she was called to the Countess of Nottingham's deathbed that he had in fact asked her for mercy.

The dying Countess had supposedly reminded Elizabeth how she had once given Essex a ring, saying that if he ever needed her help or protection he should send the ring to her and it would be forthcoming. In the Tower, under sentence of death, he had given the ring to a boy to take to the Countess's sister, Lady Scrope, who had defended Essex to the Queen for longer than almost anyone and whose husband had been one of James's earliest supporters. Essex had intended for her to pass on his ring to the Queen as a sign that he was asking for mercy, but the boy gave the ring to the Countess instead. Her husband, Admiral Nottingham (or Cecil, depending on the version of the story), persuaded her to keep it but, having seen Elizabeth's unhappiness after Essex's death, she wanted the Queen to know the truth and beg forgiveness. According to one tradition the Queen's response was to shake her cousin in her bed with the words "God may forgive you, but I never can."[40]

The legend is at odds with all the contemporary accounts of Elizabeth's mourning of her cousin's death, but the reasons for its persistence are not hard to find—they reflect the longevity of public hatred for Robert Cecil and the Howard family. There is no record of what happened to the ring described by Lady Kildare, if it ever existed, but a gold ring set with a sardonyx cameo portrait of Elizabeth, said to have belonged to Essex, and passed through the female line of his family, is still kept at Westminster Abbey. The inside is enameled with forget-me-nots.

Essex had blamed all the problems of government on Elizabeth's gender and Manningham jotted in his diary his disgust that they had to pray to ladies (for their suits) in the Queen's time—since those physically closest to her had, inevitably, been women. Now at last James's kingship restored the proper order of the sexes and he and others rejoiced at it. In an effort to discover something more about the new king, Manningham visited Barbara Ruthven, who had fled to London from Edinburgh in January. He thought her "a gallant tall gentlewoman" but disliked "the lisping, fumbling language" she spoke. Although Barbara Ruthven would have spoken highly educated Scots, the English who heard it rarely admired it. To Manningham and others it was simply a bastardized English and one few were familiar with—there were no more than a handful of Scots in the whole of London.* Barbara Ruthven told Manningham that the King was much given to swearing, especially when out hunting. Elsewhere he learned that James leaned on courtiers as he walked—a sign of his favor, it was said.[41]

By Wednesday 30 March, courtiers were heading north in droves to see the new king for themselves and to hand him their petitions. "A new King will have new soldiers and God knows what men they will be," Sir John Harington warned his friend Lord Thomas Howard. "One says he will serve him by day, another by night; the women (who love to talk as they like) are for serving him both day and night."[42] An-

---

*There was almost no intermarriage between the subjects of the two kingdoms and very few Scots took the high road south for work. It is estimated that in the late sixteenth century there were no more than sixty Scots in the whole of London. On English attitudes to Scots it is worth recalling Thomas Howard, Earl of Suffolk, who commented to Sir John Harington on Robert Carr in 1606: "The King teacheth him Latin every morning, and I think someone should teach him English too; for, as he is a Scottish lad, he hath much need of better language." Harington, *Nugae Antiquae,* vol. 1, p. 395.

other courtier complained that the dash to Scotland gave the impression that it was "as if it were nothing else but first come first served, or that preferment were a goal to be got by footmanship." Senior figures began to fret that the "wrong sort" of people might gain royal favor.[43] Lord Burghley told Cecil that he was on his knees asking God that "our corrupt court may not corrupt [James] nor such about the King as hereafter have credit with him,"[44] and Sir Roger Wilbraham was also busy praying that "the wealth of England and the flattery of the Court do not in time deprave his government."[45] The men heading north certainly included enemies of the present government—Lord Cobham and a Puritan gentleman from Northamptonshire called Sir Lewis Pickering among them—and the Council sent others to countermand whatever they might say.[46]

Sir John Harington, anxious to avoid any trouble, left London, not for Scotland but for his estate in Somerset. "Good caution never comes better, than when a man is climbing," he observed; "it is a pitiful thing to set a wrong foot and, instead of raising one's head, to fall to the ground and show one's baser parts."[47]

❊   ❊   ❊

James was in an ebullient mood as his English suitors and officials poured into Holyroodhouse. His master huntsman, Sir Roger Aston, is said to have described him as being "like a poor man, wandering above forty years in a Wilderness and barren soil, and now arrived at the Land of Promise."[48] He greeted everyone with familiarity and courtesy, anxious to send no one away disappointed.

The first suitor to reach Holyrood was the Puritan Sir Lewis Pickering. The new English edition of the *Basilikon Doron* had raised the hopes of the "hotter sort" of Protestant, as the preface appeared to sympathize with those who thought the Prayer Book ceremonies too Popish. James assured Pickering that the case for reform would be thoroughly examined. Hard on Pickering's heels, however, came Archbishop Whitgift's emissary, Dr. Thomas Neville, Dean of Canterbury. James assured Neville that he was resolved to maintain the Church "as it had been settled by the late queen"—not quite the impression he had given Pickering, but James hoped to keep both types of Protestant happy, initiating reforms here, rejecting others there and enjoying the debates along the way.

Indeed, a religious settlement was one of James's top three priorities, along with peace with his neighbors and the union of England with Scotland.[49] The throne of England was within James's grasp, but to secure it and keep hold of the Scots throne he had to ensure that his English and Scots subjects had a stake in his crown. This required a wider distribution of wealth and honors. The distribution of the latter was easy: James had showered the Scots elite with honors for years and he would now do the same for the English. When John Peyton, the son of the Lieutenant of the Tower, arrived in Edinburgh, James dubbed him his "first knight"—there would soon be many others. Distributing wealth, however, could only be achieved with peace and union, for without peace there would be no money and without union he would not be able to share it with the Scots.

Sir John Harington and the Earl of Northumberland had warned James that the English would resent seeing English money spent on Scotland, but they had never grasped the sacrifice the Scots were making in sending their King south. The Scottish lawyer Sir Thomas Craig had once predicted that "no prince born in Scotland will ever rule that country after ... His Majesty's son. Our kings will be Englishmen, born in England, residing in England. They will naturally prefer Englishmen as their attendants and courtiers ... London will be the seat of government and the capital of the whole island. Thence for the most part will the laws that govern us proceed." It was important that the Scots felt that they had something significant to gain by James's accession to the English throne.

Intimations of James's intentions were not long in coming. The royal engraver in London was sent instructions to make new signets with the union of the arms of England and Scotland, and a court official called Sir Thomas Lake reported back from Scotland that James would "be loath to give the first blow between Spain and him." James had sent the Dutch rebels in the Netherlands assurances that he would not abandon them, but it was evident to Lake he was on good terms with the emissary to the Archdukes Albert and Isabella and that it was France whom he viewed with the most suspicion: "He told me the French Ambassador never looked merrily since he heard of his Majesty's success in England."[50] Lake also gained the impression that James was prepared to accept peace with Tyrone "upon any terms."

Fortunately Lord Mountjoy had received Tyrone's submission at Mellifont Abbey on the afternoon of Wednesday the 30th. An on-looker recorded that Elizabeth's "Monster of the North" appeared utterly exhausted, throwing himself to the ground as he entered the room and "grovelling to the earth, with such a dejected countenance, that the standers by were amazed and my Lord Mountjoy had much ado to remember the work in hand."[51] He was left on his knees for an hour. It was not until he made his final formal submission before the Irish Parliament on Sunday 3 April that he was informed that Elizabeth was dead. Fynes Moryson watched as the news was broken and reported that he saw tears stream down Tyrone's face, "in such quantity as it could not well be concealed, especially in him upon whose face all men's eyes were cast."[52]

Lake was finding it uncomfortable and expensive in Edinburgh, but he was among the first to be able to form a judgment of the new king, noting, "He is very facile, using no great majesty nor solemnity in his access, but witty to conceive, and very ready of speech."[53] Lord Burghley's son, William, told his father that James's well-known passion for hunting was also evident. James had announced that he had heard that every gentleman in England kept a well-stocked park for hunting and that he intended to hunt as many of them as he could on his way south. He wanted to enjoy his crown and leave the minutiae of political affairs to Cecil. Roger Aston passed on a message to Cecil that the King had heard that he was "but a little man, but he would shortly load your shoulders with business."[54] This was both good news and bad for Cecil; some of the King's business was already causing him considerable concern.

James had requested huge sums to cover the costs of his journey south. The figure of £5,000 was circulating in London—money that the English Treasury simply did not have.[55] Cecil and Buckhurst had been through the accounts and found no credits whatsoever. Cecil, however, was loath to pass on the bad news and money was raised to present to James in Berwick. It allowed James to persist in the belief that he had inherited enormous wealth—and what a glorious change in circumstances that must have seemed.[56] James was virtually bankrupt and even before Elizabeth was dead he had been asking Cecil for an advance on his annuity. A flurry of activity in the Scots Council provided James with some money for his immediate needs. He ordered a purple velvet cloak lined with fur, and matching purple coats and breeches lined with taffeta, in an effort to upgrade his modest wardrobe.[57] The cost of such outfits was, however, but a drop in the ocean to what he intended to spend.

On Sunday 3 April James attended morning service at the High Church of St. Giles, Edinburgh—a church described by Fynes Moryson as "large and lightsome" but "nothing at all for beauty and ornament." James's throne was raised on wooden steps against the pillar next to the pulpit. Opposite was another seat very like it, in which those accused of acts of immorality were made to do their public penance. A few weeks before Moryson's visit, a stranger had sat in this seat, assuming it was meant for important gentlemen, "till he was driven away with the profuse laughter of the common sort, to the disturbance of the whole congregation." There were no such mistakes, however, during this service. The minister, John Hall, delivered a sermon celebrating the King's peaceful succession as the work of God. When he had finished James stood up from his throne and addressed the congregation. He reiterated that he was the lawful heir to the crown of England, as he was to that of Scotland, and he then set out his vision for the future of his two kingdoms:

> As my right is united in my person . . . my marches are united by land and not by sea, so there is no difference betwixt them. There is nae mair difference betwixt London and Edinburgh . . . than there is betwixt Inverness and Aberdeen and Edinburgh . . . But my course must be betwixt baith—to establish peace and religion, and wealth betwixt baith the countries . . . and as ane [one] country has wealth, and the other has multitude of men, sae ye may pairt the gifts, and ane [one] do as they may to help the other.'

James promised that everyone, from the least important person in his kingdom to the greatest, would have access to him to pour out

their complaints. He was not going abroad, he said, but simply traveling from one part of his isle to another, and he intended to return to
Scotland once every three years. He ended his address with the words:
"I now employ only your hearts to the gude prospering of me in my
success and journey. I have nae mair to say, but pray for me."[58] Many
of the Scots congregation wept.

James had set his departure date for Tuesday 5 April. Anna, Prince
Henry and Princess Elizabeth were to follow after Elizabeth's funeral,
when the ladies-in-waiting would be free to attend upon their new
royal family. The two-year-old Charles, Duke of Albany, was considered too young and sickly to travel with them and would not join his
family until the following year. The final preparations went ahead
rapidly. James wrote a fond letter of farewell to Prince Henry, still at
Stirling Castle, and signed an act entrusting the education of the infant Charles to Lord President Fyvie. A number of other acts established the government in James's absence. Finally on Tuesday James
kissed Anna goodbye in front of a large crowd that had gathered on
the Royal Mile. He bent low as his lips touched her throat. She was a
few weeks pregnant and both were in tears, as were many in the
crowd. James then rode off surrounded by a large train of followers. It
included English noblemen and gentlemen, the French ambassador
and his wife—who was to be carried the whole way to London in a
sedan chair—and his Scots favorites.

Despite James's promises to visit Scotland every three years he returned to his homeland only once, in 1617. He nevertheless boasted
with some justice that he ruled Scotland from England more effectively with his pen than others had ruled it with the sword. It remained peaceful and increasingly prosperous, although the huge
wealth that would be accumulated by his Scots favorites was not reflected in a wider distribution of England's wealth north of the border. These favorites included Lord Home, who had tended Carey
after his fall and whose castle at Dunglass the King was to stay at that
night; his former tutor, Peter Young; his old school friend Jocky
o'Sclaittis, the Earl of Mar; Ludovic Stuart, Duke of Lennox, the son
of his beloved Esmé d'Aubigny; his fat and jovial Treasurer, Sir George
Home of Spott, said to be "the only man of all other most inward with

the King"; the Captain of the Guard, Thomas Erskine; and Carey's old adversary, Robert Kerr of Cessford—estimated to have been present at the violent death of twenty men and destined to be a future Lord Privy Seal.

As one popular English verse of the next few years would have it:

> Then bonny Scot well witness can
> 'twas England that made thee a gentleman.[59]

❖   ❖   ❖

Late in the afternoon of Wednesday 6 April Sir John Carey and his constables, captains and Gentleman Pensioners greeted James at the "liberties" of Berwick—an area about a mile north of the city walls. They rode on together until, a witness recalls, at about five o'clock the city of Berwick rose before them "like an enchanted castle." As the town's cannon fired in thunderous salute from its angled bastions the ground seemed to tremble and the houses stagger; the whole town was wrapped in a mantle of smoke. Even the garrison's oldest soldiers, stationed at Berwick since the days of Henry VIII, swore they had never heard or seen anything like it.[60]

At the city gates Mr. William Selby, Gentleman Porter of Berwick, presented James with the keys of the town. James handed them back, knighted him and rode through cheering crowds to the marketplace. As James appeared the gathered throng fell to their knees shouting and crying "Welcome" and "God save King James." They were entreated to be quiet so that the Recorder of Berwick, Mr. Christopher Parkinson, could deliver his speech. The Mayor, Hugh Gregson, then presented James with a traditional gift of a purse of gold and the town's charter.[61] At this point Queen Elizabeth would have thanked the people for their show of devotion and as Harington recalled,

> her speech did win all affections for she would say, her state did require her to
> command what she knew her people would willingly do from their own love to
> her. Herein she did show her wisdom fully; for who did choose to lose her confi-
> dence; or who would withhold a show of love or obedience, when their sover-

eign said it was their own choice and not her compulsion? Surely did she play
her tables well to gain obedience thus without restraint.[62]

James, however, took a more aggressive view. His book of instruction
on kingship made it plain that he did not approve of populist speeches
or being "prodigal in joking and nodding at every step." He believed
that lawful kings should be obeyed whether they were loved or not.
"Your Queen did talk of her subjects love and good affections and in
truth she aimed well," Harington's friend Lord Thomas Howard later
observed; "our King talks of his subjects' fear and subjugation, and
herein he does well too, as long as it holds good."[63]

The Berwick crowds waited patiently on their knees for words of
love that never came. Eventually a burst of rain exploded over them
and James kicked his horse on, riding straight to the main church to
thank God for the good fortune of his inheritance. Berwick was a
poor town by English standards and the church was small and so
structurally unsound that the congregation would often run out of the
building if there was a sudden blast of wind, "even," we are told, "at
sermon time."[64] The sermon that day was to be delivered by Tobie
Matthew, the powerful Bishop of Durham, who was acutely aware
that his political future would depend on his saying the right thing.
The first Lord Burghley had installed Matthew in the bishopric in the
early 1590s, with instructions to crush Catholic resistance and keep a
watchful eye on Scotland. Matthew had become renowned for his ferocious pursuit of recusants, forcing them to conform through fines,
imprisonment and the threat of death. But, like the first Lord Burghley, Matthew also opposed James's inheritance of the crown, giving
credit to Catholic opinion that James "secretly hath mass and is a
Catholic." The gossips in London were certain Matthew's career was
over. All, however, was not yet lost.

Matthew was the kind of man James admired: intelligent, witty,
with a deep knowledge of theology. He had also had a stroke of good
fortune: Cecil wanted something from him, namely, Durham House,
the old bishopric palace in London, which Elizabeth had leased to
Ralegh. It lay next to Cecil's new house and he wanted to expand his

property in that direction. Confident that Ralegh would not find favor with James, he had asked Matthew if he could take it over when it reverted to the bishopric. Matthew replied from Berwick with the tantalizing answer that he could not make any immediate promises, "not knowing the state of the house, or what recompense I should require of it."[65] For now Bishop Matthew would continue to enjoy Cecil's goodwill and thus James's trust.

Matthew opened his sermon with a humble petition to James for pardon. It was obvious that it had been accepted when after the service he was asked to wait on James and say grace at his dinner table. Since Elizabeth's death, however, James's actions and pronouncements had left most none the wiser on his attitudes toward religious toleration. On the one hand, his letters to the Privy Council and city councils had promised to defend the rights of the Protestant religion and said nothing about allowing religious toleration. On the other, he had shown favor to leading Catholic figures such as Lord Thomas Howard, whom he announced was to replace the sickly Lord Hunsdon as Lord Chamberlain. When the letter sacking Hunsdon reached London from Berwick it triggered outbursts of fury from his servants; one was put in the Tower and racked "on his assertion as to the King's favouring Catholics" and "his threats against the life of the King."[66]

A request from James that Elizabeth's funeral should take place before he arrived in London also added to the confusion. It was said that he did not want to pay his respects to his mother's killer and the Venetian Scaramelli reported that "Elizabeth's portrait is being hidden everywhere, and Mary Stuart's shown instead with declaration that she suffered for no other cause than for her religion."[67] Gradually, however, James's true views were showing themselves. A Catholic priest later claimed that when an English nobleman had asked James in Scotland whether he really was going to offer toleration, he had replied: "Na Na, good faith, we's not need the papists now!" Whether or not he used these words, they neatly summed up how he viewed the issue.[68] James would tolerate Catholics but not Catholicism, a distinction that not everyone understood but which would eventually be spelled out as the invitation to hypocrisy and dishonesty that it was.

On James's second day in Berwick he was given a tour of the walls of the city and inspected the garrison. Berwick was considered to be one of the least desirable postings in England: the weather was often cold and damp and the storms could be terrible. In January 1595 several soldiers had been blown off the city walls. The garrison's victualing was also a constant ground of complaint. The soldiers often went hungry despite the cheap and plentiful supplies of salmon and shellfish available in the town.*

James fired one of the garrison's cannon and commended the soldiers for their actions in bringing an end to the robberies of the "Busy Week."[69] He was accompanied by large numbers of Gentlemen Pensioners and courtiers. Among them was Henry Howard, who had been sent to Berwick by Cecil "to possess the King's ear and countermine the Lord Cobham."[70] It was a task in which he was proving entirely successful. Cobham was getting nowhere in his efforts to attract the King's goodwill, and neither was his brother, George Brooke. Brooke had been pushing for the mastership of the St. Cross hospital near Winchester during the last months of Elizabeth's life. He had only a fraction of his brother's wealth and the added expense of keeping his wife's sister as his mistress. The mastership was the ideal solution and although Cecil had blocked his suit with Elizabeth he hoped to have better luck with James.[71] When he finally caught the King's attention he offered to spy on any malcontents, hoping for a promise of preferment in return. None, however, was forthcoming and there were soon other suitors to take Brooke's place.

The king's train had swollen to over 500. James hated the crush of strangers around him, any one of whom could have been carrying a knife and a grudge. He was also concerned that so many important figures should be away from their positions of responsibility, and questioned how the numbers already in his train could be fed and housed as he journeyed south. He had issued a proclamation two days earlier ordering all those who held office or who were of significant standing to stay in their counties and at their posts. In London, Ralegh was caught hold of as he prepared to ride north with a large

---

*The garrison at Berwick would close that summer, as it was no longer needed after the Borders became the Middle Shires of Britain. Many of the old soldiers who fired the salute to James that April were thrown into destitution.

group of suitors and ordered "to spare his labour"—but others were still arriving. James ordered the issuing of a further proclamation "for attendance on the King's person, and for receiving of him by the sheriffs of the several counties, at his first coming into England." It demanded that the county sheriffs "take special care and regard, that all manner victuals and other provisions necessary ... for his Majesty and his whole train, be in convenient time brought to all places where his Highness shall lodge or rest." If anyone proved reluctant to provide what was necessary "they are to sustain such condign punishment as their offence in that behalf deserves."[72]

James was in high spirits as he set off for Widdrington the following day, Friday 8 April.* After stopping briefly at the house of an old, blind soldier called Sir William Read, he galloped down the Great North Road, reportedly covering thirty-seven miles in four hours and leaving much of the train far behind him.[†] After a short rest at Widdrington Castle he left to go out hunting Carey's deer and killed two before he returned "with a good appetite to the house, where he was most royally feasted and banqueted that night."[‡] James's energy, generosity and bonhomie were attractive and in London Scaramelli soon received positive reports "that the King is a man of letters and of business, fond of the chase and of riding, sometimes indulging in play," qualities that men admired and which "render him acceptable to the aristocracy."[73]

On Saturday James left for Newcastle upon Tyne, the most important commercial center in Northumberland and one already famous for its coal trade. The city walls were reputed to be the most impressive in England, but Newcastle was also notorious for the numbers of its poor and for the tenacious Catholicism of its citizens. Bishop Matthew complained he had found it almost impossible to get its of-

---

*Before leaving Berwick James knighted Robert Cecil's godson Ralph Grey on the bridge.

†Sir William Read claimed that he was so honored it made him "feel the warmth of youth stir in his frost nipped blood."

‡Several gentlemen involved in the suppression of the "Busy Week" were knighted at Widdrington, including Nicholas Forster, Henry Widdrington, High Sheriff of Northumberland, William Fenwick and Edward Gorges.

ficers to enforce the law on "an infamous recusant" called Nicholas Tempest, adding: "That town is of great privilege and small trust in these affairs; upon my word, I am sorry and ashamed to say it."[74] The people of Newcastle nevertheless greeted James with even more enthusiasm than Berwick. According to tradition the shouting and crying reaching such a pitch that a shocked Scotsman in James's entourage was heard to mutter: "These people will spoil a gude king." The journal of Captain Millington, who was with the train, records that they also expressed their loyalty in practical terms:

So joyful were the townsmen of Newcastle of his Majesty being there, that they thankfully bare all charges of his household during the time of his abode with them, being from Saturday till Wednesday morning. All things were in such plenty, and so delicate for variety, that it gave great contentment to his Majesty.[75]

The truth, however, was a little more complex than these stories suggest. The description of the shocked Scotsman, which first appears in a history written a generation later, was based on a real event, but it was not one that took place in Newcastle. A diary entry written by the London-based lawyer John Manningham during the period that James was in Newcastle records that James's envoy Edward Bruce, now Lord Kinloss, was in London and that he "told our nobles that they shall receive a very good, wise, and religious King, if we can keep him so; if we mar him not."[76] These comments were not prompted by the behavior of ordinary people in Newcastle, or anywhere else, but by continuing concerns about the corrupting influence of flattering courtiers. Captain Millington's remarks on the willing generosity of the people of Newcastle also paint a distorted picture, as they were written for the King to read at a later date. The reality was that behind the scenes arguments were raging over who should pay for what and how much they should pay.

At the end of March Lord Burghley had asked the city officials of York—a much larger and richer city than Newcastle—to loan the King £3,000 to cover his expenses (James had already had to declare Scots money valid tender in England in order to save his Scots entourage from financial embarrassment). After some debate the York city officials sent £1,000 to Newcastle, "by way of loan towards the defraying of some small part of his present occasions."[77] And Alderman Askwith, who delivered the loan, was instructed to ensure that the King knew where the money had come from and to "procure such warrant as you think sufficient for the repayment thereof." The instructions continued: "If any demand be made of the wealth of the town, you may allege that it is very poor."[78] The people of Newcastle, like those of York, were doing no more than was expected and, indeed, demanded of them.

James used some of his new money to buy Newcastle's debtors out of prison and ordered the release of all other prisoners "except those that lay for treason, murder" and, significantly, "papistry."[79] It was the first solid evidence of his attitude toward Catholics and it sent a shiver through the north. As Bishop Godfrey Goodman later explained, although Catholics were persecuted under Elizabeth, "they did live in some hope that after the old woman's life they might have some mitigation, and even those who did then persecute them were a little more moderate, as being doubtful what times might succeed." If James was determined to continue with the persecution, their situation was now far worse, for he was young with sons to follow him and Catholics could expect "the utmost rigour of the law should be executed."[80]

James, however, saw only unalloyed delight at his accession, not only in the faces of the welcoming crowds but in the seemingly endless flow of petitions given to him requesting reforms in the Church and the corrupt Elizabethan state. James wrote to the Privy Council from Newcastle asking that they announce his intention "to hold our Parliament at our City of Westminster as soon as conveniently may be . . . and that the same shall be chiefly assembled for the relief of all grievances of our people."[81] He could now reflect that this was the moment when the prophecy of the cradle king marked with a lion was being fulfilled:

> . . . *Arthur I am, of Britain King,*
> *Come by good right to claim my seat and throne,*

My kingdoms severed to rejoin in one,
To amend what is amiss in everything

—WALTER QUIN, 1595

As James's progress continued to Durham he stopped briefly at the medieval Lumley Castle. Lord Lumley had been involved in the plot to marry the Duke of Norfolk to Mary, Queen of Scots, and Cecil had chosen to send his son William to live with the Lumley household after his removal from the care of the Raleghs. It was an excellent way for Cecil to mark the break with his father's role in the death of James's mother. In Lumley's absence Dr. James, Dean of Durham, showed the King around the castle. Lumley had carved his ancient lineage on the west side of the castle courtyard in the form of a double pile of sixteen shields. As they reached it the Dean launched into a long-winded explanation of its details. Members of the nobility had often complained that under Elizabeth they had lost much of their former power and influence to families such as the Cecils. Here was an opportunity for James to demonstrate his respect for them. But as the Dean droned on James exploded, "Oh, mon, gang na further; let me digest the knowledge I have gained, for I did na ken Adam's name was Lumley." It was a minor incident but it did indicate that James was not going to be too reverent in his future treatment of them.

Durham itself provided the kind of company James preferred and as the brilliant Bishop Matthew entertained the King at Durham Castle with "his merry and well seasoned jests," the King's favor was sealed.[82] James assured Matthew he could do what he wished with Durham House in London, currently occupied by Ralegh. Matthew in turn agreed that Norham Castle, which also belonged to the bishopric, should be taken from Robert Carey and passed to Lord Home, who had cared for Carey so tenderly in Edinburgh. Before James left Durham he issued another general pardon from which Catholics were again excluded—this time despite the pleading of Scots Catholics such as Home.

The country on the road to York was growing richer. The views of the Tees with its woodlands, pastures and fields were so beautiful that James is said to have stopped for a time at Haughton-le-Side to gaze at the panorama from a spot that became known as the Cross Legs. The houses of the local gentry also gave him some insight into the wealth of his new kingdom. In Scotland they still lived in ancient manses furnished only by a few basic necessities. In England, by contrast, they had new, light, airy houses embellished with elaborate plaster ceilings and carved chimneypieces and furnished with wall hangings, carpets and furniture, crystal and silks.

On the night of 14 April James stayed at High Walworth Manor, whose large mullioned windows were decorated with painted glass representing the arms of important figures—a show of loyalty that was particularly important for James's hostess, a widow called Elizabeth Jenison. Three of her sons were Catholic converts who had spent time in prison for recusancy—proof to James of the dangers of allowing priests to remain in England.*

Mrs. Jenison paid for the entertainment of James and his train, something that must have represented an almost intolerable financial burden. Despite the orders for officials to stay at their posts, courtiers continued to stream northward and the pressure on the country had driven up the price of provisions to exorbitant levels. Officials were sent south to turn people back on the roads and James issued another proclamation telling courtiers to stay away. Only those on government business were allowed access and some "of great name and office" were sent home.[83]

James's mood was not improved when he reached the town of Topcliffe. When James was in Berwick he had written to the Privy Council asking that Anna be sent "such jewels and other furniture which did appertain to the late Queen."[84] He wanted Anna to share in the pleasure he was having on his progress and to be well prepared for her journey south. They had now replied that they were not prepared to send any of Elizabeth's possessions into Scotland. It suggested that despite James's announcement in Edinburgh that the two kingdoms were now one, the Councilors still regarded Scotland as a foreign and potentially hostile country. Significantly, the man in charge of the

---

*The younger two were married to the sisters of the brilliant missionary Jesuit John Gerard. Bishop Matthew's son and namesake actually became a Jesuit.

Great Wardrobe was Sir John Fortescue, believed to have supported Grey of Wilton's motion that James be given the crown with conditions. James was further angered when the Council announced that they would greet him in York rather than farther south, as he had wished (he had suggested Burghley House, the extravagant palace built by William Cecil). It set a bad example to the rest of the court and James penned them an acid letter:

> *To our right trusty and well beloved Cousins and Councillors, our Keeper of our Great Seal of England, our High Treasurer of England, our Admiral of England, and our Principal Secretary* for the time being. [my emphasis]
> . . . *For answer to the contents of your letter, we would have you remember, that you may perceive by our former letters that we never urged your personal repair to us further or sooner than our affairs there would permit you . . . But that now being altered, we desire that you do not remove from the charge in hand . . . Touching the jewels to be sent for our wife, our meaning is not to have any of the principal jewels of state to be sent so soon nor so far off, but only such as, by the opinion of the Ladies attendant about the late Queen our Sister, you shall find meet for the ordinary apparelling and ornament of her the rest may come after, when she shall be nearer at hand.*[85]

The Councilors were left in no doubt that their decisions had put their jobs at risk. James intended to enter York the following day and the city government and citizens of York continued a frantic rush of activity as they prepared for his visit. At a public meeting on 30 March the Recorder had "declared unto the said commoners and others assembled" that every inhabitant should "remove all clogs . . . dung hill and filth out of the streets, and shall also paint the outside of their houses with some colours." Vagrants were to be sent to Hull en route for the army in the Low Countries and the newly cleaned streets were to be strewn with "rushes, flowers and herbs."[86] Lord Burghley added orders for the citizens to hang tapestries and painted cloth in the streets James was to pass through. A York schoolmaster called Smith was commissioned to write a welcoming speech based on the advice of Alderman Askwith, the man who had been sent to Newcastle with the loan. The traditional gifts for a visiting monarch were also ordered: a double gilt silver cup, "having the City arms on it," and a hundred pounds in gold. Similar but lesser gifts were ordered for the King's favorites and chief officers.[87] Lord Burghley, anxious about where they were to be housed, had asked to be informed "how many beds my Lord Mayor and every Alderman and other citizens have, and are able to make and furnish . . . for the placings of the nobles and other attendants upon the King's Majesty at their houses."[88]

But just as everything seemed to be coming together, Lord Burghley issued new demands. No one was to carry arms, save a rapier. The ceremonies were to be held in open places, "and the press or crowd kept as far and wide from [the King] as may be, so that he may have space and room to stir his horse up and down and not to stand still."[89] Trusted people were to be employed to stand at the front and hold back the press. Heads of households were to be instructed that all weapons should be taken to the mayor, and to ensure they had done so, houses were to be searched. Finally, the areas around James's lodgings were to be kept free of people. Burghley had been advised to "tell the mayor it is for avoiding of heat, evil air, and that the King may be better seen, and what other colours it shall please your Lordship [to] allege."* It was an insult to the citizens of York that their loyalty should be considered suspect, and James's fear of assassination suggested an estrangement from his subjects that Elizabeth had never shown, even with a papal bull of excommunication on her head.[90]

On 16 April James was dutifully met on the east end of York's Skip Bridge by scarlet-gowned sheriffs attended by "all the gentlemen and the best sort of yeoman (which are men of comely personages and such as have decent and good apparel and good horses)."[91] They presented James with their white staffs of office. Half a mile further, the rituals continued as Lord Burghley and the knights and gentlemen of

*Nearly one-sixth of all recusant Catholics registered with the Exchequer between 1590 and 1625 came from Yorkshire. It was possible that one of them might try to kill James, but a particular comparison with Elizabeth is instructive. The Jacobean bishop Godfrey Goodman recalled a night in December 1588 when he and a group of friends had seen the Queen on her way to Council. A huge crowd gathered and she stopped to speak to them although, as he recalled, this was the year of the Spanish Armada, "when she had most enemies and how easily might they have gotten into the crowd and multitude to have done her a mischief." Goodman, *Court of James*, vol. 1, p. 163.

the shire greeted James and, with a blast of trumpets, the sergeants at arms delivered up their maces. A waiting coach carried James to the city gates, where the schoolmaster's oration was delivered. The mayor stood on a platform attended by a footman in a new coat embroidered with the city's arms. Those citizens who stood nearby also had new clothes made in accordance with orders that they should look their best.

The mayor gave James the usual gilt cup filled with gold, together with the city's sword and keys. He expected to then be given the sword of state to carry in front of James through the city. It was, however, handed instead to George Clifford, the third Earl of Cumberland, in an effort to honor the nobility, after the feelings James had displayed at Lumley Castle. The public celebration began after a service in York Minster as James was escorted under a canopy to the Manor of St. Mary's. A fountain featuring a mermaid, designed by Mr. Rawlings, ran with wine and York's "butteries, pantries, and cellars" were "held open in great abundance for all comers."[92] Lord Home, Sir George Home, Sir Thomas Erskine, Sir Roger Aston and Sir John Ramsay were presented with personal gifts from the city of gilded cups, bowls and jewels. James, pleased and relieved by the welcome, declined the offer of a coach the next morning, saying "the people are desirous to see a King, and so they shall, for they shall see his body as his face." It was an unfortunate consequence that James was to find himself face-to-face with a Catholic priest.

As James walked back to his lodgings from another religious service, a man dressed as a gentleman stepped forward. His name was Thomas Hill, a priest considered to be a troublemaker, even by the Vatican. He had been condemned by Pope Clement VIII in 1597 as a "factious man" and subsequently had been refused papal permission to carry out his priestly functions, but he was intent on delivering a petition on behalf of England's Catholics. James had already been presented with a number of petitions from Catholics. Typically they pointed out that Puritans and atheists were tolerated in England and asked for the same treatment, drawing attention to the good effects of religious toleration in France. This one, however, had a very different tone. Hill's petition demanded the suppression of penal laws and compared the lot of England's Catholics to that of the Israelites under King Jeroboam, whose tyrannies had given them "a just occasion to leave their due obedience."[93] In short, Hill's petition threatened treason.

James asked Hill what college he was from. Hill replied "that he belonged to the true college of Christ, and that in this kingdom he had forty thousand of his religion." James quipped back, "Well then, amongst so many, have you never found a chief to take ten of your tribes and lead them elsewhere?"[94] Hill was arrested soon after and hauled off to the Gatehouse prison in London.

That evening was James's last in York, but Cecil's arrival had been delayed "by his fat horses failing him."[95] He was carrying a number of papers from his fellow Councilors, some of whom had considerable anxieties about their futures. Edward Bruce of Kinloss had advertised that James wanted half the Council to be Scots, provoking Councilors and noblemen to complain to the Venetian ambassador that "no one but Englishmen should hold honours and office in England."[96] Cecil, however, had already accepted the inevitable and was working to ingratiate himself with the Scots favorites.

Although Cecil knew that the Treasury was almost empty, he had found £1,000 in state funds as a gift for Sir George Home—an astute move.[97] The contemporary Scottish historian Spottiswoode described Home as a man of deep wit and few words who achieved the most difficult political tasks without noise. The restoration of episcopacy in Scotland had been one such and James trusted him completely. Home's friendship would prove central to the success of Cecil's future career. Cecil had also fawned over Home's fellow countryman, Kinloss, writing to James when Kinloss had arrived in London on 10 April to beg humble thanks for the King sending a Scot who was "already so good an Englishman."[98] The phrase was significant because James had asked the Council to naturalize all Scots—something that would enable him to give them English land as well as English offices. The Council had been horrified by the proposal but did not dare oppose it openly and their reply suggested a middle road. The naturalizing of all Scots would require an Act of Parliament, but in the meantime, they suggested, individuals could be provided for under the Great Seal.[99] Cecil's letter had implied that Kinloss would be particularly welcome to English citizenship.

Cecil was also carrying the Council's instructions to settle the dates for Elizabeth's funeral and James's coronation. They had suggested a joint coronation with Anna, as this would save an estimated third of the costs. It was to take place about a month after the funeral, which they hoped could be held the Friday after Easter. Elizabeth had already lain unburied for long enough. The shoddy work of the embalmers and the warm spring weather had allowed the Queen's body to deteriorate with horrific consequences. Elizabeth Southwell described how as the ladies were kneeling by the dead Queen one night they heard a crack. It was discovered on investigation that the wood of the coffin, the lead underneath it and the cerecloth had split as the fumes from the decomposing corpse had burst out. In the morning the body "was fain to be new trimmed up . . . but no man durst speak of it publicly for fear of displeasing Secretary Cecil."[100] There was a danger that reports of such horrors would be taken as an ill omen for the future or a judgment against James's accession.

When Cecil eventually arrived in York it was night and James was asleep. The next morning, however, Cecil was given an hour of James's time before he went for breakfast with the city's mayor. His first impression cannot have been far removed from that of his cousin Sir Francis Bacon. Reporting back to the Earl of Northumberland, Bacon describes

> a prince the farthest from the appearance of vainglory that may be, and rather like a prince of the ancient form than of the latter time. His speech is swift and cursory, and in the full dialect of his country; and in point of business, short; in point of discourse, large. He affects popularity by gracing such as he hath heard to be popular, and not by any fashions of his own. He is thought somewhat general in his favours, and his virtue of access is rather because he is much abroad and in press, than that he gives easy audience about serious things.

Bacon was unable to have any private conference with James and, he complained, "no more has almost any other English." The King was surrounded by Scotsmen and would not even talk to the Attorney

General without Sir George Home's say-so. Nor did he appear too sensitive about English national feelings. Bacon warned Northumberland: "He hastens to a mixture of both kingdoms and nations, faster perhaps than policy will conveniently bear," and added, "I told your Lordship once before, that (methought) his Majesty asked counsel of the time past than of the time to come."[101]

James's reluctance to listen to advice was in stark contrast with what Cecil was used to with Elizabeth, but the meeting began well. James agreed to the Council's suggestions on the dating of Elizabeth's funeral. He also agreed that there should be a joint coronation on 25 July. When Cecil suggested that no immediate announcements should be made regarding posts given to Scots, however, he discovered that James had already paired the two Gentlemen Ushers who had come up from London with two Scots. James also made it plain that he was not prepared to wait long before more significant offices were split between the two nations.[102]

With the meeting over James had his breakfast with the mayor and rewarded him with a knighthood. It was no longer the honor it had been a month earlier. People were discovering that a payment to one of James's Scots favorites was all that was required of those who wished for a knighthood. James made a dozen more that afternoon at Grimston, the house of the High Sheriff of Yorkshire, Sir Edward Stanhope. One of those James dubbed was Thomas Gerard, brother of the notorious Jesuit John Gerard. James made much of the fact that Gerard's father had been imprisoned after trying to help Mary, Queen of Scots, escape from imprisonment in 1571. "I am particularly bound to love your family on account of the persecution you have borne for me," he told Thomas. The Jesuit was infuriated by what he recognized as James's attempt to seduce his brother into loyalty to the crown at the expense of loyalty to the Catholic Church. He railed in his memoirs that to be made a knight by James "was to him no advancement whose ancestors had been so for sixteen generations"—but Thomas would also accept the newly invented title of baronet from James in 1611 and have James's arms carved on the chimneypiece in the hall of the family house.[103]

The mood as James set out on the second leg of his journey was captured by the seventeenth-century historian Arthur Wilson: "Now every man that had but a spark of hope, struck fire to light himself in the way of advancement, though it were to the consumption both of his estate and his being. The court being a kind of lottery, where men that venture much may draw a blank, as such as have little may get the prize."

CHAPTER FIVE

"HOPE AND FEAR"

Winners and Losers, April–May 1603

The head of the Jesuit order in England, Henry Garnet, had shown several soldiers the papal edict calling on Catholics to defy the accession of a Protestant—among them the future gunpowder plotter Robert Catesby. But since resistance to the proclamation declaring James king had proved negligible a new response was called for. Within days of Elizabeth's death, the stocky, flaxen-haired priest had written to "a Catholic nobleman," probably the Earl of Worcester, asking him to tell James that the Jesuits offered him "all the love, fidelity, duty and obedience which can be desired or yielded by any Christian heart."[1] It was a strategic response: they had no choice but to accept James's fait accompli, and in secret they would continue to seek means and opportunities to advance their cause of restoring the Catholic faith.

While the Jesuits had never supported James's accession, and nothing he was likely to do was therefore going to disappoint them, many of the Catholic secular clergy had backed James's candidature and they now realized their mistake. The royal pardons that had left Catholics in prison alongside murderers had put paid to the lie that James had ever intended to offer religious toleration. Catholics such as the Howards might be allowed to play a leading role in government, but they would not be allowed the free exercise of their faith; the price of their power was to risk their souls. As James left York the Venetian ambassador Scaramelli reported that James's Scots agents had confirmed that the most Catholics could hope for was the remission of recusancy fines—and he warned that even that was in doubt.[2]

In the winter James had told Cecil that he expected the seculars to be expelled from England along with the Jesuits. He was not interested in "the distinction in their ranks"; both were subject to the authority of the Pope and he wanted both "safely transported beyond the seas, where they may freely glut themselves on their imagined gods."[3] Cecil was now trying to work out how this could be best achieved. It was important that people not feel inclined to pity the Catholic clergy or resent their treatment. The most effective way to achieve that was for them to be tarnished by treason. In the past plots had been "wakened" by corralling malcontents into actions against the state and there was an outstanding candidate to play such a part now: the most vocal of James's supporters within the seculars had been a short, cross-eyed priest called William Watson, whose personal history is illustrative of the extraordinary bitterness between the Jesuits and those who sought to compromise with the state.

❈   ❈   ❈

The story of the Elizabethan Catholic priesthood was not straightforwardly one of Catholic priests versus a savage absolutist state: sometimes it was one of Catholic priest against Catholic priest. Watson, now in his thirties, had left England at the age of sixteen to train as a priest at Douai, a Catholic college founded by William (later Cardinal) Allen, which was then at Rheims. He returned to work as a missionary in June 1586, when Mary, Queen of Scots, was the outstanding candidate for the succession. Just eight months later she was dead. In common with most moderate Catholic opinion, the secular clergy accepted that this ended all likelihood of a Catholic monarch succeeding Elizabeth and restoring their faith. They hoped that instead proofs of loyalty would eventually earn them a place as an accepted minority. The Jesuits, however, remained doggedly determined that England should have a Catholic monarch.

The Society of Jesus, founded earlier in the century by the Basque-born soldier and courtier Iñigo López de Loyola,[4] was informed by a strongly Spanish mentality, one shaped by hundreds of years spent fighting the Moors. Their intellectual rigor and personal determination stood them in good stead in the battles of the Counter-Reformation and their English members demonstrated particular discipline and courage in the face of torture and death. Each grim butchering on the scaffold at Tyburn and elsewhere was advertised as a martyrdom and used as propaganda for their cause. Indeed, by the turn of the century they were claiming that the penal laws in England were the basis of all their success at home and abroad, and they were certain that they could bring England back into the fold of the mother church. It had taken the Spanish 800 years to erase Islam from Spain. The Jesuits were not going to give up England to heretics after less than seventy.

Most Jesuits had supported Philip II's Armada, whereas the secular students at the English College in Rome had greeted the news of its defeat with cheers. Five years later the Jesuits had been behind the Doleman book advocating the candidature of the Infanta, while the seculars had condemned it as "the most pestilential thing ever written," claiming that its main achievement had been to inflame Protestant fears of Catholics and bring greater persecution.[5] Hitherto the English government had barely differentiated between the two sides—both John Gerard, SJ, and William Watson were imprisoned and tortured during the 1590s—but by the end of the decade Cecil had become aware that there was virtual civil war between them.

Ironically, the issue that set their conflicts alight arose out of Pope Clement VIII's attempts to impose discipline on his quarreling flock. Before the Reformation the secular, or diocesan, priests would have been subject to bishops, but the last member of the ancient hierarchy of English Catholic bishops, Goldwell, Bishop of St. Asaph's, had died in 1585, and persecution had since made it impossible to replace him. The Pope's solution was to impose an archpriest to oversee the English missionaries. The seculars, however, complained that the title "Archpriest" was unknown to canon law and they distrusted the man appointed to the post, George Blackwell, a tactless individual who was close to Henry Garnet. The seculars appealed against Clement's decision, but despite this, on 6 April 1599, the Pope confirmed Blackwell in his new position. The Jesuits had then accused the Appellants—as the faction of the appealers became known—of schism. If such a charge was proved, the Appellants would have faced the choice of obedience to Blackwell and his Jesuit allies or being excommunicated. As they saw it, treason could be made an article of faith. In the autumn of 1600 Thomas Bluet, one of around thirty priests imprisoned at Wisbech Castle on the Isle of Ely, told his jailer that he feared the Jesuits would "swear all priests to be true to the Infanta of Spain," and that he was ready to be "starved to death in the Castle of Wisbech before he would take such an oath." The incident was reported to the authorities and from this point on Cecil became involved, taking a close interest in events as they unfolded.

On 17 November 1600 thirty-three secular priests signed a second appeal to Rome and published a flurry of pamphlets in England. William Watson wrote one warning that if the Pope's decision on the Archpriest was allowed to stand, "all Catholics must hereafter depend upon Blackwell, and he upon Garnet and Garnet upon Persons, and Persons upon the Devil, who is the author of all rebellions, treasons, murders, disobedience and all such designments as this wicked Jesuit had hitherto contrived."[6] Cecil was astonished and delighted by the hatred Watson had expressed for the Jesuits. Here at last was a way to stanch the increase in the number of Catholic converts. He would use the Appellants to expose the treachery of the Jesuits, discredit all of them and thereby sow further divisions.

In March 1601 the Bishop of London, Richard Bancroft, summoned the Appellant priest Thomas Bluet from his cell to meet with him at his palace in Fulham. Bluet was shown letters and books allegedly written by Jesuits inviting the King of Spain to invade England and urging individuals to assassinate Elizabeth. Bluet willingly agreed to help the government and in return the Appellant priests were encouraged to prepare a supplication for toleration to the Queen. Elizabeth responded in July 1601 with an icy reminder that she had been excommunicated—a judgment that still stood: "if I grant this liberty to Catholics," she told them, "by this very fact I lay at their feet my honour, my crown and my life."[7] But the priests were encouraged to continue to strive to prove their loyalty and in November 1601 the Privy Council sent Bluet and four or five of his companions to Rome for a new appeal on the matter of the Archpriest. Meanwhile Bancroft, the licensing authority for printing, encouraged the Appellants to publish more literature,[8] and he soon informed Cecil that William Watson was proving to be particularly "tractable to whet his pen against the Jesuits."[9]

Another of these sixteenth-century "useful idiots" was a gentleman poet and friend of Watson called Anthony Copley. His writings claimed that the courtly Jesuit Robert Persons was the bastard son of a plowman, "a common ale house squire, and the drunkest sponge in all the parish where he lived," and that he had "two bastards, male and female, upon the body of his own sister" before "he ran away . . . and so became a Jesuit."[10] Eighteen such books attacking Persons and his designs upon the English throne appeared between 1601 and 1603, and eventually Persons responded.

In his "Manifestation of the Great Folly and Bad Spirit of Certain in England calling themselves secular priests," published in 1602, Persons sank to the same level as Copley. He sneered that the cross-eyed William Watson "looks nine ways at once" and was so short-sighted "he can discern nothing that touches not his eye." Watson, he wrote, was remembered at his seminary in Rheims for being as clumsy as he was stupid and for arriving so poor that he licked "the dishes which other men had emptied." Other priests received similar treatment while Copley was dismissed as "a little, wanton idle headed boy."[11] Bancroft was so pleased when he saw the pamphlet that he told the man who brought it to him "that if he had brought him a £100 he could not have done him a greater pleasure, and, scratching his elbow, said that this was that he looked for all this while, viz, that one should write against another."[12] The propaganda war was, however, only part of a very dirty business. Some members of the Appellant faction were persuaded that the best way to prove their loyalty to the state was to betray their Jesuit enemies directly to the government. Here again Watson stood out.

In April 1602 three priests were hung, drawn and quartered at Ty-burn on the same day and all, according to Garnet, "like our Saviour were betrayed by false brethren." Watson, in contrast, was "permitted to live where he will" and "though he be known generally, yet he go-eth in his chain of gold, white satin doublet and hose and velvet jerkin"[13]—quite an outfit for a man who had once been obliged to feed himself by licking others men's plates. The appeal to Rome by the sec-ular priests finally came to a conclusion on 5 October when Clement VIII issued a new brief. It attempted to end the friction by forbid-ding the Archpriest from communicating with either the Head of the English Jesuits (Garnet) or their Principal (Persons). It cleared the Appellants of schism and insisted that three of the Appellant priests should be appointed as Blackwell's assistants in succession. It did not, however, establish episcopal government, as the Appellants had hoped. The post of Archpriest was to remain. Nor did it restrain priests from interfering in political affairs, or bind them to release any information of plots against the monarch. On the contrary, Pope Clement then issued his secret brief that no Catholic should consent to *any* Protestant successor to the Queen.

Elizabeth had by now grown anxious to put an end to calls for reli-gious toleration, and in November 1602 the Privy Council published its Proclamation Against Jesuits and Others. It repeated what Eliza-beth had already told the Appellants in 1601—namely, that she would never permit two religions to exist in her realm. The proclamation or-dered the Jesuits to leave the country within thirty days; the Appel-lants had until the end of January 1603. Behind the scenes, Cecil and Bancroft maintained contact with the Appellants, but James was in-furiated that the November proclamation was not being carried out, and the letter he sent to Cecil from Scotland left the Secretary with no option but to confront this inaction. The Appellants' search for common ground concluded on 31 January 1603, the day Elizabeth made her last journey to Richmond, when they presented a Protestation of Allegiance to Bancroft. It affirmed that the thirteen priests who signed it would maintain their allegiance to the Queen despite her excommunication, but they also reasserted their adherence to the Catholic faith and submission to the Pope in spiritual matters.

Bluet and the three other priests who delivered the Protestation were taken straight to the Clink prison in Southwark (at least one and possibly two signatories of the Protestation would become martyrs). The rest of the secular clergy were given a further forty days' grace before banishment. Watson had refused to sign the Protestation, telling Bancroft he was "much moved with this [the priests'] presumption in taking upon them to prescribe in effect their own conditions" for staying in England.[14] But he took advantage of the forty days' grace to set off for Scotland, looking for assurances of toleration from James and hoping to achieve the breakthrough the other priests had failed to make. He had returned when Elizabeth was dying, claiming that James "was neither heretic, as Persons and other Jesuits had blazed him to be; neither would he afflict [Catholics] as they had been: and therefore [he] wished them by me not to be afraid."[15] Since Catholics remained in prison, as afflicted as they had been when Elizabeth was alive, Watson was now looking very foolish. Fellow Catholics bitterly referred to James as "Watson's King" and he was seething with resentment.

The first person Watson shared his disappointment with was his good friend Sir Griffin Markham, Sir John Harington's Catholic first cousin. Once an excellent soldier, he had served as Essex's Colonel of the Horse in Ireland until a gunshot wound to the arm almost killed him. Sir Griffin had financed Watson's trip to Scotland and Watson had arranged to meet him in Doncaster, where Sir Griffin hoped to be given an audience with James. The Markham family history had been one of total loyalty to Elizabeth: they had remained true to her even in the aftermath of Wyatt's revolt against Mary I. Elizabeth had duly rewarded them with the lease of Beskwood Park, nine square miles in the Forest of Nottingham. These woodland stewardships had become the basis of Sir Griffin's high standing in the county and he was anxious to prove his loyalty to James in the hope of continuing royal favor—not least because the Markhams had urgent need of his help. They had recently found themselves in severe financial difficulty. This had been not through extravagance but the consequence of misplaced family loyalty. Sir Griffin's brother-in-law, John Skinner, the Deputy Governor of Berwick, had persuaded Sir Griffin's father to guarantee his debts. He had then defaulted, leaving the Markhams facing ruin. Sir Griffin had written to Cecil in December asking for his help in resolving the crisis. They were kinsmen and he hoped Cecil would pressure Skinner into selling his house in Berwick to pay his debts. Cecil was no friend of Skinner, but he did nothing to help the Markhams. Only the King could now save the family from disaster. Sir Griffin hoped that Watson would express his family's loyalty to James and he intended to match those words with deeds. While the priest had traveled through the north in March, "longing much to drive all doubtful conceits and dangerous attempts, tending to disloyalty, out of all English but especially all Catholic hearts," Sir Griffin kept his ear to the ground for Jesuit plots.[16]

Sir Griffin was friendly with a priest called William Clark, who had just published an answer to Persons's tract on the secular priests.[17] Clark wrote to Sir Griffin early in April warning that the Jesuit John Gerard was seeking the means to depose James. Watson later elaborated on this, claiming that Gerard had been telling Catholics that they would be excommunicated if they did not resist the crowning of a heretic.[18] Sir Griffin hoped his information would please James, and as Cecil was still traveling with the King, he was in a position to create an occasion on which Sir Griffin could present his suit.

On 19 April James stayed at the Sun and Bear Inn at Doncaster.* The Council had originally intended that James spend the night at the eight-towered Pontefract Castle, but it had proved to be in too poor a condition to accommodate the royal party. Such decay was a direct result of a deliberate policy of Tudor neglect, an attempt to prevent such castles from being used as strongholds by rebellious sub-

---

*The town was then famous for its manufacture of stockings—a commodity of which James VI had once been so short that he had to borrow a pair from a courtier so as not to look too shabby in front of a visiting ambassador.

jects. Only those in the north and west, which were needed as bulwarks against the Scots and the Spanish, were still maintained. England's inns, by contrast, were famously comfortable. Fynes Moryson boasted, "There is no place in the world where passengers may so freely command as in the English Inns; they are attended for themselves and their horses as well as if they were at home, and perhaps better, each servant being ready to call, in hope of a small reward in the morning."[19] James's bedchamber and dining place at Doncaster had been dressed especially for his stay, but even an ordinary traveler could expect rooms to be well furnished and to be offered a wide selection of fresh meat and fish.

Sir Griffin must have cut a distinctive figure among the press of people around the inn, with his dark complexion, broad face and badly disfigured hand. We do not know whether he saw Cecil, but he was refused an audience with James. Watson wasted no time in expressing his own sense of betrayal to the former soldier, as Cecil must surely have guessed he would. He also knew that if Watson was caught and condemned for involvement in any future plot his fellow secular priests would be damaged by association. Sir Griffin, who was well connected at court and a neighbor of Arbella Stuart, might in turn involve other malcontents. He was friendly with both Grey of Wilton, who had demanded James be invited to accept the crown with conditions, and Cobham's brother, George Brooke. Once compromised, he would either hang with the rest or act as a spy—but Sir Griffin's hopes in James were not yet entirely spent.

❖   ❖   ❖

From Doncaster James traveled to Worksop Manor in Nottinghamshire, the first of the great Elizabethan palaces the King was to see. Worksop was one of nine houses the Earl of Shrewsbury owned in the area and the nobleman was grateful the King had chosen to visit it. The actions of Arbella Stuart at Christmas had made her more of a liability than an asset to the family and Shrewsbury knew he would have to work hard to charm the King.

The builder of Worksop, Robert Smythson, had honed his trade as a mason on Longleat and he knew how to impress. The façade was

180 feet long, reaching six stories at its wings, with lantern turrets above. For much of this length it was only one room wide, which must have made it a cold house, but it was light and Cecil judged the gallery to be "the fairest in England."[20] James was greeted in Worksop Park by a band of huntsmen dressed in green, the chief of whom delivered a speech of welcome and asked if he would like to see some game—an offer, of course, James accepted.[21] After his kill James retired to the house. Shrewsbury had invited all his local friends to meet the King, adding by way of postscript to his letters: "I will not refuse any fat capons and hens, partridges and the like." His neighbors had responded generously and there was a feast for rich and poor. The Shrewsburys had also added a special touch, the "most excellent soul-ravishing music, wherewith his Highness was not a little delighted."[22] James had been an enthusiastic patron of music in Scotland and it is likely the musicians included Thomas Greaves, a lutanist to the Countess of Shrewsbury's brother-in-law at nearby Holme Pierrepont.*

When James was suitably relaxed the Shrewsburys seized the opportunity to assure him that Arbella's attempts to escape Hardwick and marry Edward Seymour had sprung entirely from unhappiness at the severity of her grandmother. James asked with whom she would be happier. Shrewsbury suggested the Earl of Kent, whose nephew had recently married his daughter. James immediately drafted Kent a letter ordering him to take his cousin in.

> *Forasmuch as we are desirous to free our cousin the Lady Arbella Stuart from that unpleasant life which she hath led in the house of her grandmother with whose severity and age she, being a young lady, could hardly agree, we have thought fit for the present to require you, as a nobleman of whose wisdom and fidelity we have heard so good report, to be contented for some short space to receive her into your house, and there to use her in that manner which is fit for her calling.*

*The Pierreponts were parents to Mary Stapleton, whose recusant husband, Richard, had tried to help Arbella escape from Hardwick in March. Mary Stapleton was also goddaughter to Mary, Queen of Scots, and was raised in her retinue from the age of four, often sharing the Queen's bed. Greaves's *Songs of Sundry Kinds* was published in 1604: my thanks to Robin Brackenbury for this information.

A copy was sent to the Dowager Countess of Shrewsbury at Hardwick. Arbella must have been delighted at her grandmother's discomfiture, but when James asked her to act as chief mourner at Elizabeth's funeral she refused with ill grace, saying that since she had been denied access to the Queen during her lifetime she would not be brought onto the stage for a public spectacle after her death. It was poor repayment for the effort James had made on her behalf and a source of further embarrassment for the Shrewsburys, though before James left he knighted the Shrewsburys' son-in-law, Henry Grey.

The events of that day cast a long shadow over James's future reputation. He stopped at the Nottinghamshire town of Newark, which according to one visitor boasted a "fair church . . . richly adorned with monuments," a "neat market place . . . in a manner four-square," and streets full of "handsome creatures, well furnished."[23] It was, however, to be the scene of an ugly incident.

A young cutpurse who had followed the royal train disguised as a gentleman had been caught with a large amount of coin on him. The sentence for any thief caught and convicted of stealing more than 12 pence was death.* The end for this cutpurse was thus never in doubt and by tradition the house at number 63 London Road, Newark, bearing the name "Gallows Field," was the place where the execution took place. What was unusual—and disturbing—was that James simply directed a warrant to the Recorder of Newark to have the young man executed.[24] "I hear our new King has hanged a man before he was tried," Sir John Harington wrote soon afterward; " 'tis strangely done: now if the wind blows thus, why may not a man be tried before he has

---

*Cutpurses and pickpockets were very common in England and it was usual for them to dress as gentlemen—according to a disgusted Fynes Moryson, even actors did so. A report written by Fleetwood, the Recorder of London, in 1585 described how these cutpurses and pickpockets operated. A school for such scoundrels had been founded at an alehouse near Billingsgate. Young thieves were shown "two devices, the one was a pocket, the other was a purse. The pocket had in it certain counters, and was hung about with hawks bells." The purse was similarly dressed with bells hanging over the top. Those who could take the counters out of the pocket without ringing the bells graduated as pickpockets and those who could do so from the purse as cutpurses. When they graduated they worked in pairs. But the teammate of the Newark cutpurse escaped and was never tried (Rye, *England as Seen by Foreigners,* p. 268n; Ashton, *James I,* p. 65).

offended?"[25] Harington's comments would be quoted down the centuries, with James's action described as the first example of Stuart despotism in England. It was not, however, quite as shocking as writers would later make out.

Scottish law did not require cutpurses to be tried before execution. The same applied to some areas of England—Fynes Moryson records, for instance, that the town of Halifax still had the privilege to behead "anyone found in open theft... without delay."[26] James never repeated his offense, presumably having had the English legal norms explained to him, but it is significant that Harington, hitherto such an advocate of James's cause, was so quick to pass judgment. Harington was clearly disappointed that James was not going to offer toleration of religion, as he had hoped, but he was also close to Sir Griffin Markham, under whom he had served in Ireland—so close, in fact, that he had secured his debts. If Sir Griffin defaulted on his creditors, they would pursue Harington. It seems possible that Sir Griffin had been in contact with Harington, expressing his irritation that he was unable to get an audience with James at Doncaster as well as describing the death of the cutpurse in Newark.*

James stayed at Newark Castle that night, one of two key fortresses guarding the crossings of the Trent and so in a reasonable state of repair. The second, at Nottingham, was well known to Harington. It was famous for having held David II of Scotland a prisoner between 1346 and 1357. Tourists were often shown the cell where "the said king with his own hands (without any instrument than the nails of his fingers) did engrave and claw out the form of our Saviour's life, death and passion."[27] The scratches could still be seen on the walls and Harington had shrewdly had one of these scenes copied onto the lantern he had sent James as a New Year's gift. The king had sent Harington his thanks for the gift shortly before he left Scotland, but the words of the good thief crucified alongside Christ inscribed on it—"Lord remember me when you come into your kingdom"—would soon have a

---

*Another possible source is Lord Hunsdon, who greeted James in Newark with the Band of Gentlemen Pensioners. Having lost his post as Chamberlain, he had reason to spread malicious stories about James, as did his servants.

desperate ring. Harington was already beginning to understand what he had lost in his royal godmother and as he considered what he had learned of the new king he moaned to his friends: "I have lost the best and fairest love that ever shepherd knew, even my gracious Queen."[28]

James hunted all the way from Newark to Belvoir—another fortress that, like Pontefract, Newark and Nottingham, would be pulled down after the Civil War when they had shown how dangerous a weapon of war they could still be. This was the seat of the Earl of Rutland, with whom Sir Griffin Markham had been having frequent rows over his attempts to acquire the Beskwood stewardships in perpetuity. Rutland considered the lieutenancy of the forest to be the hereditary property of the Manners family. Sir Griffin knew Rutland was a bad enemy to make at this juncture. The Earl had been a leading supporter of the Essex revolt and had only been released from the Tower in February—he was thus one of James's "martyrs." At Belvoir Rutland offered James lavish entertainments including a mock battle—which appeared to frighten the King—and an exhibition of Ben Jonson's masque *The Metamorphosis of Gypsies,* which proved more to his liking. James, in turn, realized Sir Griffin Markham's worst fears by rewarding Rutland with a gift of the parks on which Sir Griffin's honor and wealth rested.[29]

Harington, meanwhile, had arranged for one of his friends to greet the King at Burghley House, Lincolnshire, on 23 April, with an elegy celebrating his peaceful entry into England:

> *Here James the sixth, now James the first proclaimed.*
> *See how all hearts are healed that erst were maimed:*
> *The peer is pleased, the knight, the clerk, the clown;*
> *The mark at which the malcontent has aimed*
> *Is missed; succession 'stablished in the crown.*[30]

Succession was not "'stablished in the crown" until the coronation, as Harington well knew, but James was getting an ever greater sense of just how rich this new kingdom was.

Burghley, one of the grandest and largest palaces to have been built during Elizabeth's reign, was a statement of power and wealth. Its exterior presents an exuberant display of fantastic Gothic architecture, with obelisks, Ionic columns and arches sprouting across its roofline, while the interior, now lost, seemed "so rich, as it had been furnished at the charges of an Emperor." Lord Burghley had complained bitterly to his brother Cecil that he would pay dearly for his office by the time he had finished entertaining the King, but the rewards of royal favor were there for all to see.

As the Scots gawped a number of leading courtiers arrived to celebrate Easter with the King the following day. Essex's friend, the Earl of Southampton, was said to be "well used," that is, treated with honor, and when Henry Howard presented his nephews, Lords Thomas and William Howard, James declared that he loved the whole family.[31]

But on Monday, when the feasting was over, Sir Walter Ralegh appeared. After he had been prevented from leading a party of suitors to Berwick he had been sent personal orders from James that he was to remain with Elizabeth's body until the funeral. According to the French ambassador, the Comte de Beaumont, Ralegh was nevertheless determined to protest to James about the disinformation Cecil and Howard had been feeding him.[32] His pretext for gaining an audience was the need for letters "for continuance of process and the course of justice in the Duchy of Cornwall." This was, however, just a formality, and James snorted to Sir Thomas Lake "that this was all that he had to allege for excuse of his coming and . . . promised to write those letters, and willed . . . they might be speedily delivered that he were gone again."[33]

That afternoon, as an angry Ralegh returned to London, James went hunting on the estate of Sir John Harington's elderly cousin, Sir John Harington of Exton. In the course of the chase he fell heavily from his horse. With "his blood yet hot" he made light of his injuries, but the next day he was unable to ride and had to travel by coach. He had broken his collarbone. It could very easily have been his neck and his heir was still only a child. The accident was a timely reminder of just how fragile the political situation was and it was a subdued train that arrived at Apethorpe, the Northamptonshire seat of Sir Anthony Mildmay, the following day.

Sir Anthony's father had been a judge at the trial of Mary, Queen of Scots, but no mention was made of the events at nearby Fotheringay: James was uninterested in pursuing vendettas on his mother's account, as his stay was doubtless intended to demonstrate.* Mildmay's wife, Grace, had personally prepared some of the food for the day's feast. The appearance of food was considered at least as important as the taste in England and enormous *pièces montées* in pastry, jelly or sugar were very fashionable. Ben Jonson described the work of a typical "master cook" of the period:

> He paints, he carves, he builds,
> He fortifies,
> Makes citadels of curious fowl and fish.
> Some he dry-ditches, some motes round with broths,
> Mounts marrow-bones, cuts fifty
> Angled custards,
> Rears bulwark pies; and for his outer works,
> He raiseth ramparts of immortal crust.

At Apethorpe "everything that was most delicious for taste, proved more delicate, by the art that made it seem beauteous to the eye; the Lady of the House being one of the most excellent confectioners in England."[†] But the feast was soon interrupted by the delivery of a supplication from the poor of the royal parks of Brigstock, which Cecil had acquired from the dying Queen in January. Cecil had wasted no

---

*Sir Anthony's father had at least had the foresight to refuse to house Mary's executioners. James would return several times to Apethorpe and it is here that he is believed to have met his greatest favorite, George Villiers, the future Duke of Buckingham. Apethorpe is now in poor condition, but it still retains its magnificent plaster ceilings bearing James's arms and houses a statue of the King. Its then owner, Sir Anthony Mildmay, was a diplomat, although not always a very diplomatic one: Henri IV of France had taken against Sir Anthony for listening coldly to his praise for Essex and on one occasion in 1597 Henri was so irritated by Mildmay that he actually struck him.

†Nichols, *Progresses, Processions*, p. 97. James had little time for such food, but if Grace Mildmay's confectionery was wasted on the King, her herbal medicines—for everything from headaches to syphilis—would surely have come in useful in easing the pain of James's broken collarbone. (Her cures are still extant.) Grace was a pious Protestant,

time in overthrowing the extensive common rights the inhabitants had enjoyed under Elizabeth's cousin, Lord Hunsdon. The land was now being enclosed rapidly, with heavily defended sheep pastures being erected and trees chopped down and sold—depriving the poor of fuel as well as food. Such behavior was not unusual. The rise in population during the sixteenth century created valuable grain and meat markets and the more successful farmers had bought or leased land near their own, but as the population continued to grow and the numbers of farms had shrunk land hunger set in. Large numbers of landless peasants were now entirely dependent on wages, and if the new, bigger farms converted to pasture, their only protection against starvation became the animals they grazed on common land. In areas where there was most pressure on the land, however, the big farmers were grazing this common more intensely and enclosing ever larger parts of it.

Northamptonshire was the worst affected area in England. Between 1578 and 1607, at least 27,335 acres were enclosed and 1,444 people displaced.[34] Aggrieved peasants in the country had already accosted James when he was hunting through common land near Stamford. It had begun with the extraordinary spectacle of what seemed like a hundred men, at least fourteen feet high, striding toward the hunting party. At first James had wondered what they were but as they came closer a witness observed that "they proved a company of poor honest suitors, all going upon high stilts, preferring a petition against the Lady Hatton."[35] James assured them he would consider their petition when he reached London. The supplication delivered at

but her sister Olive was not. She fell in love with Shrewsbury's brother John Talbot, to the disapproval of her father. Undaunted, she pursued the relationship. John Aubrey describes what happened: "Discoursing with him one night from the battlements of the Abbey Church, said she, 'I will leap down to you.' Her sweetheart replied he would catch her then; but he did not believe she would have done it. She leap't down, and the wind, which was then high, came under her coats and did something to break her fall. Mr Talbot caught her in his arms, but she struck him dead: she cried out for help, and he was with great difficulty brought to life again. Her father told her that since she had made such a leap she should e'er marry him." Cited by Linda Pollock, *With Faith and Physic: The Life of a Tudor Gentlewoman, Lady Grace Mildmay 1552–1620*, p. 70, and John Britton (ed.), *Aubrey's Natural History of Wiltshire*, 1969.

Apethorpe was more problematic, since it concerned Cecil's property. James refused to reply to it and as he left Apethorpe he found himself confronted by large crowds, shouting their complaints.[36] He ignored them and almost as soon as he had passed, riots broke out, with people "resisting them that offered to carry the wood already felled, and not suffering the deer to be driven out of the park into the forest."[37]

A little further down the road James passed through another common that had suffered from enclosures. This time it was at the hands of Sir John Spencer, who, like Cecil, had a reputation as one of the most ruthless commercial farmers of the day.* Again James was met by protestors begging him to open the common, "for the comfort of the poor inhabitants about," and, as at Stamford, James promised them "their hearts desire."

In the future James would be inclined to favor the side of the peasantry in such disputes, but Cecil knew how to get his own way. When James reached London Cecil convinced him that the disturbances in his parks had to be suppressed so that he could improve the area to allow James to hunt there. James promptly ordered local justices of the peace "to prevent injuries to the game in Brigstock park," and Cecil continued enclosing land until 1607, when a peasant rebellion swept Northamptonshire.[38] It was far more serious than anything seen in the 1590s, but it was a struggle the peasants were bound to lose. By the time Cecil died in 1612 he had a very profitable property at Brigstock, which he leased to a large-scale grazier at a rent of over £1,200 a year.[39]

❈   ❈   ❈

On Thursday 28 April Elizabeth's funeral took place in London. The court official, John Clapham, found Westminster packed "with multitudes of all sorts of people in their streets, houses, windows, leads, and gutters," straining to watch the spectacle. The mourners processed from Whitehall Palace to Westminster Abbey, in a river of black. Twelve thousand yards of dark cloth had been ordered for the occasion:

---

*Spencer had been Mayor of London during the riots of 1595, when a scaffold had been built in front of his house.

First went two hundred and sixty poor women, four in a rank, apparelled in black, with linen kerchiefs over their heads; the inferior officers of the Household and gentlemen of meaner quality following after them. The standards of the Dragon, of the Greyhound, and the Lion, the supporters of the arms of England . . . intermingled with the train; among which also there were led . . . two great horses, the one covered with black cloth, the other with velvet; whereto the escutcheons of the Arms of England and France were fastened. Then came the gentlemen and children of the Chapel in copes and surplices, singing in a mournful tune. The ensigns of the earldom of Chester, of the Duchy of Cornwall, of the Principality of Wales, and of the Kingdom of Ireland were severally borne by some of the nobility . . . Between them were placed the Aldermen of the City of London, the Justices of the Benches, and the Gentlemen Pensioners, whose pole axes were covered in black and the heads of them carried downwards. Then followed the Mayor of the City, the Privy Councillors, the Lords Spiritual and Temporal, and the chief officers of the Kingdom.[40]

The Venetian ambassador Giovanni Scaramelli had refused to attend the funeral of a heretic, but the French ambassador, de Beaumont, walked behind the chief officers dressed in a long black cloak. The heralds carrying banners bearing the royal arms followed him and then came Elizabeth's hearse, draped in black velvet and pulled by four horses. On top of Elizabeth's coffin was a full-size effigy of the Queen carved in wood, the face and hands painted to appear lifelike, with a crown upon its head, a ball and scepter in either hand, the body dressed in her parliamentary robes of red velvet and ermine.[41] As it passed there was "such a general sighing, groaning and weeping, as the like hath not been seen or known in the memory of man," and the playwright Thomas Dekker declared: "Her hearse (as it was borne) seemed to be an island swimming in water."[42]

In the absence of Arbella, the role of chief mourner had fallen to the Marchioness of Northampton, who walked behind Elizabeth's hearse, her black train carried by the Vice Chamberlain, John Stanhope, and three countesses. Admiral Nottingham and Lord Buckhurst assisted her, and Elizabeth's Ladies and Maids of Honor followed. Sir Walter Ralegh and the Guard, walking five abreast, brought up the rear, their halberds held downward. The train disappeared inside the Abbey and as Elizabeth was interred her chief officers had their white staffs of office taken and "broken upon their heads."[43] Outside, meanwhile, Clapham listened as "the people then began to talk diversely." His memoirs recall that many simpler people remained fixated on any strange coincidence thrown up by the Queen's death. The latest story was that an old lion bearing Elizabeth's name had died in the Tower after pining away during her illness. The more educated, however, discussed her life and the manner of her government.

The pessimists noted "the long and peaceable time of [Elizabeth's] reign, her clemency and other virtues; wishing that things might continue in no worse state than they had done." They quoted the old proverb that "seldom cometh the better" and, indeed, questions were already being asked about some of James's decisions. The numbers of knights James had created was causing consternation at court: there had been eighteen at Worksop and forty-nine at Belvoir alone. Most were respectable men such as the Earl of Rutland's brothers, George and Oliver Manners—the kind of men Elizabeth should have dubbed years before (although Oliver was one of John Gerard's converts)—but some of those newly honored were considered to be of "mean quality."[44] The courtier Philip Gawdy was certain that James regretted making so many knights "and is very angry with some Scots, for he has heard they took money for making of them."[45] But there were other concerns.

At York James had created two Scots Gentlemen Ushers and it was reported that at Burghley he had gone on to bestow the deaneries of Lichfield and Norwich "upon Mr Peter Young his schoolmaster, the other upon one Montgomery at the suit of the Earl of Mar."[46] The Jesuits and the Archpriest Blackwell had picked up on fears at court that other offices might also go to the Scots, and a Catholic gentleman called Anthony Dutton was on his way to Valladolid carrying descriptions of English contempt for James and his entourage. They hoped to persuade the Spanish that there would be widespread support for an invasion and Dutton's message insisted that "Walter Ralegh . . . and many others of repute, though they are Protestants, or without concern for religion, have so much declared themselves against the Scot that they will come over to us without fail."[47] Some radical Catholics appear to have been considering other drastic courses. A priest called Tillerton had informed the authorities that a few of his fellow Jesuits planned to murder James and his children. Coincidentally a suitable method of achieving mass murder had suggested itself only the previous day. A gunpowder mill had exploded at Redriffe on the Thames. It killed thirteen people instantly and injured many others. The accident was noted by the charismatic future gunpowder plotter Robert Catesby, but James was doing his best to ensure that such extremist elements would find no support in Spain or Rome.

James had already intimated, while still in Scotland, that he would be willing to negotiate peace with Spain and that he wanted to remain on good terms with the Pope—hence the messages sent by Anna. Scaramelli's absence from Elizabeth's funeral had not gone unnoticed and that afternoon a Scot, Edward Bruce of Kinloss, paid the Venetian a visit. Kinloss expressed James's gratitude to the Pope for not having excommunicated him and assured Scaramelli that as long as Catholics remained quiet and hidden they would neither be hunted nor persecuted. Scaramelli retorted that this hardly fulfilled the Pope's expectations that James would grant religious toleration or even convert. Kinloss admitted that on this front everything that Anna had suggested was wrong, and "beyond a doubt this will never happen," but he explained that James believed there was another way forward: James's dream of a Council that would work out the ground for the reunification of the Protestant and Catholic Churches:

> If the Pope wished to summon a General Council, which, according to ancient usage, should be superior to all Churches, all doctrine, all Princes, secular and ecclesiastic, none excepted, my master would be extremely willing to take the lead and to prove himself the warm supporter of so great a benefit to Christendom . . . abuses would be removed on all hands, and a sound decision would put an end, perhaps for ever, to the discords in the Christian faith, nor would his Majesty think he could act more nobly than to be the first to offer complete obedience to the Council's decrees.[48]

Scaramelli was unimpressed. James's plans struck him as nothing more than vanity. But being a diplomat, he bit his tongue.

❀   ❀   ❀

While the pessimists in the crowds outside the Abbey had claimed that "seldom cometh better," others had retorted that "they could not lightly be in worse state than they were." There was still a great deal of hope and belief in James. Many in the funeral crowd recalled Elizabeth's "continual subsidies and taxes, besides other exactions of contributions extorted by corrupt officers," with "the meaner sort commonly sustaining the greater burden"; how wrongs were winked at "for private respects"; and how the few had gained trading and other privileges at the expense of the many.[49] Plenty of people, particularly among the Puritans, still believed that James was to be the instrument of much-needed change, whatever the Jesuits were telling the Spanish.

James's host on the day of the funeral was one such Puritan. Oliver Cromwell, uncle of the future Lord Protector, had first met James in 1594 when he arrived in Scotland as part of the English delegation sent for the christening of Prince Henry. His brother-in-law, Henry Bromley, had traveled with him. Bromley had been recently released from jail, having been imprisoned for being a co-signatory to Peter Wentworth's petition that Elizabeth name an heir. He was sent back to jail in 1601 for his part in the Essex revolt and, freshly released in May, he had again traveled with Cromwell to see James, this time in Berwick. Bromley's spells in prison had proven his loyalty to James's cause and the King was happy to listen to the views of Bromley and his brother-in-law. The nature of the reforms they sought was outlined in an anonymous "Memorial," addressed to James, which had probably been handed to him in Northumberland.

The first section of the "Memorial" attacked the Cecilian administration for its corruption. Cecil himself was singled out for abusing his position as Master of the Wards, selling wardships "at the second hand, as men do horses and other cattle."[50] The second section addressed the desire for the continuation and restoration of the radical reforms in the Church made during the reign of Edward VI: the introduction of more preaching ministers, an end to profanation of the Sabbath, the ring in marriage and other relics of popery. They also advocated harsher penalties for fornication and adultery and attacked members of the nobility for living with women other than their wives. The "Memorial" alluded to a similar petition yet to be delivered, now thought to have been the Millenary Petition—so called because of the thousand signatures it claimed to bear—which it is believed was delivered at Cromwell's family seat, Hinchingbrooke, near Huntingdon.

Hinchingbrooke stood as a virtual monument to the Reformation. It had once been a small Benedictine nunnery called the Priory of St. James but Henry VIII's chief minister, Thomas Cromwell, threw out the nuns during the dissolution of the monasteries and gave the priory to his nephew, Richard Williams, the son of a Welsh brewer who had settled in Putney. Williams adopted his mother's name of Cromwell in gratitude for Thomas's generosity. Oliver Cromwell, who was Richard's grandson, had further improved the family fortunes with his recent marriage to the widow of the financier Sir Horatio Palavicino. A good part of this new wealth had now been used to prepare what was said to be the greatest feast ever provided by a subject for a king. James's train was offered vast quantities of food, beer and wines "and those not riff raff but ever the best kind." There were also "many open beer houses erected where there was no want of beef and bread for the comfort of the poorest creatures," and these stayed open for a fortnight after James left.[51]

Cromwell's personal gifts for the King were almost as generous: there was a gold cup, several good horses, "fleet and deep mouthed hounds, divers hawks of excellent wing" and £50 to be distributed among James's Scottish officers. Other gifts were presented by guests waiting to greet James, among them the heads of the University of Cambridge, clad in their scarlet gowns and corner caps. One gave an oration in Latin and another offered the King several books "published in commendation of our late gracious Queen."[52] But these gifts were politically loaded, for in praising aspects of Elizabeth's reign they suggested what was and what was not expected of the new monarch. There was approval for the persecution of Catholics, but also condemnation of any proposed union of England and Scotland. The

"Memorial" was more supportive on this point—and James assured Cromwell as he left after breakfast on 29 April: "Marry, man, thou hast treated me better than any man since I left Edinburgh."[53] Cromwell would be well rewarded for his tact as well as his generosity in the weeks ahead.

❀   ❀   ❀

With Elizabeth's funeral over, the nobility and Privy Councilors were gathering to greet James at Broxborne, the Hertfordshire seat of the Cofferer, Sir Henry Cock. It was a frantic few days as he tried to gather the supplies fit to feed a king and countless hungry peasants, but as Sir Henry observed to Cecil, "better to lack good meat than good company." James eventually arrived on Monday 2 May, escorted by Sir Edward Denny, the Sheriff of Hertfordshire, and a mounted escort of 150 of the most handsome men in the county. Each was dressed in the Denny colors, with white doublets, blue coats with split sleeves and feathered hats tied with red and yellow bands. Even the horses had new red saddles. But it was James that people wished to see and the crowds had grown immense with "nobility, gentry, citizens, country people, and all," pressing together and kicking up clouds of dust in an effort to see him.[54]

The Lord Keeper Egerton, Lord Admiral Nottingham and the Treasurer, Lord Buckhurst, were among those waiting at Broxborne, but Cecil had gone to his own house, Theobalds, to prepare for the King's much anticipated stay there. It proved to be a wise decision. James complained angrily to Cock about the dust thrown up by the crowds and Sir Henry was obliged to send Cecil a message warning that the King "is desirous to have some private way made for him." The next day, as James left for Cecil's great palace, thousands streamed out of London to witness the greatest spectacle of the King's progress thus far, among them the writer John Savile and two friends. They stopped for a while to sit by an upstairs window at the Bell Inn at Edmonton and counted the numbers who passed by. Within half an hour they saw 309 on horse and 137 on foot, and the landlord assured them that the traffic had been as heavy since four that morning.

James arrived at Theobalds at half past one that afternoon and, "as his Highness was espied," Savile tells us, "for very joy many ran from their carts, leaving their team of horses to their own unreasonable directions." Savile and his friends decided to split up and each watch the spectacle from a different spot and then compare notes later. Savile was by the gates, watching as James rode down a long drive lined with ash and elm surrounded by nobles and gentlemen, "observing no place of superiority, all bare headed." As James approached he saw a palace of red brick and white stone covering over a quarter of a mile rising before him. Innumerable turrets surmounted by golden lions holding golden vanes flashed in the sun; fountains set in huge formal gardens sprayed up almost as high as the roofline. Sir John Harington had called it the "paradise of Theobalds" and so it must have seemed to James, who would one day make Theobalds his own.

As James reached the end of the avenue, he was greeted by a fanfare of trumpets. The courtiers around him dismounted and four noblemen stepped forward and walked on either side of James's horse with their hands touching its flanks as he rode to the entrance of the forecourt. There a young gentleman stepped forward and handed James yet another petition. It is believed that this was the Poor Man's Petition, another call for assurance of uniformity in religion and for reform in public life. "A pox take the proud covetous Attorney and merciless lawyer!" its authors cried; "fye upon all close biting knaverie!"[55] Sir Walter Ralegh was picked out by name as it condemned the abuse of monopolies. James assured the young man that his petition would be heard and he would receive justice. Cecil then escorted the King through the doorway and the vast crowd cheered and threw their hats in the air.

"We were first led into a beautiful room panelled with chestnut wood, and in many places richly gilt. In the windows were placed the coats of arms of the principal potentates of the world," the Duke of Stettin's secretary recorded.

> *All the other rooms were most magnificently decorated with splendid hangings, and velvet beds and chairs. Especially noteworthy were the three galleries. In the first were representations of the principal emperors and knights of the Golden Fleece, with the most splendid cities in the world and their garments and fashions. In the next, the coats of arms of all the noble families of*

England . . . the labours of Hercules and the game called billiards on a long
cloth covered table. In the third, all England, represented by fifty two trees,
each tree representing one province. On the branches and leaves the coats of
arms of all the . . . noblemen residing in the county; and between the trees, the
towns and boroughs, together with the principal mountains and rivers.[56]

James rested in his bedchamber for an hour before he was persuaded to show himself to the crowds. He stood by the window for
half an hour without speaking and then went for a walk in the gardens, wandering in the cool with "bays, rosemary, and the like over-
shadowing his walk, to defend him from the heat of the sun, till
supper time."[57] The King stayed at Theobalds for four days and we are
told that "to speak of Lord Robert's cost to entertain him, were but to
imitate geographers, that set a little round O for a mighty province;
words being unable to express what was done there indeed." James
was introduced to Elizabeth's servants and officers of the Household
as well as her Guard. "It was a most stately sight, the glory of that
reception, where the nobility and gentry were in exceeding rich
equipage," John Aubrey tells us, but adds that James, far from being
pleased, regarded the bejeweled and armed courtiers with a "secret
dread . . . and an inward envy." Sir Walter Ralegh particularly attracted the King's distrust. Although his long, wavy hair had grown
gray and he walked with a limp from a gunshot wound received fighting the Spanish years before, he remained perhaps the most striking
figure from Elizabeth's court. "He had that awfulness and ascendancy
in his aspect over other mortals," Aubrey recalled. His dress was also
notoriously extravagant even by the standards of Elizabeth's court.
Ralegh particularly liked pearls and wore them head to toe—from
pearl hat bands to large drop earrings, pearl-embroidered suits and
even shoes; he once owned a pair worth £6,000.

According to Aubrey, writing decades later, James quipped testily
to Ralegh as his name was announced, "O my soul mon, I have heard
rawly of thee." The pun on Ralegh's name had been used for years, but
James had indeed heard badly of him from Howard and Cecil and, as
Ralegh had already shown in his misjudged visit to Burghley, he was

determined to counter their slanders. Unfortunately, if Aubrey is to be believed, he made another hash of it. At one point James, provoked by the displays of wealth and power around him, boasted anxiously that he could have taken the crown by force of arms if it had proved necessary. Ralegh quickly responded that he wished that James had been forced to fight for his crown, because then he would have seen who his real friends were. The impression on James was exactly the opposite of what Ralegh had intended and Aubrey tells us "that reason of Sir Walter was never forgotten nor forgiven."[58] But is this story true? Captain Millington's account, written contemporaneously, contradicts Aubrey's later piece and claims that all the Guard were "courteously received [by James] to their own content."[59] Millington, however, was writing to please the new King and would be rewarded for doing so with Felley Priory in Nottinghamshire. Aubrey, although writing later, was writing more freely. His tales—passed down from people who were either there or knew people who were there—also have a ring of truth: hadn't Harington told James he would have been able to invade England successfully?

James was certainly aware of the stark contrast between the great finery of Elizabeth's court and begrimed appearance of his own favorites, which was already attracting a great deal of unfavorable comment. There was a comic story doing the rounds at Theobalds that a religious fanatic dressed like a serving man had managed to sneak into the palace. When the guards caught up with him and asked whom he served he had responded, "The Lord Jehovah," to which a weary constable replied, "Well let him pass; I believe it is some Scottish Lord or other."[60] Similarly, the Countess of Cumberland and her daughter, the thirteen-year-old Lady Anne Clifford, were horrified to discover that they had caught lice after sitting in Sir Thomas Erskine's chamber.

James hoped money would solve such problems. He had already started enriching his countrymen by allowing them to sell knighthoods: a further twenty-eight were dubbed at Theobalds, bringing the numbers made on James's progress thus far to 237, not far short of the number Elizabeth had made in her entire reign—but this was only tinkering. A much deeper and wider distribution of wealth could only be achieved with a Union of the kingdoms and James was anxious to make progress on it.

The Privy Council was now expanded to include Lords Henry and Thomas Howard, Lord Mountjoy, and five Scots, including the Earl of Mar, Duke of Lennox, James Elphinstone, Lord Kinloss and Sir George Home. Plans were laid for Home to replace Sir John Fortescue as Chancellor of the Exchequer and for Kinloss to be made Master of the Rolls in Chancery. The top financial and legal jobs in England were thus to have Scottish seconds in command—and Cecil only narrowly averted having a Scottish partner in the Secretaryship. For the time being James retained his Scottish Bedchamber with its English addition, Sir Robert Carey, but the titles were anglicized. The "Chalmer" became the Bedchamber and the "Varlets" Grooms. A Privy Council committee dominated by Home and Cecil was set up to shape the final settlement, to be announced from the Tower a week later.[61] The issue of the reform of corruption was addressed in a royal proclamation. It announced the recall of all monopolies and licenses for consideration, including Ralegh's monopoly on tin. Lawyers were ordered to desist from charging excessive fees, household officials were warned not to abuse their position in acquiring provisions for the court, and there was a Puritan-inspired Sunday ban on bear- or bull-baiting, listening to music, watching plays or indulging in any other "disordered exercises."

Having thus addressed matters of business as well as pleasure, James left Theobalds for London on Saturday 7 May. The Lord Mayor, Robert Lee, waited at Stamford Hill, where the pushing, shoving crowds "covered the beauty of the fields; and so greedy were they to behold the countenance of the King, that with much unruliness they injured and hurt one another, some even hazarded to the danger of death."[62] One man made a small fortune renting out his cart to onlookers. Eight people at a time could stand in it and watch the spectacle in safety for fifteen minutes at a cost of a groat a head. Alongside the Mayor they saw the City aldermen dressed in scarlet gowns, heralds, trumpeters and 500 mounted citizens in velvet coats and chains of gold.

When James arrived he was given the usual oration on behalf of the sheriffs, but this proved to be no bland speech of welcome. The speaker warned against the evils of flattery and demanded that

the people shall sit under his own olive tree, and anoint himself with the fat thereof, his face not grinded with extorted suits, nor his marrow sucked with most odious and unjust monopolies. Unconscionable lawyers and greedy officers shall no longer spin out the poor man's cause in length to his undoing and the delay of justice. No more shall bribes blind the eyes of the wise, nor gold be reputed the common measure of a man's worthiness.

The speech called for an end to the sale of benefices, to the neglect of the nobility and to the promotion of men who "mean to sell the King to his subjects at their own price, and abuse the authority of his Majesty to their private gain and greatness." It claimed hopes had been raised by the recent publication of James's *Basilikon Doron,* "now fresh in every man's hand," and as such, it concluded, James was welcome.[63] A pack of hounds was brought out for James and put in pursuit of a carted deer. James hunted as far as Islington where he was to stay at Lord Thomas Howard's Charterhouse. The children of the nearby Christ's Hospital had lined themselves up in its garden to sing for the King, but the crowd pushed right through them, scattering the children to left and right, as they threw their hats and shouted out in greeting to the King.* James must have been relieved to take refuge inside the Charterhouse. His hostess, the beautiful and rapacious Catherine Howard, was an intimate of Cecil's—some even claimed she was his mistress—and according to the malicious courtier Anthony Weldon she later proved an expert in finding James "choice young men, whom she daily curled and perfumed."[64] His host, Lord Thomas—a friend of Harington's—was fat and genial with a con-

---

*The former French ambassador, de Maisse, recorded that "at London there are infinite houses of charity and hospitals, and almost throughout the whole realm . . . insomuch that one hardly sees a beggar." There were also "several fair colleges where the children are taught at the expense of the Queen and the public," and, he commented, "there is no youth in the world, poor or rich, that has greater chance of learning than in England." De Maisse, *Journal,* pp. 12–13.

science sufficiently flexible to allow him to attend the Protestant divine service on the Sunday despite his Catholic faith. The service proved rather more uncomfortable for James: People hadn't liked all they read in the *Basilikon Doron* and Thomas Blague's sermon suggested disapproval of some of James's theories of absolutism, warning the King that "he that blows his nose too hard wrings out blood."[65]

A number of matters were tidied up at the Charterhouse. Ralegh was brought before the Council to be officially relieved of his post of Captain of the Guard. He was offered £300 compensation and, sensibly, he "most humbly submitted himself." Arbella was sent an invitation to join the court when it reached Greenwich and James created a further 134 knights, the last being dubbed on the morning of 11 May shortly before he took a carriage to Whitehall. From there he took a barge along the river to the Tower. The journey allowed him to avoid the crowds crammed together in the narrow streets—something that was all the more important now that the weather was growing warmer, for besides his fears of a lurking assassin there was a new threat: plague. An epidemic had been spreading across Europe. It had devastated Lisbon in 1599, Spain in 1601 and the Low Countries in 1602. By January 1603 over 200 people were dying every week in Ostend and English ships had returned home carrying infected rats.

The Catholic spy Anthony Rivers had reported plague deaths in the poor areas of Southwark and Stepney in February, but with the drama of Elizabeth's death and James's arrival the rising toll had attracted little comment. Throughout April and May people had poured into London in anticipation of James's arrival. A courtier had sent a letter to Anne Newdigate in Warwickshire promising that "London streets shall be hanged with cloth of gold when the King comes" and warning that they would never have the opportunity to see the like again.[66] Many had responded to such calls, and craftsmen and others hoped to take advantage of the business opportunities offered by the large numbers of gentry and foreign diplomats arriving in the capital. There were smiths, tailors, vintners and tobacconists. It was said that even "trades that lay dead and rotten started out of their trance."[67]

Of the dying and the dead, people reasoned that there was always the odd suspicious death. They dreaded triggering the plague orders under which whole households were shut up, healthy and sick together. But as the sun rose higher in the sky the number of plague victims had also begun to climb. Scaramelli had noted fourteen deaths from plague in London in the week before James arrived at Whitehall; another eleven succumbed in the next three days. The sick began shivering about a week after exposure. Their pulse rates rose and they became lethargic, then violently ill with muscle and backaches, nausea and diarrhea. As the disease progressed they became confused and giddy; bright light became painful and their tongues were coated white. Inflamed lymph nodes, called buboes, filled with pus until the blood vessels broke. They turned black as they dried under the skin, giving the plague its sobriquet of the Black Death. The majority of the victims died within four days.

The Tower cannon fired a noisy salute as James disembarked from his barge accompanied by Lord Thomas Howard and the Earls of Worcester and Nottingham. Most of the Tower's prisoners had been released to celebrate the occasion of his visit, among them the Jesuit William Weston, who had noticed the bells of London falling silent as Elizabeth was dying; like other priests, he was to be sent into exile. Weston had watched frantic efforts being made to get the Tower into good order: leaking roofs were plugged, while the derelict Great Hall had its walls boarded and a temporary roof built of fir poles covered with canvas. Finally, however, the day came when he was to have his freedom. He had spent five years in the Tower and a total of seventeen in prison. "The hour was after dinner," he recalled in his memoirs; "a large company followed me. However I was not yet a free person, for a triple guard was to escort us as far as Calais."[68] No chances were being taken that such an individual should escape.

The Lieutenant of the Tower, Sir John Peyton, escorted James around the sights: the Armory, the Wardrobe, the artillery, and the church. Afterward James walked in the garden and then rested for the night. The Duke of Stettin described the bedchambers as having "many fine bedsteads, gilt all over, used when visitors of high rank arrive; costly cushions of all colours and golden stuff, but especially two bedsteads, one covered with large pearls and granites, the other covered with beaten gold." But he warned that they were "not very soft to lie upon."[69] It was therefore after a possibly uncomfortable night that James faced the business of the day.* Among those prisoners who had remained in the Tower was Valentine Thomas, the Catholic who had claimed that James had ordered him to assassinate the Queen. Elizabeth had stayed his trial in 1598, hoping to save James from embarrassment, but James would now order it to go ahead and within a fortnight, on 4 June, Thomas was hung, drawn and quartered.

There was also bad news from Scotland, where the difficult issue of the Earl of Mar having care of Prince Henry had flared up once more. The nine-year-old prince had been thoroughly confused by the events of April. One day an Englishman had arrived at Stirling Castle carrying a letter from his father telling him of the "great occasion" of his accession to the crown of England. It explained that he was leaving Scotland, but "by God's grace" Henry would follow shortly and live with him in England. The letter concluded:

> Let not this news make you proud or insolent, for a king's son ye were, and no more are you yet . . . Look upon all Englishmen that come to visit you as your loving subjects, not with ceremonious[ness] as towards strangers, but with that heartiness which they at this time deserve . . . Farewell, Your loving father, James R.[70]

Henry had dutifully composed congratulations in Latin (a language with which he struggled) but all he had really understood from his father's letter was that he was going far away. When his surrogate father, the Earl of Mar, left to join James, Henry feared he had been abandoned and he did something he knew he could be punished for. He wrote to his mother, whom he had not seen for five years, pleading that without his father's visits he needed her care,

*James's itinerary for the next day included more sightseeing—"the Ordinance house and after that the Mint houses, and last of all the lions." James had his own lions at Holyrood and thought the lion house in the Tower rather poor. He would order extensive building work on the menagerie over the course of his reign.

which I have the more just cause to crave, that I have wanted it so long, to my
great grief and displeasure; to the end that your Majesty by sight may have, as
I hope, the great matter to love me, and I likewise may be encouraged to go for-
ward in well doing, and to honour your Majesty with all due reverence, as ap-
pertains to me, who is your Majesty's most obedient and truthful son, Henry.[71]

No woman with an ounce of maternal feeling could have ignored such a letter—certainly not Anna, who was keen to avenge herself on Mar. She immediately contacted courtiers she could rely on and on 7 May rode to Stirling with a large group of armed men including the Earl of Glencairne, the Master of Orkney, the Earl of Linlithgow and Lord Elphinstone. When they arrived Lady Mar refused them entry. Only the Queen and her usual officers and attendants were allowed through the gates, but they also were armed and once inside Anna demanded to see her son. Lady Mar refused. Anna threatened to use force and swords were drawn, but the redoubtable Lady Mar quickly produced James's instructions on keeping the prince in their care until he was eighteen. No one dared disobey the royal warrant and Anna's men backed down. Humiliated and grief-stricken, Anna became hysterical, and according to a later report from the Venetian ambassador, she started beating her pregnant belly.* She was carried to a bedchamber and the Countess of Mar immediately wrote to the King to tell him what had happened.

James was concerned for Anna's health—she was now four months pregnant—but he also feared her actions could stir up a hornet's nest. There were many Scots who would have liked to have Prince Henry remain in Scotland and he sent Mar north with instructions to discover who had ridden with his wife. In the meantime James created his first English nobles. They included four barons, three of whom—Sir William Knollys, Sir Robert Sidney and Sir Edward Wotton—had been close to Essex. From the opposite faction, Sir Robert Cecil was made Baron Cecil of Essendon in recognition of his role in James's ac-

---

*Men as well as women in this period were much more open and dramatic in their displays of emotion than we are today. The macho Earl of Essex would throw himself to the ground and beat himself in rage—and expect Queen Elizabeth to be told about it.

cession; Cecil's authority in the Council was reinforced by the addition of his brother Lord Burghley and Lord Zouche, who was a close ally.[72] Cecil had persuaded James not to add more Scots names to the Council, but James's hopes for the Union were reflected in his new Privy Chamber. It was to consist of twenty-four English and twenty-four Scots divided into groups of four, each on duty for three months. Cromwell and Bromley were among those named.

James's Bedchamber was to be entirely Scottish. Its members included Sir John Ramsay, the page who had killed Alexander Ruthven; Lennox's younger brother Esmé Stuart, Lord Aubigny; James's Master Huntsman, Sir Roger Aston; and his Scottish Treasurer, Sir George Home. Robert Carey had lost the post so hard won on the road from Richmond to Edinburgh—and the decision on the Bedchamber was a serious one for the entire English court. The rules of entrée to James's presence remained as they had been under Elizabeth, making the Scots gatekeepers to the King of England. The reaction was predictable, with English courtiers telling the Venetian Scaramelli that the government was

> charged with having sold England to the Scots, for no Englishman, whatever his rank, can enter the Presence Chamber without being summoned, whereas the Scottish Lords have free entrée of the Privy Chamber, and more especially at the toilette; at which time they discuss proposals which, after dinner are submitted to the Council, in so high and mighty a fashion that no one has the courage to oppose them.[73]

Even Cecil, often seen closeted alone with James for hours at a time, would find with time that he could see the King only in formal audiences. The Scots entourage would do extraordinarily well from their exclusive access to the King. Of the twenty-nine individuals who received 75 percent of all crown patronage between 1588 (the year of the Armada) and 1641 (during the reign of Charles I), ten were gentlemen of James's Bedchamber. Of the nine individuals who took 45 percent, six were in his Bedchamber. They made at least £40,000 a year, excluding grants of land and James's periodic payment of their vast debts.[74] The gravy train, set in motion with the sale of knighthoods during the progress south, would now pick up considerable speed, inspiring the following verse, among many similar ones:

Hark! Hark!
The dogs do bark,
The beggars have come to town.

Some in rags,
And some in tags
And some in velvet gowns.

CHAPTER SIX

"THE BEGGARS HAVE COME TO TOWN"

Plague and Plot in London, May–June 1603

The Venetian ambassador had his first audience with James at Greenwich Palace on 18 May. He disembarked from his barge at the great gatehouse where Elizabeth used to watch naval displays on the Thames and military reviews in the park. It was a favorite palace in the summer months and was full of mementoes of Essex. Rooms were hung with Chinese silk tapestries he had given her and even his portrait remained on display.[1] Scaramelli was astonished by the size of the crowds hoping to get just a glimpse of James: "I never saw the like even at Constantinople in time of peace. There were upwards of ten or twelve thousand persons...All the efforts of the guards hardly enabled me to reach the first, let alone the inner chamber."[2]

When Scaramelli reached the Presence Chamber he found it had more than eighty feet of windows and the brilliant light illuminated a bizarre tableau. James stood on a raised platform by his throne. He wore a chain of diamonds around his neck and a huge diamond in his hat, but his suit was a simple one of gray satin worn with a black cloak, lined with scarlet, and his arm was still in a sling from the hunting accident at Exton. Scaramelli felt he "could have been taken for the meanest among the courtiers" if he were not surrounded by his Councilors "and an infinity of other Lords almost in attitude of adoration."[3] Scaramelli was convinced that left to himself James would have continued with "the modest habit of life which he pursued in Scotland where he barely lived like a private gentleman, let alone a sovereign," but Elizabeth's court was determined to retain the Tudor magnificence they were used to. Scaramelli was instructed to greet James with the same deference he would use toward the King of Spain and he was invited to return to the Presence Chamber later in the week to watch James dine in state.

Three days later the Venetian duly returned. His dispatch to the Senate observed that James was used to sitting with his friends, "waited on by rough servants, who did not even remove their hats." Now he sat alone, his food served to him by kneeling noblemen following the strict rituals of the Tudor court. It was, Scaramelli admitted, "a splendid and unwonted sight."[4] But James would not always play the part of Renaissance monarch as well as people would have liked. Too often he proved to be full of coarse bonhomie when dignity was required, and icily arrogant when he was expected to display warmth. The Catholic Sir Griffin Markham, who was at court still angling for an audience, told his friends that James drank in an uncouth manner. His disabilities made it difficult for him to sip and Sir Griffin's comments may have referred to the way wine could pour from the corners of his mouth, but there was also a suggestion that James drank too much.

The court was used to the moderate habits of an old spinster and James came from a heavier-drinking culture. Essex's secretary in Ireland, Fynes Moryson, once claimed he would accept invitations in Scotland only if his hosts promised to protect him from the "large drinking" he feared he would be drawn into.[5] Excessive drinking is also a problem associated with ADHD and James may have inherited a susceptibility to alcohol from his father. Certainly Anna was already very worried about James's drinking and the following year she was predicting that it would eventually either kill him or turn him into an imbecile.[6] There were other examples of self-indulgence, and even worse in the minds of some courtiers was James's coldness toward his ordinary subjects. One wrote to a friend from Greenwich complaining James was rarely in Council since he spent most of his days hunting "in fields and parks"; local people came out to see their new king but were treated so dismissively that they were soon calling for "some more of that generous affability which their good old Queen did afford them."[7]

At best James ignored the knots of people at the roadsides and at worst he insulted them. In one infamous incident that took place later in the summer he responded to a request to acknowledge a small crowd of onlookers by crying out in Scots: "By God's wounds! I will pull down my breeches and they shall also see my arse!"[8] Meanwhile resentment against the Scots was growing. The price being demanded for a knighthood was dropping rapidly as the Scots sold it ever more widely. The courtier Sir Philip Gawdy, who had hoped that the King regretted making so many knights on his progress from Scotland, now wrote to his brother complaining that "all gentlemen of worth make a ridiculous jest of them that bought them so dearly."[9] He was still more dismayed to report that James was placing Scots "in all offices . . . and put out many English, meaning to make us all under the name of ancient Britons."[10]

The King's intentions for the Union had been formally announced by proclamation on 19 May and hardly a day seemed to pass without one of his Scots favorites receiving lands and office. Lord Home was made Governor of Berwick in place of Sir John Carey, who also lost the lease on Ampthill Park to Sir Thomas Erskine. In addition Erskine was made Steward of the Manor of Woking and Keeper of the Park. Sir Robert Carey, having lost his post in the Bedchamber, also lost the wardenry of the Middle Marches and Norham Castle to Lord Home, and Home was granted Carey's estates in North Durham for good measure. Carey was lucky to be offered £6,000 compensation for them. Sir George Home, meanwhile, having been granted Sir John

Fortescue's post at the Treasury, also took his posts as Chancellor of the Duchy of Lancaster and Master of the Great Wardrobe—this last decision smacking of vengeance for Fortescue's earlier refusal to allow Elizabeth's possessions to be transported to Anna in Scotland.[11]

In the years ahead, when Elizabeth's fabulous costumes disappeared, Sir George Home—by then the Earl of Dunbar—would be accused of destroying the nation's heritage for personal gain by "wickedly transporting them into the Low Countries" and selling them "for above one hundred thousand pounds."[12] In fact Anna would cut up many of them as costumes for her masques and give away others. But there remained something totemic about Elizabeth's clothes, and handing them to a Scot was an insult the English never forgave. Dunbar had remained the closest of all James's servants and was hated by the English court in like degree. They described him to a Venetian ambassador in 1607 as a man of "weak character in every respect, ungracious, ungrateful to his friends, incapable of winning friends, lacking in all the qualities that make a man beloved."[13] The strain between the English and the Scots was already such that many violent quarrels had broken out and on 26 May Scaramelli dispatched to the Senate the news that "the ill will between English and Scots goes on rising rapidly. It serves nothing that the King declares his resolve to extinguish both names, and that both people shall pass under the common name of Britons and be governed by one and the same law." In one incident a Scot killed Northumberland's page with a dagger; in another a Scot struck an Englishman in the Presence Chamber, and Scaramelli warned: "The English, who were at first divided amongst themselves, begin now to make common cause against the Scots."[14]

The radical Catholics were moving quickly to take advantage of the developing situation. Anthony Dutton, who had been sent to Valladolid to gain support for an invasion, was to be followed by a long-serving soldier in the Catholic cause in Flanders—the now infamous Yorkshireman Guy Fawkes. The future gunpowder plotter met a mysterious gentleman in Brussels in early June. This gentleman had traveled from England with papers describing the latest news from court and hoped to pass them to the Archduke Albert; having discovered that the Archduke wanted peace with England, he begged Fawkes to take his intelligence on to Spain. The most recent speculation suggests that this gentleman was none other than the spy Anthony Rivers, otherwise known as William Sterrell, secretary to the Earl of Worcester—one of James's four most trusted Englishmen (the others being Lords Henry and Thomas Howard and Robert Cecil).* The papers Fawkes was asked to carry included letters from "a leading personage at court" and "one who has charge of the letters to Spain." There was also one written and one verbal message, as well as a copy of the petition for toleration that the "factious" priest Thomas Hill had given James in York. The general thrust of these messages was that the English Catholics had asked for toleration but had been denied it, that James was unpopular with everyone except the Scots and that with some military help he could easily be overthrown.

The latest disappointment to Catholics was the requirement that Catholic MPs take the Oath of Supremacy at the next Parliament and thereby recognize the King as head of the Church in England. But they had also learned that, despite James's repeated promises that he would end recusancy fines, those that had fallen due in April were to be collected after all. The verbal message Fawkes delivered to Spain added some intriguing details about the reaction to this at court. It described the Earl of Northumberland as being deeply disillusioned. He had been rewarded for his loyalty to James with a place on the Privy Council and with the prestigious post of Captain of the Band of Gentlemen Pensioners, but his role as a champion of toleration for Catholics had been conveniently ignored. On 18 May he had been instructed to tell the Pensioners that they must take the Oath of Supremacy. It was a severe blow to his honor and he later refused to ask his Catholic kinsman Thomas Percy to take the oath—an act of defi-

*Sterrell had already benefited from his master's success and been a recipient of James's favor. On or around 19 May, when James granted a license to Shakespeare's company, Sterrell was given the post of Keeper of the Palace of St. John of Jerusalem, Clerkenwell, which housed the Office of the Revels. In his position there, and through his connections with Worcester and Lord Thomas Howard, he would have a great deal of influence on which plays and masques were performed in the years ahead. I am grateful to Professor John Finnis for this information.

ance that would land him in the Tower in the aftermath of the Gunpowder Plot (in which Percy was certainly involved, and possibly
Northumberland—though his part has never been proven).

The message also mentioned other names. It claimed that along
with Northumberland, the Earls of Worcester, Cumberland and
Shrewsbury did not want "to plan peace [with Spain] unless it is
under the condition of liberty of conscience."[15] Worcester was a
Catholic and Shrewsbury had a Catholic wife, but on the face of it
Cumberland was a more surprising name. Cumberland was Elizabeth's last champion and one of the greatest privateers of his age—
certainly no friend to the Spanish. James had also shown him favor by
making him Governor of the Scottish Borders on 8 June. Cumberland's daughter, however, tells us that he felt undervalued. The then
thirteen-year-old Lady Anne Clifford recalled that the adults around
her hoped for mountains from James but found only molehills and
that they were envious of the success of Cecil and the Howards. Cumberland also detested the Scots and favored toleration for Catholics.
State papers from the Netherlands reveal that Cumberland was already in contact with the Archduke's agent, Dr. Taylor, as to how the
cause might be advanced.[16] This strongly suggests that his well-
advertised opposition to peace with Spain had indeed more to it than
a wish to continue his piracy, as contemporaries such as Bishop Goodman assumed.

The message went on to describe the anti-Scots feeling at court
and to express concern that some anti-Spanish Catholics were now
on the point of rebelling. The fear was that if such a revolt failed it
would lead to reprisals against all Catholics, and if it succeeded it
would preempt a Spanish-backed invasion. The Jesuits were therefore desperately urging Catholics in England to show restraint. They
also attended a secret meeting in London on 13 May with all the main
Catholic parties in order to work out a common policy on how to
confront James's attitude to toleration. The Jesuit position was represented by the Archpriest Blackwell, that of the seculars by two Appellant priests called Mush and Colleton, and there was also a leading
representative of the laity—a recusant Catholic gentleman called
Robert Tempest. The result was a statement under which the parties

agreed to work together to pressure the King into a change of course. But the meeting was concealed from the cross-eyed priest William Watson, who was now as loud in his condemnation of the King as he had once been of the Jesuits.

It was probably Watson's talk of revolt the Jesuits had picked up on. His friend Sir Griffin Markham had reached the point of despair where he had begun to listen to Watson's schemes; with the former soldier's help he was now plotting in earnest.

❈   ❈   ❈

Sir Griffin's creditors had accepted that the King was not going to save him from ruin and by 21 May they were already in pursuit of the man who had secured his debts, his cousin Sir John Harington. Elizabeth's godson's first reaction was to write to Robert Cecil asking him to draw the King's attention to his plight: "I that have never committed crime in my life ... am betrayed by my kin into a debt of £40,000," he pleaded. "I look for relief from the King. Your good word may hasten it ... I beseech you show yourself a friend to us both in this."[17] Harington had been cultivating Cecil for years. Only the previous summer he had given him one of his water closets for Theobalds, but when Cecil responded, on 29 May, it was not to show his gratitude.

"My noble knight," Cecil wrote, "I shall not fail to keep your grace and favour quick and lively in the King's breast, as far as good discretion guides me." The problem was, Cecil explained, he was not entirely secure in James's favor and, as Harington knew, keeping a monarch's goodwill was a tricky business: "You have tasted a little hereof in our blessed Queen's time, who was more than a man, and (in troth) some times less than a woman." These were still more uncertain times: "I wish I waited now in her Presence Chamber, with ease at my food, and rest in my bed. I am pushed from the shore of comfort, and know not where the winds and waves of a court will bear me ... We are much stirred about counsels, and more about honours ... Farewell ... Your true friend, Cecil."[18]

There was another royal proclamation issued that day. It ordered all those not in attendance at court, or with some special reason to be in London, to leave until the coronation on 25 July, "for our people's sake as for the safety of our own person."[19] The plague was spreading rapidly. Deaths in London and the outskirts were thirty-two for the week ending 26 May and the Lord Mayor was issuing new plague orders. The paper bills marked with the words "Lord Have Mercy on Us" that denoted infected households had proved to be too easy to deface and dispose of. They were now to be replaced by a red cross "fourteen inches in length and the like in breadth upon the wall or boards in the most open place." Some of those shut up were so angry that they set out deliberately to infect others. One such, Henry Ross of St. Bartholomew's the Great, was flogged and thrown into Newgate, after he did "most lewdly presume to go to the King's Majesty's Court at Greenwich and there thrust himself in company amongst his Majesty's household servants and others."[20]

Harington was more than happy to obey the King's orders and flee London for the clean air of his Somerset estate but Sir Griffin's creditors caught up with him before he had the chance, and on 6 June they threw him into the Gatehouse prison in Westminster. London was now baking in a summer heat wave and deaths from the plague began doubling every week. If there was an outbreak in the prison, Harington would be under a virtual death sentence. Terrified, he wrote a second letter to Cecil from his "unaccustomed lodging," begging for "some comfortable answer in this my distress." He hoped that at the very least pressure might be put on Sir Griffin Markham and Sir John Skinner to sell their property and pay their debts.[21] But the only news Harington heard in the next few days was that Lord Mountjoy had returned from Ireland with Elizabeth's "Monster of the North," Hugh O'Neill, Earl of Tyrone.

Harington could hardly believe that he, a veteran of Essex's terrible Irish campaign, was in prison and Tyrone was on his way to court. Others had their dead to mourn and the mothers and wives of men who had never come back from Ireland lined the roads from the coast, shouting abuse and throwing mud and stones as Mountjoy's train and the traitor Earl passed.

The title of Tyrone was one of three earldoms created by Henry VIII in Ireland. It dated back to a time when the English had hoped to spearhead progress in Ireland by working with the chiefs. For the Irish, Tyrone's native title, "the O'Neill," was more significant. It made him the nearest thing Ireland had to a king—and a remarkable king Tyrone would have made, as Harington recalled. By a twist of fate he had met Tyrone in 1600. Essex had asked the knight to follow him back to court when he left Ireland, but Harington had found the ships full of wounded men and Essex's horses. Left in Ireland, Harington had learned that Sir William Warren had orders to extend the truce Essex and Tyrone had made and he took the opportunity to travel with Warren to Ulster.

The great rebel was already in his fifties and his red beard had turned gray, but as one contemporary recalled, he was as "fresh and active as if he had not as yet obtained forty." Courageous and spirited but also wary and patient, Tyrone was a brilliant actor who could "appear serious or joyful, pleased or angry . . . in the most natural manner."[22] He had greeted the Queen's godson respectfully and apologized "that he could no better call to mind myself and some of my friends that had done him some courtesy in England saying these troubles made him forget almost all his friends." Tyrone had traveled to court in the early 1590s with his English wife.

As Warren and Tyrone discussed the truce, Harington was left to talk to Tyrone's two children—"of goodly spirit, their age between thirteen and fifteen, in English clothes like a nobleman's sons; with velvet jerkins and gold lace; of a good cheerful aspect, freckle faced, not tall of stature, but strong and well set; both of them [learning] the English tongue." He gave them a copy of his English translation of Ariosto's *Orlando Furioso*. Later when the boys showed it to their father, Tyrone asked Harington to read some of it and they sat together gossiping over a meal set on a "fern table and fern forms, spread under the stately canopy of heaven." Tyrone's guard, he had noted, "for the most part, were beardless boys without shirts; who, in the frost, wade as familiarly through rivers as water spaniels," Harington observed, "With what charm such a master makes them love him I know not, but if he bid come, they come; if go they do go; if he say do this, they do it."[23]

Most of those boys were now dead, but although Harington felt pity for the fallen enemy he felt none for their leader: "I have lived to

Above Elizabeth's cousin Sir Robert Carey, who carried her blue ring to James in Scotland as proof of her death. His wife later had the charge of raising the future Charles I.

Right The Essex rebel, Henry Wriothesley, third Earl of Southampton, in the Tower in 1603. The Latin inscription proclaims he is "in chains but unconquered." The cat is symbolic of a desire for liberty, and one of James's first acts on the death of Elizabeth was to free him.

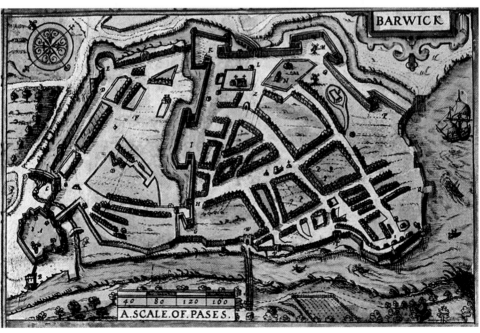

As James arrived at Berwick the town rose before him "like an enchanted castle."
Plan of Berwick by John Speed.

Left As James was being given an explanation of the Lumley family lineage, carved on the west side of Lumley Castle, he burst out impatiently, "Oh mon . . . I did na ken Adam's name was Lumley."

Right The Bishop of Durham and a hundred gentlemen in tawny livery coats met James at Durham Castle. The Tudors had never visited the city.

Left The citizens of York had their houses painted for James's arrival, and a fountain ran with wine.

Above James refused to see Sir Walter Ralegh when he arrived at Burghley House.

Right A statue of King James in the hall at Apethorpe, Northamptonshire, where in 1603 he was feasted by Lady Mildmay, "one of the most excellent confectioners in England."

Below At Elizabeth's funeral many in the crowds felt that whatever the future held, "they could not lightly be in worse state than they were." As the hearse passed by the people wept.

Left Henry Percy, Earl of Northumberland, was one of James's most powerful supporters in March 1603, but by June he was an angry enemy.

Right Dingley Hall, Leicestershire, where Anna was entertained on her progress south by the recusant Catholic Sir Thomas Griffin. The archway was engraved with "God save the King 1560"—meaning King Philip of Spain. Elizabeth had then been on the throne for two years.

Left The crossbow in Anna's hair was taken from Elizabeth's wardrobe in May 1603 and sent to her in Scotland as a gift from James. The portrait depicts her in 1617, when she was in late middle age, but shows her persisting love of jeweled ciphers. The crowned "S" pinned to her left collar refers to her mother, Sophia of Mecklenberg, and the crowned "C" on the right to her brother Christian IV of Denmark. The jeweled "IHS" monogram and crucifix are prominent symbols of the Catholic faith, to which she converted and which her husband persecuted.

Left Henry, Prince of Wales, wearing the robes and collar of the Order of the Garter, c. 1603.

Right The Princess Royal, later Elizabeth, Queen of Bohemia, from whom the current royal family is descended. Behind her is a hunting party. (Robert Peake the Elder, dated 1603)

Above left Anna's lifelong English favorite, Lucy, Countess of Bedford, in her robes for the coronation, c. 1603. *Above right* Elizabeth I's cousin, friend and servant, Charles Howard of Effingham, Earl of Nottingham, High Admiral of England, in his robes for the coronation, c. 1603. It was said that Nottingham began the Union between England and Scotland with his marriage to James's young cousin Lady Margaret Stuart, but their sex life was the source of much mirth at court.

James couldn't resist flirting with Sir Philip Herbert,
even amid the solemnity of the coronation.

James I, by Paul Van Somer.

Above left Mary Rogers, the beloved wife of Sir John Harington, age twenty-three. Her dress, with its crisscross pattern and the knots of pearls in her left hand, reflects the Harington arms. (Marcus Gheeraerts the Younger, c. 1592)

Above right The Round Table of King Arthur, which hung in the great hall at the castle in Winchester when Sir Walter Ralegh was tried there and does so today. Constructed in the fourteenth century, it bears the names of the twenty-four legendry knights of the table and a portrait of Arthur, whom James hoped to co-opt as a symbol of British Union.

Left Electrotype of the tomb of Elizabeth I. Even in death she wears a low-cut dress in accordance with the tradition for unmarried girls.

Right Designs for a new British flag made by the Earl of Nottingham. But James's hopes of union were not to be fulfilled until the next century.

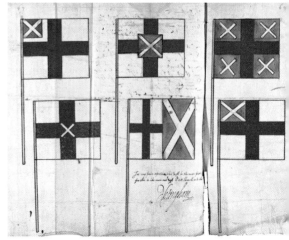

see that damnable rebel Tyrone brought to England, courteously favoured, honoured and well liked." Harington spat as he wrote to his friend, the Bishop of Bath and Wells: "Oh! My Lord, what is there which doth not prove the inconstancy of worldly matters! How did I labour after that knave's destruction! I was called from my home by her Majesty's command, adventured perils by sea and land, endured toil, was near starving, ate horse flesh at Munster; and all to quell that man, who now smiles in peace at those that did hazard their lives to destroy him."[24]

As the crowds at the roadsides grew more volatile the authorities were forced to rush Tyrone to a hiding place a few miles outside London. On 8 June James issued a proclamation "commanding that no man abuse the Earl of Tyrone" so that he could be moved once more. Tyrone remained heavily guarded for his own protection. Harington, meanwhile, had also found himself under close watch, but entirely for the protection of his creditors.

❀   ❀   ❀

A new king meant new opportunities on the diplomatic as well as the domestic front, and it was not long before ambassadors began arriving from all over Europe. The Archdukes' envoy, Charles de Ligne, Count Aremberg, had disembarked at Dover on 3 June. He was old and his gout made the journey to London an uncomfortable one, but there was some good news waiting for him.

James had announced three principal intentions: union with Scotland, the upholding of the established religion, and peace with his neighbors.[25] The first had been underscored by James's proclamation on the Union, the second by his conservative choice of Household chaplains (all eleven of those sworn in at Greenwich were veterans of Elizabeth's pulpit); the third meant that Aremberg's years of work toward peace with England could at last see a result. The Spanish, however, had not yet sent an ambassador and the Archdukes could not make peace without them. His task was primarily to gather information and prepare the ground for discussion. Aremberg's chief enemy in this regard was Henri IV's mighty chief minister, Maximilien de Béthune, the Marquis de Rosni (later the Duke of Sully).

De Rosni had arrived in England on 6 June with a train of around 250 followers, 1,200 crowns' worth of presents and a heavy baggage of diplomatic disadvantages. The gossip was that in the weeks before Elizabeth's death the French had refused to support James's inheritance unless he left one of his sons behind to rule Scotland; when James refused, their ambassador, de Beaumont, supported the attempted coup supposedly led by Lord Beauchamp on 28 March. De Beaumont had tried to defend himself from these accusations, saying "that all he ever said, when the Queen died, was that it became every good Catholic to protect and favour ladies, and this [meant] to encourage Lady Arabella"—a statement that just incriminated him further.

One of James's first actions on reaching England had been to demand that Henri IV repay the debt France owed the English crown. Henri had offered 200,000 francs as a down payment, and James had pointedly replied that he would put this toward the cost of his coronation. He had since heard that Henri gibed that he was a mere "Captain of Arts and Clerk of Arms."[26] If all this were not bad enough, de Rosni had discovered another potential difficulty while he was in Calais. Henri had ordered his chief minister to arrive at court dressed in mourning for Elizabeth, but de Rosni was warned that this "would most certainly be highly disagreeable to the court, where so strong an affectation prevailed to obliterate the memory of that great princess, that she was never spoke of, and even the mention of her name industriously avoided."

Robert Lord Sidney and the Earl of Southampton met de Rosni and his brilliant train in Canterbury and they were escorted to Gravesend. There the French were received on board royal barges— "a kind of covered boat . . . very commodious and richly ornamented," de Rosni noted with satisfaction. The barges took the French up the Thames as far as the Tower, where they were given the most impressive salute de Rosni had ever heard, "with upwards of three thousand guns, besides the discharges from several shipguns, and the musketry from the mole and fort before the Tower." They disembarked into around thirty coaches and made their way through the crowded streets.

De Rosni was placed in temporary lodgings at Sir John Spencer's palace at Crosby Place in Bishopsgate while the magnificent mansion of Arundel House was made ready for him.[27] It had been the residence of Richard III and had huge apartments, but de Rosni needed to find places for those members of his large retinue for whom there was no room, and this was proving difficult. "It is certain that the English hate us and this hatred is so general and inveterate, that one would be almost tempted to number it among their natural dispositions," he complained.[28] The ill will had almost immediate consequences and on only his second night the French minister found himself confronted with a new diplomatic problem.

De Rosni had spent the evening playing primero with friends while some of the younger gentlemen went out looking for drink and women. They returned in disarray in small groups of three or four. When he demanded to know what was going on he was told that a young cousin of de Beaumont had killed an Englishman in a brawl. The ambassador was desperate to protect the boy, who was the only son of a leading French courtier, but de Rosni decided this was an opportunity to prove France's goodwill to England. He told de Beaumont that he was determined that "the service of the king my master . . . shall not suffer for such an imprudent stripling," and asked the Lord Mayor, Robert Lee, to prepare for the young man's execution. Lee had no desire for things to go this far. It was not uncommon for English gentlemen to kill each other in brawls and they were not usually executed for it. Besides, de Beaumont had offered large sums in compensation to the Englishman's family. Lee found himself pleading for a more moderate punishment for the foreigner. "This removed at least one obstacle to the success of my negotiation," de Rosni recalled coolly, "but there remained many to encounter."[29]

Over the next few days de Rosni gathered what information he could from the envoys of other nations opposed to England making peace with Spain. Scaramelli was one such. James had gone out of his way to try to please the Venetian. He had promised he would put an end to attacks on Venetian shipping and had already withdrawn the letters of marque, which enabled privateers to carry out attacks under a cloak of patriotic respectability. He had even allowed Scaramelli to hold one of Piers the pirate's business partners as prisoner until Piers returned to Plymouth. But Scaramelli's dispatches to the Senate sketched a merciless portrait of James as an idle, vain and vulgar provincial who merely wanted " 'to enjoy the papacy' as we say, and so desires to have no bother with other people's affairs and little with his own; he would like to dedicate himself to his books and to the chase and to encourage the opinion that he is the arbiter of peace."[30] He appeared to think James incapable of actually achieving it.

The root of Scaramelli's distaste was James's treatment of the Catholics. He expressed his disgust to de Rosni over James's dishonesty in the matter of toleration, warning that the King's "dissimulation, which his flatterers complimented in him as a virtue, had always consisted in giving hopes to all, but accomplishing none." James had frequently been heard to say "that it was to such artful conduct alone he owed his security when King of Scotland" and "it was highly probable that he would put those arts into practise again, and pursue them more tenaciously than ever, at the beginning of a reign and at the head of a great kingdom, whose people, affairs, and neighbours, he was utterly unacquainted with."[31]

De Rosni found the Dutch less heated in their assessment. Their agents informed him that James wanted peace with Spain but was anxious not to drive them into the arms of the French. As yet no decisions had been made as to what help the Dutch would continue to receive and all was marked by irresolution. James had told them he wanted to be close to France and even to conclude a double marriage between the royal families, but as he was notoriously untrustworthy, they were unsure what his true intentions were.

Aremberg's audience with James was to be delayed until after de Rosni's departure, supposedly because of Aremberg's gout, but more likely to ease diplomatic tensions. In the meantime they exchanged extravagant compliments "in all which nothing was wanting but sincerity."[32] De Rosni's own audience could not go ahead, however, until he dropped his insistence that his train should come to court in mourning. He was finally forced to do so when the new Captain of the Guard, Thomas Erskine, explained to de Beaumont that arriving at court in such a manner would be taken as a deliberate affront. At last, on 15 June, de Rosni and his train "all got into their most fantastic costumes and went to Greenwich where they found the court in right sumptuous array and very crowded."[33]

Fynes Moryson described French courtiers as wearing their suits with a certain affected carelessness, "which the Germans call slovenly because they many times go without hatbands and garters, with their points untrust and their doublets unbuttoned."[34] De Rosni's vast, swaggering retinue filed into the Presence Chamber and walked toward the throne, a process that took fifteen minutes, with de Rosni bringing up the rear. When he reached the foot of the platform to the throne James stood up. He took a couple of steps down, but one of his ministers whispered in his ear that he should go no further. James announced that he only wished to show his esteem for an ambassador who shared their religion—de Rosni belonged to France's tolerated Protestant minority.

De Rosni dutifully rehearsed the history of alliances between James's family and that of Henri IV. He then passed on messages of goodwill, which James reciprocated before asking after Henri IV's health. This was no innocent question. The French king had been seriously ill after a hunting accident. Since his heir was only three years old and of uncertain legitimacy it was feared that France could be plunged back into civil war at any time. James's apparent concern implied that England would be foolish to make any long-term commitments to France at the expense of a more stable Spain. De Rosni assured James that Henri was quite well (indeed, he would survive another seven years, until killed by an assassin in 1610). The atmosphere then quickly soured as James moved on to attack the French habit of referring to the Pope as "His Holiness," a title that he declared belonged only to God. De Rosni snapped that it was no worse than "the frequent giving to princes such titles as they were well known not to deserve"—a reference to the English crown's claim to the title of King of France.[35] It was now James's turn to be annoyed and he concluded the audience after making it brutally clear that if de Rosni was to block his planned peace with Spain he would need to find a satisfactory answer to the question "How can you ask me to live at war in order that you may live in peace?"[36]

The Frenchman would, however, develop a higher opinion of James than Scaramelli had. His memoirs recalled James as "upright and conscientious, that he had eloquence and even erudition; but still more of penetration and of the show of learning. He loved to hear discourse of affairs of state, and to have great enterprises proposed to him . . . [although] . . . he naturally hated war and still more to be personally engaged in it."[37] Unfortunately for de Rosni, war was the issue at hand. As the French minister left Greenwich he was approached by Sir Thomas Erskine, who informed him of "his desire to be ranked amongst the number of my friends." Erskine had said exactly the same thing to Aremberg, and the Venetian ambassador in Madrid, Simon Contarini, had reported in mid-June that "four Scotsmen, newly added to the Council, have for a long time been in receipt of large sums from Spain."[38] De Rosni believed that, nevertheless, in their hearts, the Scots supported France. English allegiances, however, were more complex.

De Rosni identified three factions. The first was a pro-Spanish faction headed by the House of Howard. The second he described as the "old English." It was neither pro-French nor pro-Spanish but was "desirous of restoring the ancient kingdom of Burgundy . . . and sought to render Flanders independent of both."[39] All those he named as belonging to this faction had been involved in peace negotiations with Aremberg in the 1590s. They included Lord Buckhurst, Sir John Fortescue and Cecil—"at least as far as one could judge from a man who was all mystery." Buckhurst and Fortescue may well have supported the Archdukes' dream of an independent Burgundy allied to England; both were crypto-Catholics and Scaramelli also considered Buckhurst anti-French. As for Cecil, his goal remained peace with Spain, and Catherine Howard was pushing for a Spanish pension for him, as well as for herself and her husband (it would be granted the following year and Cecil would continue to receive it until his death in 1612). He must have considered an independent Burgundy an attractive idea, but little more.

De Rosni's "third faction" was described as a group of "seditious persons, of a character purely English, and ready to undertake anything in favour of novelty, were it even against the King himself."

These, he continued, "had at their heads the Earls of Northumberland, Southampton, and Cumberland, Lord Cobham, Ralegh, Griffin and others."[40] It is an interesting collection of names. The three earls had all been shown James's favor, while the others were among the greatest losers in his accession. But de Rosni's assessment was astute: names from both groups appeared in the verbal message given to Fawkes in Brussels and all, with one exception, would be arrested for plots against the state over the next thirty months (the exception being the Earl of Cumberland, who died in 1605).

De Rosni was very impressed by Northumberland: "no one amongst the English Lords has more understanding, capacity, courage, or possesses more authority than this nobleman." But Northumberland had told de Rosni quite openly that "he had no great share of fidelity or esteem for James," disliking both James's treatment of Catholics and his peace policy towards Spain.[41] The third earl named by de Rosni, Henry Wriothesley, Earl of Southampton, was a friend of the Earl of Essex, whom James had ordered to be released from the Tower in March. Southampton, still only thirty, was one of the most handsome and accomplished members of Elizabeth's court. A patron of poets, most notably William Shakespeare, he was already the recipient of the captaincy of the Isle of Wight and James would restore his earldom in July, stripped from him after the Essex revolt. Southampton should have been delighted with James becoming king, but like Northumberland and Cumberland, he resented the power and influence of the Scots, of Cecil and the Howards; he supported the principle of religious toleration and was anti-Spanish. Southampton would be arrested the following year after being "rumoured by his enemies to be plotting to slay several Scots much about the King's person."[42] His first intended victim was said to be Sir George Home, James's principal Scots favorite: nothing was proved, but the fact that the rumors were believed is suggestive of his feelings, and in the years ahead the old Essex faction—James's most loyal supporters until the Earl's death—would become a source of opposition to James's government.

The three other men named by de Rosni—Cobham, Ralegh and Sir Griffin Markham—were in a very different situation from that of the favored earls. They had been deprived of position and office.

Cecil had no need to manufacture a plot with which to ruin them; he knew from experience that it was enough to set the conditions for one. Humiliations were therefore being piled upon them and all were plotting against James. The Catholic Sir Griffin Markham was involved in an entirely English plot with the priest William Watson, while Lord Cobham and Sir Walter Ralegh were looking to Spain for support.

❖   ❖   ❖

Ralegh had fought and lost a desperate legal battle to keep Durham House and at the end of May a royal command ordered him to "deliver quiet possession" of the palace to Tobie Matthew. The Bishop demanded that Ralegh leave promptly and another royal command followed, ordering him out of the house before 24 June. Ralegh was further instructed not to remove "any ceiling, glass, iron etc.," and was informed that the stables and garden were to be vacated "instantly." Matthew had agreed to hand them over to Robert Cecil, who was looking forward to extending his new house at the earliest opportunity.

Predictably enough, Ralegh was incandescent. He had spent almost £20,000 restoring Durham House over twenty years and many of the fixtures were his. In a furious letter to the authorities on 9 June, he complained that his treatment was "contrary to honour, to custom and to civility . . . I am of the opinion that if the King's Majesty had recovered this house or the like from the meanest gentleman and servant he had in England that his Majesty would have given six months time . . . to cast out my hay and oats into the streets at an hour's warning and to remove my family and stuff in fourteen days after is such a severe expulsion as hath not been offered to any man before."[43]

On the same day Lord Cobham was with his brother George Brooke. The younger sibling's hopes that James would grant him the mastership of the St. Cross hospital in Winchester had been dashed when James had allowed his Scots agent, James Hudson, to sell it to Dr. Lake—the brother of the court official Thomas Lake, who had dealt with Ralegh at Burghley. As Brooke and Cobham discussed their disappointments Cobham revealed that he and Ralegh believed James could be overthrown in favor of Arbella Stuart. The Spanish and the French had been working toward nominating an English-born candidate before Elizabeth's death and had considered Arbella's name. It was furthermore apparent that she was discontented with her lot. The bright and optimistic seventeen-year-old seen at court in 1592 had soured into what Scaramelli described as "a regular termagant." Although she was pleased to be away from Hardwick, she found she had to plead with James for financial support and he proved humiliatingly slow to give it.

Cobham was already in contact with one of Arbella's servants and he intended to raise money from the Archdukes or Philip III to help finance a revolt in her name. The Privy Council had refused him a passport to travel abroad on 23 May but he hoped to enter into discussions with Aremberg in London instead. Brooke told Cobham that he too was discussing the genesis of a plot with his fellow soldier Sir Griffin Markham. In private, Sir Griffin's habitual loyalty was still making him reluctant to turn traitor, but there seemed to be no other way out. As Brooke and Cobham gossiped he was being given official notice that the Earl of Rutland had been granted the post of Keeper of the Parks of Beskwood and Clipston. The following day he went to see Sir John Harington in prison. He assured his cousin that Cecil intended to help him, and Harington immediately wrote to thank the Secretary. But the help was never offered and would never come. It seems Sir Griffin had convinced himself that one way or another he would soon be able to clear his debts and free Harington, but he could not tell his cousin what his plans were and so invented Cecil's goodwill to give Harington heart.

On 11 June Sir Griffin left London for York. Anna had just arrived in the city and women from all over the north were pouring into it hoping to give her supplications for toleration of religion. Sir Griffin hoped that, as a fellow Catholic, she might also see him. It was one last desperate attempt to pull back from the brink.[44]

Unlike James, Anna was completely at ease in York and spent the next few days waving to the crowds and accepting the usual gifts of goblets and gold for herself and her children. On one occasion, after a tour in the blazing sun, she spotted the wife of the mayor and her lady friends sipping from a wine cup and asked if she could join them, adding that if possible she would prefer to drink beer. Lord Burghley, who as President of the North, was at Anna's side, was captivated by his new queen and unconcerned about the approaches of Catholics, assuring Cecil, "She is wise enough how to answer them." Her refusal to see Sir Griffin Markham when he arrived on the fourteenth suggests that she was indeed prepared to take Burghley's advice, on this occasion at least.[45] Sir Griffin accepted his failure and left for Beskwood immediately. That night he invited his brothers Charles and Thomas to supper and a family meeting.

Beskwood Park was surrounded by hills where watch could be kept for any unwanted visitors; there were no entrances to it save by gates, and the house itself was hidden from view until you were virtually upon it. Sir Griffin nevertheless avoided any sensitive subjects until after they had eaten, when he took his brothers for a walk. The three men were as close as brothers could be. Charles and Thomas Markham had fought under Sir Griffin in Ireland, making them brothers in arms as well as siblings. They even looked alike: tall and muscular with swarthy complexions and large noses, Sir Griffin distinguishable by a wispy beard, a broader face and his crippled arm and hand. The brothers made small talk until Sir Griffin turned to ask Charles how happy he was with the state of the world. Charles replied that he was content if Sir Griffin was in good grace with the King. Sir Griffin told him that he was in despair about that—the parks were gone and he had been unable to speak to the King despite his best efforts. "But," he said, "let that pass, when will you go into London?" His shocked brothers, absorbing the possibility of family ruin, replied that they weren't sure. He persisted: was it possible they could be there on Thursday? Again they told him they didn't know. "Well," he said, "suppose I should have engaged myself so far into an action, that I neither could nor would withdraw, being for so good a purpose as the advancement of the Catholic faith, and peradventure the raising of our house, seeing my disability for action [would] you two . . . go with me or no?" Charles answered that as he had been commanded by him in war and other ways, so he would be commanded by him in this. "By God," he replied, "if I may have you two . . . I shall think myself safe." His brothers assured him they would not leave him.[46]

Sir Griffin explained to his loyal brothers that before he could describe his plan of action they had to take an oath. The two men duly swore to do all they could for the raising of the Catholic faith, to secure the King's person and to keep the action secret unless commanded otherwise by one of the leaders. They then discovered that chief among these leaders were the secular Appellant priests Watson and Clark—the latter being the priest who had warned Sir Griffin in April that the Jesuit John Gerard was planning to depose the King. The brothers were told that the plan was to recruit a large body of Catholics who would take the court by surprise on Midsummer Night, capture the King and take him to the Tower; the plot would be later sometimes referred to as "the Surprise." Once at the Tower the plotters would demand a royal pardon, religious toleration for Catholics and the removal of Privy Councilors associated with their repression. The inspiration for the plot was the Scots habit of kidnapping their King and there was no intention to harm James or even to overthrow him.

Sir Griffin suggested to his brothers that they should expect between 500 and 1,000 supporters and assured them that they had the support of a nobleman. George Brooke had recruited the Puritan Lord Grey of Wilton, the courtier who had demanded James's power be limited before he was offered the throne. Grey had subsequently found himself shut out of favor and abandoned by his former ally Cecil, and he had agreed to lead a hundred soldiers to court under cover of presenting the King with a petition. The promise gave the Markhams heart, but it had appalled the priest Watson. Such a prominent figure could take charge of events after the plot had succeeded and he believed that Grey was as much an enemy to Catholics as he was to the King. His real role, Watson hoped, would be to take the blame for the plot, with Catholics presenting themselves as James's "saviour" against Puritan treachery. He and Clark were now touring the country trying to gather support.

Watson promised potential recruits that once their action was effected 40,000 Catholics would rise in support. It was a figure often bandied around. Sir Edward Baynham, the wild young gentleman arrested on the eve of Elizabeth's death, had quoted the same Catholic numbers and so had the factious priest Thomas Hill—but only a handful of hotheads and extremists proved prepared to sign Watson's oath, among them the two future gunpowder plotters (and former Essex rebels) Francis Tresham and his neighbor Robert Catesby.[47] The English had learned the habit of obedience under the Tudors and were instinctively opposed to rebellion. Clark tried to convince his Catholic friends that as there was no legitimate government until James was crowned, a revolt could not be considered treason, but the Jesuits had countered that Catholics should lie low and keep out of trouble and this is exactly what they did.

In desperation Watson spun lies to gain recruits. Anthony Copley, the gentleman poet who had accused Robert Persons of incest, drunkenness and heresy, was told that they would be presenting James with a petition on 20 June and no more. Sir Edward Parham was assured that he was needed to save James from Grey's Puritan plot: "Will you not be ready to draw your sword against Lord Grey, and, if the King's servants be overmastered, help to carry the King to the Tower, for his relief from Lord Grey's control, and for the advancement of the Catholic religion?" Watson asked him.[48] Parham asked for proof of Grey's intentions. He never got it and never signed Watson's oath.

Cobham and Brooke, meanwhile, continued to discuss their plans. Cobham thought Watson's plot to kidnap the King was insufficiently ambitious and boasted to his brother that "Mr Brooke and the rest were upon the bye, but he and Sir Walter Ralegh were upon the main, which was to destroy the king and all his cubs."[49] The words eventually gave the plots their better-known names, the Bye, or secondary, plot and the Main, or principal, one. Cobham's Main plot, with its threat to murder the entire royal family, had not, however, gotten very far. Aremberg learned that Cobham was out of favor and refused to see him unless it was agreed with Cecil first. He and Ralegh had no better luck with de Rosni, who gave neutral responses to their queries as to what Henri IV's attitude might be to James's removal.

Watson and Clark's work had one result: by the third week in June rumors were spreading fast among the Catholic gentry that there was to be some sort of action against James. The Jesuits used go-betweens

to warn the government and pointed to James's insistence on collect-
ing recusancy fines as a possible recruiting ground. James was persuaded that he had to tread more carefully and in a private meeting
with de Rosni on 17 June he indicated that he intended to hold to his
original promise to remit recusancy fines. Two days later de Rosni and
de Beaumont attended a religious service at Greenwich and afterward
shared the King's table. It was impressively dressed with a heavily jeweled centerpiece displaying valuable goblets and James was served by
kneeling courtiers.

The men discussed the blazing hot weather, hunting and James's
predecessor. De Rosni's insistence on wearing mourning for Elizabeth still rankled with James and to the Frenchman's great distaste
James talked of her with contempt: "he even boasted of the dexterity
which he had employed to manage her by means of her own councillors, all of whom, he said, he had gained over during her life, so that
they did nothing but what was agreeable to him."[50] James was drinking his wine undiluted and began making extravagant toasts to Henri
IV's health. At one point he leaned over to de Rosni and whispered
promises of a marriage between the royal houses. James may have
been a little drunk, but he was not being foolish. It was unwise to fall
out with France before any peace with Spain was signed. James merrily indicated interest in a defensive treaty. De Rosni seized the opportunity and the meeting ended positively.

The following day, 20 June, James's birthday, was the day planned
for the Bye plot. The poet Anthony Copley had arrived in London as
Watson had asked him to a week earlier, only to be told that the date
of the plot had been moved to the night of the twenty-fourth. Watson
added that the plan was not, in fact, to deliver a petition, as he had
previously said, but to capture the King. Copley did his best to disguise his shock and appeared enthusiastic. The action he took next
suggests that, unlike Watson, he was aware of the meeting on 13 May
at which the secular priesthood and the Archpriest had agreed to
work peacefully together for toleration. He sought the advice of his
sister, Elizabeth Gage, who was close to the Jesuit John Gerard. He
also went to see the Archpriest Blackwell. Both promptly informed

the government of the few details they were given. They were understandably deeply suspicious of Copley, who like Watson had been a government stooge for years.

Messages were sent around the country warning Catholics that Cecil was behind Watson's plot and its true intention was to ruin them all. Nothing, however, was said to Watson, and Copley continued to see the plotters. At the most significant of these meetings Sir Griffin Markham explained exactly how the plot was to be achieved. He believed that they needed around 400 men, some to disperse around Greenwich, the rest to arrive at the palace by water on the night of the twenty-fourth. He suggested ammunition be brought to the palace in chests and hidden in advance. When the court gates were about to be shut and the watch set "and everybody in court either in or toward bed," the outer passages were to be taken "in all stillness." He sketched in pen where these passages were. Two or three men would wait for "a sign, either of fire or of horn from without, to get the porter." They had to be men who knew him and could fool him into opening the gate, or get him so drunk he would not know what he was doing. In the last resort, they were to knock him out, "whereby the gate once possessed, all the action may freely succeed; admitting no more numbers than may be competent to master all opposition."

Those not needed to surprise the court were to take command of the town and hold the river and roads so that news of their action would not reach London. With the King and Council captured their tallest men were to "clap upon their backs the guards' coats" and take them to the Tower, where the King would be forced to tell the Lieutenant, Sir John Peyton, "that imminent treason being toward his person and the state, he and it was coming thither for their defence."[51] There was much discussion about what the plotters might do after the King's kidnapping. Brooke, who was motivated by money, hoped to be Lord Treasurer; Sir Griffin, the soldier, wanted to be Earl Marshal. Lord Grey, obsessed with vengeance against Southampton, was to have his enemy's post as Captain of the Isle of Wight, while Copley, who had been dismissed by Persons as "a little, wanton, idle-headed boy," hoped the issues of the day might be resolved in trial by combat.[52] Watson alone wanted to shed blood. He took great delight in the thought of chopping off the heads of James's Privy Councilors.

The plotters waited in vain for Catholics to pour into London to aid them. At one point Watson complained angrily that the Jesuits were foiling their recruitment plans in Lancashire and Wales. The day before the plot was due to be sprung, Sir Griffin Markham heard James had decided to move to Windsor Castle and would be spending the night at Hansworth. Since Hansworth would be easier to storm than Greenwich, Markham suggested a dawn assault. He believed that Northumberland, Mountjoy and Southampton would be there and expressed anxiety that they should not be harmed—Northumberland because he was a champion of toleration, the others because they had been close to Essex.

On the day of the twenty-fourth, Anna was staying at Dingley Hall in Northamptonshire, the house of Sir Griffin Markham's cousin Sir Thomas, whose family was still more stubbornly Catholic than his own.* Sir Thomas Griffin had sold ten properties to pay recusancy fines and although he remained in debt he persisted in refusing to attend Protestant services.[53] Sir Griffin Markham, on the other hand, appears to have been what they called a "church papist," that is, one who went to the Protestant service to avoid the fines but was Catholic in his beliefs—the kind that was the first to compromise with the state.

Sir Griffin's more extreme cousin was a very odd choice of host for the Queen. It is possible that James, worried that there was a plot afoot, was redoubling his efforts to divide Catholics by showing favor to individuals, or even that he already knew the details of it. But Anna's itinerary could have been decided much earlier with the same desire to divide Catholics in mind. James's host at Topcliffe near

*You can still see the engraving made on the porch by Sir Thomas's father, Sir Edward, who had been Mary I's Attorney General: "Anno 1558. In the rayne of Felep and Marey. After darkness . . . cometh light." It refers to the darkness under the Protestant King Edward VI and the light of the restored Catholic faith under Mary. Queen Elizabeth had brought the darkness of Protestantism to Northamptonshire once more and an archway built two years after her accession was stubbornly engraved "God save the King 1560"—meaning King Philip of Spain (see *Country Life*, 16 and 23 April 1921).

York, Mr. Ingleby, was one of a group of brothers considered to be among the most dangerous papists of the north.

That night Watson's lodgings in London were packed with Catholics. They included Sir Griffin's brothers, but there was nowhere near 100 men, let alone the 1,000 Sir Griffin had originally hoped for—and Grey of Wilton was nowhere to be seen. The plan was aborted and the next day Sir Griffin Markham went to see Grey. He returned after dinner with the unwelcome news that Grey wanted nothing more to do with them. It was evident that he did not trust Watson.

Grey had also told Sir Griffin that he hoped he might get a major command in the Low Countries that would provide him with an army to carry through his own plot, in which Brooke would be involved. " 'Till then attend," he said to Markham, "for you know all things must have their opportunity."[54] Watson fled London the next day and Copley warned Sir Griffin that he had told the Jesuits of their plans and that he too should escape as best he could. Sir Griffin went straight to Cobham and asked for a passport to flee abroad. Cobham explained that he was unable to oblige. Sir Griffin then gave him the chilling news that Copley "was in question, and that if he should confess, himself must be in danger."[55] Cobham convinced himself he would be able to brazen it out. His plot was still largely in his head and its existence would be almost impossible to prove.

On 28 June the authorities began looking for Copley. De Rosni, meanwhile, was preparing to return to France. The minister had spent his last few days in England finalizing the defensive treaty James had suggested. By it France and England agreed to help the Dutch reach a settlement with Spain and that in the meantime they would cooperate in providing them with military aid. Even if an Anglo-Spanish peace went ahead, James's "neutrality" would be pro-Dutch.[56] The sense of achievement from the treaty was soon tarnished, however, by a parting shot from James. De Rosni was handed a letter for the French King addressed to "Mon très cher frère le Roi" and not the more polite "Monsieur mon frère" Henri had used when writing to James. It was a deliberate insult and de Rosni was furious about this "error." He asked that a new letter be sent after him and he left England at four in the morning on the twenty-ninth, "with a good wind and a fair passage, but in his mind much discontented."[57]

James, despite the recent attempt to kidnap him, was in a far happier frame of mind. The Bye plot was nothing compared to his terrifying experiences of kidnap in Scotland and besides, he was shortly to be reunited with Anna and his children.

❈ ❈ ❈

It had taken quite some time for the quarrel over Prince Henry to resolve itself and the last few weeks before Anna's progress south had witnessed further stresses in the royal marriage. No sooner had Mar left for Scotland, after the news of the row reached James, than other letters had followed informing him that Anna had miscarried. Groups of leading Scots gentry gathered near Stirling Castle and debated whether they should fight to keep Prince Henry in Scotland, but Lord Fife, the President of the Scots Council, warned James that "physic and medicine requires greater place with her majesty, at present, than lectures on economy or politic." James had taken this kindly advice on board and instructed the Duke of Lennox, of whom his wife was fond, "to meet Mar on the road . . . [and] beg of him to return to Stirling in his company, and pacify the queen as well as he could."

Lennox had taken four of Elizabeth's jewels with him to Scotland. They included a gold and diamond crossbow (which was to become one of Anna's favorite pieces) that was removed from the Wardrobe on 19 May—almost the same day that Fortescue was removed from his post as Master of the Great Wardrobe and replaced with Home. James had hoped that the situation around Stirling would calm once Henry was formally handed to the Queen, but although Anna accepted the jewels from Lennox she had refused to have anything to do with Mar. Anna had heard that the Mars were claiming that she wanted to raise Prince Henry as a Catholic and she wrote warning James not to believe any slanders given out by the family, adding in a postscript written in her own hand, "My hairt, for God's sake take na care nor anger, for it will renew me pain and displeasure."[58]

Since James had given Mar orders to travel with Henry to Holyrood and the boy could not be moved from Stirling without them being revoked, a request for new instructions was sent to Greenwich. James was heard swearing loudly as he read the letter. He was, however, careful not to quarrel with Anna and wrote asking instead how she could possibly believe that anyone would dare speak to him to her prejudice:

> I thank God, I carry that love and respect to you [which] by the law of God and nature [I] ought to do to my wife and the mother of my children—not for that ye are a king's daughter, for whether you were a king's or a cook's daughter ye must be alike to me being my wife. For the respect of your honourable birth, and descent I married you, but the love and respect I now bear you, is because you are my married wife and partaker of my honour, as of my other fortunes . . . God is my witness, I ever preferred you to my bairns, much more than to a subject . . . praying God, my heart, to preserve you and all the bairns, and to send me a blyth meeting with you, and a couple of them, Your awn, James R[59]

Anna nevertheless persisted in her vendetta. As a court observer later noted, she was a queen "full of kindness for those who support her, but on the other hand, terrible, proud, unendurable to those she dislikes."[60] She blamed the Erskines for causing her to miscarry and she wanted the entire family punished and for the Mars to have to apologize. They refused, arguing that they had done nothing but obey the King's commands. James suggested to Anna that she "would do wisely to forget all her grudges to the Earl of Mar, and think of nothing but thanking God for the peaceable possession they had got of England." But Anna retorted that "she would rather never see England, than be in any sort beholden to the Earl of Mar."[61] Eventually Anna got her way. Lennox was ordered to deliver Prince Henry to Anna in the place of Mar, and Anna, satisfied to have at last triumphed over her enemy, left for Holyrood accompanied by her son.

The potential rebels dispersed and when Anna and Henry arrived in Edinburgh they were greeted by a salvo of guns from the castle. A number of English ladies also waited for her. They were not those who had been chosen to attend her by the Council. The official ladies, including Cobham's wife, the Countess of Kildare, and Carey's sister,

Lady Scrope, were in Berwick, where they had been ordered to wait with more jewels and clothes from the Great Wardrobe. The ladies in Edinburgh were the female equivalent of the courtiers who had ridden to Scotland on Elizabeth's death: those ambitious and bold enough to risk the wrath of the government in order to make a strong first impression on the Queen. The beautiful, dark-haired Lucy, Countess of Bedford, immediately found Anna's approval and would remain her principal favorite for the rest of her life. The daughter of Sir John Harington of Exton, Lucy was amusing, intelligent and a renowned patron of the arts. She was also able to share Anna's grief over her miscarriage. She had lost her own baby only months before.

Anna admired the fashions of the English court ladies waiting for her and ordered a new wardrobe for the royal family's progress south: a gown of figured taffeta and a mantle of white satin and purple velvet for herself; a purple doublet and breeches for Henry; a Spanish red taffeta bodice and brown skirt for the six-year-old Princess Elizabeth. Even Anna's jester, Thomas Drury, received a new green coat.[62]

Many of Anna's old clothes were given to her Scottish ladies, as were some of her jewels and the hangings in her rooms. The extravagance of this gesture caused some sour comment in London, but the mood in Edinburgh remained sunny. A farewell service was held on Tuesday 31 May and the Queen and the Prince Henry rode by coach from Holyroodhouse to the great Kirk with the English ladies in other coaches or riding on "fair horses."[63] Henry, slim and golden-haired, waved from his mother's coach as the crowds cheered and the next day, 1 June, Anna said her final goodbyes—she would never return to Scotland. With her were her Scots ladies, her English friends, Prince Henry, mounted on a new horse, and a ragtag army of chancers. Anna also had with her her stillborn baby. It was being said that she had never been pregnant at all—if James required proof she would give it to him.

The Princess Elizabeth did not travel with the party. She was so distraught at being parted from her governess, Lady Livingston, that she was left behind for a few days, and the Countess of Kildare, who was hoping to be given custody of the Princess, was disappointed when the little girl did not arrive in Berwick. This, however, was nothing to the embarrassment of the official greeting party when Anna refused to admit any of them into her Privy Chamber. James had taken his closest Scots allies south, while Anna's friends remained in Scotland. She was determined to overcome this weakness and state her independence. The only English women Anna would accept in her chamber were Lucy Bedford and Lucy's mother, Lady Harington, and she also refused to accept Sir George Carew as the newly appointed head of her Household, announcing that she intended to keep the Scottish Mr. Kennedy as her Chamberlain. When James heard what Anna had done he shouted that "if he do find that she do bring [Kennedy] hither to attend her in that place, that he would break the staff of Chamberlainship on his head, and so dismiss him."[64]

Mr. Kennedy sensibly decided to head back to Scotland while the Duke of Lennox attempted to sort out the problems with the Ladies of Honor. It was, however, clear that Anna intended to keep her own niche in public affairs and Cecil was fearful about what exactly this might mean for him. It was possible that Anna bore a grudge for his former support for the Mar faction or for his having asked James to keep their correspondence secret from her, and her new friend Lady Bedford was from the old Essex faction, who detested him. He had taken the opportunity of the row over Prince Henry to write a groveling letter to Anna assuring her that had he been consulted by the King on her quarrel with Mar, he would have supported her cause. But he need not have worried. Anna was thankful to him for helping to make her Queen of England. "You shall find her, I know, a most gracious prince," Lord Burghley assured Cecil from York; "this I must write in clouds. She will prove, if I be not deceived, a magnificent prince, a kind wife and a constant mistress."

Anna gave Cecil further confidence in her affections when she arrived at Worksop Manor on 20 June and "took Cecil's little son in her blessed arms and kissed him twice and bestowed a jewel on him, tying it herself to his ear." The boy, who had enjoyed playing pirates with Ralegh, must have been aghast by Anna's kisses, but he bore up nobly and did everything his father could have required of him. When Anna asked Prince Henry to dance and then commanded the other children to join him, none would, save young Cecil, who "stepped forth in comely and lowly manner, and took out the young sweet Princess, and danced his galliard." Unlike Henry, young Cecil did not know the steps, but we are told "the excellence of his spirit and grace helped what he wanted in the exercise of dancing."[65] After Worksop Anna traveled to Woollaton, then to Ashby de la Zouch and on to Leicester, a city regarded even then as having "more antiquity than beauty."[66]

Anna spent the night at Sir William Skipwith's house, but the honor proved a mixed blessing for her host. Several items lent for the use of the royal party went missing, including linen and pewter. Someone even stole a poor man's horse.[67] There had been a series of "disorders in the Queen's court" on the journey, as greed and a party mood had taken hold, and large numbers had already been sent home—apparently without effect. Anna herself was as absorbed in pleasure as James had been during his journey south. The next day she was at Dingley Hall with the recusant Catholic Sir Thomas Griffin and her quarrels with James seemed forgotten. When he wrote chiding her that she had not written to him, she scribbled back merrily,

> My heart, I am glad that Haddington has told me of your Majesty's good health, which I wish to continue. As for the charge you lay me with of lazy writing, I think it rather rests on yourself, because you be as slow in writing as myself. I can write of no mirth but of practise of tilting, of riding, of drumming and of music, which is all, where with I am not a little pleased. So wishing your Majesty perpetual happiness, I kiss your Majesty's hand and rest, Your Anna, R[68]

More and more court ladies joined the party at Dingley, among them the young Lady Anne Clifford, daughter and heiress of the Earl of Cumberland. Her mother and their party had killed three horses on one day as they galloped north from Kent to be with the Queen. They had spent their first night on the road sleeping in the hall of the Earl of Kent's seat, Wrest Park, where the remainder of the house was shut up. The following evening they were at Rockingham Castle where they met up with Lucy Bedford. Anne Clifford recalled that she was already "so great a woman with the Queen as everyone much respected her," but when they arrived at Dingley, Anna generously "kissed us all and used us kindly."[69] On Saturday 25 June the royal train departed for the seat of Sir Roger Spencer, Althorp—then a moated house and the beneficiary of one of the last crenellation licenses, granted by the crown in 1512. Spencer was reputed to be the richest man in England and it was here that Anna would be introduced to one of the more expensive passions of her life: the masque.

Anna arrived at Althorp in the evening, having rested at Holdenby House on the way. As the royal train moved through the park she heard pipes being played, then a satyr perched in a tree announced the beginning of Ben Jonson's masque *The Satyr*:

> *Here! There! And everywhere!*
> *Some solemnities are near,*
> *That these changes strike mine ear.*
> *My pipe and I a part shall bear.*

When the satyr finished he leaped down and gazed at the Queen and Prince Henry: "Sure they are of heavenly race," he announced, and then ran off into the woods.[70] More music heralded the arrival of fairies, and their queen later presented Anna with a jewel. The evening ended with Spencer's young son releasing two deer that were hunted and killed in front of the Queen. It was an unforgettable spectacle and Anna was captivated. Under her patronage the masque would become the outstanding feature of the artistic life of the Jacobean court and this courtly display would serve a useful purpose in reminding the world of the wealth and power of her court.

Ben Jonson put on a further entertainment for the royal party after the midday dinner on Monday, before Anna was due to meet James at nearby Easton Neston. The work, a comedy, began with the appearance of a group of clowns, their leader dressed "in a pair of breeches which were made to come up to his neck, with his arms out at his pockets, and a cap drowning his face." But the crowds of country people had by now grown so large and noisy that each time he attempted to give his opening speech he was drowned out and the farewell speech, which was to be presented by a gentleman's young son, had to be abandoned altogether.[71]

When Anna and her train arrived that afternoon at Easton Neston—the Northamptonshire seat of Sir George Fermor—James was unusually unbothered by the vast numbers in her retinue. It was obvious that his wife was at last rejoicing in their good fortune and he greeted her in high spirits, asking Southampton "if he did not think his Annie looked passing well." He then picked up his daughter Elizabeth, adding "my little Bessy too is not an ill favoured wench and may outshine her mother one of these days."[72]

The royal family traveled together the following day to the seat of the Earl of Cumberland at Grafton. Anne Clifford's mother was estranged from her husband and was forbidden from staying overnight, even on this special occasion. The nobility and higher gentry had many couples trapped in unhappy marriages, cursing "their parents even unto the pit of hell for coupling them together."[73] Arbella Stuart's uncle and aunt Henry and Grace Cavendish were one such couple and the Puritan "Memorial" had complained how the nobility frequently took up with women other than their wives.* But although Cumberland lived openly with his mistress neither James nor Anna seems to have been troubled by the Earl's living arrangements. Indeed, Cumberland's daughter noticed that the Queen showed no favor to the respectable elderly ladies (such as Lady Scrope) who had

---

*The lives of ordinary couples were more easily controlled. The Duke of Stettin's diary describes a wooden horse—"a long large tree or beam, with a seat made upon it, reaching far over the water"—which he and his secretary spotted outside the gates of Rochester. When they asked about it they were told that in England neighbors were expected to spy on each other and if any marital differences were noted the couple had to appear before a magistrate. If it was determined that the husband was at fault, he had to pay a fine; if the wife was at fault, then he was punished anyway, "for not having been able to keep up his authority." The wife, meanwhile, was "placed on the above mentioned chair and ducked three times into the water up to the neck by the boys who roam about in the streets. When she is well drenched and well shamed, she returns home to her husband, who after the custom of the country, gives her comfort by getting her dried with warm cloths, especially in winter time." Gerschow, "Stettin," p. 65.

surrounded Elizabeth but plenty to beautiful women like Essex's sister Lady Rich, who lived openly with Lord Mountjoy and had several illegitimate children by him.*

This apparent harmony was shattered, however, by the less than generous attitude of the English courtiers to James's Scots friends. Even Cumberland was unable to disguise his contempt for James's rough-and-ready entourage. Having gone to great lengths to entertain the royal family with banquets, speeches "and delicate presents," he spoiled it all by taking on one of James's Scots favorites, Henry Alexander, in a joust and almost killing him. The ill will continued once the court had made its way back to Windsor. There were only a limited number of rooms for the nobility in the castle and the English and Scots squabbled bitterly over the division of lodgings. But the court was universally fascinated and delighted by their attractive new queen, despite her Scots accent.

Anna was England's first queen consort since Catherine Parr and the first to have been a royal princess since Catherine of Aragon. "She gives great contentment to the world in her fashion and courteous behaviour to the people," the diplomat Sir Dudley Carleton wrote to a friend—his only complaint being that she was yet to admit anyone English other than Lucy Bedford to her Privy Chamber. Prince Henry was the object of still more curiosity. The parting speech Ben Jonson had written for a young gentleman to deliver at Althorp had depicted him as the rising sun for a new generation and, with notable foresight, a martial alternative to his peace-loving father:

> O shoot up fast in spirit, as in years;
> That when upon her head proud Europe wears
> Her statliest tire, you may appear thereon
> The richest gem, without a paragon
> Shine bright and fixed and the artic star:
> And when slow time hath made you fit for war,

*In 1605 Mountjoy eventually persuaded his chaplain, William Laud, to marry them, despite the fact that Lady Rich's husband was still living. Laud complained that this deferred his preferment through Church ranks for some years, but in the end it did not prevent him being made Archbishop of Canterbury.[74]

Look over the strict ocean, and think where
You may but lead us forth.[75]

Henry was invested with the Order of the Garter at Windsor Castle on 2 July, alongside the Earls of Southampton and Pembroke, the Duke of Lennox, the Earl of Mar, and the King of Denmark (in absentia). It was the first time in nearly half a century that a Chapter of the Garter was to be held, and when the ceremony took place in St. George's Chapel all eyes were on Henry. The Duke of Stettin had seen the banners and coats of arms of the few Garters still living, as well as the silver shields that replaced them when the Garters died. He had also seen the tomb of Prince Henry's namesake, Henry VIII, which he described as being "of good Lydian stone, the emblemata of brass and bell-metal, a work so large that it would take not less than forty carts to remove it."[76] He had heard that it was to stand in the center of the choir, but it was not quite finished—and it never would be: Henry VIII is buried in the choir, but in a vault under a plain black ledger stone.

The Princess Elizabeth stood with Lady Anne Clifford in what she called "the shrine"—probably Edward IV's Chantry Chapel—and from there they watched Prince Henry being represented to his mother in his Garter robes. Prince Henry's performance during the rituals was judged as being flawless. The formidable Henry Howard and Admiral Nottingham admired his "quick, witty answers, princely carriage, and reverend performing his obeyance at the altar, all of which seemed very strange unto them and the rest of the beholders, considering his tender age."[77]

The day should have ended well, but that evening Anna showed a side to her character that the English had not seen so far. As de Rosni had remarked upon in his memoirs, Anna enjoyed intrigue and faction. In choosing the company of Lady Bedford, whose husband had taken part in the Essex revolt, and Essex's sister, Lady Rich, she had chosen friends of a very particular kind and she could not resist pouring salt in old wounds by now asking Southampton "why so many great men did so little" to support Essex's revolt. Southampton explained to Anna that once Elizabeth had been "made a party against them" and issued a royal proclamation accusing them of treason they "were forced to yield." But he assured her that "if that course had not been taken, there was none of their private enemies . . . that durst have opposed themselves."[78] Southampton's enemy, Grey of Wilton, who was listening in to their conversation, begged to differ: Grey had led the "little army" Elizabeth had sent to the City to suppress the revolt and he objected that his troops could easily have crushed Southampton and the other rebels whatever had happened. The two men drew their swords. Anna angrily ordered them to "remember where they were" and at that the guard escorted them to their chambers, from where the Council had them taken to the Tower. To Anna's irritation James released them almost immediately—but Grey's freedom was to last only a matter of days. The talkative poet Anthony Copley was under arrest and he intended to save his skin by naming as many of the Bye conspirators as he could.

PART THREE

Times go by turns, and chances change by course,
From foul to fair, from better hap to worse.
—ROBERT SOUTHWELL, Poet and Jesuit

CHAPTER SEVEN

"AN ANOINTED KING"

James and Anna Are Crowned, July–August 1603

T he secrets of the Bye plot unraveled quickly after Anthony Copley's arrest. The gentleman poet made a series of confessions, culminating on 14 July in a document outlining most of the plot's details. He named the priests William Watson and William Clark, Sir Griffin Markham, George Brooke and Grey of Wilton as planning an attempted kidnap of the King. The priests, used to hiding from the authorities, evaded capture until well into August, but the others were rounded up within the month.

Grey was arrested first, on 12 July. Four days later a frightened George Brooke wrote to the Bishop of London from hiding, insisting "that he and the Lord Grey do rather deserve thanks and favour for diverting and breaking the plot, than to be imprisoned."[1] On the same day Sir John Byron led a group of pursuivants to Sir Griffin Markham's house at Beskwood and Sir Griffin fled into the forest. Byron warned the Council that it would be impossible to arrest him there even if Byron had 1,000 men to back him. It was here that Robin Hood was said to have evaded the Sheriff of Nottingham. Sir Griffin, however, gave himself up on 23 July. Brooke had already done so on the day after his letter was sent. He hoped the authorities would believe that his actions could all be explained by his offer to the King in Berwick that he become a government spy.

Brooke buckled quickly as he did his best to prove what an effective spy he had been. Within hours of his arrival at the Tower he was volunteering that his brother, Lord Cobham, had known of the Bye plot and had a more dangerous plot of his own, the Main plot, whose aim was not merely to kidnap the King but to overthrow him in favor of Arbella Stuart. He claimed that Cobham had written to Arbella and received answers. Cobham was already being questioned. His requests to travel abroad, his blood connection to Brooke and his obvious dissatisfaction with the new regime had made him a suspect even before Brooke had opened his mouth. He was not yet in the Tower, however, and he admitted to nothing save that he had corresponded with Arbella and had then burned the letters. This he explained by informing his interrogators that his kinswoman Frances Kirton, who was in Arbella's service, "had solicited him divers times about the Lady Arbella" and that he had only responded to requests for contact—intriguingly, Kirton is the name of the Earl of Hertford's lawyer, whom Arbella had been keen to approach at Christmas about a marriage to Edward Seymour. It appears Cobham was trying to embarrass Cecil with a reminder of his past interest in Arbella as Elizabeth's potential heir. As Arbella had already discovered, however, Cecil was not easily intimidated on this matter.

Ralegh's association with Cobham made it likely that he too would be interviewed and on the morning of 18 July, when he was walking on the terrace at Windsor waiting to join the King for the day's hunting, Cecil approached him. He informed Ralegh, "as from the King," that he was to meet with the Lords in the Council Chamber and warned that they "have some questions to ask you."[2] Ralegh coolly assured the Councilors he knew nothing of any plot, but after the meeting he began to wonder how much was already known. Copley was, at this very moment, telling his inquisitors that there was a plan "for the betraying a part of the navy into Sir Walter Ralegh's hands."[3] Ralegh only guessed, however, that Brooke was betraying Cobham. It seemed to him that he could still escape a treason trial if he distanced himself from his old friend and, to this end, he wrote a note to the Council suggesting that they interview Aremberg's agent, Matthew la Renzi.

On 19 May la Renzi was interviewed. He admitted that he had carried several letters from Cobham to Aremberg and had returned answers. When Cobham was confronted with this evidence he claimed the letters were about nothing more than "dogs and ambling mares and such like things."[4] Brooke, however, was now accusing his brother of soliciting up to 600,000 crowns from France and Spain to help him overthrow James and replace him with Arbella. He also claimed that Cobham had asked him to tell Arbella to contact Philip III and the Archdukes offering peace and toleration of religion if they supported her title. He said Sir Griffin Markham and Grey of Wilton had known of the plot and that Grey was planning a further plot of his own in which he would use his command in the Low Countries to provide him with an army. That night Cobham was placed in the Tower. Come the morning, the shaken man was shown Ralegh's letter. He read it twice, unbelieving the first time. On the second, he cried out, "O wretch, O traitor!" three or four times, and then in fury and despair he told them, "I will tell you all truly."[5]

Cobham's revenge on Ralegh was fulsome. He claimed that the plot to put Arbella on the throne was all Ralegh's idea, "that he had never entered this course but at his instigation, and that he would never let him alone." Cobham outlined that the plan was for him to "travel to the Archduke, from thence to Spain for the money, for that Archduke was but poor, and from thence to return to Jersey to Sir Walter Ralegh."[6] They were to discuss how best to distribute the money as and when public discontent presented opportunities for revolt. Cobham's servant, Matthew Questor, added further details implicating Ralegh. Cobham had sent Questor to see Aremberg after the envoy's arrival, hoping to arrange a secret meeting. When Questor returned with the news that Aremberg had insisted that any meeting be cleared with Cecil, Cobham was with Ralegh, but he had made no effort to keep Questor's information secret or to hide his disappointment.

It was now Ralegh's turn to be taken to the Tower. Sir John Peyton, the Lieutenant of the Tower, had seen many brave men collapse in the face of ruin and death. Even the Earl of Essex had lost his nerve after a visit from his chaplain, confessing his crimes and casting blame on his friends and family, before recovering his courage for the scaffold. But Peyton was still shocked by the effect the Tower had on Ralegh. "I never saw so strange a dejected mind as in Sir Walter Ralegh. I am extremely cumbered with him," he complained to Cecil: "five or six times in a day he sends for me in such passions as I see his fortitude is [not] competent to support his grief."[7] It was not only the fear of death that had reduced Ralegh to this state, it was the shame of impending disgrace. He wrote to his wife, Bess, in despair:

> All my services, hazards and expenses for my country: plantings, discoveries, fights, counsels and whatsoever else, malice hath now covered over . . . Woe, woe, woe be unto him by whose falsehood we are lost . . . Oh what will my poor servants think at their return when they hear I am accused to be Spanish . . . Oh intolerable infamy. Oh God I cannot resist these thoughts. I cannot live to think how I am derided, to think of the expectation of my enemies, the scorns I shall receive, the cruel words of lawyers, the infamous taunts and despites, to be made a wonder and a spectacle.

Ralegh then swore to his wife that he was innocent of treason—"Be bold of my innocence, for God to whom I offer life and soul knows it."[8] Many since have believed him, but Ralegh was a fluent liar. Ralegh had every reason to want to see the back of James and from his perspective Arbella would have been an excellent replacement. Her aunt, Mary Shrewsbury, was a family friend.* She was acceptable to

---

*Henry Howard's letters to James the previous year had complained that Arbella's aunt, Lady Shrewsbury, was trying to persuade Elizabeth to accept Lady Ralegh back at court, from which she had been banished for marrying Ralegh behind the Queen's back. Usually this letter has been taken to refer to Bess of Hardwick, but Bess was the dowager Lady Shrewsbury and the current Lady Shrewsbury was Mary Cavendish.

the Catholic powers and Ralegh, being open-minded on religious matters, was not averse to toleration of religion. Furthermore, contrary to the belief of some of his posthumous admirers, there was no pressing reason for him not to take money from Spain. Even the fervently Protestant servant of Lord Hundson, racked in April "on his assertion as to the King's favouring Catholics," intended to go to Spain for help. It was the only possible source of the funds necessary to support a rebellion.[9]

The government's case against Ralegh was presented in a prosecution document that focused on Cobham's furious reaction to Ralegh's letter. If Ralegh had not known what he was plotting, why would he have been so concerned about it? And if Ralegh did know about the plot, why did he do nothing? The Earl of Southampton later expressed his belief that Ralegh had intended to betray the plot when Cobham reached Jersey, "and to have delivered them up to the King and made his peace."[10] Cobham himself confessed that he had feared that this was Ralegh's intention all along, but even if this was the case, by keeping such information to himself he was, at best, putting James's life at risk; the more likely truth was that he was trying to keep his options open. The evidence against Ralegh was, however, largely circumstantial. Cobham and Brooke, by contrast, had made fulsome confessions—and now had to face the fact that they were likely to be executed for treason.

James was to issue pardons to celebrate the coronation on 25 July and Cobham and Brooke looked to their former brother-in-law, Robert Cecil, to ask for the King's mercy. Cecil had loved their sister, Elizabeth Brooke, and never remarried after her death in 1598. They hoped that he might take pity on them for her sake. Cobham swore to him that although he had had treasonous thoughts he had not done anything treasonous: "For God is my witness, when I saw [Arbella] I resolved never to hazard my estate for her . . . God make you apprehensive of the affliction I am in . . . and dispose your heart to yield me comfort." Brooke also pleaded, "I perceive that I have fallen quick into hell . . . yet do I . . . entreat that you will not be weary to move the king for grace, and that he will not exempt us out of this great and universal jubilee."[11]

But as no news of mercy came Ralegh appears to have decided on suicide as his way out. "I know it is forbidden to destroy ourselves," he wrote to his wife, "but I trust it is forbidden in this sort, that we destroy not ourselves despairing of God's mercy. The mercy of God is immeasurable, the cognitions of men comprehend it not . . . Far is it for me to be tempted with Satan; I am only tempted with sorrow, whose sharp teeth devour my heart."[12] He asked her to forgive Henry Howard, "my heavy enemy," but could not forgive his old ally, Cecil: "I thought he would never forsake me in extremity: I would not have done it him, God knows." He warned his wife that she must pretend not to feel Cecil's betrayal. As Master of the Wards, he would be the guardian of their child. Ralegh listed his debts and urged her to marry again "to avoid poverty," though adding that he could not bear the thought that she might love her second husband: "let him be but thy politic husband, but let thy son be thy beloved for he is part of me and I live in him."[13]

Shortly after this letter was written, on 27 July, Ralegh took out a dagger and stabbed himself in the chest in front of Sir John Peyton, with whom he was having dinner. It was not, however, a fatal blow. Something held Ralegh back and despite his long experience with weapons he struck a rib. Cecil, who was in the Tower interviewing other prisoners, found Ralegh bleeding heavily but he judged the wound "in truth rather a cut than a stab." Perhaps Ralegh was unbalanced and had made a genuine gesture toward killing himself. If he died before his trial, it would have protected his estates from confiscation—although he would have hoped they were protected anyway since he had put them in his son's name the previous autumn. Perhaps it was all a ploy. Ralegh's letter to his wife would be circulated as evidence of his innocence and the wickedness of his enemies. His secretary, Edward Hancock, is also believed to have killed himself on the same day, which suggests the timing was planned—and there was now one less witness against him.

❈　　❈　　❈

An unofficial truce was declared between James and the Catholic gentry early in July. Sir Thomas Tresham, whose son Francis had signed Watson's oath, had led a deputation to Hampton Court and presented the King with a proclamation of allegiance signed by a large number of leading members of the Catholic laity.* James, in return, announced the remission of recusancy fines. If Catholics would also obey the law, he told the deputation, the highest places in the state should be open to them.

The Jesuits were also pondering compromise. Their Principal, Robert Persons, had written a letter on 6 July, which they received later in the month, extinguishing any hopes of a Spanish invasion or of papal support for a Catholic rising. Addressed to the spy Anthony Rivers, the letter opened with a survey of the numerous attempts to reintroduce Catholicism since the accession of Elizabeth. These disasters had culminated in the abject failure of Catholics to make "some show of union amongst themselves and of their forces at the Queen's death." If Catholics had done something to show their strength, it would have earned them the respect of the Catholic powers, but instead, Persons scoffed, they had allowed themselves to be fooled into thinking James would become a Catholic or offer toleration. Courtiers "ran after him" and "such applause was here at the new King's entrance, as if he had been the greatest Catholic in the world."

Persons warned that the Spanish and the Vatican were unmoved by complaints "about the preferring of Scottishmen. [They] say that this was a matter to be expected, and that the English are well served that would admit a stranger and nation to their government without any condition of capitulation at all." It was now too late to prevent James becoming king. He had taken possession of the country and would be very difficult to remove. There would be no invasion before September and no papal support for a rising. Persons suggested that Catholics now proceed with the utmost care. He drew attention to the fact that ambassadors were queuing up, "to seek [James's] friendship according to their need or interest." The best they could do was to ensure that Spain did not make peace without a provision for toleration of religion. The ambassador, who had yet to arrive, was to be

*Thomas Tresham built the famous triangular lodge at Rushton. His son was later involved in the Gunpowder Plot.

persuaded that without toleration the English government would continue to aid the Dutch surreptitiously and that English Catholics would turn to France for help. In the meantime, Persons warned, "Catholics must take heed lest some passion break out." The discovery of further plots could only lead to further oppression, "which is the reason why his Holiness has ordained now sundry times how to advertise thither that all such rash attempts be avoided."[14]

Unfortunately, now that the Jesuits only hoped for toleration, as the seculars long had, they would discover just how difficult this was going to be to achieve.

❊   ❊   ❊

On 20 July the Venetian ambassador was granted a royal audience at Hampton Court. He arrived with the satisfaction of knowing that William Piers was now under lock and key. The pirate's luck had turned against him in Tunis, where a number of his crew had deserted after the booty was sold, forcing him to put to sea shorthanded. There being no honor among thieves, a friend and fellow pirate called William Cunliffe had seized the opportunity to board his ship and steal his plunder. Cunliffe had then sailed back to England with Piers in hot pursuit. As soon as Cunliffe reached shore he was clapped in irons and Piers met the same fate when he was recognized while attempting to flee London for Portsmouth.

Piers had been brought to Scaramelli's house on 7 July, "like a murderer," with a mob in pursuit. He proved to be "under twenty five years of age, squarely built and bold looking."[15] When Scaramelli questioned him he told a stream of lies and so the Venetian put him in "a prison that he merits, loaded with all the irons and chains that he can carry." He intended to torture Piers until he revealed where he had kept his treasure, assuring the Senate that the young man's courage was a mere façade and he would quickly crack. Within a week, however, he was informed that Piers was spending four ducats a day on good food and sweetened wine. Scaramelli chose to interpret this as the consequence of his having fallen "prey to despair and the dread of death."[16] There was, however, the niggling concern that Piers might somehow have planned to escape execution and Scaramelli wanted James to give him assurances that Piers would not be set free.

Hampton Court, with its forest of turrets and gilded weather vanes, made a deep impression on the ambassador. It was "far larger than the other seven palaces belonging to the crown," he reported: "They say Hampton Court has one thousand eight hundred inhabitable rooms, or at least all of them with doors that lock. The furnishings of the royal apartments are the richest that the crown possesses." This magnificence was, however, seated amid death and disease. In the tents around the palace two or three of the court's hangers-on were dying every day from plague.

Scaramelli entered the royal presence "midst a babble of voices discussing the plot(s)." He was aware that two of the Bye conspirators were "priests, of a kind," but as far as he could see, the causes of the conspiracies had more to do with frustrated ambition and hatred of Elizabeth's Councilors than religion: "both nobles and people thought that the advent of the new King would mean the downfall of certain members of the Council, instead of which those persons have managed things so cleverly that they are in greater authority than ever," he observed, accurately enough. He was convinced that James would soon be facing more problems since the Scots courtiers were only interested in making money and the King himself appeared "lost in bliss," pursuing his stags.

James gave Scaramelli his word that Piers would stay in prison and talked cheerfully to the Venetian until the new Chamberlain, Lord Thomas Howard, told Scaramelli that the Queen was waiting for him in her apartments. He knew the competition for Anna's favor was almost as ferocious as it was for that of James. The Earl of Worcester was soon bemoaning that "the plotting and malice amongst these ladies is so great, that I think envy hath tied an invisible snake around their necks, to sting each other to death."[17] Frances Pranell, the beautiful wife of the Earl of Hertford, was Anna's latest favorite. She had run off and married a poor vintner's son for her first husband and taken the opposite course with the second, marrying the aged Earl for his money and in the process breaking the heart of the young knight,

Sir George Rodney, to whom she was promised. The wretched man had written a suicide note to her in his own blood before falling on his sword.

When Anna saw Scaramelli she rose with a bow. Scaramelli mounted the steps to Anna's throne and kissed her hand. "She remained standing, all grace and fairness, of a fine height and moderately fine presence." He was told to speak French, as she did not speak Italian. He paid her some formal compliments and said, "No other Prince had a higher esteem for her Majesty than the Republic, for reasons too long to relate. At that she laughed fancying that I alluded to her being a Catholic, and returned thanks. After a brief reply I again kissed her hand and took my leave."[18] Scaramelli was unable to see the royal children at Hampton Court, as they were being installed at Oatlands Palace in Surrey with their own Households, but he visited them later in the month. He found Prince Henry "little of body and quick of spirit," but also ceremonious beyond his years. He had put his hat on during the interview and gravely asked Scaramelli to do the same. He then gave "a long discourse on his exercises, dancing, tennis, the chase" before escorting Scaramelli down a flight of steps and up another to see his little sister, whom Scaramelli found surrounded by her servants under a canopy of state.[19] Cobham's wife, Lady Kildare, had fallen from grace and Lucy Bedford's mother, Lady Harington of Exton, had been given charge of the care of the Princess Elizabeth in her place.* Her husband, meanwhile, had been raised to the peerage on 21 July along with ten others, including Anna's host at Althorp, Sir Roger Spencer, and two Catholics: Lord Thomas Howard, who became Earl of Suffolk, and the recusant Sir John Petre, who became Lord Petre of Writtle. The following three days leading up to the coronation had seen other celebrations. On the twenty-second the Earl of Worcester was made Earl Marshal (senior officer of the peerage in England), and on 23 July James knighted 300 individuals in the gardens at Whitehall. James's sale of the honor had become increasingly outrageous. Francis Bacon called it "this almost prostituted title"

*The Prince's chief officer was the linguist and naturalist Sir Thomas Chaloner, whom Cecil had sent to Scotland before Elizabeth's death and who had become a great favorite of James.

and the courtier Philip Gawdy described recent recipients of the honor as "a scum of such as it would make a man sick to think of them." They included the sons of London pedlars and a clapped-out lawyer who bought the honor for under £8.[20]

The twenty-fourth of July, the eve of the coronation, was the only time a king could create Knights of the Bath, but this was strictly for individuals of some rank. The ceremony began with the sixty-two men James had chosen riding from St. James's to the court at White-hall, where they "made show with their squires and pages about the tiltyard, and after went into the park of St James, and there lighted all from their horses, and went up to the King's Majesty's presence in the gallery."[21] Those who received the honor included Oliver Cromwell of Hinchingbrooke and James Hay, a Scot whom de Rosni had brought over from France and whom even the English found charming. Cecil was particularly pleased with the choice of Hay; he considered him "an excellent good instrument to conserve his Majesty's good opinions" and pressed for him to be added to the Bedchamber along with Sir Philip Herbert, the younger brother of the Earl of Pembroke.[22] According to the royalist historian Edward Hyde, Earl of Clarendon, Herbert "pretended to no other qualification than to understand horses and dogs very well," but since James spent so much time with horses and dogs that was not such a bad recommendation. He was also rather pretty and it appears that if Cecil was unaware of James's sexuality before he came to England, he knew something of his tastes by now, and with Herbert he had picked well. As Clarendon records, he was "the first who drew the King's eyes towards him with affection" and the only Englishman promoted to the Bedchamber before the appearance of the beautiful George Villiers.

❋   ❋   ❋

By ancient tradition the coronation was held on a holy day. James's choice, 25 July, was the feast day of his namesake, St. James, and an eminently suitable choice. The hotter sort of Protestant disapproved of holy days, but the commemoration of the life of an apostle was less offensive than that of an ordinary saint. The only difficulty with the date was that it fell during the height of summer, when the plague spread fastest, and the current epidemic was proving the worst in living memory.

A proclamation issued on 6 July had announced that James's formal entry into London would be abandoned until the winter, leaving the crafted wooden triumphal archways under which James would pass to rot where they stood. (In the event the plague was so bad that his formal entry could not take place until the following March.) A further proclamation on 11 July had limited the numbers of noblemen and gentlemen who could attend the coronation and canceled the St. James's Fair, traditionally held in Westminster on 25 July. The area around St. Paul's grew quiet in the brief lull that followed before people flooded back into London for the coronation, stubbornly ignoring the mounting death toll. About a thousand people were now dying each week, "in every house grief striking up an alarum: servants crying out for masters: wives for husbands, parents for children, children for their mothers," Dekker recalled. At night it was like being boarded up "in a vast silent charnel house . . . hung (to make it more hideous) with lamps dimly and slowly burning, in hollow and glimmering corners."[23]

When the great day of the coronation finally arrived low clouds hung over London and the streets reeked of the rosemary and other herbs used to ward off infection. In Newgate, a terrified Catholic prisoner wrote to a friend describing how they were waiting in desperation for the expected royal pardon: "We are in great danger of the sickness. The bell of St Sepulchres parish never ceasing day nor night. The common jail on the other side of us is diversely affected, many of them being now sick and others buried of the plague. . . ." The prisoner had heard rumors that Catholics were to be excluded from the pardon and was so certain he could not survive that he asked his friend if he would to divide his possessions after his death.[24] The rumors were correct. Catholics and those accused of witchcraft were indeed to be excluded, along with the Bye and Main plotters.

Sir John Harington also remained under lock and key. New bars had been put on his windows and he was checked hourly to ensure that he could not escape the prison or his debts. But there was good news for Piers the pirate. Despite James's promises to Scaramelli, he was released. Too many powerful men still had a vested interest in piracy.

As the crowds began to gather, the authorities did their best to keep them away from Westminster. This was not only out of fear of disease. There was the possibility of riots against the new king. Catholic feeling had inspired some of the dissent: ordinary people were also counted among the ranks of recusants and instead of losing land and wealth to fines they lost more immediate things such as the beds they slept on and the cow whose milk fed their children. But trade had also been badly disrupted by the plague and many people were going hungry. Guards were placed at the City gates to keep people from the roads and Scaramelli heard that the death penalty had been decreed for anyone bringing boats up the Thames. James's subjects, however, refused to be intimidated. Boats filled the river that morning and their occupants proved well placed to see the King and Queen.

Instead of the customary ride from the Tower through the City, James and Anna traveled the short distance between Whitehall Stairs and the Privy Stairs of Westminster in a gilded barge. The crowds saw they were dressed in red velvet and ermine and crowned with large golden coronets. Anna's pale blond hair hung over her shoulders in a symbol of modesty and chastity, its bright color shining in the spitting rain. James remained as stiff as always, but Anna played to the gallery and a witness records that "she so mildly saluted her new subjects, that the women, weeping, cried out with one voice, 'God bless the royal queen! Welcome to England, long to live and continue!' "[25] At ten o'clock the royal couple disembarked from the barge for the short walk toward the Abbey. The buildings on the route were hung with white cloth and the side streets with violet cloth, which was stripped down as soon as the procession passed by and divided among the crowd.

The first sight of the procession was of twelve heralds carrying wands and dressed in cloth of gold with open tabards displaying the arms of the four kingdoms. They were followed by the merchant companies and city officers, the Mayor of London coming last. "All wore long gowns of red cloth with sleeves," Scaramelli reported. Two drummers and ten trumpeters came next, then twenty-five judges and the Lord Chief Justice wearing "a broad gold chain, as wide as the collar of the order." This was the collar of SS, which started life as the Lancastrian livery collar. Behind the judge came the Knights of the Bath dressed in long purplish-red robes, "reaching half to the knee," and carrying white plumed hats and gilded swords with a "leather belt and tassels; no other device." The peers came next: about thirty barons, then about fifteen earls, each dressed more richly than the last; the barons in scarlet cloth and ermine, carrying plumed hats, the earls in scarlet velvet and ermine, carrying "a cap of crimson velvet with fillet of ermine and a small crown of plain gold, with a small thin sceptre in their hands."

The coronation of the Kings and Queens of England had been held in the Abbey since it was built by Edward the Confessor and although this was to be a Protestant ceremony only the most modest changes had been made to the pre-Reformation ritual.[26] Archbishop Whitgift belonged to a school of thought that believed the Anglican Church to be a purified Catholic Church directly descended from the primitive Christian church. He was anxious that the coronation be a visible demonstration of religious continuity and Scaramelli reported that James was equally keen to "have the full ceremony so as not to lose his prerogative." It would emphasize that he drew his rights from God rather than man. The changes planned for the service were characterized chiefly by a literal translation of the service into English and the offering of communion in both kinds—a privilege the Catholic Church usually restricted to the Kings of France or those crowned in Rome.[27] This was enough, however, to keep many Catholic ambassadors away. Aremberg, who had been embarrassed by the Main plot and was desperate to demonstrate his good intentions, was one of the few Catholic ambassadors to attend. Scaramelli's dispatch was based on reports of the service.

The procession entered the Abbey at the west door. Three earls walked abreast carrying swords embodying three aspects of the sword of state. The first sword was the pointless Curtana, the sword of mercy; the second represented justice for churchmen, the third justice for the laity.* The Constable of England, the Lord Great Chamberlain and the Earl Marshal also walked abreast. The honor of carrying the crown of St. Edward the Confessor went to Lord Buckhurst, who bore it on a velvet cushion: James later explained to Prince Charles in his "Pattern for a King's Inauguration" that it was a symbol of his people's love. Other relics included the scepter of St. Edward, the hard-stone chalice of St. Edward with its paten or communion plate, the royal spurs and another scepter surmounted with a dove.

Trumpets blew as James entered the Abbey. He walked under a canopy of cloth of gold supported by four silvered staves hung with a silver bell and carried by the barons of the Cinque Ports of Hastings, Romney, Hythe, Dover and Sandwich. The Bishop of Durham, Tobie Matthew, and the Bishop of London, Richard Bancroft, had the honor of greeting him. It was a mark of the dignity of the reformed Church, their submission to the King and the importance of episcopacy—a message to the Puritans in the congregation. "The King was followed by the gentlemen of his court, with vests of crimson velvet, reaching to the knees. Then one hundred and fifty halberdiers of the guard, in the ordinary crimson livery but with extra gold embroidery, which covered the breast and back." The choir sang as the bishops accompanied James to the railed dais between the choir and the high altar. It was covered with tapestries and scarlet velvet, and two octagonal pedestals, each six steps high and covered with embroidered taffeta, were erected on it about seven feet apart; the one for James was set a little higher than the one for Anna. On each was a chair covered in silver brocade, with a seat and cushion in crimson silk.

Two other chairs were set at the base of the thrones for James and Anna to sit on before they were crowned. All four faced the altar. Between the dais and the altar was the wood and gesso chair of St. Edward containing the Stone of Scone, taken from the Scots by Edward I—the chair on which James would be crowned.[†] According to a "prophetical fancy" quoted by the seventeenth-century century historian Arthur Wilson,

*The tradition dates back to the reign of Richard the Lionheart.

†It was returned to Scotland just a few years ago.

Fate hath designed
That wherefore this Stone
The Scots shall find
There they shall hold the throne.[28]

As James took his place, Anna was processed into the Abbey under a canopy like the King's, accompanied by Arbella Stuart; both wore dresses that bared their bosom. Behind walked the countesses in plain robes of crimson velvet lined with ermine, their hair worn up and their coronets carried under their left arm. When Anna reached the dais she and James faced the altar from the seats below the thrones. The altar in front of them, decked with gold brocade and flowered yellow silk, was covered with basins, flagons and cups in the Protestant fashion. The Archbishop, supported by the Admiral and the Chancellor and led by the Earl Marshal, walked to the four corners of the dais and the herald cried: "Listen, listen, listen!" He then formally presented the King to the people, "calling on any who denied James the Sixth of Scotland and First of England to be legitimate King of England to say so now, otherwise he would be held a traitor." It was a novel addition to the ceremony and some may have reflected that it supported the contention of the Bye plotters Watson and Clark that there could be no treason before the King was crowned. No one, however, spoke against James. The Archbishop announced that he was about to crown His Majesty in the confidence that he would govern his people well and with prayers to God to grant him long life. The congregation shouted in response: "Yea, yea, God save the King!"

Thomas Bilson, Bishop of Winchester, delivered the sermon, which emphasized that James's power came from God and that his subjects were bound to serve him as he was bound to serve God.* Then it was time for James to take the new coronation oath. He swore to

---

*Elizabeth had employed Bilson to write an answer to Dr. William Allen's "Defence of English Catholics" in the 1580s and the result had been a powerful and brilliant work. However, it argued that a king's subjects could rise against him if he broke his coronation oath. His arguments would one day be used against Charles I.

*confirm to the people of England the laws and customs to them granted by the
kings of England, your lawful and religious predecessors, and namely, the laws
customs, and franchises, granted to the clergy by the glorious king St Edward,
your predecessor according to the laws of God, the true profession of the Gospel
established in this Kingdom.*

Archbishop Whitgift had rewritten the oath in favor of the Elizabethan Settlement and it struck at Puritan hopes of a return to the
Protestantism of Edward VI, but also at the exercise of arbitrary royal
power. The bishops then sang the litany and Whitgift opened the ceremony of the anointing with the thanksgiving "Lift up your hearts."
According to Scaramelli: "The oil was taken from a vase, enclosed in a
goblet, and covered with a white cloth, standing on the altar along
with other regalia." He had heard that the oil "was consecrated long
ago, and is kept in the Tower of London." By tradition it had been delivered to St. Thomas of Canterbury by the Blessed Virgin. Mary I
had nevertheless refused to be anointed with it, believing that it had
lost its blessing at the Reformation. Elizabeth had, but she complained to her ladies "that the oil wherewith she was anointed was a
kind of grease and that it smelt ill." Whitgift held the oil and "the
Earls then unrobed the King, leaving him in vest and hose of white
satin, unlaced; he then knelt before the altar, and the Archbishop
anointed him on various parts of his person, touching the skin."* The
Archbishop first anointed James's palms, then his breast, spine, shoulder and head, praying:

*Let these hands be anointed, as Kings and prophets have been anointed, and as
Samuel did anoint David to be King, that thou maist be blessed, and established a King in his Kingdom over this people, who the Lord thy God hath
given thee to rule and govern . . . Look down Almighty God with thy
favourable countenance upon this glorious King . . . Give unto him of the dew
of heaven, and of the vastness of the earth, abundance of corn, and wine and
oil, and plenty of all fruits of thy goodness long to continue, that in his time*

---

*James I was the last monarch to kneel for the anointing.

there may be health in our country, and peace in our kingdom, and that the
glorious dignity of his royal court, may brightly shine as a most clear lightning,
far and wide in the eyes of all men.

The anointing imprinted James with God's mark as King of England. His head was "rubbed with a white handkerchief," then smoothed with the ivory comb of Edward the Confessor, and "he was robed again, but in other vestments: a long vest of crimson velvet lined with white, a Royal tunic over that, the Garter, the sword and collar of the order, over all a mantle of purple brocade." These ancient robes, which had been kept in the St. Edward Chapel for this moment, had also belonged by tradition to Edward the Confessor. The purple color, James later explained to his son Charles, was intended to be redolent of the "ancient purple [which] was of a reddish colour." It represented "the continuance and honour of their function." The resemblance to ecclesiastical garments was also significant, for kings, "as God's deputy—judges upon earth—sit on thrones clad in long robes . . . as mixtae personae . . . being bound to make a reckoning to God for their subjects souls as well as their bodies." Fully robed, James was invested with what were called the Confessor's Spurs—in fact they dated no earlier than the twelfth century.* He was then shown the Imperial Crown before it was replaced on the altar and was led to the gesso seat of St. Edward, containing the Stone of Scone, on which Jacob was said to have rested his head on the plain at Bethel.

The Crown of St. Edward was lifted up. The ambassador to the Duke of Wutternberg described it as "so heavy, with large precious stones, that two bishops had to hold it on [James's] head." An anthem was sung and a ring was placed on the fourth finger of James's left hand. A coronation ring—usually a ruby—had been part of the ceremony since at least the tenth century, but placing it on James's wedding finger was new. The idea may have been inspired by the contention of Mary I and Elizabeth that they were married to their

---

*The ritual of making a knight in the later Middle Ages included the buckling of a pair of spurs to his heels and probably inspired this part of the ceremony.

kingdom; in the future James often referred to himself as England's groom—although this relationship was reflective of a husband's dominance over a wife rather than the partnership suggested by Elizabeth.* With the ring placed on his finger James put on a pair of linen gloves—another part of the official regalia—took off his sword, and placed it on the altar. This "sword of offering" was redeemed with a payment to the Church, symbolizing the belief that the monarch's authority came from God via the Church.

The chief peer, who was to bear the "sword of offering" out of the Abbey, took it up and James was asked by Whitgift to "receive the sceptre, the sign of kingly power." The scepter of St. Edward, first seen on the coins of Edward the Confessor in 1057, was described by Scaramelli as "two spans long . . . the staff touches the ground, and has the globe and crown on the top." James held it in his right hand as the Archbishop delivered the rod and dove into the left, saying, "Receive the rod of virtue and equity. Learn to make much of the Godly and to terrify the wicked. Show the way to those that go astray. Offer thy hand to those that fall. Repress the proud. Lift up the lowly, that our Lord may open to thee the door." The rod appeared to be made of solid gold but at the time of the Commonwealth, when the ancient regalia were broken up, Cromwell's men found it was iron covered in silver gilt. Its inspiration came from the biblical reference to the Messiah coming to rule with "a rod of iron." The dove represented the gentler pastoral role of the King and was a peculiarly English insignia. Europeans preferred the imperial eagle.

When the Archbishop's prayer was finished he blessed James, who in turn kissed him and the assisting bishops. Finally the Archbishop, the Admiral, the Chancellor, and two bishops carrying the crown led the King to the octagonal dais and placed him on the throne. The earls then covered their heads and took the oath, then the barons, but uncovered. Finally the earls, Councilors and barons knelt before the

---

*The ruby was rivaled in value only by the sapphire, which was considered more feminine and often represented chastity. The blue ring carried to Scotland on Elizabeth's death was a sapphire.

King on a red brocaded cushion, kissed the King's hand and touched the crown. Some kissed it, but one went still further: "The Earl of Pembroke, a handsome youth, who is always with the King and always joking with him, actually kissed his Majesty's face, whereupon the King laughed and gave him a little cuff." As the congregation looked on aghast, a herald shouted "Listen!" three more times. It was Anna's turn to be anointed and crowned.

The Queen was brought to the altar and a white veil, signifying chastity, was held above her head as the Archbishop prayed over her. She had the last of the Virgin's ointment (new oil would have to be made for the coronation of Charles I). A scepter and an ivory rod were placed in her hands and a ring placed on a finger of her right hand. Her countesses put on their coronets and she was conducted to her throne a little beneath her husband's. "Then the King approached the altar, and from the hands of the Archbishop he received the Lord's Supper in bread and wine out of the chalice, which was borne before him." Anna, however, remained seated. She had made it clear to James and the Archbishop that morning that as a Catholic she would not take their communion.

As the service drew to an end James and Anna were once more presented to the people, this time as King and Queen of England. "They then retired to some chambers behind the altar, and the King exchanged his crown for a lighter one, and the Queen doffed her crimson mantle and remained in black. They took some refreshments, and then went back in the same order as that in which they had arrived." It was almost four o'clock in the afternoon, five hours since they had disembarked from the royal barge. James and Anna waved to the crowd for a time before retiring at last to Whitehall.[29]

Five years later the Earl of Hertford would find the clergyman who had married him to Catherine Grey in December 1560, thereby legitimizing their children—the rightful heirs to the English throne on Elizabeth's death under the will of Henry VIII as confirmed by Parliament. It was, of course, by then all too late. As Shakespeare's Richard II reminds the audience before his enforced abdication, "Not all the water in the rough rude sea, can wash the balm from an anointed King." At the coronation James's dream of becoming King of England came true at last and to stop any doubts he had his first Parliament lay aside Henry's will, as well as the law precluding heirs of foreign birth.

❊   ❊   ❊

As soon as the coronation was over people streamed out of the capital. Some were already infected with the plague and the villages around London became packed with victims carrying their flea-ridden bedding. Sir William Waad, a clerk of the Privy Council, complained to Cecil that in Hampstead they were finding corpses every week in hedgerows, yards, outhouses and barns. As the City emptied, grass began to grow on the usually busy streets of Cheapside and those left behind found that with the City aldermen and other figures of authority gone, the regulations designed to halt the spread of the disease had collapsed.

Waad reported crowds appearing at funerals, strewing the streets with flowers for unmarried girls, "and for bachelors they wear rosemary, as if it were at marriages." At least one victim actually was a bride who fell ill and died on her wedding day, aged twenty-one. Many other victims listed in the parish records were younger still: a "poor boy that died under St John's wall"; a "poor child found at Mistress Bake's door"—and not all are so anonymous. Ben Jonson lost his seven-year-old son on 6 September. People tried to protect themselves by smoking tobacco or chewing orange peel and angelica root. Others used posies of medicinal herbs. One day a "fearful pitiful coach" was seen dashing through the capital, "all hung with rue from the top to the toe of the boot, to keep the leather and the nails from infection; the very nostrils of the horses were stopped with herb grace."[30]

Outside London the court was on the run. Cecil described it as a "camp volant" driven by plague from palace to palace, "up and down so round I think we shall come to York." In mid-September the court settled briefly at the small and ancient palace of Woodstock. "This place is unwholesome all the house standing upon springs," Cecil wrote with a shudder; "it is unsavoury for there is no savour but of cows and pigs. It is uneaseful, for only the King and Queen, with the privy chamber ladies, and some three or four of the Scottish Council, are lodged in the house, and neither Chamberlain, nor one English Councillor have a room."[31] Instead the most powerful men in England lived in tents among which one person a week died of plague.

Philip III's envoy, Don Juan de Tassis, Count of Villamediana, who had finally arrived in England in August, also suffered. He had settled at first in Christ Church College, Oxford, where he made himself very popular with the ladies of the court with his gifts of gloves, hawks' hoods, leather for jerkins and perfume, but within a week or two he had lost one of his servants to plague. He upped and moved to Southampton and to James's disappointment the audience he had hoped to give de Tassis at Woodstock had to be delayed. The Venetian Scaramelli did, however, make an appearance that month. There had been further acts of piracy against the Republic and he was furious that William Piers had been released in the general amnesty at the coronation. What kind of message did that send out to others? That piracy was still supported by the English government?

James, embarrassed, listened to Scaramelli "with extreme impatience, twisting his body about, striking his hands together, and tapping with his foot" before finally shouting, "By God, I'll hang the pirate with my own hands, and my Lord Admiral as well."[32]

As soon as the meeting was over James drew up a proclamation outlawing piracy once and for all. It was issued at the end of September and became the basis of future English law on piracy. Coincidentally it also inspired the first positive example of progress on James's dream of a British union. Admiral Nottingham needed to compensate for the drop in his income after having to forgo piracy and, as he explained to his friends, the simplest way to do so was to make a profitable marriage alliance. His first wife, Elizabeth's cousin, Elizabeth Carey, had died in February. His second was to be a cousin of James: the young Lady Margaret Stuart, daughter of the Duke of Lennox. The marriage united two of the greatest families in England and Scotland—and James, who owed his crown to a similar Anglo-Scots match, was delighted. The age gap between the sixty-eight-year-old victor of the Armada and his young bride was, however, the source of much derision among Nottingham's peers.

"My Lord Admiral ... greatly boasts of his acts the first night," Worcester wrote to Shrewsbury: "the next day he was sick of the ague; but now holds out very well saving that my lady singeth the greatest part of the night—whether to bring him asleep or to keep him awake I leave to your Lordship's judgement, that are more cunning than I in these matters."[33] Even Anna thought the match absurd: "You have guessed right that I would laugh—who would not laugh," she wrote in reply to a letter from her husband; "if I were a poet I would make a song of it and sing it to the tune of three fools well met."[34] Nottingham, however, had the last laugh. He was rewarded with a large pension, and several other Anglo-Scots unions would follow.

Progress was also made on the matter of reform of the Church of England. James had announced that he intended to hold a conference on religion on 1 November, as soon as the winter cold subdued the plague. Meanwhile, he continued to spend most of his time hunting, accompanied by a small group of mainly Scots companions.

Decades later James was remembered on this summer progress dressed in clothes "as green as the grass he trod on, with a feather in his cap, and a horn instead of a sword at his side."[35] To Arbella the endless hunting had seemed "everlasting." They galloped across the farmers' crops, uncaring that famine was following hard on the heels of the plague, and the goodwill that had been extended to James on his journey south continued to vanish. Through the late summer and autumn individuals were indicted for speaking against the King in Sussex, Kent, Essex and Hertfordshire. A saddler complained that "no foreign prince should inherit the crown," a tailor declared that "there were as wise men in England to be king as the King of Scots" and Henry Collyn of Writtle in Essex announced bluntly that he did not "care a turd neither for the king nor his laws."[36] Their feelings, however, were of little consequence while the "better sort" remained loyal and the English court had more sycophants in its ranks than rebels.

Courtiers began imitating James's dismissive attitude to their poorer countrymen, leaving Arbella to complain to her uncle Gilbert

Shrewsbury that "if ever there were such a virtue as courtesy at the court I marvel what is become of it? For I protest I see little or none of it but in the Queen."[37] The late Earl of Essex was once praised for stopping in the street to "vail his bonnet to an oyster wife," but that time was now well and truly past.[38] The old tradition that James saw many times on his journey from Scotland, where the lord of a great house invited all comers to a feast, would die out with the Stuarts. Instead a new courtly extravagance took hold. The entertainments James had been offered in April had convinced him that England was rich enough to support his every whim and Shrewsbury learned from Cecil that "our Sovereign spends £100,000 yearly in his house, which was wont to be but £50,000," and how the Lord Treasurer Buckhurst was "much disquieted how to find money to supply the king's necessities."[39]

Desperate attempts were made to stop the flow of gifts to the Scots but hardly a day passed that autumn without the same men receiving more money or land: a manor in Yorkshire for Sir Thomas Erskine, a pension and a grant for Ramsay, manors and parks in Suffolk for Mar, grants and manors for Sir George Home, a trading license for Argyll. James may have felt that he had to compensate the Scots for failing to find them more places on the Council—something about which they complained loudly—but his munificence was such that Anna was even able to persuade him to grant £2,000 to Barbara Ruthven "in commiseration of her late distress; because, although her family is hateful on account of their abominable attempt against the King, she has shown no malicious disposition."[40] It was particularly remarkable given the fate of her surviving brothers.

When James was at Burghley on 25 April he had issued a royal proclamation accusing them, without any evidence, of "contriving dangerous plots, and desperate attempts against his royal person" and warning that anyone who helped them escape arrest would "answer to the contrary to their uttermost peril."[41] William Ruthven had already escaped to Europe but Patrick was captured and put in the Tower, where he would remain for the next twenty years.* Even that was not

---

*Patrick Ruthven's life has an interesting postscript. When he was eventually released he married the widow of Lord Gerard and one of their daughters married the artist Sir Anthony Vandyke.

the end of the matter. James had insisted that the English court dedicate 5 August to celebrate his escape from the Gowries and it was commemorated in the sermons at court every Tuesday. He may have hoped that this would be taken as warning to future enemies, as he had intended in Scotland, but instead it was taken as evidence that he had failed to grow beyond his role as King of Scotland.

In late September the court moved to Winchester and de Tassis at last had his audience. It proved to be a prickly affair. The envoy kept his hat on until he was halfway down the chamber and then addressed James in Spanish instead of a language they had in common, such as French or Italian. Two days later, however, James arranged for them to meet in private. He was disappointed to discover that de Tassis was not instructed to treat for peace but he was to make preliminary investigations, and it was clear that the Spanish Council had come around to the viewpoint of the Archduke and wanted peace; better still, they would not demand toleration of religion in return. Catholics had poured in to see de Tassis in Oxford and at Southampton, all trying to persuade him that it was in Spain's interest to insist on toleration before they signed any peace settlement, just as Robert Persons suggested they should. One such was Thomas Wintour, the soldier who had been offered money by the Spanish in 1602 to buy the loyalty of discontented Catholics. Unfortunately, once de Tassis had learned the details of the Bye plot he concluded that the English Catholics were too fearful and disunited to be worth supporting, and in October he advised Philip III to ignore their situation in any subsequent negotiations.

The peace conference was arranged for the following spring; meanwhile, the conference of religion was delayed. It was apparent that the plague had not subsided sufficiently for the conference to occur in November and so the date was moved until after Christmas, when it would be held at Hampton Court. The winter months were to be dominated instead by the trials of the Bye and Main plotters.

CHAPTER EIGHT

"THE GOD OF TRUTH AND TIME"
Trial, Judgment and the Dawn of the Stuart Age

Sir Walter Ralegh recovered his courage after his failed suicide bid in July and determined to fight for his life. He knew that those who were indicted for treason were almost never found innocent. A treason trial was considered to be a public demonstration of guilt, not an opportunity to clear one's name. The evidence against him was, however, largely circumstantial. In Bishop Goodman's words, the Main plot to overthrow James with Spanish backing was "as yet but in embryo." Not enough had happened for anyone to be certain what his role would have been in it—if any.

Ralegh wrote to the Council in August warning them that their case was so weak that to put him on trial for treason could be interpreted as an act of murder. People would not believe that someone with his record in fighting the Spanish would betray his country to them and leaving him "to the cruelty of the law of England" would damage their own reputations. The Council, however, was unmoved by Ralegh's threat. "Who is Sir Walter Ralegh?" the prosecution document drawn up in August asked. "A man by nature of an extraordinary wit, and thereby the better furnished to shadow his misdoing."[1] People would expect Ralegh to cover his tracks and the Council believed that he was so unpopular they would also be happy to believe the worst of him. The indictments were read in September and the gossip was that "there is a strong purpose to proceed severely in the matter" against all the principals with the exception of the young Grey of Wilton, for whom there were hopes of compassion.[2]

The plague was by now in the Tower, where it had already killed several warders, and Cobham, who had been so stalwart when he was first arrested, was now in a state of absolute misery. He wept bitterly to his jailers "that the ladies of the court loved him not, who had they been his friends he was sure to have found more comforts in his affliction."[3] He was being bombarded with demands from Lady Kildare that he sue for his life by giving a full account of Ralegh's role in the plot and from Ralegh that he retract all accusations against him. Ralegh had managed to contact Cobham as early as July, having befriended the young Sir John Peyton, son of the Lieutenant of the Tower, and persuaded him to send messages for him. He assured Cobham that he could yet be found innocent of treason. Ralegh's father-in-law, Sir Nicholas Throckmorton, had received an acquittal after Wyatt's revolt against Mary I because only one witness had spoken against him and two were required for a conviction. Ralegh pointed out that they also had only one accuser: George Brooke in Cobham's case—and Cobham in Ralegh's.

It wasn't long before the Council intercepted a letter from Cobham to one of his servants in which he outlined how he hoped to use the "two witnesses" argument in his defense. He was already withdrawing most of his accusations against Ralegh and they quickly guessed that Ralegh must have found himself an errand boy. That it proved to be the first man James had knighted was an embarrassment. To prevent it from becoming common knowledge, Peyton senior was promoted to Ralegh's old post as Governor of Jersey and his family

left the Tower for the new posting in August. Far from proving de-
spondent about this double blow, however, Ralegh used the full force
of his personality to recruit other messengers: first a servant in the
Tower, Edward Cottrell, and eventually Gawen Harvey, the son of
the incoming governor, Sir George Harvey. By a stroke of good fortune Gawen had been on Ralegh's voyage in search of El Dorado in
the 1590s.

Come October Cobham cracked under Ralegh's assault and sent a
letter that Ralegh hoped would save him. It swore: "To clear my conscience, satisfy the world and free myself from the cry of your blood, I
protest upon my soul and before God and his angels, I never had any
conference with you in any treason; nor was ever moved by you to the
things I hereto accused you of . . . and so God deal with me and have
mercy on my soul, as this is true." Ralegh hid the letter for future use
before sending Cobham another message hidden in an apple, reminding Cobham how the Earl of Essex had been persuaded to clear his
conscience by betraying his friends and relations. Ralegh warned
Cobham to be careful not to fall into the same trap. He then wrote to
Cecil pleading with him for mercy and, in another lesson learned
from the Essex affair, laid the blame for his situation on unnamed enemies. His wife had already had some success in circulating passages
from his "suicide" letter, with the French ambassador, de Beaumont,
dispatching home Ralegh's argument that his attempt on his life
"arose from no feeling of fear, but was formed in order that his fate
might not be seen as a triumph to his enemies, whose power to put
him to death despite his innocence is well known."[4]

Ralegh was determined that his reputation would be restored, even
if he did not survive the accusations of treason. Cecil, however, was
equally determined not to have his traduced, as it had been in the aftermath to the Essex revolt. He went out of his way to distance himself from any impression of prejudice against Ralegh and told
courtiers that he thought Ralegh "bedashed, but not bemuddied," by
the accusation of treason and that his old friend would "clear himself
of hanging work."[5] Not everyone was convinced and there were some
who were happy to take Ralegh at his word, or even to promote the
suggestion that the whole case against Ralegh was fabricated—among

them Sir John Harington. Harington's hope that Cecil would come to his rescue had persisted even when he had realized that he was not going to be included in the general pardon at the coronation. He had written to Cecil on 27 July with the good news that Sir Thomas Erskine had assured him that James "has said in his Princely word" that he would have the forfeiture of Sir Griffin Markham's estates. They could then be sold to pay his debts. He asked only that Cecil should push for the decision to be confirmed. But Cecil had done nothing and as the summer weeks passed with the plague raging across London, the sense that he was trapped became almost unbearable.[6]

On the evening of 22 September there was a mass breakout of thirty prisoners from the King's Bench prison in the suburban slum of Southwark. The prisoners were soon rounded up and committed to an even stricter ward, but when plague broke out in the Gatehouse, Harington determined that he too had to try to escape. His "Sweet Mall" used her dowry to bribe his jailers to release him behind the backs of his creditors, and to his great relief he succeeded in fleeing all the way to Somerset, where he waited for Mary to join him. In the meantime Harington's creditors went straight to Cecil, who proved so sympathetic that he signed a warrant giving them permission to smash down the doors of Harington's London house in Channon Row and seize him or his goods. When they broke into his hallway, however, they found themselves confronted not by a terrified knight but by his angry wife and her friends.

As the creditors battered in the door, Lady Harington had fled to her neighbors, begging for help. They had returned with her and one of them pronounced that the creditors' warrant was legal only if her husband had been accused of treason. As he had not, she ordered the men to leave her house, and they were then ejected. The creditors went straight back to Cecil, who promptly sent her a sharp letter berating her for dismissing a warrant from the Secretary of State and for her cruelty toward the creditors. This was too much for Harington. "My escape was an honest escape, I shunned the plague and not the debt," he wrote furiously to Cecil; "they cannot deny the plague to be in the Gatehouse and seven dead and the eighth sick; and therefore I might think him as much my friend [as one who] would wish me to the gallows as to the Gatehouse." Harington apologized if his wife had caused Cecil any offense, but observed acidly that it was understandable that she found it hard to believe that a Secretary of State would "lend the countenance of state to such a wrangle as debt." He added that it also seemed extraordinary that Cecil should show so much sympathy for the "suffering" of his creditors and not "me and nine children." He wondered if Cecil himself owed the creditors money and if, perhaps, Sir Griffin Markham's troubles also had some private cause. Sir Griffin's mother had often attacked Cecil, he recalled.

Cecil fired a letter back hotly denying Harington's accusations and warning him that if he thought that his attacks on Elizabeth's reputation the previous winter had gained favor with James, he was wrong.[7] Cecil, however, was nervous. Harington had some powerful friends. The Earl of Shrewsbury was giving him loyal support in furthering his suit for the Markham estates, as were Sir Thomas Erskine, the Earl of Mar and Lord Kinloss. He decided to leave Harington alone. The knight, for his part, kept away from court. "I will leave you all now to sink or swim as seems best to your own liking," Harington wrote to a friend from Bath; "I only swim now in our baths wherein I feel some benefit and more delight." He did, however, continue to keep in touch with events, and to spite Cecil he wrote a letter to the Bishop of Bath and Wells intimating that the Bye and Main plots were fabrications.

Harington claimed that Lady Ralegh's uncle, Nicholas Carew, had been asking questions about Anthony Copley's role in exposing the plots. Copley was a well-known government agent and Harington commented, "I much fear for my Lord Grey and Ralegh . . . Cecil doth bear no love to Ralegh as you well understand." He suspected that Ralegh's reputation as an atheist would be used against him and unfairly so:

> *He seems wondrously fitted, both by art and nature, to serve the state, especially as he is versed in foreign matters, his skill therein being wonderfully estimable and praise worthy. In religion he hath shown (in private talk) great depth and good reading, as I once experienced at his own house, before many learned men. In good troth, I pity his state, and doubt the dice not fairly thrown, if his life be the losing stake.*[8]

Harington's letters to the Bishop also expressed his continuing anger about the Earl of Tyrone's welcome at court, from where the rebel was now departing for home and a bleak future.

Although there were no repeats of the terrible famine of the previous winter, James's rule was to prove a bitter experience for the Irish people. Harington, despite his resentment of Tyrone, had hoped for a policy of reconciliation. Now that the war was over, as he later told James, his was a vision of an Ireland where "noble men might build palaces and solace themselves with parks and ponds, and their tenants live in as good peace and plenty as here in England."[9] But harsher voices prevailed and it drove Tyrone to attempt another revolt. In 1607 Tyrone left Ireland with his ally the Earl of Tyrconnell, hoping to gather Spanish support for his rebellion. He soon discovered that James's policy of peace with Spain had put paid to such schemes and he was abandoned by the Spanish as absolutely as the English Catholics had been. The so-called flight of the earls came to mark the end of a Gaelic polity in the north of Ireland, and James introduced Scottish settlers and new English immigrants, who reduced the Irish and old English to impoverished tenants.

※　※　※

On 26 October Cobham and Grey were taken from the Tower under an escort of fifty horses to Wolvesey Castle, the ancient episcopal palace at Winchester, where the trials were to take place. They were followed on 13 November by Sir Walter Ralegh, George Brooke, Sir Griffin Markham, Sir Edward Parham, Anthony Copley, the priests William Watson and William Clark and a Catholic gentleman from Leicestershire called Bartholomew Brookesby. The crowds lining the streets screamed abuse as Ralegh's carriage passed, and hurled stones, clods of earth and tobacco pipes—an allusion to the story that he had blown smoke in Essex's face as he had been led to his execution. Ralegh viewed the abuse with evident contempt, "as proceeding from base and rascally people," and he puffed defiantly on his silver pipe.[10] His warders commented that he seemed much changed from the shaken figure who had entered the Tower in July.

The Bye plotters—Grey of Wilton, Sir Griffin Markham, Anthony

Copley and the priests Watson and Clark—all came to trial on 15 November, along with Bartholomew Brookesby and Sir Edward Parham. Several other Catholic gentlemen had been linked to the plot, but it was clear to Scaramelli that "the Council does not think it wise to press deeply into this." Putting too many members of the gentry on trial for treason would have exposed the government's unpopularity. Brookesby and Parham appear to have been chosen as examples to the rest and Scaramelli reported that the Council let it be known, verbally and in writing, that if Catholics gave up their plots, "they may rest assured that all intention of shedding blood will from now onward vanish from the king's mind."[11] James sent similar assurances to the Pope that month, adding a detailed outline of his hopes for the calling of a General Council that would lead to the reunification of Christendom.[12] But just as his hopes for a Council would fall on deaf ears in the Vatican so did his message among the most radical sections of the Catholic gentry. Two of the future gunpowder plotters had signed Watson's oath: Robert Catesby and Francis Tresham (as well as a third name associated with it, that of Sir Edward Baynham). Of them Catesby was already trying to arrange a meeting with his cousin Thomas Wintour to discuss a plan that would "at one instant deliver us from our bonds without foreign help." The explosion at the gunpowder mill at Redriffe on the day before Elizabeth's funeral had suggested that it might be possible for a handful of men to wipe out the entire establishment.*

The proceedings against the Bye plotters were to be held in Wolvesey's great hall. On its eastern wall hung what was believed to be the simulacrum of King Arthur's Round Table with its portrait of the mythical king gazing blankly ahead. Courtiers and other curious onlookers crowded in to watch the proceedings, among them friends and foes of the men being tried.

---

*Anthony Copley had also named several others as being interested in a future "Catholic" action that never occurred. They included Lord Windsor, who was a friend of Shrewsbury, Leicester's son, Sir Robert Dudley, who became a Catholic and ran off with Elizabeth's former Maid of Honor Elizabeth Southwell in 1605, and Lord Byrdges, who later married Lady Anne Stanley, the daughter of Ferdinando, Earl of Derby, and a descendant of Mary Tudor.

The first defendant was Anthony Copley. He had no legal representation—those tried for treason had to make their own defense—but he had the advantage of being the government's main witness and it was evident that he had been carefully coached. Onlookers thought that "his declaration was extraordinarily well penned" and concluded that he would "live for the service he did."

The priest William Clark went up next. A well-built man in his mid-thirties with red-blond hair and a close-cut beard, he delivered his testimony with conviction, insisting that he had broken no laws because no king had any authority before his coronation. The judges rejected his argument, but he had made a good impression. The same could not be said of the cross-eyed William Watson. He explained to the judges that he had wanted to preempt a Jesuit plot to invite the Spanish into England, but then damaged his case by insisting loudly that his plot was also the result of James having reneged on promises of toleration.

Some Protestants feared that James secretly intended still to offer toleration and voices were expressing concern that James was too pro-Catholic. "It is hardly credible in what jollity [the papists] now live," one gentleman had complained on 12 November; "They are already labouring tooth and nail for places in the Parliament, and do so mightily prevail . . . as I cannot see how their dangerous course can be stopped unless some higher authority speedily interpose itself."[13] When Sir Griffin Markham stepped forward to make his declaration and confessed that he too had believed that James would offer toleration, Cecil intervened and assured the court that "the king had promised a moderation of religion but not a toleration." By "moderation" he meant the end to recusancy fines—which punished all Catholics regardless of their loyalty—and this had been agreed to in June, although James was already regretting the move. Not only was it costing him the significant sum of £7,000 in lost revenue but large numbers of church papists who previously attended Protestant services to avoid the fines were now staying away. He feared that further leniency could result in an explosion of Catholic numbers, and after he received a negative response from the Vatican regarding his call for a General Council in February he reintroduced them.[14] By 1605 much

of the money raised was going to Scots favorites, a factor in the fero-
ciously anti-Scots character of the Gunpowder Plot.*

Sir Griffin Markham handled the rest of his case admirably. He
freely admitted himself guilty of treason and expressed regret that he
had accepted the argument that James was not king until he was
crowned, making "many men sorry for him, and my Lord Cecil weep
abundantly."[15] The tears indicated that Cecil intended to save Sir
Griffin's life—but it is notable that he had no tears left for his former
brother-in-law, George Brooke. Here was the one figure connected to
the Bye, the Main and Lord Grey's plots. Brooke insisted that the
links were explained only by the fact he was working for the government and he relayed how he had told the King in Berwick that he
hoped to expose any plots against him. His argument was demolished,
however, when the government lawyers passed on James's answer that
although he had "embraced" Brooke's offer to expose plots against
him, "since that time, [Brooke] having long speech with the king,
he touched not that string at all, but only spoke of his own private
business."

The Leicestershire gentleman Bartholomew Brookesby was also
found guilty of treason, despite having refused to take part in the Bye
plot. This seems to have been an act of revenge for his being caught in
the company of priests on several occasions and as a warning to his
sisters, who were believed, correctly, to be running a network of safe
houses. They, however, were not to be intimidated and their names
and safe houses would also be linked to the Gunpowder Plot. Remarkably, Edward Parham, who had also declined to take part in the
plot, was acquitted. It was the first such judgment in forty-four years,
but then Cecil had something else in mind for him. Parham was expelled from England and sent to the Netherlands, where he worked as
a spy for Cecil for the rest of his life. He eventually married Francis
Tresham's sister and became Colonel of the English Catholic Regi-
ment—an indication of just how deeply penetrated the Catholic
community was.

---

*As soon as the gunpowder had done its work, the plotters intended to kill every
Scot in London.

The trial of the Main plotters opened on 17 November with that of Sir Walter Ralegh. The Lord Chief Justice, Sir John Popham, "a huge, heavy, ugly man" who "lived like a hog," presided from a raised platform under a brocade canopy. Alongside him were three other judges and seven commissioners: Robert Cecil, William Waad, Henry Howard, Lord Wotton, Sir John Stanhope and the new Earls of Suffolk and Devonshire (formerly Lord Thomas Howard and Lord Mountjoy). All were close allies of Cecil or long-standing enemies of Ralegh. The chief prosecutor was the Attorney General, Sir Edward Coke, a self-made, "very handsome, proper man," rather in the mold of Ralegh himself.

At eight in the morning Ralegh walked into the hall. He saluted some friends in the crowd and went to stand by a stool put out for him. The jury, all drawn from Middlesex, listened intently as the indictment was read: "That he did conspire, and go about, to deprive the King of his government; to raise up sedition within the realm; to alter religion, to bring in the Roman Superstition and to procure foreign armies to invade the kingdom." The allegation that he wanted to restore Catholicism was a straightforward smear. As the indictment continued, however, specific incidents were alleged: that Ralegh had given Cobham a book "written against the title of the King to the crown of England"; that meetings had taken place where they had discussed plans "to advance Arbella Stuart to the crown and royal throne of this kingdom"; that they had agreed that Arbella should write letters to the Archduke Albert, the King of Spain and the Duke of Savoy promising peace, toleration of religion and a willingness to take their advice in her choice of husband; that Cobham was to negotiate with the Archduke Albert's emissary, the Count of Aremberg, to raise £5,000 or £6,000 from the King of Spain to finance the rebellion; that he was to meet with Ralegh in Jersey to discuss "the fulfilling of said treasons, when discontentments in England should afford opportunity"; and that £8,000 or £10,000 was to be given to Ralegh personally to effect the treasons. When it finished Ralegh pleaded not guilty.

Coke opened his case by reminding the jury of the details of the Bye plot, to surprise the court, kidnap James, take him to the Tower and "keep him there until they had extorted three things from him: first, their own pardon; secondly toleration for the Romish supersti-tion . . . and thirdly the removal of certain Privy Councillors." Ralegh interrupted him: "You gentlemen of the jury, I pray remember, I am not charged with the Bye being the treason of the priests." Coke per-sisted. The Bye and the Main were, he said "like Sampson's foxes, which were joined in their tails though their heads were severed." Coke recalled Brooke's description of how Cobham had told him that he, Markham and the priests were merely on the Bye, or secondary plot, while he and Ralegh were carrying through the Main plot, which was to "kill the King and his cubs." He then turned on Ralegh: "To whom do you bear malice?" he demanded, "to the children?" Ralegh replied coolly:

> Mr. Attorney, I pray to whom, or to what end, speak you all this? I protest I do not understand what a word of this means, except it be to tell me news. What is the treason of Markham and the priests to me?

> [COKE] I will then come close to you. I will prove you to be a most notorious traitor that ever came to the bar. You are indeed upon the Main, but you have followed them of the Bye in imitation; I will charge you with the words.

> [RALEGH] Your words cannot condemn me; my innocency is my defence. I pray you go to your proofs. Prove against me any one thing of the many where-with you have charged me, and I will confess all the indictment, and that I am the most horrible traitor that ever lived, and worthy to be crucified with a thousand torments.

> [COKE] Nay I will prove all; thou are a monster; thou hast an English face, but a Spanish heart: Now you must have money: Aremberg was no sooner in England (I charge thee Ralegh) but thou incitest Cobham to go unto him, and to deal with him for money, to bestow on discontented persons, to raise rebel-lion in the kingdom.

Coke went on to describe how Ralegh intended for Cobham to pretend that the money was to be used to advance the cause of peace with Spain, when in reality it was to be used for "Spanish invasion and Scottish subversion." It was just as Henry Howard had hoped in June 1602 when he had told Cecil that it was their dealings over Spain that would be the key to their destruction. Ralegh had often expressed his belief that England would be vulnerable to invasion from Scotland and Scaramelli had observed on 28 April that James was also concerned that Spanish money might be used to foment rebellion there if he failed to make peace. But as Coke steamrollered on, Ralegh interrupted: "Let me answer."

[COKE] *Thou shalt not.*

[RALEGH] *It concerns my life.*

The bleakness of the plea shifted the mood in the courtroom toward Ralegh. Cecil, restive, spoke out: "Mr Attorney, when you have done with this general charge, do you not mean to let him answer every particular?" Coke answered, "Yes, when we deliver the proofs to be read." Coke insisted that Lord Cobham could not have dreamed up the plots on his own, for "all your Lordships all know" he "was never a politician, nor a swordsman . . . Sir Walter Ralegh was a man fitting for both. And such was Ralegh's secrecy and machiavellian policy in these courses, that he would never confer but with one at once; because saith he 'one witness can never condemn me' . . . Notwithstanding this, the Lord Cobham did once charge Ralegh; but knowing afterwards that Ralegh had excused him, then he retracted."

[RALEGH] *I do not hear yet, that you have spoken one word against me; here is no treason of mine done. If my Lord Cobham be a traitor what is that to me?*

[COKE] *All that he did was by thy instigation, thou Viper; for I thou thee thou traitor.*

"Thou" was a term used to address social inferiors and Coke's use of it was a mark of contempt.

[RALEGH] *It becomes not a man of quality and virtue, to call me so: but I take comfort in it, if it is all you can do.*

[COKE] *Have I angered you?*

[RALEGH] *I am in no case to be angry.*

Ralegh's infuriating composure was costing the prosecutor his dignity and the substantial figure of Chief Justice Popham stirred: "Sir Walter Ralegh, Mr Attorney speaks out of the zeal of his duty, for the service of the king, and you for your life, be valiant on both sides." Coke took a deep breath and read out Cobham's confession of 20 July, which claimed Ralegh was the instigator of the Main treason and outlined how he had feared all along that Ralegh would betray him when he reached Jersey from Spain and "would send him to the King." Ralegh demanded to see the accusation, then, turning to the jury, said: "This is absolutely all the evidence that can be brought against me; poor shifts! You gentlemen of the jury, I pray you understand this. This is that which must either condemn, or give me life; which must either free me, or send my wife and children to beg their bread about the streets."

Ralegh proceeded to question whether Cobham was such a weak man that he could be led into treason. He reminded the court that Cobham had a notoriously violent temper. "Is he so simple? No; he has a disposition of his own . . . he is no babe." He then asked whether it was not also unlikely that he himself would

devise with Cobham that he should go to Spain, to persuade the King to disburse so much money . . . I knowing England to be in better state to defend herself than ever she was. I knew Scotland united; Ireland quieted, werein of late our forces were dispersed; Denmark assured, which before was suspected. I knew, that having lost a lady whom time had surprised, we now had an active king, a lawful successor, who would himself be present in all his affairs. The State of Spain was not unknown to me [he continued]. I knew the Spanish had six repulses; three in Ireland and three at sea . . . I knew he was discour-

*aged and dishonoured. I knew the King of Spain to be the proudest prince in
Christendom; but now he comes creeping to the king my master for peace. I
knew whereas before he had in his port six or seven score of ships, he has now
but six or seven . . . And to show I am not "Spanish"—as you term me—at
this time I had writ a treatise to the King's Majesty of the present state of
Spain, and reasons against the Peace.*

It was an impressive performance and when Coke returned to
Cobham's confession Ralegh showed his final hand: "You try me by
the Spanish Inquisition, if you proceed only by the circumstances,
without two witnesses." Here, however, he made his first mistake.
As Coke had already made plain, he knew Ralegh had planned such
a defense and he informed him that the law had been amended, with
the loophole requiring two witnesses to convict a man of treason
closed years before. Ralegh realized that the only option that remained was for him to destroy the credibility of Cobham's confession. Cobham's wife, the Countess of Kildare, had persuaded her
husband to abandon his recent promises to Ralegh, but Ralegh believed that if he faced him in court he could bring Cobham around
once more and he asked for him to be brought to the hall to accuse
him in person. Popham refused, arguing that to introduce such an
uncertain witness might give him an unfair advantage over the
crown!

Coke then addressed the matter of the book written against the
Stuart claim which Ralegh was alleged to have given Cobham. The
book had been written when Mary, Queen of Scots, was alive and had
belonged to the first Lord Burghley. Ralegh had taken it from his library some years before. The claim that Ralegh had passed it on to
Cobham was suggestive of Ralegh the manipulator, persuading Cobham to treason, and Ralegh insisted that Cobham must have picked
the book up off a table: "I remember that it lay upon my board at a
time when he was with me." It was not very convincing and his continued insistence that Cobham be brought to face him in court gave a still
firmer impression of Cobham as a weak man who could be easily dominated. But Ralegh fought on against the odds, reiterating the paucity
of the evidence against him as the pale winter light began to fade:

> *I am accused concerning Arabella, concerning money out of Spain. My Lord*
> *Chief Justice says, a man may be condemned with one witness, yea without any*
> *witness. Cobham is guilty of many things . . . what can he hope for but mercy?*
> *My Lords, vouchsafe me this grace: let him be brought, being alive, and in the*
> *house; let him avouch any of these things, I will confess the whole indictment,*
> *and renounce the King's mercy.*

Suddenly there was a dramatic interruption to the proceedings as
Cobham's father-in-law, the tall, silver-haired figure of Admiral Nottingham, walked forward with Arbella Stuart on his arm. Cecil stood
up to point out that she was "a near kinswoman of the king's" and that
the trial had touched on her honor: "Let us not scandal the innocent
by confusion of speech: she is as innocent of all these things as I, or
any man here; only she received a letter from my Lord Cobham to
prepare her; which she laughed at and immediately sent to the king."

Nottingham added, "The lady doth here protest upon her salvation
that she never dealt in any of these things and so she willed me to tell
the court."

❁   ❁   ❁

Arbella's uncle, Henry Cavendish, who had tried to help her escape
from Hardwick, had been questioned to discover what links, if any, he
had to the Main plotters. Nothing was revealed by these interviews,
however, which was convenient for Cecil and for James. Cecil would
not have wished to have Arbella repeating her allegations that his
long-standing friend, the Earl of Hertford, had sought to marry her to
his grandson; James, who was already accused of complicity in his
mother's execution, would not have wanted to damage his reputation
further by ordering the beheading of his first cousin. The public declaration of Arbella's innocence also served to suggest that Ralegh was
guilty of abusing an innocent woman's reputation. Ralegh, however,
saw immediately that in bringing her forward Nottingham had made
a mockery of the court's refusal to call Cobham and again demanded
that Cobham be brought before the court. He recalled that even the
Jesuit martyr Edmund Campion "was not denied to have his accusers
face to face." Cecil, seeing the danger, interrupted the proceedings

once more: "I am afraid my often speaking . . . will make the world think I delight to hear myself. My affection to you Sir Walter, was not extinguished, but slaked, in regard of your deserts. You know the law of the realm that my Lord Cobham cannot be brought." Ralegh insisted: "He may be my Lord."

Cecil repeated that he was Ralegh's friend but that Cobham could not be brought before the court. Another witness was, however, brought forward—a ship's pilot called Dyer who claimed he had heard gossip that Ralegh and Cobham were to cut the King's throat. Ralegh was contemptuous: "What infer you upon this?" he asked. "That your treason hath wings," Coke retorted. Ralegh reiterated that they had "not proved any one thing against me, but all by circumstances." Coke sat down "in a chaffe" and refused to get up again until urged to do so by the commissioners. He repeated the evidence thus far. Ralegh interjected that he was doing him wrong and Coke, goaded beyond reason, finally turned on him in a black fury:

[COKE] *Thou are the most vile and execrable traitor that ever lived.*

[RALEGH] *You speak indiscreetly, barbarously and uncivilly.*

[COKE] *I want words sufficient to express thy viperous treasons.*

[RALEGH] *I think you want words indeed, for you have spoken one thing half a dozen times.*

Ralegh had caught the sympathy of the onlookers and to Cecil's horror Coke was loudly hissed. At last, however, Coke put aside the blunt instrument of personal abuse in favor of a stiletto, a letter from Cobham describing how Ralegh had passed him a message in an apple warning him not to confess to a preacher. The letter added that Ralegh had told him to get Aremberg to give him a pension of £1,500 a year in exchange for intelligence. The court had been awash with Aremberg's offers of bribes in June and Ralegh freely admitted that he had been offered one but he insisted he had never taken it. In a last throw of the dice he brought out the letter Cobham had written proclaiming his innocence. He asked Cecil, who knew his brother-in-law's writing, to read it. When Cecil had finished Ralegh concluded: "You shall see how many souls this Cobham has, and the King shall judge by our deaths which is the perfidious man."

It was nearly seven in the evening when the jury was asked to consider its verdict. Less than fifteen minutes later the foreman delivered it in the flickering candlelight: guilty. Ralegh was allowed one more statement before sentence was pronounced. He denied the charge of treason and submitted himself to the King's mercy. Then Lord Chief Justice Popham delivered his judgment:

> I thought I should never have seen this day, to have stood in this place to give Sentence of Death against you; because I thought it impossible, that one of so great parts should have fallen so grievously. God has bestowed on you many benefits. You had been a man fit and able to have served the king in good place . . . if you had entered into a good consideration of your estate, and not suffered your own wit to have entrapped yourself, you might have lived in good comfort . . . Two vices have lodged chiefly in you; one is an eager ambition, the other corrupt covetousness . . . I am sorry to hear that a gentleman of your wealth would become a base spy for the enemy, which is the vilest of all others . . . You have been taxed by the world, with the defence of the most heathenish and blasphemous opinions, which I list not to repeat, because Christian ears cannot endure to hear them . . . You shall do well before you go out of the world, to give satisfaction therein, and not to die with these imputations on you . . . Now it rests to pronounce the Judgement, which I wish you had not been this day to receive from me; for if the fear of God in you had been answerable to your other great parts you might have lived to have been a singular good subject. I never saw the like trial and I hope never to see the like again. But since you have been found guilty of these horrible Treasons, the judgement of this court is, that you shall be had from hence to the place whence you came, there to remain to the day of execution, there to be hanged and cut down alive, and your body shall be opened, your heart and bowels plucked out, and your privy members cut off, and thrown into the fire before your eyes; then your head to be stricken off from your body, and your body shall be divided into four quarters to be disposed of at the king's pleasure. And God have mercy upon your soul.[16]

Ralegh begged Devonshire and the judges to ask the King for a more honorable death than the hideous tortures to which Popham had sentenced him. They promised their best endeavors. The court rose and Ralegh was escorted from the room.

The news of the guilty verdict on Ralegh was taken to the King by his huntsman Roger Aston and a fellow Scot. The court was already abuzz with discussion of Ralegh's astonishing performance. The diplomat Dudley Carleton told his friend John Chamberlain that "in the opinion of all men, he had been acquitted." He described how the first of James's messengers "affirmed that never any man spoke so well in times past, nor would do in the world to come; and the other said that whereas when he saw him first he was so led with the common hatred, that he would have gone a hundred miles to have seen him hanged he would, ere he parted, have gone a thousand to have saved his life." "In one word," Carleton concluded, "never was a man so hated and so popular, in so short a time."[17]

James made light of the fact that Ralegh had been cleared at the bar of public opinion but not by the court, joking that he would be glad not to be tried by a Middlesex jury. There was a real danger, however, that Ralegh would become a martyr and Cecil, Howard and the King his murderers, just as he had warned the Council in August. With this in mind the trials of Cobham and Grey were delayed so that Cobham could be interviewed again. He obligingly gave the Council new information that Ralegh had urged him to tell the King of Spain that he should invade England at Milford Haven in Wales. Such an eventuality had been the nightmare of military and naval men for years and Ralegh proved ill-equipped to confront the accusation. Alone in his cell he had been contemplating the traitor's death he had witnessed so many times as Captain of the Guard. It filled him with dread and he had just penned a letter to the King begging for his life when the news of Cobham's latest confession was delivered. It dashed all his hopes of mercy and his answers to his interrogators were barely coherent.

The next day Ralegh found the strength to write to the commissioners and deny Cobham's story but the fire had gone out of him and he pleaded for his execution to be stayed, if only for a year, "to give to God in prison and to serve him." Cobham was in no better state than

Ralegh. He was brought before the court for his trial on 25 November. The hall at Wolvesey was packed with leading Scots and English courtiers hoping for a great spectacle, but Cobham cowered and shook as the indictment was read. In response to the questions he bleated that the plot was all Ralegh's idea and that Ralegh had wanted the Spanish to invade at Milford Haven; he called his brother a viper and added that Brooke was guilty of incest as well as treason and that he had a child by his wife's sister. "Having thus accused all his friends, and so little excused himself," the courtier Dudley Carleton wrote to Chamberlain, "the Peers were not long in deliberation what to judge; and after sentence of condemnation given, he begged a great while for life and favour, alleging his confession as a meritorious act."[18]

On 28 November came the last trial, that of Lord Grey of Wilton. The hot-blooded young peer spoke "with great assurances and alacrity" and made eloquent speeches to the Lords, the Council and the judges until eight at night. Despite the strong evidence given by Markham and Brooke, the judges took a long time to agree on Grey's sentence. Finally, however, the Lord Chief Justice prepared to deliver judgment and Grey was asked if he had anything to say before the sentence of death was pronounced. He replied that "the house of the Wiltons had spent many lives in their Princes' service and Grey cannot beg his." This flash of pride irritated his judges but Dudley Carleton could not help but admire "so clear and fiery a spirit." The executions were set to proceed immediately. "They say the priests shall lead the dance tomorrow," Dudley Carleton wrote to Chamberlain on the twenty-seventh, "and Brooke next after; for he proves to be the knot that tied together the three conspiracies; the rest hang indifferent betwixt mercy and justice."[19]

Watson and Clark were brought to the scaffold in the first week of December. The two men showed no fear although they faced the full horror of being hung, drawn and quartered. Clark insisted to the last that he had broken no laws. He told the crowd he was dying because he was a priest and therefore faced a kind of martyrdom. Watson wished he could die for everyone that he had brought into his plot, and regretted writing against the Jesuits. The man in charge of their executions, Benjamin Tichborne, was the first sheriff in England to proclaim James king and he and his son had been rewarded with a pension of £100 a year for their loyalty. As a Catholic, he might have ensured that the priests were hanged until they were dead, but he chose not to. Instead they were "very bloodily handled," as Carleton recorded with disgust, "and Clark, to whom more favour was intended had the worse luck; for he both strove to help himself and spake after he was cut down." When at last the grisly rituals of castration and disembowelment were over and the corpses dismembered, the priests' quarters were set on Winchester gates and their heads mounted on the first tower of the castle.*

On Monday 6 December it was George Brooke's turn to die. As a member of a noble family, Brooke had had his sentence commuted to beheading. The Bishop of Chichester accompanied him to the scaffold, where a small crowd had gathered, no bigger than that for an ordinary execution. The court was in the grip of a new hedonism and had no interest in watching the conclusion of a failed life. While Brooke faced his maker, Anna's ladies were playing children's games, from ten at night until two or three in the morning. Arbella listed several of these to her uncle Shrewsbury: "Viz, I pray my Lord give me a course in your park. Rise pig and go. One penny follow me etc." Often the games were fueled by drink and she confessed, "I daily see some even of the fairest amongst us and willingly and wittingly ensnared by the prince of darkness."[20] Only two significant courtiers, both Catholic, had torn themselves away from the flirting and drinking— the young Earl of Arundel and one of Worcester's sons.

Brooke delivered a short speech to the few townsfolk and others who looked on, claiming his faults had been errors rather than capital crimes, "which he referred to the God of truth and time to discover; and so left it, as if somewhat lay yet hid, which would one day appear for his justification." It was a desperate, last-minute bid to salvage his reputation, and Carleton, who was also there, observed that one of Brooke's final views was of the medieval buildings of the St. Cross hospital, whose lucrative mastership he had been denied. Brooke nev-

---

*Clark left a mark behind on the wall of his cell in the Tower, "W. Clarke P [priest] 1603," along with the merchants' mark, number eight.

ertheless "died constantly (and so seeming) religiously." The crowd remained subdued and when the axeman held his head aloft only Tichborne replied: "God save the King."[21] The Bishop of Chichester, who had attended Brooke, immediately left to see Cobham and offer confession, while the Bishop of Winchester was sent to Ralegh, on the express orders of the King.

Ralegh had written another farewell letter to his wife and in this one it seems he really had accepted he was going to die:

You shall now receive (my dear wife) my last words in these my last lines. My love I send you, that you may keep it when I am dead, and my counsel, that you may remember it when I am no more. I would not by my will present you with sorrows (dear Bess). Let them go into the grave with me and be buried in the dust . . . Remember your poor child for his father's sake, who chose you and loved you in his happiest times. Get those letters (if it be possible) which I writ to the Lords wherein I sued for my life. God is my witness, it was for you and ours I desired life. But it is true I distain myself for begging it. For know it (dear wife) that your son is the son of a true man, and one who, in his own respect, despises death, and all his misshapen and ugly shapes. I cannot write much. God knows how hardly I steal this time while others sleep, and it is also high time that I should separate my thoughts from this world. Beg my dead body which living was denied thee and either lay it at Sherborne (if the land continue) or in Exeter church by my mother and father. I can say no more, time and death call me away . . . My dear wife farewell. Bless my poor boy. Pray for me and let my good God hold you both in his arms. Written with the dying hand of sometime thy husband but now (alas) overthrown, Wa. Ralegh.[22]

If in sending the Bishop of Winchester James hoped for new revelations, he was to be disappointed. Neither Cobham nor Ralegh had anything new to say. If there was news, it came when Arundel and Somerset returned to court from Brooke's execution with the doomed man's last words about "hidden matters" yet to be revealed. It triggered yet more gossip on whether the plots had been fabricated or at least "awakened" by powerful figures to dispose of their enemies. Sir Thomas Tresham, who had led the delegation of Catholic gentlemen to Hampton Court in July, had no sympathy for the priests Watson and Clark, but having seen Catholics encouraged into plots in the past, he admitted, "I partly . . . do suspect: *Latet anguis in herba* [a snake lies hidden in the grass]."[23] His suspicion must have hardened in February when the Bye plot was used as the pretext for a royal proclamation ordering all Jesuit and seminary priests to depart the kingdom before 19 March. Others suspected that Grey, Cobham and Ralegh were paying the price for their demand that James be accepted as king with conditions. Their dismay increased when they discovered James was to hand some of Cobham's great estates to a Scot. Within three days of Elizabeth's death there had been rumors that a Scots woman had complained "nothing did discontent them more than that their king should be received peaceably," since it meant they would not be getting their hands on attainted land.[24] It seemed their wish had now come true—with James's Scots huntsman, Sir Roger Aston, having already been promised Cobham's park at Cowling in Kent. The day after Brooke's death, 7 December, a Scots divine further embittered the atmosphere by delivering a sermon before the King in which he implied that clemency to traitors was a deadly sin. Councilors, nervous about the effect on their reputations if so many former luminaries of Elizabeth's court were to die, petitioned the King for mercy and the Countess of Pembroke asked her son, who was James's host at Wilton, to use his influence to gain a pardon for Ralegh if he could. Large bribes were offered to the Scots to put in a word and Sir Griffin Markham's friends assured him that his life at least was safe—though James had, in fact, signed his death warrant that day, along with those of Grey and Cobham. The date of their executions was set for the tenth, Ralegh's for the thirteenth, and another, less significant Englishman also found himself in James's sights.

On Thursday 8 December two new envoys arrived from Venice for an audience with James. Councilors argued with the Venetians that James could not legally retract the general pardon that had freed the pirate William Piers, whatever he might wish. The Venetians wanted to know from James directly whether he was going to accept that or fulfill his promise to have Piers executed. James, angry that his wishes had so far been denied, readily agreed that the pirate should hang and on 9 December he appeared at a meeting of the Privy Council to insist in person that Piers should die for his crimes. They reluctantly agreed to have him rearrested.

The next morning at ten o'clock Cobham, Markham and Grey were brought to the scaffold in torrential rain. Dudley Carleton, who was once more a witness to events, thought, "A fouler day could hardly have been picked out, or a fitter for such a tragedy." Markham was the first to be taken up onto the platform where the block was placed in the castle yard. His stricken face registered his shock that he was to die despite the promises he had been given. He gave a speech complaining that he had been fed false hopes and that he wished he were better prepared. A friend offered him a cloth to tie over his eyes, but "he threw it away, saying he could look upon death without blushing." He said goodbye to his friends who were standing nearby and recited his prayers in Latin, the language of the Catholic Church. The ten-year-old Prince Henry stood near the scaffold, having been sent by his father.

As Markham prayed, John Gibb, a Scots groom of the Bedchamber, pushed desperately through the crowd toward Tichborne. Eventually he found himself stuck and, still struggling, he shouted out. The sheriff turned and, having spotted him, ordered him to come aside. The execution was stayed for a few moments as Gibb showed Tichborne a new warrant from the King. Carleton watched as Markham was "left upon the scaffold to entertain his own thoughts which, no doubt, were as melancholy as his countenance." When Tichborne had finished reading the warrant he informed Markham that since he had been poorly prepared for death his beheading would be delayed by a couple of hours. Markham was then escorted off the scaffold and locked in the hall, where Prince Henry was waiting to walk with him. James had hoped the boy might persuade the condemned man to a last-minute confession. Lord Grey was now led to the scaffold by a troop of young courtiers. Two of his best friends walked on either side of him and Carleton thought there was "such gaiety and cheer in his countenance that he seemed a dapper young bridegroom."

Grey prayed at length for the King, keeping the crowd standing in the icy rain for half an hour. But as he made himself ready for the block Tichborne again interrupted the proceedings, this time to say that the King had decided that Cobham should be beheaded first. A confused Grey was taken to the hall and Lord Cobham brought out. He was a changed man compared to the trembling creature who had appeared before the court. He calmly craved pardon of the King and swore that, "for Sir Walter Ralegh, he took it, upon the hope of his soul's resurrection, that what he had said of him was true." It seems likely that he had been told his life was to be spared and been asked, in return, to convict Ralegh from the scaffold. The sheriff duly stayed the execution, telling him he had to face some other prisoners. Grey and Markham were then brought from the hall, "and the three, looked strange one upon the other like men beheaded and met again in the other world," Carleton observed.

The sheriff announced that the King had mercifully granted the lives of all three men—and Ralegh, who was watching this grotesque theater from his window, realized that he too was safe. Relief and delight swept the crowd and as the news spread first the town began to celebrate and then the court.[25] Even Arbella took the risk of expressing to her uncle her pleasure at "the royal and wise manner of the King's proceeding therein."[26]

Almost unbelievably, Piers was also to evade execution. Six pirates were hanged at Southampton on 22 December, but he was not among them. James was so angry when he heard about it that he threatened to hang the Admiralty judge instead. The judge, however, persisted in keeping the young man alive, and he appears to have persuaded the Venetians to accept money and information on the whereabouts of their goods in exchange for his life. Piers disappears from the Venetian state papers in the spring of 1604 and no mention is made of his ever having been hanged. James would prove equally unsuccessful in stamping out Piers's profession. As this story suggests, pirates made too much money for their investors to be sacrificed by them to the hangman.

Predictably, the Bye plotters, Copley and Sir Griffin Markham, were sent into exile to join Sir Edward Parham as spies for the government. Sir Griffin's wife, who remained in England, made strenuous efforts to infiltrate the Gunpowder Plot, in the hopes that she could earn her husband a passport home, but without success. His estates were granted to Sir John Harington in June 1604. The Main plotters were no use as spies and they suffered worse fates. Cobham, who had been one of the ten richest men in England, fell into utter destitution in the Tower while his wife and his former brother-in-law, Robert Cecil, shared the spoils of his ruin. Most unusually, Lady Kildare was granted his attainted estates in May 1604 and eventually Cecil acquired the bulk of Cobham's estates by buying Lady Kildare's interest in her husband's land and helping her to break the male entail to George Brooke's son. Cobham was released from the Tower on grounds of ill health in 1617 and died the following year. His corpse was left unburied for some time after his death, as no one could be found to pay his funeral expenses.*

The fiery-spirited Grey of Wilton died in the Tower in 1614, the last of his line, but Sir Walter Ralegh was released in 1617 after thirteen years. James was desperate for money and prepared to listen to Sir Walter's promises that he would succeed in doing what he had failed to do in the 1590s: find El Dorado, the land of the golden man. By then Ralegh's cherished estate at Sherborne had been lost to James's Scots favorite, the handsome young Robert Carr, and he hoped El Dorado would restore his own fortunes as well as the King's. Instead the quest cost him the life of his elder son, Wat, who died during an assault on the town of San Tomé in what is now Venezuela. The action infuriated the Spanish, and James, anxious to keep on good terms, agreed to lift the stay of execution bestowed on Ralegh in December 1603. He was beheaded in front of a large crowd in 1618. On the scaffold Ralegh denied the story that he had blown smoke in Essex's face before his execution in 1601 and observed that those who had destroyed Essex had also destroyed him. It took only two blows to strike off Ralegh's head and it fell amid the groans of a sullen crowd.

There is a famous story about Ralegh, written later in the seventeenth century, in which as a young man walking with Elizabeth he

---

*Stories later circulated that Cobham had died of starvation in the house of his laundress. These were not true, but his real fate was not much less dreadful.

took a diamond ring from her and scratched on a window: "Fain would I climb, yet I fear to fall." Elizabeth immediately scratched underneath: "If thy heart fails thee, climb not at all." Among those possessions found on his body after his death was a diamond ring Elizabeth had given him.[27] Ralegh remains an extraordinarily romantic figure; given his striking good looks and his brilliant mind, it is sometimes hard to envisage the other side of Ralegh—the murderer with blood-soaked hands and scented hair, who his friend Lord Cobham believed was ready to sacrifice him on the altar of his ambition. But many of his contemporaries had no such difficulty and his fate, like that of Grey of Wilton, was often linked to the massacre of unarmed prisoners at Smerwick Fort in Ireland. In December 1603 Sir John Harington recalled that it was Ralegh who had carried out the orders of Grey's father to kill his Italian and Spanish prisoners, and after Ralegh's death Bishop Goodman recorded that "a soldier who was then present [at Smerwick] and did see the execution done, told me that in his certain knowledge most of those soldiers who were employed therein came to a very unhappy end."[28] The bones of the victims of the massacre at Smerwick Fort are still being unearthed.

The object of the Main plot, Arbella Stuart, suffered a fate every bit as grim as those who had plotted for her to become Queen. The French emissary de Rosni, now the Duke of Sully, recalled how the Sultan of Turkey, Mahomet the Third, had twenty of his brothers strangled in 1603 "to secure himself, as he thought, on the throne."[29] Arbella was merely kept "without mate and without estate," as a Venetian neatly phrased it. The humiliation of her dependence on James, however, encouraged her obsession with the Seymour family to return. In 1610 she married Edward Seymour's younger brother, William, without royal permission. James placed Arbella under house arrest and William was put in the Tower. He escaped to France, but Arbella was caught on her way to join him. The bill of arrests of those who had tried to help her flee to France included many names associated with the Bye and Main plotters: her Catholic aunt, the Countess of Shrewsbury, who had been a friend of Lady Ralegh; William Markham, a cousin of Sir Griffin Markham; and Edward Kirton, whose wife was a kinsman of Cobham.* Arbella was placed in the Tower, where she starved herself to death in 1615. Dodderidge, the servant who had taken her message to the Earl of Hertford in December 1602, was with her until the end.

Just how close had England come to civil war in 1603? James's accession looks so smooth in retrospect, but at the time people commented often on the providential character of James's peaceful inheritance. As Dekker recalled in his *Wonderful Year*:

> *Who did expect but ruin, blood, and death,*
> *To share our kingdom, and divide our breath?*

James had gained widespread support by promising wealth, titles and office to key figures, offering the hope of toleration to Catholics and of reform to Puritans while also reassuring conservatives that he would maintain the Established Church—in short, being all things to all men. But his achievement owed almost as much to luck as to political talent. Despite all his promises, James was not loved in England and he was fortunate that Elizabeth died when she did. Two years earlier and Essex might have taken the crown from under him, or accepted him with conditions, while Cecil might have used his political cunning to back a different candidate. Any later and Spain, France and the Vatican would have chosen an English candidate on whom they could all agree. Arbella's name was high on the list, and Anthony Rivers had heard gossip that some courtiers were plotting to marry her to a Seymour and so unite the lines of Margaret and Mary Tudor. A son from such a marriage would have had a powerful claim—but as it was, Elizabeth's death caught James's opponents by surprise. In Europe on the morning of James's accession, 24 March 1603, the Spanish were still discussing what candidate they should support. In England Ralegh was not even at court. When he returned the day after her death, he faced a fait accompli.

---

*Arbella's closeness to the Markham family was also illustrated by the fact that Sir Griffin Markham's sister, Lady Skinner, nursed her through smallpox in 1609.

Subsequent plans to overthrow James were exposed at a very early stage and the fate of the Main and Bye plotters offered a warning to other malcontents, while James's peace efforts worked to ensure that Spain was no longer prepared to offer financial or military help to overthrow him. Only a small group of Catholic extremists was prepared to risk one last, desperate attempt to overthrow him, and after the dud that was the Gunpowder Plot of 1605 both he and Cecil were secure.

❊   ❊   ❊

Sir John Harington was confident enough of a welcome at court to return for the Christmas celebrations. This year they were held at Hampton Court instead of Whitehall and Anna's passion for the arts had already made itself felt. Thirty plays were planned, including several works by William Shakespeare. The playwright had never been greatly favored by Elizabeth. He was, after all, the author of *Richard II*, the play that Essex had used to stir public feeling against her. Now any association with Essex was a positive advantage and his company had been promoted on 19 May from the Lord Chamberlain's Players to the King's Players.

Among the plays performed by the King's Players were *A Midsummer Night's Dream* and Ben Jonson's controversial *Sejanus, His Fall.* It painted a horrifying picture of Tiberian Rome, where men lived in terror of informers, arbitrary justice and the executioner. Any resemblance to the present age was entirely deliberate. There was even an allusion to Ralegh's trial in the character of Silius, who attacks his prosecutor for failing to supply proof of his treason. Meanwhile, courtiers were still talking of "matters yet hidden" behind the plots and Cecil was complaining anxiously to Shrewsbury about some undefined "base and viperous" accusation circulating against him.[30] None of this, however, troubled Anna. She and her ladies requested many private showings of plays as well as keeping busy with arrangements for the forthcoming masque, *The Vision of the Twelve Goddesses,* in which the Queen was to perform as Pallas Athene and the Ladies Bedford and Rich were to be Vesta and Venus.

In the past masques had been a predominantly male form of

courtly display and the younger and most handsome of James's fa-vored courtiers set the standard on 1 January 1604 with the *Masque of the Chinese Magician*. Heaven was re-created at the lower end of the hall at Hampton Court, where torchbearers and other lights revealed the masquers. They were dressed as Indian and Chinese knights in red satin robes embroidered with gold and bordered with silver lace. Anna was determined that her masque was to be still more dramatic and Harington learned that she had given Lady Suffolk and Lady Walsingham warrants to take Elizabeth's best apparel out of the Tower to be cut up and rearranged as costumes. She was clearly un-concerned that they were regarded as state treasure or that they held something of the iconic status of the queen who had once worn them. She had her own costume cut to the knee, prompting Dudley Carle-ton to joke that she must have done so in order that "we might see a woman had both feet and legs which I never knew before."

The eventual cost of *The Vision of the Twelve Goddesses* was estimated to be between £2,000 and £3,000, but Anna believed she could well afford it. James had granted her a jointure larger than any Queen of England had ever had before. While Anna set about highlighting the status of her personal court, James was occupied chiefly with enter-taining all the visiting ambassadors. There were at least seven at Hampton Court and the kitchens were overhauled to ensure that the elaborate banquets held in their honor never failed to impress. The French and Spanish ambassadors quarreled endlessly over matters of precedence, but happily for James and Anna they also vied to give the best gifts. The Queen of France, Marie de Médicis, sent Anna a cabi-net, "very cunningly wrought, and inlaid all over with musk and am-bergris, which maketh a sweet savour; and in every box was a different present of jewels and flowers, for head tiring," while the Queen of Spain had sent a mulberry-colored satin gown, ornamented with gilded cut leather.[31]

Cecil had been given the task of preparing for the coming Parlia-ment. The most important matter on the agenda was James's plans for Union between the kingdoms, but Cecil's lobbying was coming up against a brick wall and he confided in Shrewsbury that "whosoever is absent [from Parliament] I will protest they do it purposely because they say no to the Union."³² It must have seemed extraordinary to Harington that Cecil was still on the Privy Council. His hopes that James would bring sweeping changes to the Council had been disappointed, but now at last he was to meet the King he had backed as Elizabeth's heir. He described his audience in detail in a letter to his friend Sir Amias Paulett. He had at first been taken to kneel before the King in the Presence Chamber along with many others, but he was soon taken on one side and asked to wait in a room nearby. He was then escorted to another small room, this time furnished with a table that was covered with James's papers, ink and pens. James himself came in shortly afterward.

The King was in a jovial mood and he asked Harington if he was a cousin to Lord Harington of Exton, whose wife had the care of the Princess Elizabeth. Harington acknowledged that he was and James added that he had heard a great deal about Harington's learning. He proceeded to show off his own, quoting "profound sentences from Aristotle, and such like writers, which I had never read and which some are bold enough to say," Harington observed acidly, "others do not understand." James then cross-questioned Harington until, he confessed to Paulett, he began to feel that he was up before his old examiner at Cambridge. When at last this interrogation concluded James asked Harington what he thought "pure wit was made of; and whom did it best become? Whether a King should not be the best clerk in his own country; and if this land did not entertain good opinion of his learning and wisdom?" Harington took the hint and assured James that everyone admired his knowledge and wisdom. Given the opportunity, however, he would have concurred with Scaramelli, who had observed in the summer that the fact James believed that he knew more than anyone else rendered him incapable of conversation. But James did, at least, give Harington an insight into what he thought of the English court.

It was clear, for example, that James was shocked by the prevalence of smoking. The habit had become fashionable after Ralegh's discovery of Virginia and courtiers lavished as much as £300 or £400 a year on it. James was ahead of his time in recognizing smoking as unhealthy, and he warned Harington that tobacco "would, by its use, infuse ill qualities on the brain, and that no learned man ought to taste it, and [he] wished it forbidden." He was already planning a treatise on the subject, A *Counter-blast to Tobacco*, which would be published anonymously a few months later. He may well have been writing it at the table in the little room in which they stood.*

Another cause for alarm, in James's eyes, was the slack attitude the English had toward the threat from witchcraft. Although in later years he would become more questioning about how widespread witchcraft actually was, his experience of the Berwick witches and their efforts to kill him in the year of his marriage remained fresh in his mind. He had noted that while women were strangled and burned regularly as witches in Scotland, in England the death penalty was invoked in cases of witchcraft only if murder was proven—and that was very rare. James pressed Harington hard for his opinion, "touching the power of Satan in the matter of witchcraft," and asked him gravely if he knew why it was that the Devil so often worked in old women. Harington confessed to Sir Amias Paulett that at this point he could not resist "a scurvy jest" and replied that "we were taught hereof in scripture where it is told, that the Devil walketh in dry places." James enjoyed Harington's jokes, filthy though they were, but he was also in deadly earnest about the need to address the problem of witchcraft: he would see to it in the spring Parliament that its practice was made a capital offense.

The only moment that made Harington nervous, however, was when James brought up the subject of the execution of Mary, Queen of Scots, and the role of Sir William Davison, the man who had delivered her death warrant. Courtiers remained uncertain whether James might yet seek revenge against individuals connected with her fate. Harington tried to change the subject back to witchcraft, only to have James tell him that his mother's death had been foreseen in Scotland in visions of "a bloody head dancing in the air." James claimed that he knew a great deal about the gift of foresight and that he had a sure way to discover the future. He did not own any magic mirrors but he listed

---

*Ralegh, Essex and Kit Marlowe were among the more famous smokers of the period, though we can be certain none of them died as a result of its effects—two having been beheaded and one murdered.

a number of relevant books, warning Harington that he should not read them because an ordinary man was not as spiritually strong as a king and they might have a corrupting effect. Harington reassured James that he feared that the power of Satan had already wrought too much damage on his body for him to risk courting "his friendship, for my souls hurt." At this the conversation turned at last to James's favorite subject: religion.

Harington accepted that the issue of toleration for Catholics was a dead letter. James had announced to an Irish delegation in August that "he would rather fight in blood to the knees than give toleration of religion,"* and therefore Harington gave the subject of Catholicism a wide berth.[33] This was not hard to do, as the religious topic of the moment was the conference on the English Church that was to be held at Hampton Court only a week or two later. James intended to thrash out a middle ground between those who wanted the English Protestant Church to stay as it was and the radical reforms demanded by the more extreme Puritans. Anything that smacked of Presbyterianism was to be ruled out and the extremists who represented such views expelled or repressed.

Harington hoped to witness the conference and James, aware that Harington was bound to write about it, asked, "I pray you, do me justice in your reports," adding the warning that "in good season, I will not fail to add to your understanding, in such points as I may find you lack amendment." Elizabeth's godson "made courtesy hereat, and withdrew down the passage, and out at the gate, amidst the many varlets and lordly servants who stood around."[34] He promised Paulett that he would tell him more when they were alone at his house in Somerset: "I must press to silence hereon, as otherwise all is undone."

❋ ❋ ❋

The previous December, 1602, Harington had complained that England had been left to rack and ruin by an old Queen who lived "shut

---

*In the summer the judicial murder of Catholics would begin anew with a priest and his servant executed at Warwick in July and two laymen at Lancaster in August. The persecution of Catholics was to be less intense than it had been under Elizabeth, but as the Gunpowder Plot demonstrated, the despair was greater.

up in her chamber." His *Tract on the Succession* predicted that after Elizabeth's death the English would turn their backs on the recent past, embracing "a man of spirit and learning, of able body, of understanding mind"—one good Stuart who would "set all in order."[35] Within weeks of Elizabeth's death, however, Harington had performed a volte-face. As James journeyed south from Scotland, Harington bemoaned that he had "lost the best and fairest love that ever shepherd knew, even my gracious Queen," and he condemned James for hanging a man without trial. His later writings painted a beguiling portrait of his godmother's charm, intelligence and toughness of character. In retrospect he found that even her faults "did seem great marks of surprising endowments." Beside such a paragon, James would always be found wanting—and not only by Harington.

The glorification of Elizabeth's memory became a popular means of criticizing her successor. The Jacobean bishop Godfrey Goodman recalled how after only a few years the public began to express their hatred for the "Scottish government" by celebrating the date of Elizabeth's coronation with more enthusiasm than that of James. Her neglect of the English Church came to be overlooked and her pursuit of peace with Spain forgotten: she was now seen as a Protestant amazon, contrasted with James, the effeminate seeker of conciliation and compromise. Even the rottenness of the Elizabethan state was wiped from history by the national amnesia. In 1623, two years before James died, a paper was found in the hand of the statue of Queen Elizabeth at Westminster bewailing the state of England and looking for redress, just as the petitions of 1603 had once looked to James to end the corruption of Elizabethan public life. Matters had come full circle—and there they have stayed. Elizabeth is still remembered as the Gloriana celebrated on her accession day, while the young king who came south in 1603 is largely forgotten. Instead James remains fixed in the public imagination as the grotesque described by the sacked Jacobean official Sir Anthony Weldon in his *Character of King James.* Weldon's witty descriptions of a king who wore stiletto-proof doublets, slobbered at the mouth and walked about fiddling with his codpiece have come to define one of the most intellectually brilliant men ever to sit on the English throne.

Where did it all go so wrong for James? It was perhaps inevitable that someone who had raised the hopes of opposing groups before his accession would create disappointment when the time came for decisions. The first to feel betrayed were those who had hoped James would introduce toleration of religion for Catholics, among them Sir John Harington. The Hampton Court conference left many Puritans feeling equally let down. In the months leading up to the conference James had begun to associate English Puritans with Scots Presbyterians. In part this was the work of conservative bishops blackening their names, but the Puritans had also damaged their own cause. When James announced his intention to hold the conference in August he unleashed frantic lobbying for the abolition of episcopacy, wedding rings and even crucifixes. By the end of October the extreme views expressed had forced him to issue a proclamation against those who "seditiously seek reformation in church matters" and made him all the more determined to stamp out radicals. Harington, who attended the Hampton Court conference, observed that in dealing with the Puritan leaders James often "rather used upbraidings than arguments; and told the petitioners that they wanted to strip Christ again and away with their snivellings."[36]

James was, in fact, to introduce substantial reforms to the Church of England. He fulfilled promises to support a full preaching ministry and to clamp down on the publication of popish books. He also sponsored a new catechism and translation of the Bible—the now much-loved King James version. He showed far more care for the Church than Elizabeth ever had, but it was still much less than many Puritans had hoped for. When Archbishop Whitgift died shortly after the conference ended, the Northamptonshire Puritan Lewis Pickering composed a bitter elegy accusing Whitgift of being "masked impiety, cunning hypocrisy, Prelates pope, Jesuits hope."[37] Pickering had been the first courtier to see James after he had the official notice of Elizabeth's death in Scotland and he had left Edinburgh with James's assurances of support ringing in his ears. Someone pinned a copy of his elegy to Whitgift's coffin at his funeral and he was punished with a long term of imprisonment.

Meanwhile, Pickering's fellow Puritan, Sir Oliver Cromwell, was similarly disappointed in many of his political objectives. Negotiations over possible reforms of wardship and purveyance ground to a halt in May 1604 and Cecil was to remain Master of the Wards as well as Secretary of State until his death in 1612. He was in addition raised to the title of Earl of Salisbury in 1605 and made Lord Treasurer in 1608. The corruption in public life with which Cecil was so associated continued and even worsened while the grandeur of Elizabeth's court declined into decadence.

Harington wrote a memorable description of the entertainment of the King of Denmark at Theobalds in 1606 where he had seen "the ladies ... roll about in intoxication" and the men excel each other in "wild riot, excess, and devastation of time and temperance."[38] It was a long way from the prayers at James's coronation that "the glorious dignity of his royal court, may brightly shine ... far and wide in the eyes of all men." And James's personal behavior further diminished his prestige. In the months before he was crowned he had already revealed many of the flaws by which he is remembered: his incontinence with money, his intemperate attraction to young men, his arrogance and lack of charm or dignity. Above all, ordinary people complained that they missed "that generous affability that their good queen did afford them," and Harington came to concur. "We did all love [the Queen], for she said she loved us," he recalled, and James's Privy Councilor, the Earl of Suffolk, acknowledged: "These things are no more the same."[39] One of Scaramelli's successors as Venetian ambassador recalled that the consequence of the King's failure to "caress the people" was that James was "despised and almost hated."[40] There was never any national cult of King James and attempts to turn the figure of Arthur from a chivalric symbol to one of British Union failed. The Parliament of 1604 made it clear that they would not exchange the ancient name of England for Britain and the attitude remained the one expressed in the Doleman book on the succession: there was no possible advantage to England in it.

Those who hoped for a revival of the mythical glory days of the past and a monarch who could embody the old national aspirations looked to Prince Henry, the rising sun on the political horizon. Harington was one of those involved in the young Prince's education, but it was old members of the Essex faction such as Cromwell, who held the position of Master of the Prince's Game, who were at the center of his court. Prince Henry grew to be loved and admired for being everything that his father was not: he was gracious and elegant, a young man who enjoyed sports and soldiery. While James's policy of peace with Spain came to be seen as a threat to national security and the national religion, Henry was held up as a future champion of Protestantism in Europe and of a sea-borne empire.

In 1612 Henry Peacham's book *Minerva Britannia* had Elizabeth, the Fairy Queen, passing her scepter to Henry as Oberon, the Fairy Prince. It was to be a year of many changes. Harington's health was deteriorating and on 18 May, "sick of a dead palsie," he was brought to Bath, where in 1598 he had spent time with Elizabeth's dying Treasurer, Lord Burghley. He now found himself alongside Burghley's son, Robert Cecil, Earl of Salisbury, who was suffering from an advanced state of scurvy. Ulcerous and weeping sores covered the Secretary's body and he endured further agony from cancerous tumors in the stomach, liver and neck.

Cecil died on 24 May, only a few days after Harington saw him, and the news was greeted with an outpouring of public loathing. Popular verses compared him to that other hunchback, Richard III, claimed that he had died of syphilis contracted from the Countess of Suffolk and recalled his theft of common land and his role in the destruction of the Earl of Essex,

> And now these lecherous wretched all,
> That plotted worthy Essex's fall,
> May see by this foul loathsome end,
> How foully then they did offend.[41]

But if some of the bitterness of the past could be buried with Cecil, the hopes vested in Prince Henry were also to be snuffed out. Just as Harington was weakening during the summer months so was Prince Henry, who had contracted typhoid. He died in November at the age of eighteen. To Bishop Hacket it seemed as if so much light was extinguished that England had fallen into a darkness akin to hell. Harington was unable to make his own feelings known: he had passed away within days of Prince Henry and was buried at Kelston, leaving his "Sweet Mall" to see out James's reign. Queen Anna never recovered from Henry's death. She had broken the power of the Earl of Mar over Prince Henry and seen him raised by allies of her friends from the old Essex faction, but it had come to nothing. She could not bring herself to attend the ceremony in which Prince Charles was installed as Prince of Wales in 1616 and she died only three years later. James's new heir would never prove as popular as his brother, and in part this was surely because he had never been surrounded with men of the same caliber as Prince Henry was.

The three-year-old Charles had been too weak to be brought south in 1603, and when he had finally arrived in England in August 1604 the ladies who had offered to take charge of the little Duke were so concerned he might die that they demurred from taking responsibility for him. Only the wife of Sir Robert Carey had stepped forward. The woman Carey had married "more for her virtues than her fortune" raised the future Charles I with devotion and courage. When James wanted the membrane under Charles's tongue cut to help him speak and his legs put in irons to help him walk, she protested against it until she got her way. As the Prince flourished Carey was put in charge of his household. He kept his position until Charles was eleven and was later made the Prince's Master of the Robes and Lord Chamberlain—extraordinary good fortune for a member of the Boleyn family, all the more so when it was the consequence of a marriage that was one of those rare acts in court life that were free of cynicism. But a man who was still despised for racing to Scotland before Elizabeth's corpse was cold could do little political good for his young master's image.

Despite increasing poor health James outlived Anna by six years, dying at Theobalds on 27 March 1625 after a stroke. One of Charles I's earliest decisions was to raise Carey to the title of Earl of Monmouth, a mark, perhaps, of his poor political judgment. But the verdict of history has generally been harsher on James than on the son, who led England and Scotland into civil war. If the first Stuart King of England could defend his reign, he might point out to us that when he first arrived in London he announced that he had three specific aims: the preservation of religion, peace and the unification of his three kingdoms. He proved to be remarkably successful in the first two. Although James's ecumenical hopes were well ahead of their time his interest in the Church of England left it in a considerably better state than he had found it, with a well-educated and confident clergy. His success in keeping his three kingdoms at peace earned some respect, even from Sir Anthony Weldon, and at his death he was lauded as "James the Peaceful and the Just." If his biggest regret was his failure to found a united kingdom of Britain, James did help create a British identity by continuing the process of integrating the great families of his kingdoms begun with the Nottingham-Lennox marriage in September 1603.

In the end, however, we are left with Weldon's image of the "wisest fool in Christendom." James's lack of dignity, his self-indulgence, his evident contempt for ordinary people and his failure to appreciate the importance of Elizabeth's role as a symbol of national aspirations counted for more than his good intentions and high intellect. "It is a true old saying," James informed Prince Henry in the *Basilikon Doron,* "that a King is as one set up a stage, whose smallest actions and gestures, all the people gazingly do behold: and therefore although a King be never so precise in the discharging of his Office, the people, who seeeth but the outward part, will ever judge of the substance, by the circumstances and according to the outward appearance."

The contrast between the vulgar James and the iconic Elizabeth was so startling and the perceptions of him so negative that the political nation never learned to trust him. The respect in which the English crown was held was thus diminished and the nation that shaped and worshiped Gloriana has never forgiven him for it.

NOTES

The following abbreviations are used in the notes:

Border papers: *Calendar of Letters and Papers Relating to the Affairs of the Borders of England and Scotland*

CSPAS: *Calendar of Letters and State Papers Relating to English Affairs Preserved in or Originally Belonging to the Archives of Simancas, vol. 4, 1587–1603*

CSPD: *Calendar of the State Papers, Domestic Series, of the Reign of Elizabeth, 1601–1603; with Addenda 1547–1565; and 1603–1610*

CSPS: *Calendar of the State Papers Relating to Scotland, vol. 2, 1547–1603*

CSPV: *Calendar of the State Papers Relating to English Affairs, Existing in the Archives and Collections of Venice, vol. 9, 1592–1603; vol. 10, 1603–1607*

DNB: *Dictionary of National Biography*

HMC Rutland: *Historical Manuscripts Commission, Manuscripts of His Grace the Duke of Rutland, KG, 2 vols.*

HMC Salisbury: *Historical Manuscripts Commission, Manuscripts of the Marquis of Salisbury, vols. 12, 14, 15 (Calendar of the Manuscripts of the Most Honourable the Marquess of Salisbury . . . Preserved at Hatfield House, Hertfordshire)*

PRO: Public Record Office

CHAPTER ONE
"The World Waxed Old"
1. Sir John Harington, *A Tract on the Succession to the Crown*, AD 1602, p. 51.
2. Fynes Moryson, *An Itinerary, 1617*, vol. 4, pp. 231–6.
3. Simon Thurley, *The Royal Palaces of Tudor England*, pp. 54–5; Sir John Harington, *Nugae Antiquae, being a miscellaneous collection of original papers*, with notes by Thomas Park FSA, vol. 1, p. 168.
4. Harington, *Nugae Antiquae*, vol. 1, p. 168.

5. For a detailed discussion of Elizabethan patronage see MacCaffrey, *Place and Patronage:* he estimates there were 2,500 politically active people in England, and also Malcolm R. Smuts, *Court Culture and the Origins of a Royalist Tradition in Early Stuart England.* For a contemporary view see Thomas Wilson's *State of England in 1600.*

6. Harington, *Nugae Antiquae,* vol. 1, p. 168.

7. John Chamberlain quoted in Smuts, *Court Culture,* p. 77.

8. Harington, *Tract,* p. 40.

9. *Camden Miscellany,* vol. 16, p. 2.

10. *Camden Miscellany,* vol. 16, p. 5.

11. John Clapham, *Elizabeth of England,* edited by E. Plummer Read and C. Read, p. 97.

12. Frederic Gerschow, "Diary of the Duke of Stettin's Journey through England in 1602," *Transactions of the Royal Historical Society,* vol. 6 (1892), p. 15.

13. J. E. Neale, "The Sayings of Queen Elizabeth," *History New Series,* 10 (1925), p. 383.

14. Gerschow, "Diary of Duke of Stettin," p. 25.

15. De Maisse, *A Journal of All That Was Accomplished by Monsieur de Maisse, Ambassador in England, from Henri IV to Queen Elizabeth,* edited by G. B. Harrison, p. 23.

16. Godfrey Goodman, *The Court of James the First,* vol. 1, p. 164.

17. Harington, *Nugae Antiquae,* vol. 1, pp. 320–4.

18. "Rivers," December 1601 in Henry Foley, SJ (ed.), *Records of the English Province of the Society of Jesus,* vol. 1, p. 8.

19. Harington, *Nugae Antiquae,* vol. 1, p. 323.

20. Harington, *Nugae Antiquae,* vol. 1, p. 321.

21. Harington, *Nugae Antiquae,* vol. 1, pp. 320–4.

22. Thurley, *Royal Palaces,* p. 209.

23. R. Doleman, *A Conference About the Next Succession to the Crowne of Ingland,* part 2, pp. 1–2; Harington, *Tract,* p. 23.

24. Harington, *Tract,* p. 41.

25. Right Rev'd John Spottiswoode, *The History of the Church and State of Scotland,* edited by Right Rev'd M. Russell, vol. 2, pp. 11–13.

26. Spottiswoode, *Church and State,* vol. 2, pp. 10–13.

27. Harington, *Tract,* p. 106; the Protestant John Manningham also notes: "Religion must be persuaded not enforced," *The Diary of John Manningham of the Middle Temple 1602–1603,* edited by Robert Parker, p. 244.

28. John Guy, *Tudor England,* pp. 331–2, and John Guy, *My Heart Is My Own, The Life of Mary Queen of Scots,* p. 475.

29. Letter 16, Sara Jayne Steen (ed.), *The Letters of Arbella Stuart,* p. 167; Harington, *Tract,* p. 42.

30. John Aubrey, *Aubrey's Brief Lives,* edited by Oliver Lawson Dick, p. 255.

31. P. M. Handover, *Arbella Stuart: Royal Lady of Hardwick and Cousin to King James,* p. 75; Francis Edwards, *Plots and Plotters in the Reign of Elizabeth I,* p. 75.

32. Handover, *Arbella Stuart,* p. 77; Steen (ed.), *Letters of Arbella Stuart,* p. 20.

33. Harington, *Tract,* p. 45.

34. Henry Wotton, *The Life and Letters of Sir Henry Wotton,* edited by Logan Pearsell Smith, p. 487.

35. Smuts, *Court Culture*, pp. 76–9.
36. See *Camden Miscellany*, vol. 16, pp. 42–3.
37. Clapham, *Elizabeth of England*, p. 87.
38. Guy, *Tudor England*, p. 396.
39. Goodman, *Court of James*, vol. 1, pp. 96–7; John Guy (ed.), *The Reign of Elizabeth I, Court and Culture in the Last Decade*, p. 4.
40. Harington, *Nugae Antiquae*, vol. 1, p. 168.
41. Manningham, *Diary*, p. 219.
42. Doleman, *Conference*, part 2, p. 424.
43. Harington, *Tract*, p. 33.
44. Edwards, *Plots and Plotters*, p. 186.
45. De Maisse, *Journal*, p. 115.
46. Harington, *Tract*, p. 106.
47. Doleman, *Conference*, part 2, p. 191.
48. Thomas Phelipps, CSPD, 12, addenda, p. 407.
49. Doleman, *Conference*, part 2, pp. 94, 96.
50. Christopher Hill: "The many-headed monster in late-Tudor and early-Stuart thinking," in C. H. Carter (ed.), *From the Renaissance to the Counter-Reformation*, p. 305.
51. Doleman, *Conference*, part 2, p. 183.
52. Doleman, *Conference*, part 2, p. 189.
53. Doleman, *Conference*, part 2, p. 196; Antonia Fraser, *The Gunpowder Plot: Terror and Faith in 1605*, p. 7.
54. Harington, *Tract*, p. 106.
55. Moryson, *Itinerary*, vol. 2, p. 261.
56. Harington, *Nugae Antiquae*, vol. 1, pp. 179–80.
57. Cuffe to Cecil, HMC Salisbury; appendix; Edward Edwards, *The Life of Sir Walter Ralegh*, vol. 2, pp. 82–3.
58. Mervyn James, *Society, Politics and Culture, Studies in Early Modern England*, p. 45. For a detailed account of the coup attempt see CSPD, 1603–1610, pp. 109–10.
59. James, *Society, Politics and Culture*, p. 462; HMC Rutland, 1, p. 373.
60. De Maisse, *A Journal*, p. 82.
61. Harington, *Nugae Antiquae*, vol. 1, p. 317.
62. Guy, *Reign of Elizabeth I*, p. 5.
63. Guy, *Tudor England*, p. 401.
64. J. E. Neale, *Queen Elizabeth I*, p. 389.
65. Sir Roger Wilbraham, *The Journal of Sir Roger Wilbraham for the Years 1593–1616*, edited by Harold Spencer Scott, *Camden Miscellany*, vol. 10, p. 45.
66. Rivers in Foley (ed.), *Records*, p. 24.
67. Henry Howard to Edward Bruce, 1602, in Goodman, *The Court of James*, p. 97.
68. Lucy Aikin, *Memoirs of the Reign of Queen Elizabeth*, vol. 2, p. 487.
69. Rivers in Foley (ed.), *Records*, p. 47.
70. Rivers in Foley (ed.), *Records*, p. 37.
71. Rivers in Foley (ed.), *Records*, p. 50. I am grateful to Professor John Finnis, co-author of a forthcoming biography of Sterrell, for the identification of Rivers.
72. Harington, *Nugae Antiquae*, vol. 1, pp. 325–35.

CHAPTER TWO

"A Babe Crowned in His Cradle"

1. Dickinson, William Croft, *Scotland from the Earliest Times to 1603,* p. 397; Bruce Galloway, *The Union of England and Scotland 1603–1608,* pp. 6–7.
2. Dickinson, *Scotland,* p. 397; Galloway, *Union of England,* pp. 6–7. John Napier would go on to invent the decimal point.
3. Moryson, *Itinerary,* vol. 3, pp. 497, 498, and vol. 4, pp. 177, 180.
4. A. L. Juhala, "The Household and Court of King James VI of Scots, 1567–1603," unpublished Ph.D. thesis, pp. 124, 125, 126, 153, 154.
5. Cited in Robert Ashton, *James I, by His Contemporaries,* pp. 4, 5.
6. Moryson, *Itinerary,* vol. 4, pp. 228, 235, 183.
7. Moryson, *Itinerary,* vol. 4.
8. Francis Osborne, "Some Traditionall Memorialls on the Raign of King James," in *The Works of Francis Osborne,* pp. 1–143.
9. Ashton, *James I,* pp. 1–3; Harris D. Willson, *King James VI and I,* pp. 53–4.
10. See A. W. Beasley, "The Disability of James VI & I," in *The Seventeenth Century,* vol. 10 (1995).
11. Harington, *Tract,* p. 121; HMC Salisbury, 13, p. 495.
12. James VI of Scotland, *Correspondence with Sir Robert Cecil and Others in England,* Camden Society, p. 37.
13. W. B. Patterson, *King James VI & I and the Reunion of Christendom,* pp. 17, 18.
14. Patterson, *King James,* p. 38.
15. James VI, *Basilikon Doron,* in Johann P. Somerville (ed.), *Political Writings,* p. 28.
16. Spottiswoode, *Church and State,* vol. 2, p. 165.
17. Harington, *Nugae Antiquae,* vol. 1, pp. 367–71.
18. Quoted in Willson, *King James,* p. 30.
19. Willson, *King James,* p. 36.
20. Osborne, "Some Traditionall Memorialls," p. 128.
21. *Basilikon Doron,* in Somerville (ed.), *Political Writings,* p. 23.
22. For a detailed discussion of James's sexuality see Michael B. Young, *James and the History of Homosexuality.*
23. Somerville (ed.), *Political Writings,* p. xxxix.
24. Jenny Wormald, "The Neighbour to the North," in *Queen Elizabeth I: Most Politick Princess,* p. 37.
25. Willson, *King James,* p. 53.
26. Maxwell Scott, *The Tragedy of Fotheringay,* p. 256.
27. Maxwell Scott, *Fotheringay,* appendix; Spottiswoode, *Church and State,* vol. 4, p. 120n. The above is drawn mainly from Bourgoing, pp. 417–23, here translated from the French, M. R. Chantelauze, "Marie Stuart son Procès et son Execution," *Journal of Bourgoing* (Paris 1876).
28. *Basilikon Doron,* in Somerville (ed.), *Political Writings,* p. 120.
29. Quoted in Agnes Strickland (ed.), *Lives of the Queens of England,* pp. 26–7.
30. David Stevenson, *Scotland's Last Royal Wedding: The Marriage of James VI and Anne of Denmark,* p. 104.
31. Stevenson, *Last Royal Wedding,* pp. 59, 104, 105.
32. Maximilien de Béthune, Duc de Sully, *Memoirs of Maximilian de Bethune, Duke of Sully,* translated by Charlotte Lennox, vol. 4, p. 57.

33. Edmund Lodge (ed.), *Illustrations of British History, Biography and Manners, selected from the manuscripts of the noble families of Howard, Talbot and Cecil*, 3, pp. 1–2.

34. Sully, *Memoirs*, vol. 4, p. 57.

35. Juhala, "Household and Court," pp. 159, 160, 299, for the descriptions of Anna's clothes and jewels.

36. Barbara Kiefer Lewalski, *Writing Women in Jacobean England*, pp. 17, 177.

37. Stevenson, *Scotland's Last Royal Wedding*, p. 105.

38. William Forbes-Leith SJ, *Narratives of the Scottish Catholics Under Mary Stuart and James VI*, pp. 263–5.

39. Sully, *Memoirs*, vol. 4, p. 57.

40. Forbes-Leith, *Narratives*, pp. 263–5.

41. Strickland (ed.), *Lives*, p. 58, from a report of a quarrel sent to England 25 May 1595.

42. Strickland (ed.), *Lives*, pp. 60, 61.

43. Joel Hurstfield, *The Succession Struggle in Late Elizabethan England: Elizabethan Government and Society*, p. 393.

44. HMC Salisbury, 10, p. 388; W. F. Arbuckle, "The Gowrie Conspiracy," *Scottish Historical Review*, 36 (1957), p. 106.

45. Arbuckle, "Gowrie Conspiracy," p. 11.

46. Willson, *King James*, p. 128.

47. Arbuckle, "Gowrie Conspiracy," p. 129.

48. Arbuckle, "Gowrie Conspiracy," pp. 96–7.

49. Paul E. J. Hammer, *The Polarisation of Elizabethan Politics: The Political Career of Robert Devereux, 2nd Earl of Essex, 1585–97*, p. 167, 88n.

50. James VI of Scotland, *Correspondence with Sir Robert Cecil and Others in England*, pp. 35–6.

51. Goodman, *Court of James*, vol. 1, pp. 31–2. In another version of the story he told her the bag stank and needed to be aired before she looked through it. Wilson, Arthur, *The History of Great Britain, Being the Life and Reign of King James the First*, p. 2.

52. *Camden Miscellany*, vol. 16, 3rd series, pp. 42–3.

53. *Camden Miscellany*, vol. 16, 3rd series, pp. 42–3.

54. Goodman, *Court of James*, vol. 1, pp. 66–7.

55. Clapham, *Elizabeth of England*, p. 92.

56. Clapham, *Elizabeth of England*, p. 93.

57. P. M. Handover, *The Second Cecil, 1563–1604*, p. 218.

58. See John Finnis and Patrick Martin's forthcoming biography of William Sterrell, and my thanks to John Finnis for showing me his draft article for *American Literary Review*, 2003.

59. Edwards, *Life of Sir Walter Ralegh*, vol. 2, p. 331.

60. Letters from Cecil to Carew, *Letters to Sir George Carew*, ed. Jon McLean, Camden Society, pp. 108–16.

61. Edwards, *Life*, vol. 2, p. 261; Handover, *Cecil*, p. 262; Cecil, *Letters to Sir George Carew*, Camden Society, pp. 84–5.

62. D. D. Hailes, *Memorials and Letters Relating to the History of Britain in the Reign of James the First*, p. 16.

63. Handover, *Cecil*, p. 250.

64. Handover, *Cecil*, p. 257.

65. Hailes, *Memorials*, pp. 24–5.
66. Edwards, *Life*, vol. 2, pp. 313, 314; Hailes, *Memorials*, p. 65.
67. Edwards, *Life*, vol. 2, pp. 436–44.
68. The paper in question was anonymous but current thinking is that it was written by Ralegh.
69. June, 1602, Letter X, quoted in Edwards, *Life*, vol. 2, p. 312.
70. James VI, *Correspondence*, pp. 53–61.
71. James VI, *Correspondence*, p. 54.
72. James VI, *Correspondence*, pp. 55–6.
73. Harington, *Tract*, p. 104.
74. See Michael Questier, "Clerical Recruitment, Conversion and Rome c. 1580–1625," in *Patronage and Recruitment in the Tudor and Early Stuart Church*, edited by Claire Cross.
75. Northumberland to James, in James VI, *Correspondence*, p. 56.
76. From a letter translated by John Finnis, Vatican Archives, Borghese II, g.I.ff. 69–70v.
77. James VI, *Correspondence*, pp. 30–2.
78. James VI, *Correspondence*, pp. 30–2.
79. James VI, *Correspondence*, pp. 34–5.
80. James VI, *Correspondence*, p. 37.
81. Albert J. Loomie, *Guy Fawkes in Spain: The Spanish Treason in Spanish Documents*, pp. 11, 12, 21; HMC Salisbury, 17, p. 512; CSPAS, 4, 1587–1603, p. 724.
82. CSPAS, 4, pp. 719–29.
83. John Chamberlain, *The Letters of John Chamberlain*, edited by Norman Egbert McClure, p. 180.
84. Stone, Lawrence, *The Crisis of the Aristocracy 1558–1641*, p. 221; Stone mentions that they were brought by William Cavendish for Chatsworth, but William did not buy the house from his brother until some years later.

CHAPTER THREE
"Westward . . . Descended a Hideous Tempest"

1. Thomas Dekker, *Wonderful Year of 1603*, in Dekker, *Non-Dramatic Works*, p. 85.
2. Thurley, *Royal Palaces*, p. 209.
3. W. B. Rye, *England as Seen by Foreigners in the Days of Elizabeth and James the First*, pp. 134, 272; also Gerschow, "Stettin," p. 57.
4. Goodman, *Court of James*, vol. 1, p. 164.
5. Diana Scarisbrick, "Anne of Denmark's jewellery," p. 52; also Steen (ed.), *Letters*, Letter 1, p. 119.
6. CSPV, 9, p. 532.
7. Moryson, *Itinerary*, vol. 4, p. 219.
8. CSPV, 9, p. 532.
9. Alberto Tenenti, *Piracy and the Decline of Venice 1580–1615*, pp. 64, 68.
10. CSPV, 9, p. 533.
11. William Camden, *The History of Elizabeth, Late Queen of England*, Book IV, p. 659.
12. Rivers in Foley (ed.) *Records*, pp. 55, 56.
13. HMC Salisbury, 12, pp. 583–7; Letter 3, Steen (ed.), *Letters*, p. 121.
14. Henry Howard had described to James how Mary had tried and failed to per-

suade Elizabeth to forgive Lady Ralegh for marrying Sir Walter behind her back.

15. CSPD, 1580–1625, addenda, pp. 407–8.
16. Harington, *Tract*, p. 44.
17. Brouncker to Elizabeth, HMC Salisbury, 12, pp. 593–4.
18. Brouncker to Cecil, HMC Salisbury, 12, p. 595.
19. Recent biographers of Arbella have referred to Stapleton as "Henry" Stapleton, but Bess's letters to Cecil describe him as the son and heir to "Stapleton of Carlton." This was not Henry Stapleton, but Richard. The only Henry Stapleton was a Protestant kinsman and neighbor at Wighill, then age twenty-nine (see H. E. Chetwynd-Stapleton, *The Stapletons of Yorkshire*, pp. 159–61, pp. 231–5). For Bess's letters see HMC Salisbury, 12, p. 689.
20. HMC Salisbury, 14, pp. 252, 253, 254.
21. Letter 8, Steen (ed.), *Letters*, p. 135.
22. Steen (ed.), *Letters*, p. 34.
23. CSPV, 9, pp. 539, 540, 541, 542.
24. CSPV, 9, p. 549.
25. Richard Berleth, *The Twilight Lords*, p. 292.
26. Harington, *State of Ireland*, p. 3.
27. Cyrall Falls, *Elizabeth's Irish Wars*, pp. 333–4; Berleth, *Twilight Lords*, pp. 292–3; Goodman, *Court of James*, vol. 2, pp. 43–6.
28. Rivers in Foley (ed.), *Records*, p. 52.
29. Rivers in Foley (ed.), *Records*, p. 54.
30. Rivers in Foley (ed.), *Records*, p. 53.
31. Letter 8, Steen (ed.), *Letters*, p. 151–4.
32. Letter 15, Steen (ed.), *Letters*, p. 156–7.
33. Rivers in Foley (ed.), *Records*, pp. 52–5.
34. Rivers in Foley (ed.), *Records*, pp. 54–7.
35. Cecil, *Letters*, Camden Society, pp. 52–4.
36. Camden, *History of Elizabeth*, p. 659.
37. Rivers in Foley (ed.), *Records*, p. 53.
38. Hill, "The many-headed monster," p. 297.
39. Roger B. Manning, *Village Revolts, Social Protests and Popular Disturbances in England, 1509–1640*, pp. 209–10.
40. HMC Salisbury, 12, p. 672.
41. Letter 16, Steen (ed.), *Letters*, pp. 158–75.
42. HMC Salisbury, 12, p. 689.
43. Northumberland to James VI, *Correspondence*, p. 72.
44. Clapham, *Elizabeth of England*, p. 98.
45. James VI, *Correspondence*, pp. 72–3.
46. Manningham, *Diary*, p. 208; Clapham, *Elizabeth of England*, p. 99; Wilbraham, *Journal*, p. 54.
47. Northumberland to James, *Correspondence*, pp. 72–5.
48. CSPV, 9, p. 558.
49. CSPV, 9, p. 558. Scaramelli mistakenly wrote "9th" as "19th," which I have corrected here to save confusion.
50. CSPV, 9, p. 558.

51. I would like to thank Dr. Paul Davenport and Dr. Sharon Mitchell for information on this condition.

52. CSPV, 9, pp. 559, 560.

53. CSPV, 9, pp. 559, 560.

54. CSPV, 9, pp. 559, 560.

55. HMC Salisbury, 15, p. 4.

56. For Carey's memoirs see *Stuart Tracts 1603–1693*, pp. 2–10.

57. Clapham, *Elizabeth of England*, p. 98.

58. CSPV, 9, p. 566.

59. *Stuart Tracts*, pp. 2–3; report of parliamentary commissioners quoted in *Country Life*, 14 April 1944.

60. Chamberlain, *Letters*, p. 189.

61. Gerschow, "Stettin," p. 7.

62. William Weston, *Autobiography of an Elizabethan*, p. 222.

63. Catherine Loomis, "Elizabeth Southwell's Manuscript Account of the Death of Queen Elizabeth," *English Literary Renaissance*, p. 485; also Elizabeth Cooper, *The Life and Letters of Arabella Stuart*, vol. 2, p. 254. In his *Diary*, pp. 207–8, John Manningham notes Elizabeth was still not taking physic and "princes must not be forced"—a phrase he seems to have heard from her clerics, who may have been repeating her own words.

64. W. Kelly, *Royal Progresses and Visits to Leicester*, p. 317.

65. *Stuart Tracts*, p. 4; Loomis, "Elizabeth Southwell's Manuscript," p. 486; CSPV, 9, p. 562.

66. Manningham, *Diary*, pp. 207–8; Chamberlain, *Letters*, p. 189.

67. Loomis, "Southwell's Manuscript," p. 486; *Stuart Tracts*, p. 4.

68. Loomis, "Southwell's Manuscript," p. 486, and p. 493 on "rascals" being repeated by de Beaumont and Manningham.

69. HMC Salisbury, 14, p. 247.

70. William Cobbett, *Cobbett's Complete Collection of State Trials and Proceedings for High Treason and other Crimes and Misdemeanours*, pp. 5–7.

71. James F. Larkin and Paul L. Hughes (eds.), *Stuart Royal Proclamations 1603–1625*, pp. vi, 1, 2.

72. Larkin and Hughes (eds.), *Proclamations*, pp. 1, 2.

73. Manningham, *Diary*, p. 211.

74. Moryson, *Itinerary*, vol. 3, pp. 496–7; Harrison, *Jacobean Journal*, p. 282.

75. Gerschow, "Stettin," p. 29; Manningham, *Diary*, pp. 208, 209; John Stowe, *Annales of England*, p. 817.

76. Dekker, *Wonderful Year*, pp. 86–7.

77. Letter to Dr. Dun from Simon Theloal, 26 March 1603, cited in Goodman, *Court of James*, vol. 2, p. 57.

78. Clapham, *Elizabeth of England*, p. 99.

79. Manningham, *Diary*, p. 209.

CHAPTER FOUR
"Lots Were Cast upon Our Land"

1. Joseph Hall, in a sermon commemorating the death of Elizabeth and accession of James, 24 March 1613. Hall, *Collected Works*.

2. Goodman, *Court of James*, vol. 1, pp. 24–5.

3. DNB entry for Grey of Wilton; Edwards, *Life*, vol. 2, p. 474.

4. Harington, *Nugae Antiquae*, vol. 1, p. 271.

5. Aubrey, *Brief Lives*, p. 257; see also Osborne, "Some Traditionall Memorialls," and DNB entry for Grey of Wilton.

6. HMC Salisbury, 15, p. 11; also Manningham's diary and Chamberlain letters.

7. Goodman, *Court of James*, vol. 1, p. 25.

8. S. R. Gardiner, *A History of England from the Accession of James I to the Outbreak of Civil War*, vol. 1, pp. 85–6.

9. Moryson, *Itinerary*, vol. 3, p. 479 and vol. 4, p. 169.

10. Brydges, *Peers of England*, vol. 1, p. 402.

11. Galloway, *Union of England*, pp. 10, 229; S. J. Watts and Susan J. Watts, *From Border to Middle Shire: Northumberland 1586–1625*, pp. 37–53.

12. John Nichols, *The Progresses, Processions and Magnificent Festivities of James the First*, p. 33n; Brydges, *Peers of England*, vol. 1, pp. 10–12.

13. *Basilikon Doron*, in Somerville (ed.), *Political Writings*, p. 24.

14. *The Register of the Privy Council of Scotland*, edited by David Masson, vol. 6, 1599–1604, p. 558.

15. John Taylor, *Travels Through Stuart Britain: The Adventures of John Taylor, the Water Poet*, edited and selected by John Chandler, pp. 29–31; Moryson, *Itinerary*, vol. 2, pp. 118–19.

16. As soon as James received this letter he signed an act making it a treasonable offense to conduct a raid into England, *Register of the Privy Council of Scotland*, p. 548.

17. For Carey's story see Brydges, *Peers of England*, vol. 1, pp. 412–15. There may have been other unofficial messengers already in Scotland. John Manningham's London diary mentions that Carey's fall had slowed him so much that someone else had overtaken him. There are three possible names. A letter exists from a John Ferrour to Cecil referring to himself as a "prime messenger." Other accounts state that Thomas Berkeley was an official bearer of the news of the Queen's death. The great Victorian historian S. R. Gardiner mentions a third, called George Marshall. Only Carey, however, held the proof of the ring (Lodge, *Illustrations*, vol. 3, p. 1; Brydges, *Peers of England*, vol. 1, p. 22; Gardiner, *History of England*, p. 86).

18. H. Lonchay, J. Cuvelier and J. Lefèvre (eds.), *Correspondance de la cour d'Espagne sur les affaires des Pays-Bas au XVIIe siècle*, pp. 141–2.

19. Spottiswoode, *Church and State*, vol. 3, p. 135.

20. HMC Salisbury, 15, p. 10; Spottiswoode, *Church and State*, vol. 3, p. 135.

21. CSPV, 10, p. 5.

22. Letters, 27 March, HMC Salisbury, 15: Sir George Carew to Sir Robert Cecil, pp. 8–9; James to Cecil, pp. 9–10; Thomas Burghley to Cecil, pp. 10–11.

23. Wilbraham, *Journal*, p. 55; Nichols, *Progresses, Processions*, pp. 27, 28, 30; Francis Drake, *Eboracum of the History and Antiquities of the City of York*, p. 130.

24. Watts and Watts, *Border to Middle Shire*, p. 136.

25. Watts and Watts, *Border to Middle Shire*, p. 136.

26. Moryson, *Itinerary*, vol. 2, p. 235.

27. Nichols, *Progresses, Processions*, p. 59.

28. R. Bakan, *Medical Hypothesis*, 17 (3): pp. 277–84. What is a little curious is that

none of Henry VIII's daughters had children. Not just Elizabeth and Mary—
who was said to have had menstrual problems since childhood—but also the
illegitimate Ethelreda.

29. Manningham, *Diary*, p. 223.

30. Chamberlain, *Letters*, p. 189.

31. The Stowe inventory is listed in full in Janet Arnold's *Queen Elizabeth's Wardrobe Unlocked*.

32. Clapham, *Elizabeth of England*, p. 110; CSPV, 10, p. 3.

33. Peter E. McCullough, *Sermons at Court: Politics and Religion in Elizabethan and Jacobean Preaching*, p. 102; Manningham, *Diary*, p. 211.

34. Sir Henry Whithead, *Sir Henry Whithead's Letter Book*, vol. 1, 1601–1640, pp. 16–17; Manningham, *Diary*, p. 211.

35. Manningham, *Diary*, pp. 211, 212.

36. McCullough, *Sermons at Court*, p. 102; Manningham, *Diary*, p. 211.

37. Manningham, *Diary*, p. 210. Dr. Boleyn was a member of Cambridge University. Sir John Harington described his lack of pretension, saying that when Dr. Boleyn took off his gowns he would put aside all gravity and be "as good a fellow as the best of you." He claimed he admired the same quality in James. Harington, *Tract*, p. 84.

38. Manningham, *Diary*, p. 222.

39. Nieves Matthews, *Francis Bacon: The History of a Character Assassination*, p. 47.

40. See for example Francis Osborn's *Political Reflections: Historical Memoirs on the Reigns of Queen Elizabeth and King James*, pp. 92–5, and F. Tanner, *Recollections of a Westminster Antiquary*. In contrast to Lady Nottingham, Lady Scrope was the most loyal of Essex's defenders among Elizabeth's ladies—her husband was Henry Howard's nephew.

41. Manningham, *Diary*, p. 219.

42. MacLure, *Paul's Cross Sermons*, p. 99.

43. Chamberlain, *Letters*, p. 189.

44. HMC Salisbury, 15, p. 31.

45. Wilbraham, *Journal*, p. 55.

46. Chamberlain, *Letters*, p. 189.

47. Harington, *Nugae Antiquae*, vol. 1, p. 339.

48. Weldon, *Court and Character*, pp. 2–3.

49. H. Lonchay et al. (eds.), *Correspondance*, p. 149.

50. HMC Salisbury, 15, p. 31.

51. Falls, *Elizabeth's Irish Wars*, pp. 333–4; Berleth, *Twilight Lords*, pp. 292, 293.

52. Moryson, *Itinerary*, vol. 3, pp. 303–4.

53. HMC Salisbury, 15, p. 30.

54. CSPD, 1603, p. 1; HMC Salisbury, 15, p. 31.

55. Manningham, *Diary*, p. 218.

56. Handover, *Cecil*, p. 298.

57. Juhala, *Household and Court*, p. 168.

58. Chambers, pp. 12–14.

59. Pauline Croft, "The Reputation of Robert Cecil: libels, political opinion and popular awareness in the early seventeenth century," *Transactions of the Royal Historical Society*, p. 277.

60. Nichols, *Progresses, Processions*, p. 63.

61. Nichols, *Progresses, Processions*, p. 65; Sykes, *Local Records or Historical Records of Northumberland and Durham, Newcastle upon Tyne and Berwick upon Tweed*, vol. 1.

62. Lucy Aikin, *Memoirs of the Court of Queen Elizabeth*, vol. 2, p. 445.

63. Harington, *Nugae Antiquae*, vol. 1, pp. 354–63.

64. Border papers, 2, p. xxii.

65. HMC Salisbury, 15, p. 37.

66. Intriguingly this servant was said to be intending to go to Spain for help; CSPD, 1603, p. 4.

67. CSPV, 10, pp. 9–10.

68. Mark Nicholls, "Treason's Reward: The Punishment of Conspirators in the Bye Plot of 1603," *Historical Journal*, 38, p. 832. The priest William Watson claimed he heard the story from a nobleman who had been in Scotland, probably Lord Cobham.

69. Border papers, 2, p. xx; Moryson, *Itinerary*, vol. 2, pp. 116–17; Watts and Watts, *Border to Middle Shire*, pp. 210–11.

70. Chamberlain, *Letters*, p. 192.

71. Chamberlain, *Letters*, p. 181.

72. Larkin and Hughes (eds), *Proclamations*, p. 8.

73. CSPV, 10, p. 9.

74. Roland G. Usher, *The Reconstruction of the English Church*, p. 140.

75. Nichols, *Progresses, Processions*, pp. 70–1.

76. Manningham, *Diary*, p. 245.

77. 255r, *York Corporation House Books for Reign of James I*, transcribed by Professor Toshio Sakata.

78. 255a, *York Corporation House Books*.

79. Nichols, *Progresses, Processions*, p. 70.

80. Goodman, *Court of James*, vol. 2, p. 100n.

81. Quoted in R. C. Munden, "James I and the growth of mutual distrust," in *Faction and Parliament*, edited by K. Sharpe, p. 45. The Council declined to do so, but a Parliament was to be held the following year.

82. Matthew had also been with the King in Newcastle, where he gave the sermon in St. Nicholas's Church on Sunday 10 April.

83. Nichols, *Progresses, Processions*, pp. 75–6.

84. Nichols, *Progresses, Processions*, p. 122.

85. Nichols, *Progresses, Processions*, p. 124.

86. *York Corporation House Books*, p. 154.

87. *York Corporation House Books*, pp. 139, 152.

88. *York Corporation House Books*, pp. 139, 144.

89. *York Corporation House Books*, p. 155.

90. *York Corporation House Books*, p. 155. Burghley had received the instructions via his deputy secretary John Fern.

91. *York Corporation House Books*, p. 148. The yeomen were from Ainsty.

92. Nichols, *Progresses, Processions*, p. 83.

93. Loomie, *Spanish Treason*, pp. 22–3; CSPD, 1603, p. 5.

94. CSPV, 10, p. 26.

95. HMC Salisbury, 15, p. 52.

96. CSPV, 10, p. 10. Scaramelli's dispatches do not mention any names, but Lord Grey of Wilton, Lord Cobham and Sir John Fortescue had all spoken out against accepting Scots into the government, and the Earl of Northumberland had warned James against giving posts to Scotsmen.

97. In 1607 a Venetian emissary wrote that "Home, grown rich by great presents, is the chief cause why Salisbury [Cecil] is maintained in his present place of reputation and power," CSPV, 10, p. 515.

98. 10 April 1603, quoted in Jenny Wormald, "The creation of Britain," *Transactions of the Royal Historical Society*, p. 179; Goodman, *Court of James*, vol. 1, p. 27.

99. HMC Salisbury, 15, p. 49.

100. Loomie, *Spanish Treason*, pp. 493–7, and p. 487.

101. James Spedding, *An Account of the Life and Times of Francis Bacon*, Book III, pp. 413–14; Bacon's comments are undated and may have been made at some other stage during James's progress.

102. Neil Cuddy, "The Anglo-Scottish Union and the Court of James I, 1603–1625," *Transactions of the Royal Historical Society*, vol. 39, p. 109.

103. Philip Caraman, *Henry Garnet, 1555–1606, and the Gunpowder Plot*, p. 213.

CHAPTER FIVE
"Hope and Fear"

1. Quoted in John Gerard, *Autobiography of an Elizabethan*, translated by Philip Caraman, p. 306.

2. CSPV, 10, p. 10.

3. James VI, *Correspondence*, p. 37.

4. He is known to history as Ignatius because of a clerical error when he matriculated at the University of Paris.

5. MacCulloch, *Reformation*, p. 392.

6. Thomas Graves Law, *Jesuits and Seculars*, p. lxv.

7. Law, *Jesuits and Seculars*, pp. xcviii–xcix.

8. Handover, *Cecil*, p. 290.

9. Bancroft to Cecil, HMC Salisbury, 12, p. 350.

10. Law, *Jesuits and Seculars*, p. xcii. Some of this gossip still survives: historians who are Catholics usually spell "Persons" with an "e"; Protestants spell it with an "a"—an allusion to his supposed origins as the bastard son of a parson.

11. Law, *Jesuits and Seculars*, pp. xciv–xcv.

12. Rivers, 18 June 1602, in Foley (ed.), *Records*, vol. 1, p. 39.

13. Garnet to Persons, quoted in Philip Caraman, *Henry Garnet, 1555–1606, and the Gunpowder Plot*, pp. 540–1.

14. Usher, *Reconstruction*, vol. 1, p. 185.

15. Watson to Privy Council, Goodman, *Court of James*, vol. 2, p. 62.

16. Watson to Privy Council, Goodman, *Court of James*, vol. 2, p. 62.

17. Entitled "A reply unto a certain libel lately put forth by Father Persons."

18. HMC Salisbury, 15, p. 35.

19. Moryson, *Itinerary*, vol. 3, p. 480.

20. Timothy Mowl, *Elizabethan and Jacobean Style*, pp. 98–9.

21. The park was described in 1636 as covering over 2,000 acres and having 800 fallow deer as well as a mill and a trout stream.

22. Nichols, *Progresses, Processions*, p. 87.
23. L. G. Wickham Legg (ed.), *A Relation of a Short Survey of Twenty-Six Counties Observed in a Seven Week Journey Begun on August 11th, 1634*, p. 10.
24. Ashton, *James I*, p. 65.
25. Harington, *Nugae Antiquae*, vol. 1, p. 16.
26. Moryson, *Itinerary*, vol. 4, p. 158.
27. Taylor, *Travels*, p. 163.
28. Harington, *Nugae Antiquae*, p. 180, and *Tract*, p. 51.
29. James would also name Rutland his ambassador to Denmark in June.
30. "A congratulatory elegy of the peaceable entry of King James, given to his Majesty at Burghley 1603" by Sir John Harington, cited in Nichols, *Progresses, Processions*.
31. Quoted in Linda Levy Peck, *Northampton, Patronage and Policy at the Court of James I*, p. 23.
32. Gardiner, *History of England*, p. 95n.
33. HMC Salisbury, 15, p. 57.
34. C. G. A. Clay, *Economic Expansion and Social Change: England 1500–1700*, vol. 1, p. 76.
35. Nichols, *Progresses, Processions*, pp. 94–5.
36. HMC Salisbury, 15, p. 60.
37. HMC Salisbury, 15, p. 71.
38. CSPD, 1603–1610. p. 9; HMC Salisbury, 15, p. 60.
39. Lawrence Stone, "The Fruits of Office: The Case of Robert Cecil First Earl of Salisbury, 1596–1612," in F. J. Fisher (ed.), *Essays in the Economic and Social History of Tudor and Stuart England*, pp. 107–8.
40. Clapham, *Elizabeth of England*, p. 111.
41. Stowe, *Annales of England*, p. 815; HMC Salisbury, 15, p. 56; CSPV, 10, p. 22.
42. Stowe, *Annales of England*, p. 815; Dekker, *Wonderful Year*, pp. 87–8.
43. Philip Gawdy, *Letters of Philip Gawdy*, edited and introduced by Isaac Herbert Geaves, p. 128.
44. HMC Salisbury, 15, p. 62.
45. Gawdy, *Letters*, p. 128.
46. HMC Salisbury, 15, p. 57.
47. Loomie, *Spanish Treason*, pp. 17–18; Lonchay et al. (eds.), *Correspondance*, p. 155.
48. CSPV, 10, pp. 21–2.
49. Clapham, *Elizabeth of England*, p. 113.
50. See Nicholas Tyacke, "Puritan Politicians and James VI and I, 1587–1604," in *Politics, Religion and Popularity in Early Stuart Britain*, edited by Thomas Cogswell, Richard Cust and Peter Lake.
51. Nichols, *Progresses, Processions*, p. 99.
52. Goodman, *Court of James*, vol. 1, pp. 28–9.
53. Robert Chambers, *The Life of King James the First*, vol. 1, p. 33.
54. Nichols, *Progresses, Processions*, pp. 103–4.
55. Nichols, *Progresses, Processions*, p. 127.
56. Gerschow, "Stettin," p. 31.
57. Nichols, *Progresses, Processions*, pp. 98–113.
58. Aubrey, *Brief Lives*, p. 257.
59. Nichols, *Progresses, Processions*, p. 107.

60. G. P. V. Akrigg, *A Jacobean Pageant: the Court of King James*, pp. 49–50.

61. Cuddy, "The Anglo-Scottish Union," pp. 109–10, and "Revival of the Entourage," p. 176.

62. Nichols, *Progresses, Processions*, p. 113.

63. Nichols, *Progresses, Processions*, pp. 128–32.

64. Weldon, *Court and Character*, p. 376.

65. Peter E. McCullough, *Sermons at Court: Politics and Religion in Elizabethan and Jacobean Preaching*, p. 105.

66. Lady Newdigate-Newdegate, *Gossip From a Muniment Room*, p. 55.

67. Wilson, *Plague*, pp. 84–8.

68. Weston, *Autobiography*, p. 224.

69. Gerschow, "Stettin," p. 15.

70. Strickland (ed.), *Lives of the Queens*, p. 80.

71. Strickland (ed.), *Lives of the Queens*, p. 80.

72. Lord Zouche had been appointed President of Wales in June 1602. The courtier John Chamberlain complained he had been playing king there ever since. DNB entry.

73. CSPV, 10, p. 33.

74. Young, *James and Homosexuality*, pp. 28–9; see also Stone, *Crisis of the Aristocracy*.

CHAPTER SIX
"The Beggars Have Come to Town"

1. Gerschow, "Stettin," p. 63.

2. CSPV, 10, p. 39.

3. CSPV, 10, p. 39.

4. CSPV, 10, p. 46.

5. Moryson, *Itinerary*, vol. 4, pp. 184–5. The rather less prim "Water Poet" John Taylor later joked that he consumed so much wine and ale when he was in Edinburgh "that every night before I went to bed, if any man had asked me a civil question, all the wit in my head could not have made him a sober answer," Taylor, *Travels*, p. 30.

6. Young, *James and Homosexuality*, p. 28.

7. Nichols, *Progresses, Processions*, p. 188.

8. Willson, *James VI and I*, p. 165.

9. Gawdy, *Letters*, p. 134.

10. Gawdy, *Letters*, p. 131.

11. CSDP, 1603–1610, p. 11; Gawdy, *Letters*, p. 131; Brydges, *Peers of England*, vol. 1, p. 415.

12. D'Ewes quoted in Janet Arnold, *Elizabeth's Wardrobe Unlocked*, p. 174.

13. CSPV, 10, p. 515.

14. CSPV, 10, p. 44; Loomie, *Spanish Treason*, p. 62.

15. Loomie, *Spanish Treason*, pp. 61–2.

16. Lonchay et al. (eds.), *Correspondance*, vol. 1, p. 156.

17. HMC Salisbury, 15, p. 98.

18. Nichols, *Progresses, Processions*, p. 146.

19. Larkin and Hughes (eds), *Proclamations*, p. 22.

20. Wilson, *Plague*, pp. 60, 64.

21. HMC Salisbury, 15, p. 125.

22. Peter Lombard, *De Regno Hiberniae*, quoted in Hiram Morgan, *Tyrone's Rebellion: The Outbreak of the Nine Years War in Tudor Ireland*, p. 4.

23. Harington, *Nugae Antiquae*, vol. 1, pp. 249–51.

24. Harington, *Nugae Antiquae*, vol. 1, pp. 340–1.

25. Lonchay et al. (eds), *Correspondance*, vol. 1, p. 149.

26. CSPV, 10, p. 48; de Béthune, Maximilien, Duc de Sully, *Memoirs of Maximilian de Bethune, Duke of Sully*, vol., Book XIV, p. 56.

27. Nichols, *Progresses, Processions*, p. 159.

28. Sully, *Memoirs*, vol. 3, XIV, pp. 43–6.

29. Sully, *Memoirs*, vol. 3, XIV, pp. 50–9.

30. CSPV, 10, pp. 49–50.

31. Sully, *Memoirs*, vol. 3, XIV, p. 66.

32. Sully, *Memoirs*, vol. 3, XIV p. 67.

33. CSPV, 10, p. 54; Nichols, *Progresses, Processions*, p. 161.

34. Moryson, *Itinerary*, vol. 4, p. 228.

35. Sully, *Memoirs*, vol. 3, XV, pp. 74–9.

36. CSPV, 10, p. 55.

37. Sully, *Memoirs*, vol. 3, XIV, pp. 56–7.

38. CSPV, 10, p. 57.

39. Sully, *Memoirs*, vol. 3, XIV, pp. 54–5.

40. Sully, *Memoirs*, vol. 3, XIV, pp. 44–5.

41. Sully, *Memoirs*, vol. 3, XV, pp. 78–9.

42. Cuddy, "Anglo-Scottish Union," pp. 113–14.

43. Agnes Latham and Joyce Youings (eds.), *The Letters of Sir Walter Ralegh*, pp. 245–6.

44. The Queen's itinerary from Berwick to York was as follows: "Monday 6 June—From Berwick to Chillingham, Sir Ralph Grey; Tuesday 7 June—Thence to Alnwick to dinner and to Witherington to bed; Wednesday 8 June—Thence to Bottell to dinner and to Newcastle to bed; Thursday 9 June—Thence to Durham to dinner and to Auckland to bed; Friday 10 June—Thence to Smeton to dinner and to Brackenborough to bed; Sir Thomas Lassells, Saturday 11 June—Thence to the High Sheriffs to dinner and to York to bed," HMC Salisbury, 15, p. 126.

45. HMC Salisbury, 15, p. 119.

46. HMC Salisbury, 15, p. 233.

47. Nicholls, "Treason's Reward," p. 836.

48. Edwards, *Life*, vol. 1, p. 350.

49. PRO, SP 14/3/34.

50. Sully, *Memoirs*, XV, p. 105.

51. Revd M. Tierney, *Dodd's Church History of England*, vol. 1, appendix, pp. vi–vii.

52. Law, *Jesuits and Seculars*, pp. xciv–xcv.

53. Manningham, *Diary*, p. 220.

54. Nicholls, *Two Winchester Trials*, p. 32.

55. Nicholls, *Two Winchester Trials*, p. 38.

56. Maurice Lee Jr., *James I and Henry IV: An Essay in English Foreign Policy, 1603–1610*, pp. 26–7.

57. HMC Salisbury, 15, p. 154.

58. Chambers, *The Life of King James the First*, vol. 1, pp. 50–1.

59. Hailes, *Memorials and Letters*, pp. 185–7.
60. CSPV, 10, p. 513.
61. Spottiswoode, *Church and State*, vol. 3, p. 140.
62. Carleton Williams, *Anne of Denmark*, pp. 73–4.
63. Quoted in *Register of the Privy Council of Scotland*, p. 572.
64. Nichols, *Progresses, Processions*, p. 161.
65. Charles Topclyffe to Cecil, HMC Salisbury, 15, p. 143.
66. Moryson, *Itinerary*, vol. 4, p. 152.
67. T. Fielding Johnson, *Glimpses of Ancient Leicester*, p. 201.
68. Strickland (ed.), *Lives of the Queens*, p. 94.
69. Anne Clifford, *The Diary of the Lady Anne Clifford*, p. 8.
70. Nichols, *Progresses, Processions*, p. 176.
71. Nichols, *Progresses, Processions*, pp. 184–7.
72. Willson, *James VI and I*, p. 165; Carleton Williams, *Anne of Denmark*, p. 81.
73. Thomas Becon, *Book of Matrimony*, quoted in A. Esler, *The Aspiring Mind of the Elizabethan Younger Generation*, p. 59.
74. Nichols, *Progresses, Processions*, p. 190.
75. Nichols, *Progresses, Processions*, p. 187.
76. Gerschow, "Stettin," p. 49.
77. Stowe, *Annales of England*, p. 826; Nichols, *Progresses, Processions*, pp. 193–4.
78. Nichols, *Progresses, Processions*, p. 197.

CHAPTER SEVEN
"An Anointed King"
1. HMC Salisbury, 15, pp. 194–5.
2. Edwards, *Life*, vol. 1, p. 366.
3. Nicholls, "Treason's Reward," p. 833.
4. Nicholls, "Two Winchester Trials," p. 38; PRO, SP 14/2/65.
5. Nicholls, "Sir Walter Ralegh's Treason: A Prosecution Document," *English Historical Review*, 110, 1995, p. 919.
6. Nicholls, "Ralegh's Treason," p. 921.
7. HMC Salisbury, 15, p. 208.
8. Agnes Latham and Joyce Youings (eds.), *Letters of Sir Walter Ralegh*, pp. 248–9.
9. CSPD, 1603, p. 4.
10. Aubrey, *Brief Lives*, p. 257.
11. Edwards, *Life*, vol. 2, p. 448.
12. Latham and Youings (eds.), *Letters of Sir Walter Ralegh*, p. 248.
13. Latham and Youings (eds.), *Letters of Sir Walter Ralegh*, pp. 248–9.
14. Robert Persons, "A political retrospect, being Fr Persons letter to Fr Anthony Rivers, July 6th 1603," Catholic Record Society, *Miscellanea*, vol. 2, pp. 214–18.
15. CSPV, 10, p. 66.
16. CSPV, 10, p. 67.
17. Lodge, *Illustrations*, vol. 3, p. 88; Strickland (ed.), *Lives of the Queens*, vol. 5, pp. 108–9.
18. CSPV, 10, p. 72.
19. CSPV, 10, p. 74.
20. HMC Salisbury, 15, p. 167; Gawdy, pp. 135, 163.

21. Nichols, *Progresses, Processions*, p. 221.
22. Cuddy, "Revival of the Entourage," p. 197.
23. Dekker, *Wonderful Year*, pp. 102–5.
24. HMC Rutland, vol. 1, p. 392.
25. Strickland (ed.), *Lives of the Queens*, p. 105.
26. It is almost certain that King Harold was crowned at Westminster Abbey.
27. Elizabeth I had taken communion in both kinds at her coronation, which was marked by three amendments to the traditional Latin service: (1) the epistle and gospel were read in English; (2) the host was not elevated, and instead a vernacular ritual of preparation was read prior to Elizabeth receiving communion; (3) Elizabeth took communion in both kinds.
28. Arthur Wilson, *The History of Great Britain, Being the Life and Reign of King James the First*, p. 5.
29. Scaramelli's descriptions (which are from CSPV, 10, pp. 74–7) are supplemented with information drawn from other witnesses, particularly a Roman called Giovanni degli Effeti. The works of reference are: *The Ceremonies, Form of Prayer and Services used in Westminster Abbey at the Coronation of King James 1st and Queen Anne* (1685); J. Wickham Legg (ed.), *The Coronation Order of King James I*, and most important: Claude Blair (ed.), *The Crown Jewels*, vol. 1. My thanks to Claude Blair for his advice on this section; any mistakes are, of course, my own. For a history of the coronation and more thorough descriptions and explanations see Sir Roy Strong's forthcoming book: *Coronation: A History*.
30. Wilson, *Plague*, pp. 90, 94, 95, 97, 98.
31. Lodge, *Illustrations*, vol. 3, p. 38.
32. CSPV, 10, p. lxi.
33. Lodge, *Illustrations*, vol. 3, pp. 40–1.
34. Carleton Williams, *Anne of Denmark*, p. 87.
35. Osborn, *Works of Francis Osborn*, p. 54.
36. Jenny Wormald, "Gunpowder, Treason and Scots," in *Journal of British Studies*, vol. 24, p. 160; CSPD, 1603, p. 43.
37. Steen (ed.), *Letters*, p. 184.
38. Croft, "Reputation of Robert Cecil," p. 273.
39. Lodge, *Illustrations*, vol. 3, pp. 21, 34.
40. CSPD, 1603, p. 43.
41. Larkin and Hughs (eds.), *Proclamations*, vol. 1, p. 9.

CHAPTER EIGHT
"The God of Truth and Time"

1. Nicholls, "Sir Walter Ralegh's Treason," p. 918.
2. Lodge, *Illustrations*, vol. 3, p. 30.
3. HMC Salisbury, 15, p. 311.
4. Edwards, *Life of Sir Walter Ralegh*, I, p. 367.
5. Gawdy, *Letters*, p. 137,
6. Harington, *The Letters and Epigrams of Sir John Harington Together with The Prayse of Private Life*, edited and introduced by Norman McClure, pp. 103–4.
7. Harington, *Letters*, pp. 104–6.
8. Harington, *Letters*, pp. 108–9.

9. Sir John Harington, *State of Ireland*, p. 6.

10. Lodge, *Illustrations*, vol. 3, p. 75.

11. CSPV, 10, p. 94.

12. Patterson, *Reunion of Christendom*, p. 41.

13. HMC Salisbury, 15, p. 283.

14. The Vatican's response to James's call for a General Council expressed the view that there had already been several councils, all of which had confirmed the truth of the Church's "holy doctrine" and the Council of Trent had dealt with those issues that needed to be resolved. Henri IV of France had once called for another General Council, but, the Vatican reminded James, Henri had eventually accepted the truth without the need for one. The Pope had hopes that Anna might be instrumental in bringing James to "see the light" and sent her relics, rosaries and other devotional objects to encourage him. James was so angry that he had the messenger put in the Tower. On 19 February James protested "his utter detestation of their superstitious religion and that he was so far from favouring it, as if he thought his son and heir after him would give any toleration thereunto, he would wish him fairly buried before his eyes." Recusancy fines were introduced and all priests ordered into exile within a month.

15. Nicholls, "Treason's Reward," p. 829.

16. For trial transcript see Cobbett, *State Trials* and Edwards, *Life*.

17. William Cobbett, *Cobbett's Complete Collection of State Trials and Proceedings for High Treason and other Crimes and Misdemeanours* (1809), p. 47.

18. Cobbett, *State Trials*, pp. 48–9.

19. Cobbett, *State Trials*, p. 50.

20. Steen (ed.), *Letters*, pp. 191–2.

21. Edwards, *Life*, vol. 1, pp. 441–2; Cobbett, *State Trials*, p. 51.

22. Ralegh, *Letters*, pp. 263–5.

23. Anstruther, Godfrey, *Vaux of Harrowden*, Newport, 1953, p. 262.

24. HMC Salisbury, 15, pp. 8–11.

25. Cobbett, *State Trials*, pp. 52–4.

26. Steen, *Letters*, p. 197.

27. "Inventory of Such Things as Were Found on the Body of Sir WR etc," in Edwards, *Life*, vol. 2, p. 496.

28. Goodman, *The Court of James the First*, vol. 1, pp. 66–7.

29. Sully, *Memoirs*, Book XIV, vol. 3, p. 160.

30. Lodge, *Illustrations*, vol. 3, p. 81.

31. Strickland (ed.), *Lives of the Queens*, vol. 5, p. 114.

32. Lodge, *Illustrations*, vol. 3, p. 81.

33. Wilbraham, *Journal*, p. 62.

34. Harington, *Nugae Antiquae*, vol. 1, pp. 367–71.

35. Harington, *Nugae Antiquae*, vol. 1, p. 354.

36. Harington, *Nugae Antiquae*, vol. 1, pp. 181–2.

37. Croft, "The Reputation of Robert Cecil," p. 275.

38. Harington, *Nugae Antiquae*, vol. 1, p. 352.

39. Harington, *Nugae Antiquae*, vol. 1, pp. 354–63.

40. CSPV, 10, p. 513.

41. Croft, "The Reputation of Robert Cecil," pp. 52, 53, 55, 60 and 61.

BIBLIOGRAPHY

Adams, Robert M., *Ben Jonson's Plays and Masques* (New York and London, 1979)

Aikin, Lucy, *Memoirs of the Court of King James I,* 2 vols. (London, 1823)

———, *Memoirs of the Court of Queen Elizabeth,* 2 vols. (London, 1818)

Akrigg, G. P. V., *A Jacobean Pageant: The Court of King James* (London, 1962)

Anstruther, Godfrey, *Vaux of Harrowden* (Newport, 1953)

Arbert, E., *Stuart Tracts 1603–1693* (London, 1903)

Arbuckle, W. F., "The Gowrie Conspiracy," *Scottish Historical Review* 36 (1957)

Arnold, Janet, *Queen Elizabeth's Wardrobe Unlocked* (Leeds, 1988)

Ashton, Robert, *James I: By His Contemporaries* (London, 1969)

Aubrey, John, *Aubrey's Brief Lives,* edited, and with a life of John Aubrey, by Oliver Lawson Dick (Boston, 1999)

Bakan, R., *Medical Hypothesis* 17 (3): 277–84 (July 1985)

Barroll, Leeds, *Anna of Denmark, Queen of England; A Cultural Biography* (Philadelphia, 2001)

———, "The Court of the First Stuart Queen," in *The Mental World of the Jacobean Court,* edited by Linda Levy Peck (Cambridge, 1991)

Batho, G. R., "The Finances of an Elizabethan Gentleman," *Economic History Review* 9 (1957)

Beasley, A. W., "The Disability of James VI & I," in *The Seventeenth Century,* vol. 10 (1995)

Berleth, Richard, *The Twilight Lords* (London, 1978)

de Béthune, Maximilien, Duc de Sully, *Memoirs of Maximilian de Bethune, Duke of Sully,* 5 vols., translated by Charlotte Lennox (London, 1810)

Binny, Marcus, "Holme Pierrepont Hall, Nottinghamshire," *Country Life* 20 (September 1979)

Blair, Claude (ed.), *The Crown Jewels: The History of the Coronation Regalia in the Jewel House in the Tower of London,* vol. 1 (London, 1998)

Border papers: *Calendar of Letters and Papers Relating to the Affairs of the Borders of England and Scotland,* edited by Joseph Bain, vol. 2, 1595–1603 (Edinburgh, 1896)

Bossy, John, "Henry IV, the Appellants and the Jesuits," *Recusant History,* August 2002

——, "The English Catholic Community, 1603–1605," in *The Reign of James VI & I,* edited by A. G. R. Smith (London, 1973)

Bradley, E. T., *The Life of the Lady Arabella Stuart,* 2 vols. (London, 1889)

Brereton, Sir W., *Notes of a Journey Through Durham and Northumberland in the yr 1635* (Newcastle, 1844)

Brown, Cornelius, *A History of Newark on Trent,* vol. 2 (London, 1891)

Brydges, Sir S. E., *Memoirs of the Peers of England During the Reign of James 1st* (London, 1802)

Calendar of Letters and State Papers Relating to English Affairs, Preserved in or Originally Belonging to the Archives of Simancas, vol. 4, 1587–1603, edited by Martin A. S. Hume (London, 1899)

Calendar of the State Papers, Domestic Series, of the Reign of Elizabeth, 1601–1603; with addenda 1547–1565; Preserved in Her Majesty's Public Record Office, vol. 6, edited by Mary Anne Everett Green (London, 1870)

Calendar of the State Papers, Domestic Series, 1603–1610, Preserved in Her Majesty's Public Record Office, edited by Mary Anne Everett Green (London, 1857–59)

Calendar of the State Papers Relating to Scotland, vol. 2, 1547–1603 (London, 1858)

Calendar of the State Papers Relating to English Affairs, Existing in the Archives and Collections of Venice, vol. 9, 1592–1603 (London, 1897)

Calendar of the State Papers Relating to English Affairs, Existing in the Archives and Collections of Venice, vol. 10, 1603–1607 (London, 1900)

Camden, William, *The History of the Most Renowned and Victorious Princess Elizabeth, Late Queen of England,* Book IV, 3rd edition, by E. Flesher (London, 1675)

The Camden Miscellany, vol. 16 (London, 1936)

Caraman, Philip, *Henry Garnet, 1555–1606, and the Gunpowder Plot* (London, 1964)

Carleton Williams, Ethel, *Anne of Denmark* (London, 1970)

Carter, Charles Howard, *The Secret Diplomacy of the Habsburgs, 1598–1625* (New York, 1964)

Catholic Record Society, *Miscellanea*, vol. 2 (London, 1906)

Cecil, R., *Letters to Sir George Carew*, edited by Jon McLean, Camden Society, 88 (1864)

———, *The Secret Correspondence of Sir Robert Cecil with King James VI of Scotland*, edited by Edmund Goldsmid FRHS, FSA (Scot), 3 vols. (Edinburgh, 1887)

The Ceremonies, Form of Prayer and Services used in Westminster Abbey at the Coronation of King James I and Queen Anne (London, 1685)

Chamberlain, John, *The Letters of John Chamberlain*, edited by Norman Egbert McClure, 2 vols. (Philadelphia, 1939)

Chambers, Robert, *The Life of King James the First*, 2 vols. (Edinburgh, 1830)

Chantelauze, M. R., "Marie Stuart son Procès et son Execution," *Journal of Bourgoing* (Paris, 1876)

Chetwynd-Stapleton, H. E., *The Stapletons of Yorkshire* (London and Bombay, 1897)

Clapham, John, *Elizabeth of England*, edited by E. Plummer Read and C. Read (London, 1951)

Clay, C. G. A., *Economic Expansion and Social Change: England 1500–1700*, vols. 1 and 2 (Cambridge, 1984)

Clifford, Anne, *The Diary of the Lady Anne Clifford*, with an introductory note by V. Sackville-West (London, 1923)

Clifford, Henry, *The Life of Jane Dormer, Duchess of Feria*, translated from manuscript by Canon E. E. Escort (London, 1887)

Cobbett, William, *Cobbett's Complete Collection of State Trials and Proceedings for High Treason and Other Crimes and Misdemeanours*, vol. 2 (1809)

Cooper, Elizabeth, *The Life and Letters of Arabella Stuart*, 2 vols. (London, 1866)

Country Life, "Apethorpe": 20 March 1909; 27 March 1909; "Hinchingbrooke": 2 November 1907; 6 April 1929; 13 April 1929; "Lumley Castle": 18 June 1910; "Dingley Hall": 16 and 23 April 1921; "Richmond Palace": 14 April 1944

Croft, Pauline, *King James* (New York and Basingstoke, 2003)

———, "The Reputation of Robert Cecil: Libels, Political Opinion and Popular Awareness in the Early Seventeenth Century," *Transactions of the Royal Historical Society*, 6th series, 1 (March 1991)

———, "Robert Cecil and the Early Jacobean Court," in *The Mental World of the Jacobean Court,* edited by Linda Levy Peck (Cambridge, 1991)

Cuddy, Neil, "The Anglo-Scottish Union and the Court of James I, 1603–1625," *Transactions of the Royal Historical Society,* vol. 39 (1989)

———, "The Revival of the Entourage: The Bedchamber of James I, 1603–1625," in David Starkey et al., *The English Court: From the Wars of the Roses to the Civil War* (London, 1987)

Dekker, Thomas, *The Non-Dramatic Works of Thomas Dekker,* vol. 1 (London, 1884)

———, *The Seven Deadly Sinnes of London,* The Percy Reprints, no. 4 (London, 1922)

De Maisse, *A Journal of All That Was Accomplished by Monsieur de Maisse, Ambassador in England from Henry IV to Queen Elizabeth, Anno Domini 1597,* edited by G. B. Harrison (London, 1931)

Dickens, A. G., "The Extent and Character of Recusancy in Yorkshire, 1604," *Yorkshire Archaeological Journals* 37 (1945)

Dickinson, William Croft, *Scotland from the Earliest Times to 1603* (Oxford, 1977)

Dodd, A. H., "North Wales and the Essex Revolt of 1601," *English Historical Review* 59 (1944)

———, "Wales and the Scottish Succession 1570–1605," *Transactions of the Cymmrodorion Society,* 1937 Sessia (1938)

Doleman, R., *A Conference About the Next Succession to the Crowne of Ingland* (n.p. [Antwerp], 1594)

Donaldson, Gordon, *Foundations of Anglo-Scottish Union, Elizabethan Government and Society, Essays Presented by Sir John Neale* (London, 1961)

Drake, Francis, *Eboracum of the History and Antiquities of the City of York* (London, 1736)

Durant, David N., *Bess of Hardwick* (London, 1999)

Edmondes, Sir Thomas, *The Edmondes Papers,* edited by Geoffrey G. Butler (London, 1913)

Edwards, Edward, *The Life of Sir Walter Ralegh,* 2 vols. (London, 1868)

Edwards, Francis, *Plots and Plotters in the Reign of Elizabeth I* (Dublin, 2002)

Ellis, Steven G., *Tudor Frontiers and Noble Power: The Making of the British State* (Oxford, 1995)

Emery, Anthony, *Greater Medieval Houses of England and Wales 1300–1500,* 2 vols. (Cambridge, 1996)

Esler, A., *The Aspiring Mind of the Elizabethan Younger Generation* (Durham, N.C., 1966)

Falls, Cyrall, *Elizabeth's Irish Wars* (London, 1970)

Ferguson, William, *Scotland's Relations with England: A Survey to 1707* (Edinburgh, 1977)

Fielding Johnson, T., *Glimpses of Ancient Leicester* (Leicester and London, 1906)

Fincham, Kenneth, *Prelate as Pastor: The Episcopate of James I* (Oxford, 1990)

Fincham, Kenneth, and Peter Lake, "The Ecclesiastical Policy of James VI & I," *Journal of British Studies* 24 (1985)

——, "Popularity, Prelacy and Puritanism in the 1630s: Bishop Hall Explains Himself," *English Historical Review* (1996)

Forbes-Leith, SJ, William, *Narratives of the Scottish Catholics Under Mary Stuart and James VI* (Edinburgh, 1885)

Forster, A. M., "A Durham Family: The Jenisons of Walworth," *Recusant History*, March 2001

Fraser, Antonia, *The Gunpowder Plot: Terror and Faith in 1605* (London, 1996)

——, *Mary, Queen of Scots* (London, 1969)

Fuller, T., "The History of the University of Cambridge Since the Conquest," part 5, *Church History of Britain*, for John Williams (1655)

Galloway, Bruce, *The Union of England and Scotland 1603–1608* (Edinburgh, 1986)

Gardiner, S. R., *History of England from the Accession of James I to the Outbreak of Civil War*, 10 vols. (London, 1883)

Gawdy, Philip, *Letters of Philip Gawdy*, edited and introduced by Isaac Herbert Geaves (London, 1906)

Gee, Henry, and William Jon Hardy (eds.), *Documents Illustrative of English Church History* (New York, 1896)

Gerard, John, *Autobiography of an Elizabethan*, translated by Philip Caraman (London, 1951)

Gerschow, Frederic, "Diary of the Duke of Stettin's Journey Through England in 1602," *Transactions of the Royal Historical Society* 6 (1892)

Goldberg, Jonathan, *James I and the Politics of Literature* (Baltimore and London, 1983)

Goodare, Julian, "Scottish Politics in the Reign of James VI," in Julian Goodare and Michael Lynch (eds.), *The Reign of James VI* (East Lothian, 2000)

Goodman, Godfrey, *The Court of James the First* (from the original manuscript), 2 vols. (London, 1839)

Gristwood, Sarah, *Arbella, England's Lost Queen* (London, 2003)

Guy, John, *Tudor England* (Oxford, 1988)

——, *My Heart Is My Own: The Life of Mary, Queen of Scots* (London, 2004)

—— (ed.), *The Reign of Elizabeth I, Court and Culture in the Last Decade* (Cambridge, 1995)

Hailes, D. D., *Memorials and Letters Relating to the History of Britain in the Reign of James the First,* published from the originals (Glasgow, 1766)

Hall, Joseph, *The Works of Joseph Hall,* 12 vols., edited by Miles Flesher (London, 1647)

Haller, William, *Foxe's Book of Martyrs and the Elect Nation* (London, 1967)

Hammer, Paul E. J., *The Polarisation of Elizabethan Politics: The Political Career of Robert Devereux, 2nd Earl of Essex, 1585–97* (Cambridge, 1999)

Handover, P. M., *Arbella Stuart: Royal Lady of Hardwick and Cousin to King James* (London, 1957)

——, *The Second Cecil, 1563–1604* (London, 1959)

Harington, Sir John, *A briefe view of the state of the Church of England . . . to the year 1608. Being a character & history of the bishops of those times. And may serve as an additional supply to Dr Goodwin's catalogue of bishops,* for Jos. Kirton (1653)

——, *The Letters and Epigrams of Sir John Harington Together with The Prayse of Private Life,* edited by Norman McClure (Philadelphia, 1930)

——, *The Metamorphosis of Ajax* (London, 1814)

——, *Nugae Antiquae, being a miscellaneous collection of original papers,* with notes by Thomas Park FSA, 2 vols. (London, 1804)

——, *A Short View of the State of Ireland* (Oxford and London, 1879)

——, *A Tract on the Succession to the Crown, AD 1602,* (London, 1880)

Harrison, G. B., *A Jacobean Journal, Being a Record of Those Things Most Talked of During the Years 1603–1606* (London, 1941)

Hill, Christopher, "The Many-Headed Monster in Late-Tudor and Early-Stuart Thinking," in C. H. Carter (ed.), *From the Renaissance to the Counter-Reformation: Essays in Honour of Garrret Mattingley* (New York, 1965)

Historical Manuscripts Commission, *Calendar of the Manuscripts of His Grace the Duke of Rutland, KG,* preserved at Belvoir Castle, 2 vols.

Historical Manuscripts Commission, *Calendar of the Manuscripts of the Most*

Honourable the Marquess of Salisbury . . . Preserved at Hatfield House, Hertfordshire, vols. 12, 14 and 15

Hurstfield, Joel, *The Succession Struggle in Late Elizabethan England: Elizabethan Government and Society,* essays presented by Sir John Neale, edited by S. T. Bindoff, J. Hurstfield and C. H. Williams (London, 1961)

James VI & I, *Political Writings,* edited by Johann P. Somerville (Cambridge, 1994)

James VI of Scotland, *Correspondence with Sir Robert Cecil and Others in England,* Camden Society (London, 1861)

James, Mervyn, *Society, Politics and Culture, Studies in Early Modern England* (Cambridge, 1986)

Juhala, A. L., "The Household and Court of King James VI of Scots, 1567–1603," unpublished Ph.D. thesis, University of Edinburgh, 2000

Kay, David W., *Ben Jonson: A Literary Life* (New York, 1995)

Kelly, W., *Royal Progresses and Visits to Leicester* (Leicester and London, 1884)

Klingenstein, L., *The Great Infanta Isabel* (London, 1910)

Larkin, James F., and Paul L. Hughs (eds.), *Stuart Royal Proclamations 1603–1625,* vol. 1 (Oxford, 1973)

Latham, Agnes, and Joyce Youings (eds.), *The Letters of Sir Walter Ralegh* (Exeter, 1999)

Laurence, Anne, *Women in England 1500–1760: A Social History* (London, 1994)

Law, Thomas Graves, *Jesuits and Seculars, with Illustrative Documents* (London, 1889)

Lee, Maurice, Jr., *Government by Pen: Scotland Under James VI & I* (Chicago and London, 1980)

———, *Great Britain's Solomon: James VI & I in His Three Kingdoms* (Urbana, Ill., 1990)

———, *James I and Henry IV: An Essay in English Foreign Policy, 1603–1610* (Urbana, Ill., 1970)

Letters of Queen Elizabeth and James VI of Scotland, Camden Society (1849)

Levack, Brian P., *The Formation of the British State* (Oxford, 1989)

Lewalski, Barbara Kiefer, *Writing Women in Jacobean England* (Cambridge, Mass., 1993)

Lodge, Edmund (ed.), *Illustrations of British History, Biography and Manners, selected from the manuscripts of the noble families of Howard, Talbot and Cecil,* 3 vols. (1838)

Lonchay, H., J. Cuvelier and J. Lefèvre (eds.), *Correspondance de la cour d'Espagne sur les affaires des Pays-Bas au XVIIe siècle*, 6 vols. (Brussels, 1923–37)

Loomie, Albert J., SJ, *Guy Fawkes in Spain: The Spanish Treason in Spanish Documents* (London, 1971)

———, "King James I's Catholic Consort," *Huntington Library Quarterly* 34
(August 1971)

———, *Spain and the Early Stuarts, 1585–1655* (London, 1996)

———, *The Spanish Elizabethans* (London, 1965)

Loomis, Catherine, "Elizabeth Southwell's Manuscript Account of the
Death of Queen Elizabeth (with text)," *English Literary Renaissance,* Autumn 1996

MacCaffrey, Wallace T., *Place and Patronage in Elizabethan Politics,* essays presented by Sir John Neale (London, 1961)

———, *Elizabeth I, War and Politics 1588–1603* (Oxford, 1992)

MacCulloch, Diarmaid, *Reformation: Europe's House Divided, 1490–1700* (London, 2003)

MacGibbon, David, and Thomas Ross, *The Castellated and Domestic Architecture of Scotland from the Twelfth to the Eighteenth Centuries,* 3 vols. (Edinburgh,
1889)

MacLure, Millar, *The Paul's Cross Sermons 1534–1642* (Toronto, 1958)

Manning, Roger B., *Village Revolts, Social Protests and Popular Disturbances in England, 1509–1640* (Oxford, 1988)

Manningham, John, *The Diary of John Manningham of the Middle Temple
1602–1603,* edited by Robert Parker Sorlien (Hanover, N.H., 1976)

Martin, Patrick, and John Finnis, "The Identity of Anthony Rivers," *Recusant History,* May 2002

Mathew, Nieves, *Francis Bacon: The History of a Character Assassination* (New
Haven and London, 1996)

Maxwell Scott, the Hon. Mrs., *The Tragedy of Fotheringay,* appendix contains
three contemporary accounts of the execution of Mary, Queen of Scots
(London, 1895)

McCullough, Peter E., *Sermons at Court: Politics and Religion in Elizabethan and Jacobean Preaching* (Cambridge, 1998)

Mears, Natalie, "Regnum Cecilianum? A Cecilian Perspective of the
Court," in *The Reign of Elizabeth I, Court and Culture in the Last Decade,* edited
by John Guy (Cambridge, 1995)

Meikle, Maureen M., *A Meddlesome Princess: Anna of Denmark and Scottish Court Politics, 1589–1603,* in Julian Goodare and Michael Lynch (eds.), *The Reign of James VI* (East Lothian, 2000)

Melville, *Sir James, Memoirs* (Edinburgh, 1827)

Middlebrook, Sydney, *Newcastle—Its Growth and Achievement* (Wakefield, 1968)

Morgan, Hiram, *Tyrone's Rebellion: The Outbreak of the Nine Years War in Tudor Ireland* (London, 1993)

Moryson, Fynes, *An Itinerary written by Fynes Moryson Gent. (Containing his ten yeeres travel through the twelve dominions of Germany, Bohmerland . . . France, England, Scotland, and Ireland),* 3 vols. (Glasgow, 1617)

Mowl, Timothy, *Elizabethan and Jacobean Style* (London, 1993)

Munden, R. C., "James I and the growth of mutual distrust," in *Faction and Parliament,* edited by K. Sharpe (London, 1978)

——, "The defeat of Sir John Fortescue: Court Versus Country at the Hustings?" *English Historical Review* 93 (1978)

Naunton, Sir Robert, *Fragmentia Regalia,* reprinted from 3rd posthumous edition 1653, edited by Edward Arber (London, 1870)

Neale, J. E., *Queen Elizabeth I* (St. Albans, 1979)

——, "The Sayings of Queen Elizabeth," *History New Series* 10 (1925)

Newdigate-Newdegate, Lady, *Gossip from a Muniment Room* (London, 1897)

Newton, Diana, "Sir Francis Hastings and the Religious Education of James VI and I," *Historical Journal* 61 (1998)

Nicholls, Mark, "Sir Walter Ralegh's Treason: A Prosecution Document," *English Historical Review* 110 (1995)

——, "Treason's Reward: The Punishment of Conspirators in the Bye Plot of 1603," *Historical Journal* 38 (1995)

——, "Two Winchester Trials: the Prosecution of Henry, Lord Cobham, and Thomas, Lord Grey of Wilton, 1603," *Institute of Historical Research* 68 (1995)

Nichols, John, *The Progresses, Processions and Magnificent Festivities of James the First,* 4 vols. (London, 1828)

Osborn, Francis, *The Works of Francis Osborn,* especially "Some Traditionall Memorialls on the Raign of King James" (London, 1673)

Parker, Geoffrey, *Europe in Crisis 1598–1648* (Sussex, 1980)

Parry, Graham, *The Golden Age Restor'd: The Culture of the Stuart Court, 1603–42* (Manchester, 1981)

Patterson, W. B., *King James VI & I and the Reunion of Christendom* (Cambridge, 1997)

Peck, Linda Levy, *Court, Patronage and Corruption in Early Stuart England* (London, 1993)

—— (ed.), *Northampton, Patronage and Policy at the Court of James I* (London, 1982)

—— (ed.), *The Mental World of the Jacobean Court* (Cambridge, 1991)

"A political retrospect, being Fr Persons' letter to Fr Anthony Rivers, July 6th 1603," Catholic Record Society *Miscellanea*, volume 2 (London, 1906)

Pollen, J. H., SJ, "The Accession of James I," *The Month*, 1901

——, "A Letter from Mary, Queen of Scots to the Duke of Guise" (contains Lethington's account of negotiations with Elizabeth over the succession), *Scottish History Society* 63 (January 1904)

Pollock, Linda, *With Faith and Physic: The Life of a Tudor Gentlewoman, Lady Grace Mildmay 1552–1620,* includes the autobiography of Grace Mildmay (London, 1993)

Questier, Michael, "Clerical Recruitment, Conversion and Rome c. 1580–1625," in Claire Cross (ed.), *Patronage and Recruitment in the Tudor and Early Stuart Church* (York, 1996)

——, "The Politics of Religious Conformity and the Accession of James I," *Research Bulletin of the Institute of Historical Research* 71 (1998)

Records of the English Province of the Society of Jesus, vol. 1, edited by Henry Foley, SJ (London, 1877)

The Register of the Privy Council of Scotland, edited by David Masson, vol. 6, 1599–1604 (Edinburgh, 1884)

Richards, Judith M., "The English Accession of James VI: National Identity, Gender and the Personal Monarchy of England," in *English Historical Review* 117, 472 (June 2002)

Rowse, A. L., *Ralegh and the Throckmortons* (London, 1962)

——, *Shakespeare's Southampton, Patron of Virginia* (London, 1965)

Rye, W. B., *England as Seen by Foreigners in the Days of Elizabeth and James the First* (London, 1865)

"Sabretache," *Monarchy and the Chase* (London, 1948)

Sanderson, William, *A Complete History of the Lives and Reigns of Mary, Queen of Scotland, and of Her Son and Successor, James* (London, 1656)

Scarisbrick, Diana, "Anne of Denmark's Jewellery," *Apollo* 123, ii (April 1986)

Schramm, P. E., *The History of the English Coronation* (Oxford, 1937)

Seton, Walter W., "The Early Years of Henry Frederick, Prince of Wales and Charles, Duke of Albany 1593–1605," *Scottish Historical Review* (1916)

Sharpe, J. A., *Early Modern England: A Social History 1550–1760* (London, 1987)

Sheils, W. J., "Catholics and Their Neighbours in a Rural Community: Egton Chapelry, 1590–1780," *Northern History* 43 (1998)

Slack, Paul, *The English Poor Law 1531–1782* (London, 1990)

Smout, T. C., *A History of the Scottish People* (London, 1969)

Smuts, Malcolm R., *Court Culture and the Origins of a Royalist Tradition in Early Stuart England* (Philadelphia, 1887)

Spedding, James, *An Account of the Life and Times of Francis Bacon*, vols. 1 and 3 (London, 1878)

Spence, Richard T., *The Privateering Earl: George Clifford, 3rd Earl of Cumberland 1558–1605* (Stroud, 1995)

Spottiswoode, John, *History of the Church of Scotland: Beginning at the Year of Our Lord 203, and Continued to the End of the Reign of King James VI*, with a biographical sketch and notes by M. Russell (Edinburgh, 1848–1851)

Steen, Sara Jayne (ed.), *The Letters of Arbella Stuart* (Oxford, 1994)

Stevenson, David, *Scotland's Last Royal Wedding: The Marriage of James VI and Anne of Denmark—with a Danish Account of the Marriage Translated by Peter Graves* (Edinburgh, 1997)

Stone, Lawrence, *The Crisis of the Aristocracy 1558–1641* (Oxford, 1965)

———, "The Fruits of Office: The Case of Robert Cecil First Earl of Salisbury, 1596–1612," in F. J. Fisher (ed.), *Essays in the Economic and Social History of Tudor and Stuart England* (Cambridge, 1961)

Stowe, John, *Annales of England . . . Continued and Augmented by Edmund Howes* (London, 1631)

Strickland, Agnes (ed.), *Lives of the Queens of England*, vol. 5 (1854)

Stuart Tracts, 1603–1693: An English Garner, with an introduction by C. H. Firth (London, 1903)

Summerson, John, "Theobalds: A Lost Elizabethan Palace," *The Listener*, 31 March 1955

Sykes, John, *Local Records; or Historical Records of Remarkable Events Which Have*

    Occurred in Northumberland and Durham, Newcastle upon Tyne and Berwick upon Tweed, vol. 1 (Newcastle, 1833; reprinted 1865)

Tanner, Lawrence E., *Recollections of a Westminster Antiquary* (London, 1969)

Taylor, John, *Travels Through Stuart Britain: The Adventures of John Taylor, the Water Poet,* edited and selected by John Chandler (Stroud, 1999)

Tenenti, Alberto, *Piracy and the Decline of Venice 1580–1615* (London, 1967)

Thompson, Michael, *Medieval Bishops' Houses in England and Wales* (Aldershot, 1998)

Thompson, M. W., *The Decline of the Castle* (Cambridge, 1998)

Thurley, Simon, *The Royal Palaces of Tudor England* (New Haven and London, 1993)

Tierney, Rev'd M. A., *Dodd's Church History of England,* vol. 4 (London, 1841)

Tyacke, Nicholas, "Puritan Politicians and James VI and I, 1587–1604," in *Politics, Religion and Popularity in Early Stuart Britain, essays in honour of Conrad Russell,* edited by Thomas Cogswell, Richard Cust and Peter Lake (Cambridge, 2002)

Usher, Roland G., *The Reconstruction of the English Church,* vol. 1 (London and New York, 1910)

Warrender, Sir Victor, *The Warrender Papers,* vol. 2, edited by Annie Isabella Cameron, introduction by Robert S. Rait, Scottish History Society Publications, 3rd series, 18, 19 (Edinburgh, 1931–32)

Watts, S. J., and Susan J. Watts, *From Border to Middle Shire: Northumberland 1586–1625* (Leicester, 1975)

Weiner, Carol Z., "The Beleaguered Isle: A Study in Elizabethan and Early Jacobean Anti-Catholicism," *Past and Present* 51 (1971)

Weldon, Sir Anthony, *The Court and Character of King James* (London, 1650)

Welford, Richard (ed.), "History of Newcastle and Gateshead," 3 vols. (London, 1884–87)

Wernham, R. B., *The Return of the Armadas: The Last Years of the Elizabethan Wars Against Spain 1595–1603* (Oxford, 1994)

Weston, William, *Autobiography of an Elizabethan,* translated by Philip Caraman (London, 1955)

Whithed, Sir Henry, *Sir Henry Whithed's Letter Book,* vol. 1, 1601–1614 (Winchester, 1976)

Wickham Legg, L. G. (ed.), *A Relation of a Short Survey of Twenty-Six Counties Observed in a Seven Week Journey Begun on August 11th, 1634, By a Captain, a Lieu-*

tenant and an Ancient, All Three of the Military Company in Norwich (London, 1934)

—— (ed.), *The Coronation Order of King James I* (London, 1902)

Wilbraham, Sir Roger, *The Journal of Sir Roger Wilbraham for the Years 1593–1616*, edited by Harold Spencer Scott, *The Camden Miscellany*, vol. 10 (London, 1902)

Williams, Penry, "The Northern Borderland Under the Early Stuarts," in *Historical Essays 1600–1750*, edited by H. E. Bell and R. C. Ollard (London, 1963)

Willson, Harris D., *King James VI and I* (London, 1956)

Wilson, Arthur, *The History of Great Britain, Being the Life and Reign of King James the First* (London, 1653)

Wilson, F. P., *The Plague in Shakespeare's London* (London, 1927)

Wilson, Thomas, *The State of England, anno Dom. 1600, The Camden Miscellany*, vol. 16 (London, 1936)

Winwood, Sir Ralph, *Memorials of Affairs of State, etc., collected (chiefly) from the original papers of the Right Honourable Sir Ralph Winwood KT*, 3 vols. (London, 1725)

Wormald, Jenny, "The Creation of Britain," *Transactions of the Royal Historical Society*, 6th series, 2 (1991)

——, "Gunpowder, Treason and Scots," *Journal of British Studies* 24 (1985)

——, "James VI and I: two kings or one?," *History* 68 (1983)

——, "The Neighbour to the North," in *Queen Elizabeth I: Most Politick Princess*, History Today publication (1984)

Wotton, Henry, *The Life and Letters of Sir Henry Wotton*, edited by Logan Pearsell Smith, 2 vols. (Oxford, 1907)

York Corporation House Books for Reign of James I, transcribed by Professor Toshio Sakata (Yuhikaku Publishing Co. Ltd, n.d.)

Young, Michael B., *James and the History of Homosexuality* (London, 2000)

INDEX

ABOUT THE AUTHOR

LEANDA DE LISLE took a master's degree in history at Oxford University before embarking on a highly successful career as a journalist and writer. She returned to her first love, history, to write *After Elizabeth,* her first book. She lives in Warwickshire, England.

ABOUT THE TYPE

This book was set in Requiem, a typeface designed by the Hoefler Type Foundry. It is a modern typeface inspired by inscriptional capitals in Ludovico Vicentino degli Arrighi's 1523 writing manual, *Il modo de temperare le penne*. An original lowercase, a set of figures, and an italic in the "chancery" style that Arrighi helped popularize were created to make this adaptation of a classical design into a complete font family.